BLACK STU

OXFORD WORKSHOP SERIES

SCHOOL SOCIAL WORK ASSOCIATION OF AMERICA

Series Advisory Board

Functional Behavioral Assessment: A Three-Tiered Prevention Model
Kevin J. Filter and Michelle E. Alvarez

School Bullying: New Perspectives on a Growing Problem
David R. Dupper

Consultation Theory and Practice: A Handbook for School Social Workers
Christine Anlauf Sabatino

School-Based Practice with Children and Youth Experiencing Homelessness
James P. Canfield

Family Engagement with Schools: Strategies for School Social Workers and Educators
Nancy Feyl Chavkin

Solution-Focused Brief Therapy in Schools: A 360-Degree View of the Research and Practice Principles, Second Edition
Johnny Kim, Michael Kelly, and Cynthia Franklin

Evidence-Based Practice in School Mental Health: Addressing DSM-5 Disorders in Schools, Second Edition
James C. Raines

Creating Trauma-Informed Schools: A Guide for School Social Workers and Educators
Eileen A. Dombo and Christine Anlauf Sabatino

The Dropout Prevention Specialist Workbook: A How-To Guide for Building Skills and Competence in Education
Howard M. Blonsky

Ethical Decision Making in School Mental Health, Second Edition
James C. Raines and Nic T. Dibble

The Art of Becoming Indispensable: What School Social Workers Need to Know in Their First Three Years of Practice
Tory Cox, Michelle E. Alvarez, and Terence Fitzgerald

Black Students Matter: Play Therapy Techniques to Support Black Students Experiencing Racial Trauma
April D. Duncan

BLACK STUDENTS MATTER

Play Therapy Techniques to Support Black Students Experiencing Racial Trauma

Dr. April D. Duncan, DSW, LCSW, RPT-S

OXFORD WORKSHOP SERIES

OXFORD
UNIVERSITY PRESS

OXFORD
UNIVERSITY PRESS

Oxford University Press is a department of the University of Oxford. It furthers the University's objective of excellence in research, scholarship, and education by publishing worldwide. Oxford is a registered trade mark of Oxford University Press in the UK and certain other countries.

Published in the United States of America by Oxford University Press
198 Madison Avenue, New York, NY 10016, United States of America.

Library of Congress Cataloging-in-Publication Data
Names: Duncan, April D., author.
Title: Black students matter : play therapy techniques to support Black
students experiencing racial trauma / April D. Duncan.
Description: New York, NY : Oxford University Press, 2024. |
Includes bibliographical references and index. |
Identifiers: LCCN 2023032467 (print) | LCCN 2023032468 (ebook) |
ISBN 9780197669266 (paperback) | ISBN 9780197669280 (epub) |
ISBN 9780197669297
Subjects: LCSH: African American children—Education—Psychological aspects. |
Racism—United States—Psychological aspects. |
Psychic trauma in children—United States. | Play therapy—United States.
Classification: LCC LC2731 .D87 2024 (print) | LCC LC2731 (ebook) |
DDC 370.89/96073—dc23/eng/20230814
LC record available at https://lccn.loc.gov/2023032467
LC ebook record available at https://lccn.loc.gov/2023032468

DOI: 10.1093/oso/9780197669266.001.0001

Printed by Marquis Book Printing, Canada

To my #1 fan and heavenly cheerleader, Walter Duncan Jr. #JunesStar

Contents

Foreword

Eliana Gil, PhD, LMFT, RPT-S, ATR

I am a licensed mental health professional and I have worked with abused and traumatized children all my professional career, always prioritizing a co-ordinated team approach—"It takes a village" is one of my strongest mantras, especially because school is an important community support and protection for young children. That lesson was reinforced as COVID rules went into effect in 2020, when we faced a global pandemic and children were home-schooled for their own health. During that time, the Council on Criminal Justice reported an 8.1% increase in cases of domestic violence and found that "the pandemic's isolating impacts increased risk for potential victims." In addition, the American Academy of Child and Adolescent Psychiatry, the American Academy of Pediatrics, and the Children's Hospital Association joined together to declare a National State of Emergency in Children's Mental Health, calling for, among other things, sustainable funding of school-based mental health programs (including suicide-prevention efforts across settings), continued availability of telemedicine, and an increase in federal funding for children and families. The idea of making mental health avail-able in the very system in which children spend so much of their time was an innovation which many believe addresses issues of access to services for many. However, in spite of the willingness of many to be of service to chil-dren and assist during times of need, by 2018, suicide became the second leading cause of death for youth ages 10–24. It also became clear that race played a part in increased vulnerability among children of color. This dec-laration of a national crisis also emphasized that "inequities that result from structural racism have contributed to disproportionate impacts on children from communities of color."

From my point of view, the pandemic created a perfect storm: more stress and fear, unemployment, families stuck at home together, and children ex-pected to set everything aside to attend to school on their home computers. As mentioned above, family isolation and stress took their toll on family life and rates of violence increased. We have relied on school personnel to provide supervision of children's needs, and, without this extra set of community eyes, children became more at risk as the family's resources decreased.

Schools lost their security as the persistence of school shootings soared. 2020 had the dubious distinction of breaking the record for school shootings over four decades and marked one of the most violent years for youth ages 12–17. Many of the school shooters are students, and many of those students have access to guns during times when they are in dispute with someone else. This suggests that children need increasing direction on problem-solving skills, and access to guns needs to be decreased. Obviously, unidentified or underserved mental health issues are often associated with student shooters as well as with family contributors. As with other catastrophes that attract intense attention when they happen, over time, people lose focus until the next horrible tragedy occurs.

Interest in children's mental health wax and wanes, and although efforts at implementing future internal systems may suffer from periods where other funding priorities take place, this book has the potential to make a significant contribution by speaking directly to school personnel about why students, especially black, Indigenous and people of color (BICOP) students, must receive sustained attention and responsible, trauma-informed care. This book provides such a focus by spotlighting the plight of children of color in school systems, and it documents many of the hardships that they endure and some of the reparative actions that can take place.

Dr. Duncan seeks to identify critical safety issues in the lives of students of color and provides clear and useful practical suggestions that allow teachers as well as guidance counselors and psychologists to provide supportive services. Given that children of color are still overrepresented in the juvenile justice system and are more likely to be reported to child protective services than their White counterparts, school personnel must design systems of care that are relevant and immediately useful to disenfranchised student populations and their parents and caretakers.

This books clearly defines racial trauma, racial stressors, and the effects of trauma on students of color. It goes beyond the typical foundational concern to empower school personnel to use therapeutic skills as a way to engage and dialogue with children about critical issues such as racial trauma, colorism, hair discrimination, discipline, suicide, community violence, coping skills, etc. Unique chapters explore how gender plays a role in how racism is experienced, processed, and addressed. The book suggests ways of working with children individually, in groups, and in the classroom, providing playful approaches that encourage the child's participation and investment in personal control and change.

I have been fortunate to be an audience member and listen to Dr. Duncan's inspiring keynotes and workshops on various topics related to working with children of color and their families. The book expands on her ideas, provides practical ideas for connecting with the experience of children of color in school, and pinpoints many of the underlying variables that make racism a pivotal lens for helping students within one of their most relevant environments.

Dr. Duncan has made a significant contribution to those of us interested in providing real assistance within the true reality of our cultural context.

Preface

From the 19th century to present, Black American children have had to endure discrimination, racism, prejudice, and microaggressions from an early age. There are pictures of young Black children being used as stepstools for their White owners and Black babies picking cotton stalks bigger than themselves. In this country, Black boys and girls have been robbed of their childhoods for centuries. It is time to break that cycle.

This book seeks to highlight the constant onslaught of negative racial experiences that shape the ways Black children learn, socialize, behave, and react to things in their environment. Black children, particularly in schools, are punished for not fitting Eurocentric ideals of how a student should behave or respond to stress. From schools to churches to the Black community, adults who engage with Black children must learn how racial stress and trauma negatively affect the emotional, social, and cognitive development of Black children. In turn, we must be able to provide that information to Black children themselves, so they are empowered to cope with their stress and trauma in healthy ways. But it starts with us. It starts with you.

In 2020, the protests for George Floyd's death ignited an international call for racial justice and equality. However, the psychological effects of negative race-based experiences, including school disciplinary practices, on Black students are often overlooked. This research gap has left school mental health professionals scrambling to find culturally sensitive and fun strategies to support Black students. This book seeks to fill that gap. This book is a blueprint for school mental health professionals to help Black students navigate the systems that push them out of the classroom and into the juvenile justice system.

I'm passionate about this topic for several reasons. I was a Black girl who grew up in White spaces and experienced first-hand the unequal treatment some teachers exhibited toward me. From my Spanish teacher kicking me out of class before the bell rang because she had a migraine and "couldn't deal with me" that day or the Child Development teacher who didn't want me to attend a field trip to a daycare because she was worried I would "hurt a child," I understand the feelings my Black clients express in sessions when teachers have unjustly singled them out. But also because, as a professional with more than 10 years of clinical experience, I know how this type of treatment negatively effects my clients. I've worked with Black children who have attempted suicide because of their inability to manage racial stressors. I've advocated for assault charges to be dropped against a 5-year-old and teachers not to hotline a mother for gluing hair weave into their 5-year-old daughter's hair. We have to do better to protect the mental health of Black children, and that starts with each us engaging in honest self-reflection to recognize how we may be personally contributing to the issue.

Using play therapy to address this issue is an innovative approach to a significant problem. Integrating music, art, sand therapy, and other expressive therapies is the most culturally competent and appropriate way to build rapport with Black students and provide a nonjudgmental place for them to write their own stories. This book includes more than 30 unique play and expressive therapy interventions that are made specifically for Black children to process their experiences while honoring their cultural traditions in healing and emotional expression.

For downloadable/reproduceable versions of the forms found in the book, please contact the author at drapril@bmhconnect.com

Introduction

Every system that touches a Black child harms them.
—*Grills et al. (2019)*

From the moment a Black child enters the world, they are at a disadvantage simply because of the color of their skin. The unfair treatment exhibited toward them often stems from racist stereotypes of Black adults passed down to innocent children because of *adultification bias*. This bias is shown toward Black children by assuming that they are older than their actual age and viewing them as less innocent and culpable for their actions (Epstein et al., 2020.) For example, the "Sapphire" stereotype that Black women are hypersexualized and promiscuous (Epstein et al., n.d.) appears when a young Black girl is blamed for being sexually assaulted due to her "acting" or "dressing grown." Or the "Savage" stereotype that labels Black men as aggressive, violent, and criminals (DeGruy, 2017), which grounds decision-making when a Black boy gets into a fight with a White boy, but the Black child is the only one punished. In every environment, Black children are treated differently because of adultification bias, which denies Black children the luxury of a childhood.

In schools, Black students are punished for not fitting Eurocentric standards of talk, dress, and behavior. As a result, these students are subjected to harsher judgments of their appearance, talk, dress, and demeanor that contribute to high rates of exclusionary discipline from preschool to high school graduation. The "preschool-to-prison pipeline" is a term used to highlight the glaring racial disparities that begin in early childhood. From

Black Students Matter. April D. Duncan, Oxford University Press. © Oxford University Press 2024.
DOI: 10.1093/oso/9780197669266.003.0001

preschool to high school, Black students are more likely to be suspended, expelled, restrained, arrested, and sent to alternative schools than any other race (Office for Civil Rights, 2021). This funnels Black students directly into the juvenile justice system, as studies have found that students who are expelled or suspended are three times more likely to have contact with the juvenile justice system the following year (Fabelo et al., 2011). This constant interaction with systems and individuals that are biased, prejudiced, and discriminatory can lead to negative mental health outcomes for Black students that mirror postraumatic stress disorder (PTSD), a condition also known as *racial trauma*.

Racial trauma occurs when Black youth suffer from continuous acts of racial discrimination that cause physical, emotional, and psychological harm (Henderson et al., 2019). A 2020 study conducted by English and colleagues found Black youth participants experienced at least five acts of racial discrimination a day. This constant interaction with systemic and direct racial stressors contributes to moods and behaviors of Black students that are often misunderstood, misdiagnosed, and punished. As a result, Black youth may experience negative mental health outcomes that contribute to negative self-worth and impaired student–teacher relationships. Experiences with racism, microaggressions, prejudice, and discrimination contribute to anxiety, depression, suicidal thoughts, and symptoms that mirror PTSD (Pachter et al., 2018; Polanco-Roman et al., 2019; Assari et al., 2017; Walker et al., 2016). However, because there is no official diagnosis for racial trauma in the most recent *Diagnostic Statistical Manual* (DSM-5), it is imperative that mental health professionals become more knowledgeable about its prevalence and its symptomatology in Black students.

Within the mental health field, there is a push for trauma-informed practices when working with children and adolescents. However, with children of color, the concept of race-based trauma is continually overlooked, which often leads to misdiagnosis and ineffective treatment goals that neglect the experiences of Black children. To truly use a systems theory approach is to account for the race-based experiences Black students encounter in all of their environments: including their schools, their communities, their peers, and their families. For some Black students, those environments may also include the juvenile justice system and the child welfare system. What makes Black students unique is that their race often contributes to the negative experiences and unequal treatment they encounter in these environments that can negatively affect their mental health, their self-worth, and sometimes their lives.

This book is a blueprint for school social workers to help Black youth navigate the various systems that push them out of the classroom and into the juvenile justice system or other unhealthy environments. In this book, I focus on the psychological effects of school discipline on Black youth; including direct stressors like bullying and hair discrimination, along with systemic stressors like the child welfare and criminal justice systems. Professionals will explore how to honor the code of ethics set forth by the National Association of Social Workers (NASW) in our duty to engage in social justice, value the dignity and worth of the person, and honor the importance of human relationships while exhibiting cultural humility and inclusivity when working with Black students and families. Complex issues require innovative solutions; therefore, I also examine the use of play therapy with Black students, caregivers and educators as a unique way to support Black students of all ages learn healthy coping skills to manage negative race-based experiences. This book contains more than 30 original play therapy interventions that were developed specifically for exploring and supporting race-based experiences and stressors in the lives of Black students, with a special focus on empowerment and self-esteem. These play therapy activities are "for the culture," meaning they are created specifically for Black children, based on familiar cultural traditions and experiences.

Readers will examine the use of expressive therapy techniques such as art, music, games, and sand trays to engage Black students in individual and group play therapy sessions. These unique activities focus on encouraging social-emotional expression in Black boys, empowering Black girls, and supporting Black LGBTQ+ students. I also provide play therapy activities to address grief and bereavement as well as suicidality in Black students. Additionally, this book will provide interventions that will focus on race-based experiences unique to Black students that contribute to racial trauma, including hair discrimination, code switching, colorism and more. These interventions are meant to honor the culture of Black children and families, in an effort to deconstruct Eurocentric ideas of what is "appropriate" or "correct."

In employing an ecosystemic perspective, I will also explain the importance of building rapport and supporting both teachers and caregivers of Black students. In my opinion, every Black student in America is dealing with some level of trauma because of their daily interactions with racial trauma. Therefore, I believe it is important to engage and educate the adults in their lives, to strengthen the support and compassion they need within their systems to navigate racism, discrimination, prejudice and microaggressions mentally and emotionally. And as we say in social work, "if you work with the child, you also work with the family," so engaging important people within a students' village is key to positive long-term outcomes for Black children. With a focus on the impact of intergenerational trauma on Black parenting practices, school social workers will learn how to build relationships with Black caregivers, along with play therapy seminal theories to engage Black caregivers in their child's treatment. Additionally, the book reviews the use of play in the classroom to address vicarious trauma in teachers and help repair impaired teacher–student relationships.

Throughout their life cycle, Black Americans experience high levels of stress that are related to negative race-based experiences. Unfortunately, Black children are not immune to this stress, which can contribute to negative short- and long-term mental health outcomes. In order to help Black students, first we must understand their experience. Black children deserve to be both seen and heard, so case examples and real-life experiences are used to tell the important stories of Black children that are often silenced or dismissed. This book seeks to help the reader develop more empathy to the unique stressors experienced by Black students daily, while also providing additional resources to support their mental health needs in all their environments, including the playroom and classroom. In doing so, we all can contribute to the mental and emotional safety of Black children while helping them learn healthy coping skills to manage the inevitable negative race-based experiences they will encounter.

Racism, prejudice, and discrimination force Black children to deal with an additional layer of stressors that other children do not experience. Adultification bias contributes to them being seen and treated as adults, further robbing them of a childhood. Using play in the lives of Black children in every environment they frequent can aid in the much-needed healthy attachments and relationships they need for optimal development. So, break out your art materials, dust off your dancing shoes, and let's play away racial trauma in Black children together.

References

Assari, S., Moazen-Zadeh, E., Caldwell, C., & Zimmerman, M. (2017). Racial discrimination during adolescence predicts mental health deterioration in adulthood: Gender differences among Blacks. *Frontiers in Public Health, 5*, 104–104. https://doi.org/10.3389/fpubh.2017.00104

Degruy, J. (2017). *Post-traumatic slave syndrome: America's legacy of enduring injury & healing.* Uptown Press.

English, D., Lambert, S., Tynes, B., Bowleg, L., Zea, M., & Howard, L. (2020). Daily multidimensional racial discrimination among Black U.S. American adolescents.

Journal of Applied Developmental Psychology, 66, 101068. https://doi.org/10.1016/j.app dev.2019.101068

Epstein, R., Godfrey, E., Gonzalez, T., & Javdani, S. (2020). Data snapshot: 2017–2018. National data on school discipline by race and gender. Georgetown Law Center on Poverty & Inequality. https://genderjusticeandopportunity.georgetown.edu/wp-content/uploads/2021/04/National-Data-on-School-Discipline-by-Race-and-Gen der.pdfx

Fabelo, T., Thompson, M. D., Plotkin, M., Carmichael, D., Marchbanks III, M. P., & Booth, E. A. (2011, July). Breaking school's rules: A statewide study of how school disci-pline relates to students' success and juvenile justice involvement. Council of State Governments Justice Center. https://csgjusticecenter.org/wp-content/uploads/2020/01/ Breaking_Schools_Rules_Report_

Grills, C., Banks, J., Norrington-Sands, K., Jackson, T. R., Steve, S. L., & Clark, M. (2019, October 15). Black child suicide: A report. National Cares Mentoring Movement & the Association of Black Psychologists. https://www.caresmentoring.org/black_child_ suicide_report.pdf

Henderson, D., Walker, L., Barnes, R., Lunsford, A., Edwards, C., & Clark, C. (2019). A framework for race-related trauma in the public education system and implications on health for Black youth. *Journal of School Health, 89*(11), 926–933. https://doi-org.libpro xy1.usc.edu/10.1111/josh.12832

Office for Civil Rights. (2021). An overview of exclusionary discipline practices in public schools for the 2017–2018 school year. U.S. Department of Education, 2017–2018 Civil Rights Data Collection (CRDC). https://ocrdata.ed.gov/assets/downloads/crdc-exclusionary-school-discipline.pdf

Pachter, L., Caldwell, C., Jackson, J., & Bernstein, B. (2018). Discrimination and mental health in a representative sample of African-American and Afro-Caribbean Youth. *Journal of Racial and Ethnic Health Disparities, 5*(4), 831–837. https://doi.org/10.1007/ s40615-017-0428-z

Polanco-Roman, L., Anglin, D., Miranda, R., & Jeglic, E. (2019). Racial/ethnic discrimi-nation and suicidal ideation in emerging adults: The role of traumatic stress and de-pressive symptoms varies by gender, not race/ethnicity. *Journal of Youth and Adolescence, 48*(10), 2023–2037. https://doi.org/10.1007/s10964-019-01097-w

Walker, R., Francis, D., Brody, G., Simons, R., Cutrona, C., & Gibbons, F. (2016, May 3). A longitudinal study of racial discrimination and risk for death ideation in African American youth. *Suicide and Life-Threatening Behavior, 47*(1), 86–102. https://doi-org. libproxy1.usc.edu/10.1111/sltb.12251

1

■ ■ ■

Exploring Black Students and Racial Trauma

Defining Racial Trauma

To truly provide trauma-informed care to Black students, it is imperative that school social workers are attuned to these children's daily experiences, which often include navigating negative race-based experiences. *Racial trauma* is defined as the physical, social, and psychological harm individuals experience due to repeated exposure to discrimination, racism, and microaggressions (Henderson et al., 2019). Physically, a Black student may encounter racial trauma through bullying from their peers. Socially, Black students may be rejected from certain spaces, as when the cops are called on them for loitering or LGBTQ+ youth are rejected from their family and/or community due to their gender identity and/or sexual orientation. The psychological harm Black children encounter because of racial trauma contributes to negative mental health outcomes including negative thoughts, anxiety, and low self-esteem, to name a few. A glossary of key terms (Appendix A) is presented at the end of this chapter to help clinicians understand important terminology when exploring the race-based experiences of Black students.

Racial trauma is an adverse interaction that can happen continuously or daily through institutional, symbolic, or individual acts of racism (Henderson et al., 2019). Racial trauma looks like posttraumatic stress disorder (PTSD), with individuals experiencing anger, depression, anxiety, hypervigilance, low self-esteem, disruptive thoughts, avoidance, and isolation (Mental Health America, 2023). However, when assessing the behaviors of Black children, particularly in school, the trauma-informed lens often is tossed out and replaced with a biased interpretation of the child's behaviors. School social workers must ensure that they themselves remember the high levels

Black Students Matter. April D. Duncan, Oxford University Press. © Oxford University Press 2024.
DOI: 10.1093/oso/9780197669266.003.0002

of race-based stress and trauma Black students experience to help advocate for the most appropriate mental health treatment and, at times, disciplinary practices.

Sometimes putting a face to the issue is helpful for people to understand how racial trauma looks in real life. Darnella Frazier was 17 years old when, while walking to the local corner store with her 9-year-old cousin, she filmed the murder of George Floyd. Darnella shared the way that event shaped her life in a post on Instagram in 2021.

> I am 18 now and I still hold the weight and trauma of what I witnessed a year ago. It's a little easier now, but I'm not who I used to be. A part of my childhood was taken from me. My 9-year-old cousin who witnessed the same thing I did got a part of her childhood taken from her. Having to up and leave because my home was no longer safe, waking up to reporters at my door, closing my eyes at night only to see a man who is brown like me, lifeless on the ground. I couldn't sleep properly for weeks. I used to shake so bad at night my mom had to rock me to sleep. Hopping from hotel to hotel because we didn't have a home and looking over our back every day in the process. Having panic and anxiety attack every time I seen a police car, not knowing who to trust because a lot of people are evil with bad intentions. I hold that weight. A lot of people call me a hero even though I don't see myself as one. I was just in the right place at the right time. Behind this smile, behind these awards, behind the publicity, I'm a girl trying to heal from something I am reminded of everyday. (Hernadez, 2021)

According to the fifth edition of the *Diagnostic and Statistical Manual of Mental Disorders* (DSM-5), Darnella meets the criteria for PTSD because she (a) witnessed the murder of George Floyd; (b) is experiencing distressing memories about the event; (c) has a persistent negative state (anxiety and panic), exaggerated negative beliefs about the world (lack of trust due to evil people with bad intentions), blaming (in a separate article, she speaks about staying up late at night apologizing to Mr. Floyd for not doing more to help him); and (d) hypervigilance (looking over her back) (American Psychiatric Association, 2013). And although it is not mentioned in this passage, it can be assumed that Darnella also showed avoidant behaviors, possibly of police officers, after her description of having anxiety attacks when she sees a police car.

Her display of PTSD symptoms in relation to this negative race-based experience is racial trauma. Another defining factor that would categorize her symptoms as racial trauma is the fact that Darnella was involved in a highly publicized incident that was fueled by systemic racism. Although she was a teenager at the time, her name was still shared in the media, which placed her in the crosshairs of racist people who threatened her emotional and physical safety. This child now must deal with stressors that will continue throughout her life as a Black woman, but especially with the notoriety that she has received for her recording. Sadly, the treatment Darnella has received is not unusual because Black children in America are not afforded the same protections as White children. This makes it even more important that school social workers educate themselves and others on the consequences of racial trauma in Black children so there are more protections in place for them, as opposed to punishments and ridicule.

Racial Trauma in Black Students

Being a Black child in America is a risk factor that creates an uphill battle that these children will have to fight to climb their entire lives. Researchers conducted a study and found that Black adolescents experience an average of five incidents of discrimination a day (English et al., 2020). Additionally, a study conducted by Assari et al. (2017) found that 90% of students reported having experienced at least one racial disturbance in their lifetime and 99% reported being "at least a little bothered" by that experience. Racial incidents for Black students can occur in various environments, from school to social media. Research has shown Black youth experience both vicarious and individual acts of racial discrimination at high rates both offline and online (Tynes et al., 2019). McNeil Smith and Fincham (2016) found that approximately 40% of Black 8th graders experienced some form of discrimination from their peers or teachers. Discrimination appears at every turn for the Black student, which is evident in the glaring differences that are shown in how they are treated in every environment they encounter.

The differential treatment of Black students by means of institutionalized and systemic racism is evident from the racial disparities found in schools, child welfare systems, and the juvenile system. Biased treatment within these systems further deepens the wounds in Black students as they are constantly shown by the adults—and sometimes peers—in their lives that they way they dress, speak and socialize is wrong or inappropriate. Black children also encounter stress within their own families and communities that is a result of intergenerational trauma that guides the negative interactions that prevent Black children from having a safe space in which to process and validate their emotions and experiences. As a result, Black children have little to no reprieve from race-based stress and trauma.

These constant negative raced-based interactions contribute to poor mental health outcomes in Black youth. Racial trauma contributes to suicidal behavior, anxiety, depression, and PTSD symptoms in Black youth (Arshanapally et al., 2018; Assari et al., 2017; Pachter et al., 2018; Polanco-Roman et al., 2019; Walker et al., 2016). The emotional stress in Black youth because of racial trauma can manifest behaviorally as insomnia, irritability, and chronic anger (Pickett, 2020). Even Black students with less frequent interactions with racial stressors are negatively affected as studies have found that even limited exposure to racial discrimination can negatively impact Black youth's psychological well-being (Lanier et al., 2017). When this stress goes unrecognized and untreated, it can contribute to behavioral issues that are rooted in trauma but often misdiagnosed in Black students as attention-deficit hyperactivity disorder (ADHD), oppositional defiant disorder (ODD), and conduct disorder (CD).

Even when these diagnoses are given correctly, Black students are still unable to receive mental health support, and their behaviors are viewed as disruptive and defiant, which leads to disciplinary actions as opposed to the mental health support they deserve. Research has also been able to highlight the long-term effects of racial trauma experienced in adolescence. Assari et al. (2017) found that perceived racial discrimination during adolescence had the most harmful long-term effects on Black males (2017). This study highlights the importance of allowing Black students to define their experiences as racially influenced, rather than prioritizing the perspective of the school social worker or other adults such as teachers and their caregivers.

Defining Racial Trauma Stressors

There are different types of racial trauma stressors. A *direct* trauma stressor directly impacts a person and can be a result of individual experiences with racism or of living in a society with systemic and structural racism (Mental Health America, 2022). For example, Darnella experienced a direct trauma stressor when she witnessed the murder of George Floyd, then again after being harassed when her name was released as the person who recorded the murder. Given the interactions with systemic and structural racism that people of color experience in America, one can assume that most Black students have experienced a direct racial stressor, even at a young age. That is not to say every Black child is suffering from racial trauma, but is to encourage clinicians to acknowledge that racial stressors to occur and may be contributing to emotional and behavioral symptoms displayed by Black children. Therefore, school social workers could benefit from beginning with this assumption in the assessment phase and rule out racial stressors as a contributing factor before labeling the student's behavior as generalized anxiety, major depressive disorder, ODD, ADHD, or CD. It is important to remember that trauma can present as behaviors associated with those diagnoses, but if school social workers are operating with a racial trauma lens, they are more likely to recognize and treat the students' behaviors with trauma-informed interventions and support.

Transmitted stressors are traumatic stressors that are transferred between generations; these can include historically racist sources or personal traumas that are passed along intergenerationally (Mental Health America, 2022). An example of a transmitted stressor in the Black community is how a Black student may respond to seeing or interacting with a police officer. They may have seen or heard how their caregivers respond when they see or interact with law enforcement, which could be with fear or anxiety. In turn, the child may have those same reactions when placed in similar situations. Last, Black students are exposed to race-based stress and trauma through *vicarious* trauma stressors. Vicarious trauma stressors are the traumatic impacts of living with indirect individual racist actions or systemic racism (Mental Health America, 2022). For example, although the death of George Floyd was not something a student directly experienced, it can still negatively impact their mental health. Black students who see and hear of people who look like them being killed or hurt are just as equally traumatized by the event as if they experienced the situation themselves. This can also affect the ways they engage with police officers, given the trauma they've experienced indirectly from Floyd's death or the death of other unarmed Black citizens. School social workers and school officials should be aware that race-based societal and community events can impact the moods of Black students and their ability to focus in school as well as their overall well-being.

Racial Stressors in Black Students

There are several direct, systemic, and transmitted trauma stressors that contribute to race-based stress and trauma in Black students. Systemically, Black students receive differential treatment that results in racial disparities in schools, the juvenile justice system, the criminal justice system, and the child welfare system. Direct stressors include bullying victimization, grief, and bereavement from the loss of loved ones due to community violence and adverse police contact. Transmitted stressors guide the cultural practices employed by parents, caregivers, and community members that have contributed to maladaptive practices and beliefs that often stifle the emotional expression and identity development of Black children. Each of these stressors should be explored in more depth to gain a better grasp of the stresses placed on Black student so school social workers can provide ethical and compassionate mental health support and advocacy.

Systemic Racial Stressors: School Discipline

From their first introduction to the school system, Black students face adversity at every turn. To discuss the experience of Black students, we must honestly acknowledge the disparities within the educational system that function as racial trauma stressors. From preschool to high school, no Black child is immune from bias in school disciplinary practices and rules of conduct that are designed to push children of color out of school and into the juvenile justice system. The "preschool-to-prison pipeline" refers to the increasing trend in which school disciplinary actions indirectly funnel children of color into the juvenile justice system and, subsequently, the criminal justice system (Al-Shamma et al., 2016). This trend is rooted in outdated and discriminatory laws and policies that disproportionately affect communities of color.

The most recent data show that Black students are three times more likely to be expelled and suspended compared to White students (Office for Civil Rights, 2021). These disparities start early: Black preschoolers account for 44% of preschool children who receive more than one out-of-school suspension even though they only represent 18% of preschool enrollment (Office for Civil Rights, 2021). The preschool-to-prison pipeline highlights how racial disparities in school discipline move Black students into the juvenile justice system. Many of these arrests can be traced back to a school system whose disciplinary tactics, which often involve police officers, place Black students at a disadvantage. Essentially, schools have become ground zero for the institutionalization and criminalization of Black behavior. Factors such as implicit bias in school policies, classroom management styles, and lack of cultural awareness contribute to the criminalization of Black behavior. In turn, the behavior of Black children is often misinterpreted, misunderstood, and mislabeled because it does not fit the Eurocentric definition of behavior.

Over the years, the preschool-to-prison pipeline has captured the attention of scholars and advocates, but few have addressed the psychological effects of harsh disciplinary practices on Black students.

Black Preschoolers and Discipline

Racial disparities in school discipline begins as early as preschool for children of color. Black preschoolers make up less than a quarter of the public school enrollment (18%) but account for half of the suspension rates compared to White preschoolers, who represent 43% of preschool enrollment and account for 28% of preschoolers with more than one out-of-school suspension (Office for Civil Rights, 2021). Additionally, Black preschoolers accounted for 38% of preschool expulsions in the 2017–2018 school year, a rate that is more than double that of Latinx preschoolers (17.6%) (Office for Civil Rights, 2021). It is important also to note gender discrepancies within preschool discipline. The discrimination these young children experience sets the tone for how Black students connect with educators and engage—or disengage—in classrooms at an early age. Black male preschoolers are almost four times more likely to receive one or more out-of-school suspensions and almost five times more likely to be expelled compared to Black female preschoolers (Office for Civil Rights, 2021). Early childhood school social workers could benefit from focusing more intensive support and interventions for Black preschool boys because of this disparity.

The early childhood setting is a child's first introduction to the educational setting, and the statistics show that Black children enter this system at a disadvantage from the very beginning. Young children are at risk for racially stressful or traumatic incidents in early childhood settings (Jones et al., 2020). Many children, especially children of color, are exposed to biased school disciplinary practices in early childhood, which sets the tone for their educational experience across their life span as students. Being rejected from the educational system at an early age can lead to Black preschoolers developing low self-esteem and self-worth. While working in a therapeutic preschool, I had a mother who had difficulty finding a preschool for her child, who had been kicked out of several preschools already. Due to funding limitations, we were unable to enroll their child, but I tried my best to assist with referrals. This mom must have talked to me five times over the course of a year. One call, I remember she shared her daughter asked her "How come nobody wants me?." That experience set the tone for how the child believes teachers perceives her. Although I do not know what happened beyond that call, I can bet that child struggled in elementary school, given the high levels of rejection she already faced by the age of five. As the numbers show, Black preschoolers often enter elementary school with the stigmas of bias, racism, and discrimination that create an environment that communicates a lack of physical or emotional safety for Black students.

School-Aged Children and Discipline

As a Black student transitions to elementary school, their trip down the pipeline continues. In the 2017–2018 school year, 50.9 million students attended public schools, with Black students accounting for 15% of enrollment (Office for Civil Rights, 2021). In that same school year, Black students made up 38% of expulsions with educational services and students with one or more in-school suspension and 33% of students with one or more out-of-school suspension (Office for Civil Rights, 2021). Mirroring gender bias in school discipline from early childhood settings, Black boys are more likely to receive an in-school or out-of-school suspension compared to Black girls (20% vs. 11% and 25% vs. 13%, respectively) (Office for Civil Rights, 2021). Seeing this disparity in gender for school discipline in Black students highlights the additional need to support Black boys throughout their educational journey.

Another way that Black students are rejected from traditional educational spaces is through transfers to alternative schools. Black students make up almost 43% of students who are transferred to alternative schools (Office for Civil Rights, 2021). A review of school disciplinary incidents across the country shows glaring examples of the criminalization of childhood behaviors. Minor infractions leading to school arrests include spraying perfume, kicking a trash can, using a fake $2 bill, and carrying a volcano that was a science experiment (Whitaker et al., n.d.). This places Black students at risk of being dehumanized and arrested for issues that could and should be addressed without involving law enforcement. Additionally, the criminalization of poverty often results when individuals turn a blind eye to how systemic racism negatively impacts poor Black children and their families.

School discipline may also be used inappropriately by educators who are unable to let go of past incidents. I worked with a Black child who got in trouble during the first few months of school but was still being punished for that same incident in February. Beyond the fact that the "time did not fit the crime," the punishment was petty and unnecessary. The child, who was in fifth grade at the time, had to skip recess and art (the activities that are the most therapeutic for a child at that developmental age) and was made to sit

---

in the classroom with kindergartners. Every day. This was punishment that was meant to embarrass and shame the child, with no effort to restore the teacher-student relationship.

Discipline Among Black Students with Disabilities

Another subset of Black students receiving harsher school discipline are those with disabilities. Black students are disproportionally diagnosed with disabilities associated with externalizing behaviors such as oppositional defiance, aggression, and hyperactivity, and they are more frequently placed in special education classrooms as a result (Bean, 2013). The Individuals with Disabilities Education Act (IDEA) of 2004 recognizes that it is the responsibility of both state and federal governments to ensure all children with disabilities have access to a quality education (IDEA, n.d.). However, these children are subjected to higher rates of suspension, expulsion, seclusions, and restraints rather than receiving the protection afforded them under the IDEA. Ironically, this is in direct violation of the IDEA Act and Section 504 of the Rehabilitation Act of 1973, which results in Black students losing more days of instruction and contributes to inequities in their access to an education (Losen, 2018).

Black students with disabilities are disproportionately secluded and restrained when compared to other races. Black students only account for 17% of students receiving services under the IDEA Act, but in the 2017–2018 school year they received 30% of in-school suspension, 46% of out-of-school suspensions, and 39% of expulsions (Office for Civil Rights, 2022). *Physical restraints* immobilize or reduce a student's ability to move their torso, legs, arms, or head freely, *mechanical restraints* are any types of equipment or device used to restrict a student's mobility, and *seclusion* is the involuntary confinement of a student in an area or room where the child is prevented from leaving (Office for Civil Rights, 2020). Black children with disabilities account for 26% of physical restraints, 34% of mechanical restraints, and 22% of seclusions in public schools (Office for Civil Rights, 2020). Instead of the support afforded them by law, these students are traumatized by the very people who are supposed to protect them. Furthermore, Black children are receiving the incorrect diagnosis of learning disabilities due to its connections with externalizing behaviors (i.e., oppositional defiance, aggression, hyperactivity) which leads to them having higher rates of placement in alternative educational settings, like special education (Bean, 2013). Overall, the racial disparities in school discipline for Black students, with or without a disability, place them at a higher risk of being arrested at school.

Sometimes Black children are unable to qualify for IDEA services, despite their mental health issues, and they are still subjected to unequal treatment and punishment. I tried helping a five-year-old receive an Individual Education Plan due to his high levels of aggression and other behavioral concerns. The child had an extensive trauma history, yet they did not qualify for services. Why? I was told "It's just trauma". So, the child went into the school without services. A few months later their foster mother called me and told me he was suspended, and was threatened with expulsion, for stabbing a girl with a pencil. The school chose to deny the child the help they needed due to their blinders, and lack of understanding of trauma, then subsequently blamed the child for not making better decisions. In many cases, this leads to Black children being arrested, which completes their trip down the pipeline.

Racial Disparities in School Arrests

The overuse of School Resource Officers (SROs) and local law enforcement to intervene in school disciplinary issues disproportionally affects students of color. A report published by the American Civil Liberties Union (ACLU), "Cops and No Counselors: How the Lack of School Mental Health Staff Is Harming Students," found that schools with a police presence report 3.5 times as many arrests as schools without such a presence (Whitaker et al., 2019). The same report found schools with high percentages of students from low-income families and Black students are more likely to experience security measures such as random "contraband" sweeps, security guards, metal detectors, and security cameras. This communicates to poor students and students of color that they are criminals not children. Black students account for 31% of school arrests and almost 29% of referrals to law enforcement (Office for Civil Rights, 2021). And this happens at an early age across the country.

Another time I attempted to get an IEP for a child going into kindergarten, I was denied. The school officials told me "Oh we know that family already." Now, by law, when a caregiver requests an evaluation for an IEP, the school district must evaluate them, regardless of their history with that child or their family. I even sent over pages of safe room reports to highlight the need for services, as the child was a great child but could become highly aggressive when triggered. Again, I get a phone call. The grandmother tells me that the child punched a teacher, and they were going to press charges against him.

He was six-years old at the time. After a few phone calls and threats, the charges were dropped, but I'm sure the impact of that situation never left that child.

Disparities in school arrests are the most glaring among Black girls, who are seven times more likely to receive at least one out-of-school suspension than White girls and had the highest risk of being arrested or referred to law enforcement (Epstein et al., 2020). Additionally, Black students represent approximately 43% of all transfers to alternative schools (Office for Civil Rights, 2021). This highlights that schools may feel ill-equipped to manage behavioral issues in Black students and so place an overreliance on law enforcement that lands Black students in the crosshairs of the juvenile justice system.

Systemic Racial Stressors: Juvenile Justice System

In the 1960s, legal rights for juveniles were expanded to provide due process considerations like protection against self-incrimination and right to counsel, which started the process of juvenile court proceedings that mimic those of the adult criminal justice system (Jenson & Howard, 1998). This paved the way for an influx of juvenile offenders into both juvenile and adult incarceration facilities. One of the biggest issues to promote this influx are *status offenses*, which are acts that are not criminally illegal for adults but carry heavy consequences for youth (Coalition for Juvenile Justice, 2014). This may include things like truancy and disobedience, which are noncriminal acts but that, in schools and for children of color, are incidents that often lead these children in front of a judge. The racial disparities in school discipline are evidence of how systemic racism negatively impacts Black students.

Studies have found that children who are suspended or expelled are three times more likely to encounter the juvenile justice system the following year (Fabelo et al., 2011). This highlights the direct correlation between school discipline and the juvenile justice system. It also shows the need for schools to find more effective solutions to discipline students, especially students of color. Black youth are five times more likely to be incarcerated or confined compared to White youth (Rovner, 2016). The same report found Black youth were 129% more likely to be arrested than their White counterparts, and Black juvenile offenders are four times more likely to be committed to secure placements compared to White juvenile offenders. Not only does school discipline lead to more frequent interactions with the juvenile justice system, but it also is a risk factor for shortened life expectancy, as a study found that Black formerly incarcerated youth were more likely to die by homicide than their White counterparts (Ruch et al., 2021). Therefore, school social workers are in a unique position to advocate for more appropriate disciplinary practices for Black students, which may then decrease their likelihood of entering the criminal justice systems as adults.

Systemic Racial Stressors: Criminal Justice System

There are also racial disparities in the criminal justice system that directly impact children of color. In the United States, people of color make up 37% of the population but make up 67% of the prison population (Sentencing Project, 2022). Exploring race and ethnicity further, Black Americans are five times more likely to be imprisoned than White Americans (Nellis, 2021). However, people often forget that individuals who are imprisoned also have family systems that are negatively impacted by their incarceration. A total of 47% of individuals in state prisons and 57% of individuals in federal prisons are parents to children under the age of 18 (Ghandnoosh et al., 2021). Adult incarceration serves as a systemic racial stressor for Indigenous and Black students, who are more likely to have a family member who has been incarcerated (20% and 30%, respectively) (Ghandnoosh et al., 2021). As a result, incarcerated family members are an important loss, and this form of attachment trauma directly impacts the well-being of Black students. Having an incarcerated family member serves as a grief event that is further explored in Chapter 8, along with an additional grief event, the child welfare system.

Systemic Racial Stressors: Child Welfare System

Another grief event for Black students that serves a systemic racial stressor is the child welfare system. There is an overrepresentation of Black children of all ages in the child welfare system. Black youth account for 22.75% of the children in foster care, although they only comprise 13% of the US population (Child Welfare Information Gateway, 2021). Black child welfare–involved youth also receive less support while in this system, which contributes to less success than their White peers. Black children in the child welfare system are less likely to receive mental health and developmental services, and they are less likely to be reunified with their caregivers than are White children (Dunbar & Barth, 2007). Both Black caregivers and children in the child welfare system receive fewer supports than their White counterparts. Black caregivers are less likely to receive equitable access to special services and economic resources, and Black children are less likely to have a court order their participation in mental health services compared to White children (Lee et al., n.d.). Chapter 8 provides more detail on how school professionals can support Black youth in the child welfare system relative to a grief event.

Direct Racial Stressors: Community Violence and Adverse Police Contact

There is no data showing Black people are more violent than White people. However, when individuals live in communities with limited resources, such as job opportunities, adequate housing, and healthy foods, they may be more likely to engage in illegal activity as a means of survival. This creates a "dog-eats-dog" mentality where violence is often used to control what limited resources are available. Add in untreated racial stress that continues to build up daily, and it can result in a higher level of violence in Black communities. For example, homicide is the second leading cause of death for Black youth ages 1–14 and the leading cause of death for Black youth ages 15–24 (Centers for Disease Control [CDC], 2019). Living in communities with high levels of violence can place a child in constant survivor mode, so they're always ready to gear up for fight or flight (Community Violence Collaborative Group, 2013). In schools, this may look like a child eloping from the classroom, avoiding certain places or people, or having difficulty concentrating due to hypervigilance. This exposure to community violence can affect a child's outlook on their future and their sense of control (Community Violence Collaborative Group, 2013).

Living in violent neighborhoods also increases the likelihood that Black children will have negative encounters with law enforcement in their communities. From preadolescence, Black children, especially Black boys, are more likely to be heavily policed and have more frequent and more aggressive encounters with law enforcement than are White children (Geller, 2021). Also, Black youth are six times more likely to be shot to death in an officer-involved incident (Equal Justice Initiative, 2020). This is important because it highlights how a child's mental health and ability to engage in self-regulation can be impacted directly by their environment, especially when those experiences spill over into their school environment. Because Black children are more likely to attend schools with law enforcement presence, it is important to recognize that they may be triggered at school due to previous adverse police contact that they directly experienced or witnessed with family and/or community members.

Direct Racial Stressors: Bullying

Bullying is another direct racial stressor Black students experience both on and off campus. As a result of bullying and violence, children of color are more likely to report not going to school because they felt unsafe at school or on their way to or from school (CDC, 2020). Bullying for Black children in school is experienced physically, verbally, and visually. In the 2019–2020 school year, 9% of students reported a gang presence, 7% reported being called hate-related words, and 23% reported seeing hate-related graffiti (Irwin et al., 2022). The same study found multiracial and Black students were more likely to report being called hate-related words in school. In the 2019–2020 school year, 3.8% of public schools reported student racial/ethnic tensions, with those tensions reported highest in middle schools, schools with an enrollment of more than 1,000 students, city schools, schools in the Midwest and West, and schools with more than 50% of enrolled students listed as minorities (Wang et al., 2022). Chapter 6 explores in detail the issue of bullying as a racial stressor in Black students, with special attention to how it also disproportionately impacts Black LGBTQ+ youth.

Vicarious Racial Stressors: Family and Community Systems

Every system that interacts with a Black child harm them (Grills et al., 2019) including their own family and community members. Most of this harm is unintentional and rooted in parenting practices that evolved from slavery. In her book, *Posttraumatic Slave Syndrome*, Dr. Joy DeGruy (2017) outlines a correlation between current parenting practices in the Black community and those from the 17th and 18th centuries. Parenting practices that started out as protective measures have developed into maladaptive practices that contribute to racial trauma in Black youth. For example, a school professional may hear a Black parent talking negatively to their child. Dr. DeGruy traces this practice back to a mother in enslaved times making negative comments about their child to the slave owner to prevent them from selling the child. However, both the parent and child may be oblivious to how this negatively impacts that child's self-esteem. The child may start to think their parents do not love them when, in fact, they love them and are very proud of them. However, since the child is unaware of that pride, it affects their self-esteem and serves as another racial trauma stressor.

Other, similar practices are encouraged in the Black community, such as using physical punishment as a means of correcting behavior. A desire to heavily punish Black children by way of physical discipline is often encouraged by members of the Black community, with the intention of preventing the child from harm or the criminal justice system. However, if everyone is tough on Black children, who is soft with them? Who nurtures them when they are hurting? School social workers may not provide family therapy, but it will be important for them to build bridges with both parents and community members to address vicarious trauma that may be appearing through maladaptive parenting practices that contribute to racial trauma and reduce the overall well-being of Black children. Engaging caregivers and other important adults in the lives of Black children is explored further in Chapter 11.

Racial Trauma Effects in Black Students

There are several ways in which racial trauma affects the behaviors and socialization of Black students. The first is *alienation*, where a student adopts the cultural and racial identity of whiteness (Humphries, 2002). For example, a Black student may wear colored contacts or hair extensions. They may wear clothes and like music that is more associated with White culture. This is different from the idea of *code-switching*, where a student may go back and forth between White and Black cultures to fit in or for safety reasons in certain environments (e.g., going into a predominately White neighborhood or school). Code-switching may be seen as a survival tactic for some Black students, whereas the act of alienation completely separates the student from their culture. Students who alienate their culture require nonjudgmental support from the school counselor while also discussing the disconnection from how they present and how the world sees them.

Internalized racism, the process of accepting the racial stereotypes of the oppressor, is another psychological effect of racial trauma in Black students (Society for Adolescent Health and Medicine, 2018). For example, a Black student may say they don't want to hang out with certain students because they're "ghetto" or they make comments about another student's complexion being "burnt." These statements are rooted in racist ideals that have been around since the 17th century and are embedded in the self-talk of many Black children and adults. These students can benefit from cognitive behavioral play therapy and mindfulness play therapy to increase their self-esteem and decrease negative thinking.

Next, *race-related fatigue*, which is the mental fatigue associated with daily exposure to and vigilance associated with racial trauma (Smith et al., 2011), is another factor in identity development for Black children. For example, a

Black student in a predominately White school may stop trying out for certain teams or doing certain activities because of being singled out as a Black student. They may be dealing with microaggressions or racist questions that they are expected to answer from curious White peers. As a result, fatigue sets in and they may disengage from those teams/activities. A student struggling with racial fatigue may benefit from learning healthy coping skills, setting boundaries with peers, and making connections with community organizations or clubs that can affirm their identity and culture.

Racial mistrust is the final psychological effect on Black students experiencing racial trauma. Black students may have developed a distrust for White people and professionals either from their own experiences with racial trauma or because of historical trauma in the Black community. Medical traumas, such as the Tuskegee experiments, forced sterilization of Black women, and gynecology built around experiments on unanesthetized slave women and children contribute to the levels of mistrust that Black students and families may have toward White helping professionals. Racial mistrust of Black children toward White teachers and mental health professionals requires these adults accept with a certain level of humility that they may not be the best fit for that student. If these professionals do not, it may hinder that students' academic and therapeutic success.

For example, a student may show up to a clinical session disengaged or not even speaking. It may have nothing to do with the professional and everything to do with the racial stressors they experienced before stepping into the session. It is natural for that professional to think "They have an attitude problem" or "They don't want to be here." It is important to remember that Black children are dealing with high levels of racial stress in every environment they encounter. Often those interactions are with White people, so they may have difficulty connecting with a White clinician. The school social worker will need to display patience and focus on gaining that student's trust, which can take months or even years.

Racial Trauma and Black Youth Mental Health

The psychological effects of racial trauma in Black youth are often overlooked as the root of behavioral issues, despite the American Public Health Association (APHA) recognizing racism as a public health crisis (2020). *Adverse childhood events* (ACEs) are potentially traumatic events a child may experience, such as witnessing violence or suffering from abuse and neglect (CDC, 2021). Black children are more likely to have higher rates of childhood adverse experiences, which, left untreated, can result in mental health issues such as anxiety and depression (Patterson et al., 2018). However, Black children are less likely to be identified as having these conditions and encouraged to receive mental health treatment compared to White children (Alegria et al., 2012). As a result, Black youth are silently suffering from a mental health crisis. In 2018, 65.4% of Black youth who received a major depressive disorder diagnosis could not receive treatment (Substance Abuse and Mental Health Services Administration [SAMHSA], 2018). Black youth are more likely to be diagnosed with depression and behavioral/conduct disorders than are White youth but are less likely to receive mental health treatment for their diagnosis (Ghandour et al., 2019). This places school social workers in a unique position to provide services to students who have limited accessibility in their communities while also using a racial trauma lens when assessing their behavior so they are receiving the most ethically and culturally appropriate care possible.

Signs of Racial Trauma in Black Students

There are some keys signs of racial trauma that mental health professionals should look for in Black students. An infographic (Appendix B) for school social workers to keep in their office will help students recognize signs of racial trauma in themselves. It is important to remember that these present as trauma symptoms identified in the DSM-5 and should be treated as such. First, a student may have increased vigilance or suspicion. This can be suspicion of social institutions like schools and agencies (Smith, 2010). It also can be a student talking about how a teacher is "out to get them." Additional signs of suspicion in Black students are avoiding eye contact or stating they only trust close friends and family (Smith, 2010). This suspicion is in relation to their previous experiences and should not be termed paranoia. Instead, the professional should validate their feelings and experiences while supporting them in ways to navigate environments where they are displaying vigilance and/or suspicion. School counselors should also use safety language when communicating with the student and provide opportunities for the student to identify safe people and places.

Increased sensitivity to threat is another sign of racial trauma in Black students. This could be defensive postures, avoiding new situations, avoiding taking risks, or a heightened sensitivity to being disrespected and shamed (Smith, 2010). Disrespect is often the catalyst for disagreements and discipline in Black students. Applying a racial trauma lens helps the counselor realize that Black students are often put into situations where they are being talked down to, called out, and sometimes even shamed for their behavior. If that student has experienced high levels of racial stress, a disrespectful event can trigger their trauma response. Psychoeducation for both the student and school officials on trauma responses specific for that child will be key to addressing the behavior rather than issuing punishment.

Black students may also exhibit an increase in psychological and physiological symptoms (Smith, 2010). Unresolved traumas contribute to increased chronic stress and compromise the immune system (Morsy & Rothstein, 2019). This could manifest in a student who has a lot of trips to the nurse because of headaches, stomachaches, or other ailments. Trauma shifts the brain to a limbic system dominance, which can diminish brain activity in the prefrontal cortex that assists in executive functioning, learning, memory, anxiety, attention, and emotional regulation (Morsy & Rothstein, 2019). The school counselor should work with the family to rule out any medical conditions before treating their symptoms therapeutically, but helping students identify signs of distress and self-regulation skills can help them learn more effective coping skills to assist with regulation.

Substance use and abuse is another sign of racial trauma in Black students. This can include an increase or a new behavior in using alcohol or drugs. The real or perceived "help" that drugs and alcohol provides may be seen as beneficial in managing their pain and the danger of unresolved traumas (Smith, 2010). This can be tricky for school social workers because a student may disclose their substance use in session. Unless it is causing direct harm to themselves or others, this does not meet criteria for breaking confidentiality. Instead, the counselor should focus on the safety issues and the potential consequences, and then focus treatment on the feelings the student is looking to avoid and/or suppress through the use of drugs and/or alcohol.

Another sign of racial trauma is increased aggression. This could be joining street gangs, incidents of interpersonal violence, defiant behavior, and trying to appear tough and impenetrable (Smith, 2010). People living in a chronic state of danger do not develop a sense of fear, therefore, Black students may develop ways of coping with danger by attempting to control their physical and social environments. One skill to manage aggression is to focus on social emotional expression, especially around Black boys who may struggle with expressing emotions that are not deemed "cool" or may make them seem "weak." For example, in over ten years of clinical experience, the Black boys I worked with would flat out deny any feelings of fear, often telling me "I'm not afraid of nothing." This is a protective factor they have developed as a means of coping with danger by trying to appear tough and putting on a facade. School social workers should focus on anger management and self-regulation skills for Black male students while also considering healthy outlets for aggression such as boxing, kickboxing or marital arts.

Finally, a narrowing sense of time can be a sign of racial trauma in Black students. They may experience *allostatic load*, which means they may be constantly operating from their "survival brain." In turn, they may not communicate long-term goals and may frequently view dying as an expected outcome (Smith, 2010). It is important to remember that many Black students have seen high levels of violence and death in their lives, either directly or indirectly through the public executions of unarmed Black people by both law enforcement and "citizens" alike. School social workers should validate their concerns around death and discuss mindfulness strategies to help them focus on the present rather than the future, which they cannot control. Also, school social workers should be mindful of these comments/behaviors as a possible risk factor for suicide and conduct a suicide risk assessment to be safe.

Assessing Racial Trauma in Black Students

Assessing racial trauma in Black students will require a systemic approach to identify the key pieces of the puzzle that will create a culturally sensitive and trauma-focused diagnosis and treatment plan for Black students. Pieces of that puzzle include the use of clinical assessments, developmentally appropriate questions for students, and play themes that develop in their therapy sessions. Each piece provides insight into how racial trauma presents in each student specifically. It is paramount that school counselors take all the puzzle pieces into consideration when advocating for mental health services and appropriate discipline for Black students.

There are three clinical assessments that can assist in screening and identifying symptoms of racial trauma in Black students. First, the *Philadelphia Expanded ACEs* screens for ACEs, including racism (Philadelphia ACE Project, 2021). This assessment is recommended for all students each school year as it gives the social worker a better idea of trauma exposure for each school year. Next, the *Race-Related Event Scale* (RES) helps identify if the student has experienced any race-related events (Waelde et al., 2010). This can be a starting point for the school social worker to identify if the client has had specific racial stressors. If that student does screen for race-based events, the school counselor should use the *Race-Based Traumatic Symptoms Scale* (RBTSS) pre- and post-intervention. This scale identifies specific presentations of race-based trauma such as hypervigilance and avoidance (Carter et al., 2013). The assessment can also be used in psychoeducation for the student, their teachers, and their families on how the students' racial trauma presents so more context is given to their behavior.

Conclusion

The behaviors of Black students are often disciplined or dismissed in every environment they encounter. This places them at a higher risk for mental health issues that may be overlooked, misdiagnosed, or punished. When racial trauma is left untreated, it puts Black students at a higher risk for disrupted development, mental health issues, and even death. This book will help school social workers use a racial trauma perspective when working with students while also encouraging self-reflection to identify how professional and personal biases may show up in clinical work with Black students and families. However, rather than only focusing on the problems, I will offer innovative solutions using play therapy to help empower school social workers to have the language and tools to help Black students heal from racial trauma. Play can serve as an innovative tool to address racial trauma with Black students while also empowering them to advocate for their mental and social-emotional needs. However, school social workers will be required to acquire high levels of cultural humility and inclusivity in their clinical work with Black students to build trusting and authentic therapeutic bonds.

References

Alegría, M., Lin, J., Green, J., Sampson, N., Gruber, M., & Kessler, R. (2012). Role of referrals in mental health service disparities for racial and ethnic minority youth. *Journal of the American Academy of Child & Adolescent Psychiatry, 51*(7), 703–711.e2. https://doi.org/10.1016/j.jaac.2012.05.005

Al-Shamma, E., Basallaje, A., Bridges, C., Elgart, A., Gee, O., Kamisugi, K., Lystrup, L., Mahomes, A., Miller, A., & Mueller, J. (2016). Breaking the chains 2: The preschool-to-prison pipeline epidemic. Equal Justice Society. https://equaljusticesociety.org/wp-content/uploads/2021/09/Breaking-The-Chains-2-The-Preschool-To-Prison-Pipeline-Epidemic-PDF.pdf

American Psychiatric Association. (2013). *Diagnostic and statistical manual of mental disorders* (5th ed.). American Psychiatric Association Publishing.

American Public Health Association. (2020, October 24). Structural racism is a public health crisis: Impact on the Black community. https://www.apha.org/policies-and-advoc

acy/public-health-policy-statements/policy-database/2021/01/13/structural-racism-is-a-public-health-crisis

Arshanapally, S., Werner, K., Sartor, C., & Bucholz, K. (2018). The association between racial discrimination and suicidality among African-American adolescents and young adults. *Archives of Suicide Research*, 22(4), 584–595. https://doi-org.libproxy1.usc.edu/10.1080/13811118.2017.1387207

Assari, S., Moazen-Zadeh, E., Caldwell, C., & Zimmerman, M. (2017). Racial discrimination during adolescence predicts mental health deterioration in adulthood: Gender differences among Blacks. *Frontiers in Public Health*, 5, 104–104. https://doi.org/10.3389/fpubh.2017.00104

Bean, K. (2013). Disproportionality and acting-out behaviors among African American children in special education. *Child and Adolescent Social Work Journal*, 30(6), 1–18. https://doi.org/10.1007/s10560-013-0304-6

Carter, R. T., Mazzula, S., Victoria, R., Vazquez, R., Hall, S., Smith, S., Sant-Barket, S., Forsyth, J., Bazelais, K., & Williams, B. (2013). Race-Based Traumatic Stress Symptom Scale (RBTSS). PsycTESTS. https://dx.doi.org/10.1037/t19426-000

Centers for Disease Control and Prevention. (2019). Ten leading causes of death, United States. National Center for Health Statistics. https://webappa.cdc.gov/sasweb/ncipc/leadcause.html

Centers for Disease Control and Prevention. (2020). Youth Risk Behavior Surveillance—United States 2019. *Morbidity and Mortality Weekly Report*, 69(1), 1–85. https://www.cdc.gov/mmwr/volumes/69/su/pdfs/su6901-H.pdf

Centers for Disease and Control. (2021). Preventing adverse childhood experiences. U.S. Department of Health and Human Services. https://www.cdc.gov/violenceprevention/aces/fastfact.html?CDC_AA_refVal=https%3A%2F%2Fwww.cdc.gov%2Fviolenceprevention%2Facestudy%2Ffastfact.html

Child Welfare Information Gateway. (2021). Child welfare practice to address race disproportionality and disparity. https://www.childwelfare.gov/pubpdfs/racial_disproportionality.pdf

Coalition for Juvenile Justice. (2014). Deinstitutionalization of status offenders (DSO): Facts and resources. http://www.juvjustice.org/sites/default/files/resource-files/DSO%20Fact%20Sheet%202014.pdf

Community Violence Collaborative Group. (2013). Community violence: Reactions and actions in dangerous times. National Child Traumatic Stress Network. https://www.nctsn.org/sites/default/files/resources/fact-sheet/community_violence_reactions_and_actions_in_dangerous_times.pdf

Craft, M., Hayes, S., & Moore, R. (2020). Supporting the mental health well-being of high school students. Center for Equity in Learning. https://www.act.org/content/dam/act/unsecured/documents/R1798-mental-health-2020-01.pdf

DeGruy, J. (2017). *Post-traumatic slave syndrome: America's legacy of enduring injury & healing*. Uptown Press.

Dunbar, K., & Barth, R. P. (2007). Racial disproportionality, race disparity and other race-related finding in published works derived from the National Survey of Child and Adolescent Well-being. Casey-CSSP Alliance for Racial Equity in Child Welfare. https://

assets.aecf.org/m/resourcedoc/aecf-CFP-RacialDisproportionalityRaceDisparityAndOth
erRaceRelatedFindingsInPublishedWorksDerivedFromTheNationalSurveyOfChildAnd
AdolescentWellBeing-2008.pdf

English, D., Lambert, S., Tynes, B., Bowleg, L., Zea, M., & Howard, L. (2020). Daily
multidimensional racial discrimination among Black U.S. American adolescents.
Journal of Applied Developmental Psychology, *66*, 101068. https://doi.org/10.1016/j.app
dev.2019.101068

Epstein, R., Godfrey, E., Gonzalez, T., & Javdani, S. (2020). Data snapshot: 2017–2018.
National data on school discipline by race and gender. Georgetown Law Center on
Poverty & Inequality. https://genderjusticeandopportunity.georgetown.edu/wp-cont
ent/uploads/2021/04/National-Data-on-School-Discipline-by-Race-and-Gender.pdfx

Equal Justice Initiative. (2020). Black children are six times more likely to be shot to death
by police. https://eji.org/news/black-children-are-six-times-more-likely-to-be-shot-to-
death-by-police/

Fabelo, T., Thompson, M. D., Plotkin, M., Carmichael, D., Marchbanks III, M. P., & Booth,
E. A. (2011, July). Breaking school's rules: A statewide study of how school disci-
pline relates to students' success and juvenile justice involvement. Council of State
Governments Justice Center. https://csgjusticecenter.org/wp-content/uploads/2020/01/
Breaking_Schools_Rules_Report_

Geller, A. (2021). Youth–police contact: Burdens and inequities in an adverse childhood
experience, 2014–2017. *American Journal of Public Health*, *111*(7), 1300–1308. https://
doi.org/10.2105/AJPH.2021.306259

Ghandnoosh, N., Stammen, E., & Muhitch, K. (2021). Parents in prison. The Sentencing
Project. https://www.sentencingproject.org/app/uploads/2022/09/Parents-in-Prison.pdf

Ghandour, R. M., Sherman, L. J., Vladutiu, C. J., Lynch, S. E., Bitsko, R. H., &
Blumberg, S. J. (2019). Prevalence and treatment of depression, anxiety and conduct
problems in US children. *Journal of Pediatrics*, *206*, 256–267. https://doi.org10.1016/
j.jpeds.2018.09.021

Grills, C., Banks, J., Norrington-Sands, K., Jackson, T. R., Steve, S. L., & Clark, M. (2019,
October 15). Black child suicide: A report. National Cares Mentoring Movement &
The Association of Black Psychologists. https://www.caresmentoring.org/black_child_
suicide_report.pdf

Henderson, D., Walker, L., Barnes, R., Lunsford, A., Edwards, C., & Clark, C. (2019). A
framework for race-related trauma in the public education system and implications on
health for Black youth. *Journal of School Health*, *89*(11), 926–933. https://doi-org.libpro
xy1.usc.edu/10.1111/josh.12832

Hernadez, J. (2021). Read this powerful statement from Darnella Fraizer, who filmed
George Floyd's murder. NPR. https://www.npr.org/2021/05/26/1000475344/read-this-
powerful-statement-from-darnella-frazier-who-filmed-george-floyds-murd

Humphries, K. T. (2002). Alienation And race-related stress: A comparison of clinical and
counseling psychology students of African descent. Seton Hall University Dissertations
and Theses (ETDs). No. 269. https://scholarship.shu.edu/dissertations/269

Individuals with Disabilities Education Act. (n.d.). About IDEA. https://sites.ed.gov/idea/
about-idea/

Irwin, V., Wang, K., Cui, J., & Thompson, A. (2022). Report of indicators of school crime and safety: 2021. National Center for Education for Education Statistics at IES. https://nces.ed.gov/pubs2022/2022092.pdf

Jenson, J., & Howard, M. (1998). Youth crime, public policy, and practice in the juvenile justice system: Recent trends and needed reforms, *Social Work*, 43(4), 324–334. https://doi-org.libproxy1.usc.edu/10.1093/sw/43.4.324

Jones, S., Anderson, R., Gaskin-Wasson, A., Sawyer, B., Applewhite, K., & Metzger, I. (2020). From "crib to coffin": Navigating coping from racism-related stress throughout the lifespan of Black Americans. *American Journal of Orthopsychiatry*, 90(2), 267–282. https://doi.org/10.1037/ort0000430

Lanier, Y., Sommers, M., Fletcher, J., Sutton, M., & Roberts, D. (2017). Examining racial discrimination frequency, racial discrimination stress, and psychological well-being among Black early adolescents. *Journal of Black Psychology*, 43(3), 219–229. https://doi.org/10.1177/0095798416638189

Lee, J., Bell, Z., Ackerman-Brimberg, M. (n.d.). Implicit bias in the child welfare, education and mental health systems. National Center for Youth Law. https://ncwwi.org/files/Cultural_Responsiveness__Disproportionality/Implicit-Bias-in-Child-Welfare-Education-and-Mental-Health-Systems-Literature-Review_061915.pdf

Losen, D. J. (2018). Disabling punishment: The need for remedies to the disparate loss of instruction experienced by Black students with disabilities. The Center for Civil Rights Remedies at the Civil Rights Project. https://today.law.harvard.edu/wp-content/uploads/2018/04/disabling-punishment-report-.pdf

Mental Health America. (2023). Racial trauma. https://www.mhanational.org/racial-trauma

McNeil Smith, S., & Fincham, F. (2016). Racial discrimination experiences among Black youth: A person-centered approach. *Journal of Black Psychology*, 42(4), 300–319. doi.org/10.1177/0095798415573315

Morsy, L., & Rothstein, R. (2019). Toxic stress and children's outcomes. Economic Policy Institute. https://www.epi.org/publication/toxic-stress-and-childrens-outcomes-african-american-children-growing-up-poor-are-at-greater-risk-of-disrupted-physiological-functioning-and-depressed-academic-achievement/

Nellis, A. (2021). The color of justice: Racial and ethnic disparities in state prisons. The Sentencing Project. https://www.sentencingproject.org/reports/the-color-of-justice-racial-and-ethnic-disparity-in-state-prisons-the-sentencing-project/

Office for Civil Rights. (2020). The use of restraint and seclusion on children with disabilities in k-12 schools. U.S. Department of Education, 2017-2018 Civil Rights Data Collection (CRDC). https://www2.ed.gov/about/offices/list/ocr/docs/restraint-and-seclusion.pdf

Office for Civil Rights. (2021). An overview of exclusionary discipline practices in public schools for the 2017–2018 school year. U.S. Department of Education, 2017-2018 Civil Rights Data Collection (CRDC). https://ocrdata.ed.gov/assets/downloads/crdc-exclusionary-school-discipline.pdf

Office for Civil Rights. (2022). Suspensions and expulsions of students with disabilities in public schools. U.S. Department of Education, 2017-2018 Civil Rights Data Collection

(CRDC). https://ocrdata.ed.gov/assets/downloads/Discipline_of_Students_with_Dis abilities_Part3.pdf

Pachter, L., Caldwell, C., Jackson, J., & Bernstein, B. (2018). Discrimination and mental health in a representative sample of African-American and Afro-Caribbean Youth. *Journal of Racial and Ethnic Health Disparities*, 5(4), 831–837. https://doi.org/10.1007/ s40615-017-0428-z

Patterson, L., Stutey, D., & Dorsey, B. (2018). Play therapy with African American children exposed to adverse childhood experiences. *International Journal of Play Therapy™*, 27(4), 215–226. https://doi.org/10.1037/pla0000080

Philadelphia ACE Project. (2021). Philadelphia ACE study. https://www.philadelphiaaces. org/philadelphia-ace-survey

Pickett, L. (2020). Three trains running: The intersectionality of race-based trauma, African American youth, and race-based interventions. *Urban Review*, 52(3), 562–602. https:// doi.org/10.1007/s11256-020-00575-x

Polanco-Roman, L., Anglin, D., Miranda, R., & Jeglic, E. (2019). Racial/ethnic discrimination and suicidal ideation in emerging adults: The role of traumatic stress and depressive symptoms varies by gender, not race/ethnicity. *Journal of Youth and Adolescence*, 48(10), 2023–2037. https://doi.org/10.1007/s10964-019-01097-w

Rovner, J. (2016). Racial disparities in youth commitments and arrests. The Sentencing Project. https://www.sentencingproject.org/app/uploads/2022/08/Racial-Disparities-in-Youth-Incarceration-Persist.pdf

Ruch, D. A., Steelesmith, D. L., Brock, G., Boch, S. J., Quinn, C. R., Bridge, J. A., Campo, J. V., & Fontanella, C. A. (2021). Mortality and cause of death among youths previously incarcerated in the juvenile legal system. *JAMA Network Open*, 4(12), e2140352. https:// doi.org/10.1001/jamanetworkopen.2021.40352

Sentencing Project. (2022). Growth in mass incarceration. https://www.sentencingproject. org/criminal-justice-facts/

Smith, W. (2010). The impact of racial trauma on African Americans. The Heinz Endowments. http://www.heinz.org/userfiles/ impactofracialtraumaonafricanameric ans.pdf

Smith, W. A., Hung, M., & Franklin, J. D. (2011). Racial battle fatigue and the miseducation of Black men: Racial microaggressions, societal problems, and environmental Stress. *Journal of Negro Education*, 80(1), 63–82. http://www.jstor.org/stable/41341106

Society for Adolescent Health and Medicine. (2018). Racism and its harmful effects on nondominant racial–ethnic youth and youth-serving providers: A call to action for organizational change. *Journal of Adolescent Health*, 63(2), 257–261. https://doi.org/ 10.1016/j.jadohealth.2018.06.003

Substance Abuse and Mental Health Services Administration [SAMHSA]. (2018). 2018: National survey on drug use and health: African Americans. U.S. Department of Health and Human Services. https://www.samhsa.gov/data/sites/default/files/reports/ rpt23247/2_AfricanAmerican_2020_01_14_508.pdf

Tynes, B., Willis, H., Stewart, A., & Hamilton, M. (2019). Race-Related traumatic events online and mental health among adolescents of color. *Journal of Adolescent Health*, 65(3), 371–377. https://doi.org/10.1016/j.jadohealth.2019.03.00

Waelde, L., Pennington, D., Mahan, C., Mahan, R., Kabour, M., & Marquett, R. (2010). Psychometric properties of the race-related events scale. *Psychological Trauma*, 2(1), 4–11. https://doi.org/10.1037/a0019018

Walker, R., Francis, D., Brody, G., Simons, R., Cutrona, C., & Gibbons, F. (2016, May 3). A longitudinal study of racial discrimination and risk for death ideation in African American youth. *Suicide and Life-Threatening Behavior*, 47(1), 86–102. https://doi-org.libproxy1.usc.edu/10.1111/sltb.12251

Wang, K., Kemp, J., Burr, R., & Swan, D. (2022). Crime, violence, discipline, and safety in U.S. public schools in 2019–2020. Findings from the school survey on crime and safety. U.S. Department of Education. Institute of Education Sciences. https://nces.ed.gov/pubsearch/pubsinfo.asp?pubid=2022029

Whitaker, A., Torres-Guillen, S., Morton, M., Jordan, H., Coyle, S., Mann, A., & Sun, W. L. (n.d.). Cops and no counselors: How the lack of school mental health is harming students. American Civil Liberties Union. https://www.aclu.org/sites/default/files/field_document/030419-acluschooldisciplinereport.pdf

Diversity Definitions

Race

A group of people who have similar physical characteristics like skin color, facial features, type of hair, etc.

•Examples: Black, White, Biracial/Multiracial, Asian, Hawaiian Pacific Islander, American Native

Racism

Believing that people belonging to a certain race are lesser

•Examples: A person believes that Black people are not as smart as people in their race.

Culture

Certain characteristics or traditions that a group of people have in common. Culture is often passed down through generations.

•Example: Music, food, religion, clothing, holidays, language, and beliefs are all a part of culture.

Discrimination

When someone is treated unfairly because of something that makes them different. This can be their race, the way they dress, age, gender, religion, or other things.

•Example: A sports team not allowing a person to try out because they are a girl.

Stereotype

An assumption someone makes about a person or group of people based on how they look or a certain group they belong to.

•Example: Believing that someone is dangerous or a threat because of their religion.

Prejudice

Prejudging: Making a judgment about a person or group without really having a reason to. This can lead to treating them unfairly before getting to know them.

•Example: A teacher thinks a Black student might be a "trouble maker", so they make them sit in the front of the class on the first day of school.

Microaggression

Hurtful things someone says or does that are subtle or something you may not notice right away.

•Example: Someone purposefully mispronouncing your name or asking you "Why did your parents name you that?"

Inclusion

Actively trying to include others and allow them fair opportunities for success.

•Example: A school decides to start teaching about LGBTQ history to students in class.

Racial Trauma Symptoms

What is Racial Trauma?

Racial trauma is the result of constant interactions with racism, microaggressions, prejudice and discrimination. A person can show the same signs of Post-traumatic Stress Disorder (PTSD) after a negative race-based experience. Below are some signs of racial trauma.

Distress

You may have issues with sleeping due to nightmares or recurring dreams about the incident. You may also be experiencing flashbacks or other distressing thoughts related to the incident. For children, it may look like regressive behaviors like bed-wetting, thumb-sucking and "baby talk".

Avoidance

You may avoid certain people, places, things or sounds that remind you of the incident. You may also avoid talking about or acknowledging the incident happened. For children, it may look like missing school or an increase in tantrums.

Anxiety & Depression

After the incident, you may notice a higher level of anxiety or depression. This may happen periodically or continuously. Anxious symptoms can include physical sickness, shortness of breath, shaky hands or panic attacks. Symptoms of depression include irritability, lack of motivation, feelings of helplessness/hopelessness and thoughts of suicide or self-harm

Villines, Z. (2020). What to know about racial trauma. medical news today. https://www.medicalnewstoday.com/articles/racial-trauma#who-is-affected

Intrusive Thoughts

You may notice you have had difficulty paying attention and focusing since the incident. Or you may be distracted because of memories or thoughts of what happened. For children, it may look like daydreaming, difficulty paying attention at school and difficulty completing tasks.

Negative Thoughts

You have have negative thoughts about yourself since the incident, which may be affecting your self-esteem. You also may have negative thoughts and may not feel like you can trust other people or even the world. This can be periodically or continuously. This can put you at a higher risk of suicidal thoughts or self-harming behaviors. You can text HOME to 741741 Crisis Text Line or call the National Suicide Prevention Hotline at 800-273-8255 if you have thoughts of harming yourself.

Increased Vigilance

Other people may describe you as "jumpy" after the incident. You may also notice you are startled more easily or more hyper-vigilant about your surroundings. For children, it may look like "clingy" behavior and have problems separating from their caregivers or worrying about their safety.

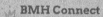

BMH Connect
Education, Connection, Empowerment

If you feel like you may be experiencing symptoms of racial trauma, you can find resources and support on our website www.bmhconnect.com.

2

███

Displaying Cultural Humility with Black Students

At every turn, Black children are met with opposition and judgment on how they should talk, dress, and behave. These standards of language, dress, and behavior are rooted in Eurocentric beliefs, which often leads to Black students being chastised or punished for not fitting into these subjective boxes of behaviors. High levels of race-based stress can have a negative effect on students' view of themselves as they are constantly told everything about them is wrong or deviant. Clinically, Black students may exhibit signs of anxiety, depression, and defiance because of racial trauma. They may disengage from school and isolate themselves from peers, which places them at a higher risk for self-harming and suicidality behaviors. Despite these difficulties, Black students are not engaged in mental health services at the same rate as their peers.

Cultural humility is an orientation and attitude held by the school social worker in which the therapist honors the reality of multiple experiences and truths based on an individual's background, identities, and experiences (Center for Play Therapy, 2022). *Cultural inclusivity* is the behaviors and actions by the social workers to include the cultural factors and nuances of individuals in the therapeutic process. School social workers should be tasked to develop both cultural humility and inclusivity when working with Black students, which includes self-reflection on implicit biases toward Black students that may be causing a blind spot in how the child's behavior is assessed, treated, and disciplined in schools and in mental health diagnosis and treatment. Everyone, regardless of their racial/ethnic background, has implicit biases, and it will require a level of humility to admit they exist, recognize how they may be negatively impacting service delivery, and take

Black Students Matter. April D. Duncan, Oxford University Press. © Oxford University Press 2024.
DOI: 10.1093/oso/9780197669266.003.0003

conscious steps to resolve them. This also requires identifying where power and privilege exist. A lack of awareness of power and privilege can recreate oppressive relationships with clients (Gill & Drewes, 2021). When working with Black students, school social workers should strive to provide a free space where Black children are seen, heard, and respected for who they are. I use the term "free space" intentionally, to emphasize the importance of providing a space for Black students to be free to be themselves. But first we must address the lack of mental health support Black children are receiving both in and out of schools.

Black Youth Mental Health

It is not news to school social workers that there are not enough hands to help manage the mental health of students, especially when accounting for racial trauma in children of color. More than 14 million children ages 3–17 were reported to have a mental, emotional, developmental, or behavioral problem in the 2020–2021 school year (Child and Adolescent Health Measurement Initiative, 2022). Schools often become a place where children can receive mental health services that may be inaccessible beyond school walls. Students are 21 more times likely to receive mental health treatment in schools (Whitaker et. al, n.d.). However, students of all backgrounds are still having difficulty obtaining mental health support. A study found that 55% of public schools provided mental health assessments to their students, but only 42% of schools provided mental health treatment to those students, which is an improvement from the 2017–2018 school year (Diliberti et al., 2019; Wang et al., 2022). The lack of treatment has been connected to two major factors: lack of financial support and too few support staff to meet the high demand for mental health treatment. In the 2019–2020 school year, 54% of public schools reported inadequate funding and 40% reported lack of access to mental health professionals as a barrier to providing mental health support to their students (Wang et al., 2022).

In addition to high levels of racial stressors, racial disparities exist in the mental health status of Black students and their ability to obtain mental health treatment. Black children are the second largest demographic (23.2% compared to 25.6% of White) of students with a reported mental, emotional, developmental, or behavioral problem (Child and Adolescent Health Measurement Initiative, 2022). It is important to note that this number may be higher because there may be Black children who are undiagnosed with mental health issues that are disguised as "misbehavior" and "defiance." However, only 9.5% of Black children received treatment or counseling from a mental health professional, with almost 17% of Black caregivers reporting it was very difficult to get their children the mental health treatment they needed (Child and Adolescent Health Measurement Initiative, 2022). Also, Black and multiracial parents were more likely to report they were unable to get their child mental health treatment when needed, and 6% reported it was not possible to obtain care at all (Child and Adolescent Health Measurement Initiative, 2022). One barrier to mental health treatment in Black students is their reluctance to seek out services. A study found Black students were less likely to reach out to a teacher or counselor if they needed mental health support (Craft et al., 2020). This highlights the need for school social workers and educators to build stronger relationships with Black students so they are comfortable asking for help when needed.

Black Youth Mental Health and COVID-19

The COVID-19 pandemic had a negative effect on students across the country. During January–June 2021, approximately half of high school students reported emotional abuse by a parent and 1 in 10 students reported physical abuse by a parent (Krause et al., 2022). The pandemic also had a negative impact on the mental health of children of color. A 2020 survey conducted by the Centers for Disease and Control (CDC) found virtual-only instruction was more commonly reported among children of color compared to White children, and parents of children receiving only virtual learning more frequently reported that their child's emotional or mental health worsened during the pandemic (2020). Black high school students were found to report higher levels of hunger and a higher prevalence of physical abuse compared to White students (Krause, 2021). On top of the pandemic, Black students had to deal with constant negative interactions with racism and discrimination. Among Black high school students, female students were more likely to report experiencing perceived racism during their lifetime than were male students (58% and 52%, respectively) (Mpofu, 2022). Among the Black students who reported experiencing perceived racism in their lifetime, 62% of those students reported poor mental health during the COVID-19 pandemic and 66% reported serious difficulty remembering, concentrating, or making decisions because of a physical, mental, or emotional problem (Mpofu, 2022). Understanding the need for mental health services for Black students is the first step. After they get into treatment, it is paramount that school social workers provide the most ethically sound and appropriate treatment possible.

Ethical Social Work with Black Students

Although social workers should adhere to all the values, principles, and standards of the National Association of Social Worker (NASW)'s (2022) code of ethics, there are three specific values school social workers should abide by when delivering therapeutic services to Black students: social justice, acknowledging the dignity and worth of the person, and the importance of human relationships. The value of *social justice* is respectful of the culture of Black students, which can serve as a protective factor for treatment planning. *Acknowledging the dignity and worth of the person* reminds school social workers to help empower Black students to address and advocate for their needs in systems that neglect them. The *importance of human relationships* will challenge school social workers to strengthen relationships, not just with Black students, but also with their caregivers and members of their communities. It will also require school social workers to build strong relationships with teachers who often struggle with their own implicit biases in the ways they connect, or disconnect, with Black students.

NASW Value: Social Justice

The ethical principle of *social justice* encourages social workers to challenge social injustice, especially with and on behalf of oppressed and vulnerable individuals and groups of people (NASW, 2022). Black students are oppressed in every system; schools, the juvenile and criminal justice systems, the child welfare system, and in their own families and communities. The lack of advocacy for fair and equal treatment for Black students in schools is a form of oppression. Therefore, school social workers are ethically responsible for advocating for their mental health needs in schools. This can include attending meetings for Individual Education Plans (IEP) and advocating for the most appropriate mental health services. This may require meeting with school officials to voice concern around harsh or unnecessary disciplinary practices toward a student. This may be difficult as no one wants to rock the boat at their place of employment. However, to sit silent is to contribute to the racial stressors experienced by Black students.

The NASW value of *social justice* also requires social workers to promote sensitivity and knowledge about oppression and ethnic and cultural diversity (NASW, 2022). School social workers experience the most success in speaking up about differential treatment in Black students by having rapport with educators first, then clearly communicating how the oppression toward the student is detrimental to their mental health. Using clinical assessments and other assessments will allow the social worker to have data to support their concerns, along with suggestions in the classroom and therapy sessions to help address the problem behaviors in a way that is free of oppression.

NASW Value: Dignity and Worth of the Person

Social workers always should respect the inherent *dignity and worth of the person* (NASW, 2022). Black students constantly enter spaces that reject who and how they are, so school social workers should provide an environment that respects each student and their culture. Ethically, social workers are expected to treat each person in a respectful and caring manner while being mindful of cultural and ethnic diversity (NASW, 2022). Working in schools, there is a higher probability that the social worker has seen or been told about the negative behaviors of the student prior to starting treatment. However, the school social worker should go into every session believing the inherent good in each student and attempt to keep subjective accounts from other adults out of the therapy session. This lets the school social worker allow the student to show who they are and what they need, rather than other people defining what is best for the child. One suggestion is to take a page from Garry Landreth, the founder of child-centered play therapy, who does not meet with the child's parents prior to the session, as they do not want background information to color their perception of the child. School social workers may benefit from avoiding any background information about the child's history to ensure they see the child for who they are, rather than their circumstances or what someone else has shared.

Like the social work value of *social justice*, the value of *dignity and worth of the person* recommends that social workers attempt to resolve conflicts between the clients' interests and the broader society's interests in a socially responsible manner consistent with the ethical principles, values, and standards of the social work profession (NASW, 2022). This can also include advocating for change in disciplinary practices at the school, state, and national levels. It may also include offering to provide a professional development workshop to staff on the negative effects of racial stressors in Black students, one that includes suggestions on ways to address classroom management and strengthen teacher–student relationships. (Chapter 9 goes into more detail about using play therapy to support teachers.)

NASW Value: Importance of Human Relationships

In their work with Black students, school social workers must acknowledge and recognize the central *importance of relationships* (NASW, 2022). Working with Black students and effectively advocating for their needs will require the school social worker to build strong therapeutic relationships with the student, their caregivers, their teachers, and, sometimes, their community members. For example, if the student has a close relationship with an extended family member or has a community mentor, the school social worker can engage those adults in the child's treatment to strengthen a relationship that goes beyond the therapy session.

The ethical value of *importance of relationships* acknowledges that social workers should attempt to engage individuals as partners in the helping process (NASW, 2022). When working with Black students, the school social worker should work collaboratively with the student to identify problem areas and develop treatment goals. Treatment goals should not be based primarily on subjective information provided by collateral contacts (e.g., teachers), although that information can provide insight into how that child's behavior, perceived or actual, looks in environments outside of therapy. Information gathered from collateral contacts should not be the only piece of the puzzle when determining the best course of treatment. The school social worker should be sure to include the voice of the student, their perceptions of their interactions with others, and their identified areas of improvement.

Implicit Bias Defined

Implicit bias is defined as those attitudes or stereotypes that affect our understanding, our actions, and our decisions in an unconscious manner (Quereshi & Okonofua, 2017). Unlike overt explicit stereotypes that we may have, implicit bias is often activated involuntarily, affecting an individual's decisions, behaviors, and judgments (National Institutes of Health, 2022). *Explicit biases*, on the other hand, exist when individuals are aware of their attitudes and prejudices toward certain individuals and/or groups (Community Relations Service, n.d.). There are several contributing factors to implicit bias, and it all comes down to the hard wiring of our brain. The human brain has so much information coming in at one time that it must put that information into boxes for the body to react quickly, especially when it comes to harmful situations (Community Relations Service, n.d.). Exposure to direct and indirect messages during a person's lifetime aids in the development of these "boxes." To provide ethically competent care, school social workers will need to have an awareness of both explicit and implicit biases they may hold toward Black students and communities of color.

Factors Contributing to Implicit Bias

Everyone is exposed to direct and indirect messages throughout their lifetime that implicitly influence their thoughts and evaluations of others (Community Relations Service, n.d.). Everyone has both explicit and implicit biases. However, as mental health professionals, the key is to be mindful of personal biases, acknowledge how they may appear toward Black students, and attempt to keep those biases outside of the clinical treatment with Black students. Regardless of race, all mental health professionals are at risk of making biased decisions toward Black children and families. An important step in developing cultural humility in working with Black students is being honest, vulnerable, and willing to engage in self-exploration to identify where such biases exist and how they can be addressed. In turn, the school social worker is more competent and capable to exhibiting cultural inclusivity when working with Black students and their families.

Another factor contributing to implicit bias is the social and cultural experiences that come from the media, our own cultures, and our own individual upbringing (Ruhl, 2020). Media representations can fuel specific biases, especially with Black children. For example, Black boys are often referred to as "men" in the media despite being as young as 13 years old. Being from the St. Louis area, I lived and worked through the Ferguson unrest when Mike Brown Jr. was killed by Darren Wilson. Sometime later, the non-profit organization I worked for had a mandatory "town hall" on race relations in the city. I vividly remember someone writing an anonymous question, "Why are we glorifying a criminal?." And this was someone working in an organization that works with predominately Black and brown communities and was expected to adhere to the NASW code of ethics. However, to them, it did not matter that Darren Wilson was unaware of the incident at the gas station and pursued Brown for a different reason. It did not matter that this was a teenager who had just graduated high school. It did not matter that he was shot while running away. The focus was on the negative because of those images from the gas station flooding into our televisions, rather than the one that should have been used, his high school graduation picture. The media aids in the dehumanizing of Black people and makes no exception for Black children.

The culture we are raised in also helps shape our biases. Because norms and rules are learned through culture, it also contributes to biased thinking and beliefs about the behaviors of others (Ruhl, 2020). In schools, Black students are often punished for being disrespectful, yet respect is defined by a person's culture and upbringing, so what is defined as "respectful" can vary across cultures. Black school social workers should also be mindful of how their cultural upbringing influences the behaviors exhibited toward Black children in a clinical setting. For example, are you tougher on a Black client because of the cultural belief in the Black community that tough love is needed to make them stronger for the world? Are you placing higher expectations on their behavior? Do you assume they are religious? All mental health professionals must be willing to ask themselves the hard questions to help keep biased language, behavior, judgments, and diagnoses at bay when working with Black students.

The final contributing factor in implicit bias is a person's environment. Where you grew up, things that were said in your families and communities, all influence the biases you have developed (Ruhl, 2020). This includes racial and stereotypical attitudes that appear in family and community systems. Each of these can influence a person's implicit prejudice as well. A lack of exposure to different cultures puts individuals at a higher risk of developing biases. In those circumstances, media misrepresentations fill in the blanks with stereotypical or biased perceptions of cultures that shape the lens that views the behaviors of Black students as appropriate or inappropriate.

Implicit Bias and Black Students

Although implicit bias is unintentional, it still fuels the fire of the everyday racial stressors that Black students encounter in their environments. To exhibit cultural humility in mental health treatment with Black students, it is important to acknowledge how stereotypes and implicit bias work together to disenfranchise children of color, because students experience bias in schools through discipline and stereotypes. Next, we explore how implicit bias shows up in schools, including stereotypes of Black girls and boys that feed implicit biases, along with how bias appears in school codes of conduct that further push Black students out of schools and into the juvenile justice system. Additionally, we explore how bias appears in the mental health care system and within the playroom itself.

Across the country, Black students are often punished for not behaving in accordance with White standards of speech, dress and behavior. They are often told that the way their hair naturally grows is unkempt and not allowed by the school dress code. If a Black student uses slang, they are told they need to talk "correctly." These examples ignore cultural differences in be-havior, speech, and dress that should be honored, not ridiculed. The privi-leged perspectives of White educators that define misbehavior can result in the suppression of the voices of Black students and their caregivers (Kayama et al., 2015). Black students should not be punished for a lack of conformity to White standards of how to behave, speak, or dress. Yet that is what is hap-pening across the United States, and it prevents Black students from authen-tically showing up in schools and extracurricular activities. Here are a few examples to paint a clear picture of the prevalence of unnecessary and biased discipline towards Black children in schools:

- In New Jersey, a Black high school wrestler was forced to cut his dreadlocks during a match because the referee deemed it an "unfair advantage" (Ortiz, 2019).
- In Florida, a Black girl attending a Christian academy reported she was being bullied for her natural hair. In response, the school deemed the child's hair a "distraction" and threatened to expel her unless she cut it (Hobdy, 2020).
- A Black teenager in Texas was suspended and unable to walk in his graduation procession because he refused to cut his dreadlocks, which school officials said violated the school district's dress code (Griffith, 2020).
- In Massachusetts, two Black female students attending a charter school were kicked off their sports teams and barred from attending prom because of wearing their hair in braids (Williams, 2017).

School social works are tasked with the important work of helping schools understand how rules of conduct and dress codes are based in implicit biases that serve as a racial trauma stressor that creates an environment where dis-crimination is allowed or even encouraged. If adults are setting the tone, and they are acting out in discriminatory ways, that then creates an environment of permissiveness for other students to act in more discriminatory ways to-ward Black students. In turn, Black students may be subjected to more race-based harassment and bullying.

Eurocentric standards of behaviors punish Black students for not behaving within the parameters defined by individuals who don't look like them or un-derstand their culture. When they do not fit into that standard, they are la-beled as defiant, aggressive, angry, and unmotivated. This bias toward Black students, particularly Black boys, which develops in early childhood, follows them throughout their education, especially if they stay in the same school district. As a result, Black students do not get a "clean slate" each school year because they often are already deemed problematic based on previous reports from other teachers or previous school years. This could lead a Black student to ask themselves "If you're still judging me for who I was last year, what's the point trying to be better this school year?" This then feeds into a constant loop of misbehavior and punishment between the student and teacher. Once a child has been subconsciously labeled a troublemaker, then a school official is more likely to inadvertently target them more often or have a shorter fuse with them. It is important to acknowledge that many of the labels that follow Black students are stereotypical and damaging.

Black Students and Stereotypes

Black children often must navigate stereotypes held by their teachers, peers, and sometimes even their own family members. The criminalization of Black people, especially Black men, has ties to the film *Birth of a Nation*. After its first showing in 1915, its depictions of the Black negro as out of control and a threat to White people, particularly White women (DuVernay, 2016), set the foundation for viewing Black people, especially Black men, as criminals. Many of the stereotypes that exist about Black adults have evolved into ways that Black children and their behavior are viewed. Within schools, Black males are seen as aggressive and dangerous, and Black females are characterized as "hot mamas," "loud," and "having an attitude" in school settings (Joseph et al., 2016; Quereshi & Okonofua, 2017). These stereotypes are often driven by media representations of Black children and families on television, in movies, and in the news (Rodgers & Robinson, 2017). Stereotypes that depict Black boys and men as aggressive/dangerous and Black girls and women as promiscuous further drive the racial disparities in how Black children receive discipline in schools (Quereshi & Okonofua, 2017).

When educators use a discriminatory lens to evaluate behavior, it can lead to social disengagement and an increase in defiance toward authority. When dealing with the stress of adapting to a racist classroom environment, findings suggest Black students tend to withdraw and even avoid going to class due to the labels and stereotypes that are placed on them (Hernadez Sheets, 1996). Unfortunately, disengagement and avoidance often become a coping skill for Black students, one misinterpreted as misbehavior, which contributes to racial disparities in school discipline.

Bias in School Code of Conduct

"Code of conduct" is the term used to describe expected behaviors in students and punishments for deviating from those behaviors. However, bias is present in how Black boys and girls are disciplined in schools, and this bias is connected to those codes of conduct that make the reasons for discipline in Black students subjective. Teachers often perceive Black students as more rule-breaking and defiant than their peers, which results in defiance being a common reason for a disciplinary referral (Gregory & Weinstein, 2008). The reasons for disciplinary referrals are subjective, therefore open to interpretation based on that educator's definition of respect, defiance, and appropriate dress. As a result, this opens the door for biased opinions of these infractions that push Black students out of the classroom as young as early childhood.

Research has found that Black students as young as 5 years are routinely expelled and suspended for minor infractions such as writing on their desks or talking back to a teacher (Rudd, 2014). Blake et al. (2011) found that Black girls were more often cited for defiance, inappropriate dress, profanity, and physical aggression, behaviors that contradict traditional standards of femininity. During the 2018–2019 school year, the National Women's Law Center (2019) conducted a study reviewing dress code policies from 29 charter and public Washington, DC high schools and found that 59% regulated the length of shorts and skirts and 48% banned hats, hair wraps, or other head coverings; 21% banned leggings or tights. These policies police the way that Black students, especially girls, dress, which is another form of oppression. Skiba (2000) found Black students were more likely to be referred to the office for less serious, subjective reasons. One could argue that removing disciplinary actions for behaviors such as defiance, disrespect, profanity, and inappropriate dress could decrease the number of disciplinary referrals in Black students. This is where school social workers can employ the NASW ethical standard of *social justice* in advocating for a change in school disciplinary policies.

Adultification Bias

Studies have shown that Black children are more likely to be seen and treated as adults. There are several ways this bias may present. One way is through social or cultural stereotypes based on how adults perceive children (Epstein et al., n.d.). For example, a Black teacher or therapist may refer to a Black boy as "little man" or may call a Black girl "little mama" as a term of endearment. They may also make comments like "he's grown" or "stop babying them." However, that perpetuates the picture of Black children being adults.

Adultification bias also is the result of a socialization process, where Black children may function at a more advanced developmental stage due to situational context and necessity, particularly in communities with little to no resources (Epstein et al., n.d.). Due to systemic and institutionalized racism through community and police violence and mass incarceration, to name a few, there is a higher probability that Black mothers may be single. Therefore, a Black boy may be told he needs to be the man of the house, or a Black girl may be expected to help take care of younger siblings. This is another way that Black children are robbed of their childhood and placed into adult roles.

Adultification of Black children can be traced back to slavery, when Black boys and girls were seen as chattel, put to work as young as 2 years old, and subjected to similar dehumanization as adults that resulted in severe punishments for displaying normal childlike behaviors (Dumas & Nelson, 2016). In the present, adultification shows up in the unequal treatment of Black students in school discipline and in the juvenile justice system. Black youth are more likely to have bias shown toward them in how delinquent conduct is referred to and handled. *Diversion* is an option here, where delinquent conduct can be addressed without involving the juvenile formally in the court system (Mendel, 2022). As you can imagine, there are racial disparities in diversions in the juvenile system. Nationally, in 2019, 52% of White youth were diverted compared to 40% of Black youth (Mendel, 2022). This disparity shows how the behaviors of Black children are viewed and punished more harshly than the behaviors of White children. Black children are often seen as responsible for their actions, while White children who may engage in the same behaviors are seen as "making mistakes" and given additional chances. The lack of diversion of Black juvenile cases fuels disparities in youth incarceration. Black youth account for 41% of youths in juvenile placements (which include detention centers, residential treatment cents, youth prisons, and group homes) (Rovner, 2021). Chapters 4 and 5 focus more specifically on adultification bias in Black boys and girls, along with ways to support optimal mental health in the face of this bias.

Bias in Mental Healthcare

Bias within the mental healthcare system leaves Black Americans struggling to obtain competent care when they need it. Studies have found that Black Americans often lack access to culturally competent care and receive a poorer quality of care than White Americans (Division of Diversity and Health Equity, 2017). When delivering services, there is a difference in how practitioners engage with Black clients. Johnson et al. (2004) found physicians were more verbally dominant and less patient-centered in their communication with Black patients compared to White patients. Another way that bias shows up in mental health care is in how symptoms are perceived. For example, a Black student may have hypervigilance toward law enforcement that could be perceived as the paranoia associated with schizophrenia, which can then lead to misdiagnosis. Studies have shown that Black Americans are more frequently diagnosed with schizophrenia and less frequently diagnosed with mood disorders compared to White Americans with the same symptoms (Bell et al., 2015).

Finally, another way that bias appears is in hotline calls. Communities of color are more likely to receive an investigation from child protective agencies because of reporting bias (Luken et al., 2021). It is not because Black mothers neglect their children at higher rates but because of bias in reporting and ignorance of cultural norms. I once had an employee who wanted to make a hotline call on a five-year old girl because her mom was gluing hair extensions in their head. My recommendation was "Go watch Good Hair. Because if you want to hotline a mother for what she does to her child's hair, you will need to hotline a majority of Black mothers." I remember my own hair experiences, receiving a perm at a young age to make my hair "more manageable." Or the first burn I got on my hair from the hot comb (a comb made out of cast iron that heats up on the stove to straighten hair). Black women are constantly told they need to change their hair to fit Eurocentric standards of beauty, yet punished for what they do to fit this standard. If a professional lacks the understanding behind behaviors such as these, they are at risk of causing irreparable harm to both the child and their family.

It also is important to remember that high-poverty communities have less resources so some of the behaviors defined as "abusive" may be driven by survival. For example, a child may be left home with their siblings because the mother must work two jobs. This can be misinterpreted as neglect and lead to an investigation, as well as to a high probability that the children will be removed from the home. In effect, poverty has been criminalized, especially for parents of color. School social workers have a duty to educate their colleagues on these cultural norms. Studies have found that a majority of hotline calls originate in schools (US Department of Health and Human Services, 2022), therefore it is important that school therapists share their knowledge of bias and advocate for both the child's and parents' culture when considering a hotline call.

Additionally, bias appears in mental health crisis care, which can lead a first responder to interpret someone in crisis as being either dangerous or violent rather than viewing them as someone who is experiencing fear or frustration during an emergency. There are countless stories of Black people who have called the police for help only to see their loved one die at the hands of those police officers who respond. Because of this, many Black people are not comfortable with calling the police whenever their family members are in crisis. So, as a mental health professional, it is important to know that it can be offensive or come off as insensitive if the treatment plan includes calling the police when a Black child is having a mental health crisis. The counselor should be aware of those emergency services in their communities that can be called as an alternative to the police. And if that is not an option, then they should communicate understanding of the parent's feelings and talk through an alternative solution that helps the parent feel better and keeps the child safe.

Bias in the Playroom

Bias also presents within play therapy and in the playroom. All social workers, regardless of their race and ethnicity, should engage in self-reflection because sometimes countertransference can appear through the biased approaches used in play therapy sessions.

I was working with a school as a contracted therapist to help with some students in need of trauma therapy. When I saw the caseload, I saw I had five Black boys in 4th and 5th grade. Being in a school, I was limited in the number of games/toys I had to use with older students. But I was also worried that they would think the activities I was trying to do with them were "wack." So I avoided the play therapy approach I use with most of my clients—sand tray—and integrated more stereotypical activities, like things having to do with sports, into their sessions. This was the school year when COVID-19 disrupted everything, so I could only see kids virtually since I was not employed by the school. Prior to lockdown, the school counselor attended my sand tray workshop. When I went to the school to get my things, she found me and said, "April! Come here, I want to show you pictures of the sand trays the boys have been making. They LOVE it!" I immediately felt guilt and shame that I had withheld a helpful intervention from them because of my own biases.

In this example, well-intentioned changes in treatment modality were rooted in implicit bias toward Black boys and based on stereotypes. However, good intentions or not, this bias got in the way of providing effective care to those students. In that situation, I made sure to acknowledge the bias, then ensure that it does not appear again in my work with Black boys by making sure I offer all activities to children regardless of their race and/or gender.

Bias may also show up in the toys and materials in the playroom. First, the social worker should avoid toys and playroom equipment that is "gendered," like a pink dollhouse or blue toolset. These colors often communicate to children they are "boy" or "girl" toys. The play therapist should also avoid setting their room up with stereotypically gendered toys, like having all the "boy" toys together and all of the "girl" toys together. From a diversity standpoint, there should be diverse skin tones and hair textures in the dolls, as well as multicultural puppets and play food. There also should be diversity within art materials. (Chapter 3 provides more insight into creating a culturally competent playroom in schools.)

Developing Cultural Humility

To develop cultural humility, social workers must have a lifelong commitment to learning and self-reflection. This includes evaluating their behaviors, comments, documentation, and diagnosis when working with Black students. This will require humility and flexibility along with the bravery to engage in critical self-reflection and a desire to learn. Another way to achieve cultural humility is to repair power imbalances. School social workers should understand that the student is the expert of their own life, their own symptoms, and their own strengths. In the playroom, both the therapist and child should collaborate with and learn from each other to achieve the best outcomes. Yes, the practitioner may hold the power in scientific knowledge; however, the student holds the power in their own personal history and strengths. The social worker should respect that expertise and acknowledge it as a protective factor for that student. Finally, school social workers should develop relationships with groups and people who advocate for others. Although individuals can create positive change, communities and groups can also have a profound impact on systems. The social worker cannot individually commit to self-evaluation and repairing power imbalances without advocating within the larger systems that Black students encounter.

An important step to developing cultural humility in clinical work with Black students is to identify both professional and personal biases. First, the therapist will have to recognize that there are disparities in both access and treatment that leave Black children and families untreated or improperly treated. Facts do not outweigh opinions in the clinical setting, and the facts show that Black students have less accessibility and quality in their mental health treatment. Next, the social worker should develop an awareness of the differences between minority individuals to provide appropriate support. This means respecting and honoring the cultures of all students and finding ways to empower them to find pride in their cultural traditions and values. It is also important that the school social worker provides a free space for clients to write their own stories and provide their own points of view on their lived experiences.

School social workers should be aware of comments that could be racist or off-putting to the student and their family. They should avoid making comments like, "I don't see color" or "I treat everybody the same." These phrases could be perceived as a microaggression toward a Black student and/or caregiver and could hinder the therapeutic relationship from growing. Although they may have positive intentions, to deny seeing color is equivalent to denying the experiences of children of color in their environments. The world sees their color and often rejects, punishes, or judges them negatively as a result. Race is the lens through which Black children receive information on how others perceive their behaviors. It is also the lens that guides the way they interact or disconnect with other people. So to deny seeing a student's skin color is to deny their existence. Furthermore, as clinicians, school social workers do not and should not treat everybody the same. Each student is unique and so are their experiences, so their treatment plans should always be individualized and personalized to that student's unique experiences and needs. This also requires that the counselor be honest with themselves about how their biased communication and behaviors with Black students could further exacerbate racial trauma in Black students and possibly contribute to treatment drop out.

Applying Cultural Humility in Mental Health Treatment with Black Students

There are several helpful suggestions for a school social worker to develop cultural humility in their clinical work with Black students. This information should also be shared with educators in the form of a professional development workshop or an article in the school's professional newsletter to help decrease bias in schools. First, school social workers should engage in critical self-awareness and self-examination (Mosher et al., 2017). This may include journaling thoughts, feelings, and behaviors after engaging with Black students. It may also include developing a support network of other professionals where you can process your actions, thoughts, and feelings in a safe place. Next, school social workers should work to build a therapeutic alliance with Black students (Mosher et al., 2018). This may require patience as the student unlearns levels of mistrust because of racial trauma. It may require talking about non–therapy related things as the relationship develops. It also includes the NASW ethical standard of *dignity and worth of the person*, where Black students are empowered to be therapeutic agents of change.

Next, the school social worker should repair cultural ruptures (Mosher et al., 2017). This may include acknowledging any cultural issues that may arise, especially if the school social worker is not Black. To ignore those differences is to aid in the rupture itself. It can also include acknowledging and/or apologizing for previous assumptions or beliefs held about the student and their culture. Finally, school social workers should attempt to navigate value differences (Mosher et al., 2017). For example, physical punishment is often used in the Black community as a means of discipline. In most states, it is not illegal unless it leaves a bruise, which then is physical abuse. A mother of a Black student may say they are going to give the child a spanking when they get home for misbehaving in school. Although that may not be something the school social work agrees with, it is important to navigate the issue free of judgment. In that case, the school social worker may point out that aggression is learned behavior and that the child's aggressive behavior may be correlated with their physical punishment. The school social worker should then work with the caregivers on ways to utilize more effective practices of discipline, such as the removal of privileges like their phone, video games, or hanging out with friends. This approach exhibits cultural humility in its respect for the parents' values while rooting the concerns in evidence rather than opinions.

Developing a Plan

After identifying personal and professional biases, school social workers should develop a plan to foster cultural humility in their clinical work with Black students. Creating a plan (Appendix A) can allow therapists and educators to create a road map to developing humility and displaying inclusivity in treatment. One way to respect the culture of Black students is to seek out competent information from reputable sources through professional development, movies, books, and documentaries on Black culture. It may also include certain organizations and social media influencers on Instagram, Facebook, and TikTok. Additionally, school social workers should attempt to look beyond their point of view, which is important when working with a Black student who may make comments that police officers don't keep people safe. It is important to honor that child's perspective and worldview while also exploring the feelings they may have about law enforcement in a nonjudgmental way. Outside of exposure to police violence toward Black Americans, a school social worker may have some students on their caseload who have been in houses where warrants have been served or who live in highly policed environments. Their personal experiences have shown them that police don't keep them safe. And the worst thing for rapport with a Black student is to deny their perspective or label it as inaccurate. Instead, that clinician should display empathy and work with the student to identify other adults in their lives who keep them safe.

School social workers can also engage in or help facilitate support groups. These support groups can provide a safe space where professionals can feel vulnerable to engage in self-reflection and receive feedback on ways to improve or decrease biased behavior, language, and thoughts. This could look like integrating important books, documentaries, and other resources with peers to increase their knowledge on Black culture and issues. Developing cultural humility is a lifelong and ongoing process that will require the support of other professionals to engage in that process. These conversations should not only occur when there are protests and community outrage around the death of unarmed Black Americans: Black students and their families experience these events every day, so mental health professionals cannot afford to take a break from the work they need to do to provide culturally respectful and competent care.

Introducing Dialogue Around Race

School social workers may struggle with finding the most appropriate way to bring up race in therapy sessions. If the school social worker is not Black but is working with Black students, there is a chance students may have some ambivalence in trusting them. Most times, it is better to address the elephant in the room rather than hide it. So, sometimes asking "Do you have any concerns with working with a White therapist?" can open the door to acknowledge the student's concerns. Below are two assessment activities that school social workers can use with Black students to introduce race and race-based experiences.

Race and Culture Conversation Cards

Race and culture conversation cards can be used in initial sessions with Black students to help assess their racial experiences. They can also provide a way to talk through any concerns that the student may have if the school social worker is of a different race/ethnicity. There are Race and Culture Conversation Cards for young students in 1st through 5th grade (Appendix B) and older students in 6th through 12th grade (Appendix C). The only preparation needed is to print and laminate the cards prior to starting the session. The card deck discusses topics that might be triggering and may bring up negative experiences, emotions, and memories for clients. These cards are designed to be used with kids, but the school social worker should read through each question to ensure that they are age appropriate for their chosen population. The Race and Culture Conversation Cards can be used for initial assessment with Black students or made easily accessible in the clinician's office so the student can freely use them in subsequent sessions if needed.

Code-Switchin' Mask

Black students are constantly in environments that communicate that who they are and how they dress, talk, walk, and even laugh is wrong. This invalidation of their existence can lead to *code-switching*. Code-switching happens when a Black student changes aspects about themselves to fit into White spaces. At times this may be done for acceptance, but it may also be a survival tactic to deal with real and/or perceived danger. The activity, Code-Switchin' Mask, uses art techniques to open dialogue around those people and places where the student tends to change. This is a variation of the "Inside/Out" mask where clients decorate the front of a mask with pictures and words that describe how they think the world sees them and decorate the inside with words and pictures that shows how they see themselves.

The Code-Switchin' Mask is an activity that is appropriate for students in 5th through 12th grades. The materials required are the handout "Code-Switchin' Mask" (Appendix D), diverse magazines, scissors, glue or a glue stick, markers, and craft masks. A variation of the activity is to use the worksheet "Code-Switchin' Mask-digital" (Appendix E) during telehealth and in-person sessions instead of a physical mask, which provides a copy of a mask for the student to complete. The student is encouraged to use the provided materials to decorate the front of the mask with people they tend to code-switch around, places where they code-switch, and the feelings they have when they must code-switch. On the inside of the mask, the student should be encouraged to identify people with whom they can be themselves, places where they do not have change, and the feelings they have when they can be their authentic selves. After completing the activity, the student should be invited to share what they decorated and give more insight into their creation. The school social worker may also ask the client which side of their mask they prefer and talk to them about ways that they may be able to be more authentic in spaces where their code-switching exists.

Conclusion

School social workers are ethically obligated to provide culturally sensitive and competent care to clients of all backgrounds. This can be difficult when working with Black students as school social workers must navigate the systemic and personal biases coming from adults who have already made up their mind about a Black child. Advocating for the fair and equal treatment of Black students will not be easy, but it is a requirement per the NASW's Code of Ethics. The first step in advocacy is developing one's own cultural humility in the clinical services delivered to Black students and families. It is a career-long journey that will require patience, humility, respect for other cultures, and a support system of your own to encourage your continual growth. In doing so, you may save the life of a Black child.

References

Bell, C. C., Jackson, W. M., & Bell, B. H. (2015). Misdiagnosis of African-Americans with psychiatric issues: Part II. *Journal of the National Medical Association, 107*(3), 35–41. https://doi.org/10.1016/S0027-9684(15)30049-3

Blake, J., Butler, B., Lewis, C., & Darensbourg, A. (2011). Unmasking the inequitable Discipline experiences of urban Black girls: Implications for urban educational stakeholders. *Urban Review, 43*(1), 90–106. https://doi.org/10.1007/s11256-009-0148-8

Center for Play Therapy. (2022). *Multicultural play therapy*. University of North Texas. https://cpt.unt.edu/multicultural-play-therapy

Centers for Disease Control and Prevention (CDC). (2020). Youth Risk Behavior Surveillance: United States 2019. *Morbidity and Mortality Weekly Report, 69*(1). https://www.cdc.gov/mmwr/volumes/69/su/pdfs/su6901-H.pdf

Child and Adolescent Health Measurement Initiative. (2022). 2020–2021 National survey of children's health (NSCH) data query. U.S. Department of Health and Human Services, Health Resources and Services Administration (HRSA), Maternal and Child Health Bureau (MCHB). [www.childhealthdata.org].

Community Relations Services. (n.d). Understanding bias: A resource guide. Department of Justice. https://www.justice.gov/file/1437326/download -:~:text=Explicit

Craft, M., Hayes, S., & Moore, R. (2020). Supporting the mental health well-being of high school students. Center for Equity in Learning. https://www.act.org/content/dam/act/unsecured/documents/R1798-mental-health-2020-01.pdf

Diliberti, M., Jackson, M., Correa, S., Padgett, Z., & Hansen, R. (2019). Crime, violence, discipline, and safety in U.S. public schools: Findings from the school survey on crime and safety: 2017–18. A first look. U.S. Department of Education. https://nces.ed.gov/pubs2019/2019061.pdf

Division of Diversity and Health Equity. (2017). Mental health disparities: African Americans. American Psychiatric Association. https://psychiatry.org/File Library/Psychiatrists/Cultural-Competency/Mental-Health-Disparities/Mental-Health-Facts-for-African-Americans.pdf

Dumas, M. J., & Nelson, J. D. (2016). (Re)Imagining Black boyhood: Toward a critical framework for educational research. *Harvard Educational Review*, 86(1), 27–47. https://doi.org/10.17763/0017-8055.86.1.27

Duvernay, A. (2016). *The 13th*. [Documentary]. Netflix.

Epstein, R., Blake, J. J., & Gonzalez, T. (n.d.). Girlhood interrupted: The erasure of Black girls' childhood. Center on Poverty and Inequality, Georgetown Law. https://genderjusticeandopportunity.georgetown.edu/wp-content/uploads/2020/06/girlhood-interrupted.pdf

Gill, E., & Drewes, A. (2021). *Cultural issues in play therapy* (2nd ed.). Guilford.

Gregory, A., & Weinstein, R. (2008). The discipline gap and African Americans: Defiance or cooperation in the high school classroom. *Journal of School Psychology*, 46(4), 455–475. https://doi.org/10.1016/j.jsp.2007.09.001

Griffith, J. (2020). Black Texas teen told to cut his dreadlocks to walk at graduation. NBC News. https://www.nbcnews.com/news/us-news/black-texas-teen-told-cut-his-dreadlocks-order-walk-graduation-n1120731

Hernández Sheets, R. (1996). Urban classroom conflict: Student-teacher perception: Ethnic integrity, solidarity, and resistance. *Urban Review*, 28(2), 165–183. https://doi.org/10.1007/BF02354383

Hobdy, D. (2020). Florida school threatens to expel African-American girl for wearing natural hair. Essence. https://www.essence.com/news/florida-school-threatens-expel-african-american-girl-wearing-natural-hair/

Johnson, R. L., Roter, D., Powe, N. R., & Cooper, L. A. (2004). Patient race/ethnicity and quality of patient-physician communication during medical visits. *American Journal of Public Health*, 94(12), 2084–2090. https://doi.org/10.2105/ajph.94.12.2084

Joseph, N. M., Viesca, K. M., & Bianco, M. (2016). Black female adolescents and racism in schools: Experiences in a colorblind society. *High School Journal*, 100(1), 4–25. https://doi.org/10.1353/hsj.2016.0018

Kayama, M., Haight, W., Gibson, P., & Wilson, R. (2015). Use of criminal justice language in personal narratives of out-of-school suspensions: Black students, caregivers, and educators. *Children and Youth Services Review*, 55(2), 26–35. https://doi.org/10.1016/j.childyouth.2015.01.020

Krause, K. H., Verlenden, J. V., Szucs, L. E., Swedo, E. A., Merlo, C. L., Holditch Niolon, P., Leroy, Z. C., Sims, V. M., Deng, X., Lee, S., Rasberry, C. N., & Underwood, J. M. (2022).

Disruptions to school and home life among high school students during the Covid-19 pandemic: Adolescent behaviors and experiences survey, United States, January–June 2021. Centers for Disease Control (CDC). *Morbidity and Mortality Weekly Report (MMWR)*, 71(3), 28–34. https://www.cdc.gov/mmwr/volumes/71/su/pdfs/su7103a5-H.pdf

Luken, A., Nair, R., & Fix, R. L. (2021). On racial disparities in child abuse reports: Exploratory mapping the 2018 NCANDS. *Child maltreatment*, 26(3), 267–281. https://doi.org/10.1177/10775595211001926

Mendel, R. (2022). Diversion: A hidden key to combating racial and ethnic disparities in juvenile justice. The Sentencing Project. https://www.sentencingproject.org/reports/diversion-a-hidden-key-to-combating-racial-and-ethnic-disparities-in-juvenile-justice/

Mosher, D. K., Hook, J., Captairi, J., & Davis, D. (2017). Cultural humility: A therapeutic framework for engaging diverse clients. *Practice Innovations*, 2(4), 221-223. http://dx.doi.org/10.1037/pri0000055

Mpofu, J. J., Cooper, A. C., Ashley, C., Geda, S., Harding, R. L., Johns, M. M., Spinks-Franklin, A., Njai, R., Moyse, D., & Underwood, J. M. (2022). Perceived racism and demographic, mental health, and behavioral characteristics among high school students during the COVID-19 pandemic: Adolescent behaviors and experiences survey, United States, January–June 2021. Centers for Disease Control (CDC). *Morbidity and Mortality Weekly Report (MMWR)*, 71(2), 22–27. https://www.cdc.gov/mmwr/volumes/71/su/su7103a4.htm?s_cid=su7103a4_w

National Association of Social Workers. (2022). Code of ethics. https://www.socialworkers.org/About/Ethics/Code-of-Ethics/Code-of-Ethics-English

National Institutes of Health. (2022). Implicit bias. https://diversity.nih.gov/sociocultural-factors/implicit-bias

National Women's Law Center. (2019). Dress coded II: Protest, progress and power in D.C. schools. https://nwlc.org/wp-content/uploads/2019/09/final_nwlc_DressCodedII_Report.pdf

Ortiz, E. (2019). N.J. wrestler forced to cut dreadlocks still target over hair, lawyer says. NBC News. https://www.nbcnews.com/news/nbcblk/n-j-wrestler-forced-cut-dreadlocks-still-targeted-over-hair-n957116

Quereshi, A., & Okonofua, J. (2017). Locked out of the classroom: How implicit bias contributes to disparities in school discipline. NAACP Legal Defense and Educational Fund, Inc. (LDF). https://www.naacpldf.org/files/about-us/Bias_Reportv2017_30_11_FINAL.pdf

Rodgers, N., & Robinson, R. (2017). How the news media distorts black families. *Washington Post*. https://www.washingtonpost.com/outlook/2017/12/29/a374a268-ea6d-11e7-8a6a-80acf0774e64_story.html

Rovner, J. (2021). Black disparities in youth incarceration. The Sentencing Project. https://www.sentencingproject.org/fact-sheet/black-disparities-in-youth-incarceration/

Rudd, T. (2014). Racial disproportionality in school discipline. Implicit bias is heavily impacted. Kirwan Institute. https://aasb.org/wp-content/uploads/racial-disproportionality-schools-02.pdf

Ruhl, C. (2020). Implicit or unconscious bias. Simply Psychology. https://www.simplypsychology.org/implicit-bias.html

Skiba, R. J. (2000). Zero tolerance, zero evidence: An analysis of school disciplinary practice. Policy research report. Indiana Education Policy Center. https://eric.ed.gov/?id=ED469537

US Department of Health and Human Services. (2022). Child Maltreatment 2020. Administration for Children and Families, Administration on Children, Youth and Families, Children's Bureau. https://www.acf.hhs.gov/cb/data-research/child-maltreatment.

Wang, K., Kemp, J., Burr, R., & Swan, D. (2022). Crime, violence, discipline, and safety in U.S. public schools in 2019–2020: Findings from the school survey on crime and safety. U.S. Department of Education. Institute of Education Sciences. https://nces.ed.gov/pubs2022/2022029.pdf

Whitaker, A., Torres-Guillen, S., Morton, M., Jordan, H., Coyle, S., Mann, A., & Sun, W. L. (2019). Cops and no counselors: How the lack of school mental health is harming students. American Civil Liberties Union. https://www.aclu.org/sites/default/files/field_document/030419-acluschooldisciplinereport.pdf

Williams, J. (2017). War on Black hair: Wearing braids gets Black girls banned from prom at Malden Charter School in Massachusetts. Newsweek. https://www.newsweek.com/wearing-braids-sends-black-girls-detention-malden-charter-school-608303

Appendix A   Anti-Bias/Anti-Racism Plan

Anti-Bias/Anti-Racism Plan

What are some things you can do to ensure you continue to monitor the way your biases may appear in the playroom with children and families of color? Use the area below to make a plan to further increase your cultural competence

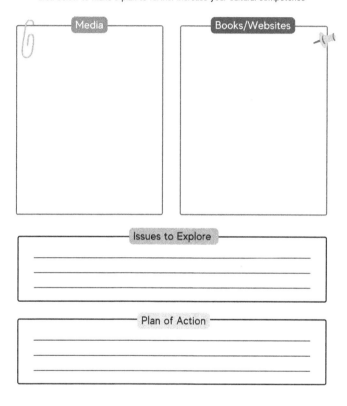

Media

Books/Websites

Issues to Explore

Plan of Action

RACE & CULTURE CONVERSATION CARDS
For Kids!

56 cards filled with prompting questions to get the conversation underway!

RACE & CULTURE
Conversation Cards
— ★★★ —

Thank you for your purchase! Please read the Terms of Use before proceeding.

Conversation Cards are designed to enhance individual or small group discussion. This particular card deck discusses topics that might be triggering and may bring up negative experiences, emotions, and memories for clients. These cards are designed to be used with kids, but please read through each question to ensure that they are age appropriate for your chosen population. Conversation Cards are not a replacement for treatment and are solely designed to be used as a supplement by a licensed professional.

How to Use

This card deck contains 56 total cards and requires printing and cutting. For best results, it is recommended to print in high quality, on card stock, and laminate, if possible, for prolonged use.

*If you would like the back graphic design on each card, then the card pages should be printed double-sided beginning on page 4. It is recommended to conduct a test print to ensure proper formatting and orientation. Cards are designed to print as traditional playing cards. Due to differences in printer functions, Mylemarks is unable to provide support if there are printing issues. To print cards without the back design, you can print the card pages Even Pages only, single-sided, starting on page 4.

Terms of Use

By purchasing this resource, you are agreeing that the contents are the property of Mylemarks LLC and BMH Connect licensed to you as a single user. To learn more about Mylemarks' licensing options, please visit: https://www.mylemarks.com/mylemarks-licensing-options.html. Mylemarks LLC and BMH Connect retain the copyright and reserve all rights to this product.

YOU MAY:

1.   Use this item with clients/students/small groups or for your own personal use and clients on your caseload only.

2.   Reference this product in blog posts, social media posts, at seminars, professional development workshops, or other such venues PROVIDED there is both credit given to Mylemarks LLC and BMH Connect and links provided to www.mylemarks.com and https://www.bmhconnect.com/.

YOU MAY NOT:

1.   Claim this work as your own, alter the files in any way, or remove/attempt to remove the copyright/watermarks.

2.   Extract any images from this file. All images are copyrighted by Mylemarks LLC.

3.   Post this document for sale or free elsewhere on the internet or in person including making the document accessible on social media platforms, shared drives, or additional places in which printed or digital copies can be accessed by unlicensed parties.

4.   Make copies of this item to share physically or electronically with others without the purchase of an additional license. This is strictly forbidden and is a violation of the Terms of Use, along with copyright law. Please direct interested parties to www.mylemarks.com to purchase a copy of their own.

5.   Obtain this product through any of the channels listed above.

If you encounter an issue with your file, notice an error, or are in any way experiencing a problem, please contact hello@mylemarks.com, and we will be more than happy to help you out!

DEFINITIONS
—★★★—

These definitions are helpful to review with your client(s) prior to use of the cards.

Race

A group of people who have similar physical characteristics like skin color, facial features, type of hair, etc. [1]

•Examples: Black, White, Biracial/Multiracial, Asian, Hawaiian Pacific Islander, American Native

Culture

Certain characteristics or traditions that a group of people have in common. Culture is often passed down through generations.

•Example: Music, food, religion, clothing, holidays, language, and beliefs are all a part of culture.

Discrimination

When someone is treated unfairly because of something that makes them different. This can be their race, the way they dress, age, gender, religion, or other things. [2]

•Example: A school makes a rule that bans common Black hairstyles like braids, cornrows, dreadlocks, etc.

Stereotype

An assumption someone makes about a person or group of people based on how they look or a certain group they belong to. [3]

•Example: Believing that *all* Black boys are aggressive or thinking that *all* Black girls are angry or loud.

Prejudice

Pre – judging. Making a judgment about a person or group without really having a reason to. This can lead to treating them unfairly before getting to know them. [4]

•Example: A teacher thinks a Black student might be a "trouble maker", so they make them sit in the front of the class on the first day of school.

Microaggression

Hurtful things someone says or does that are subtle or something you may not notice right away.

•Example: Someone purposefully mispronouncing your name or asking you "Why did your parents name you that?"

Code Switch

Changing the way you talk, dress or behave to blend into a different (often White) environment.

•Example: Talking "more proper" or not using "slang" when around White people.

1 Kids Encyclopedia Facts. (2020, October, 21). *Race (sociology) facts for kids.* Kiddle. https://kids.kiddle.co/Race_(sociology)
2 Kids Encyclopedia Facts. (2020, October 21). *Discrimination facts for kids.* Kiddle. https://kids.kiddle.co/Discrimination
3 Kids Encyclopedia Facts. (2020, October 21). *Stereotype facts for kids.* Kiddle. https://kids.kiddle.co/Stereotype
4 Kids Encyclopedia Facts. (2020, October 21). *Prejudice facts for kids.* Kiddle. https://kids.kiddle.co/Prejudice

RACE & CULTURE
Conversation Cards
—★★★— for kids!

Have you ever been treated
differently because of the way
you look? If so, how did it feel?

RACE & CULTURE
Conversation Cards
—★★★— for kids!

Has anyone ever said you
couldn't do something because
of your gender or skin color?

RACE & CULTURE
Conversation Cards
—★★★— for kids!

Has anyone ever teased
you about your hair?

RACE & CULTURE
Conversation Cards
—★★★— for kids!

Has anyone ever
teased you about the
way you talk?

RACE & CULTURE
Conversation Cards
—★★★— for kids!

Has anyone ever made
fun of the way you dress?

RACE & CULTURE
Conversation Cards
—★★★— for kids!

Has anyone ever treated
you meanly before they
even got to know you?

RACE & CULTURE
Conversation Cards
—★★★— for kids!

Name a grownup who can help
when someone is mean to you
because of the way you look.

RACE & CULTURE
Conversation Cards
—★★★— for kids!

Have you ever felt like your
teacher treated you differently
from other kids in your class?

RACE & CULTURE
Conversation Cards
For Kids!
mylemarks BMH Connect

RACE & CULTURE
Conversation Cards
For Kids!
mylemarks BMH Connect

RACE & CULTURE
Conversation Cards
For Kids!
mylemarks BMH Connect

RACE & CULTURE
Conversation Cards
For Kids!
mylemarks BMH Connect

RACE & CULTURE
Conversation Cards
For Kids!
mylemarks BMH Connect

RACE & CULTURE
Conversation Cards
For Kids!
mylemarks BMH Connect

RACE & CULTURE
Conversation Cards
For Kids!
mylemarks BMH Connect

RACE & CULTURE
Conversation Cards
For Kids!
mylemarks BMH Connect

RACE & CULTURE
Conversation Cards
—★★★— FOR KidS!

Have you ever felt like your
teacher was being mean to you,
but you didn't know how to say it?

RACE & CULTURE
Conversation Cards
—★★★— FOR KidS!

Has anyone ever made
fun of the way you and
your family smell?

RACE & CULTURE
Conversation Cards
—★★★— FOR KidS!

What have your parents told
you about how to act around
a police officer?

RACE & CULTURE
Conversation Cards
—★★★— FOR KidS!

Do you feel safe when the
police are in your school or
neighborhood?

RACE & CULTURE
Conversation Cards
—★★★— FOR KidS!

Have you ever seen someone
being hurt by the police?

RACE & CULTURE
Conversation Cards
—★★★— FOR KidS!

If you've seen someone
being hurt by the police, how
did it make you feel?

RACE & CULTURE
Conversation Cards
—★★★— FOR KidS!

How does your face look
when you're feeling angry?

RACE & CULTURE
Conversation Cards
—★★★— FOR KidS!

How does your face look
when you're feeling sad?

RACE & CULTURE
Conversation Cards
for kids!
mylemarks · BMH Connect

RACE & CULTURE
Conversation Cards
for kids!
mylemarks · BMH Connect

RACE & CULTURE
Conversation Cards
for kids!
mylemarks · BMH Connect

RACE & CULTURE
Conversation Cards
for kids!
mylemarks · BMH Connect

RACE & CULTURE
Conversation Cards
for kids!
mylemarks · BMH Connect

RACE & CULTURE
Conversation Cards
for kids!
mylemarks · BMH Connect

RACE & CULTURE
Conversation Cards
for kids!
mylemarks · BMH Connect

RACE & CULTURE
Conversation Cards
for kids!
mylemarks · BMH Connect

RACE & CULTURE
Conversation Cards
—★★★— For KidS!

Do you ever worry about
someone hurting you because
of the way you look?

RACE & CULTURE
Conversation Cards
—★★★— For KidS!

If you're angry because someone
is being mean, what's a good way
to cope with your anger?

RACE & CULTURE
Conversation Cards
—★★★— For KidS!

If you're sad because someone
is being mean, what can you do
to feel better?

RACE & CULTURE
Conversation Cards
—★★★— For KidS!

Name someone that helps
you feel better when you're
feeling angry or sad.

RACE & CULTURE
Conversation Cards
—★★★— For KidS!

If you are worried about someone
hurting you because of the way you
look, who is someone who can help
you feel safe?

RACE & CULTURE
Conversation Cards
—★★★— For KidS!

Who is a grownup you can talk to
if you're feeling confused about
how someone is treating you?

RACE & CULTURE
Conversation Cards
—★★★— For KidS!

Have you ever changed the way
you wear your hair because of
something someone said to you?

RACE & CULTURE
Conversation Cards
—★★★— For KidS!

Have you ever changed the way
you talk because of something
someone said to you?

RACE & CULTURE
Conversation Cards
For kids!
mylemarks   BMH Connect

RACE & CULTURE
Conversation Cards
For kids!
mylemarks   BMH Connect

RACE & CULTURE
Conversation Cards
For kids!
mylemarks   BMH Connect

RACE & CULTURE
Conversation Cards
For kids!
mylemarks   BMH Connect

RACE & CULTURE
Conversation Cards
For kids!
mylemarks   BMH Connect

RACE & CULTURE
Conversation Cards
For kids!
mylemarks   BMH Connect

RACE & CULTURE
Conversation Cards
For kids!
mylemarks   BMH Connect

RACE & CULTURE
Conversation Cards
For kids!
mylemarks   BMH Connect

RACE & CULTURE
Conversation Cards
—★★★— for kidS!

Have you ever changed the way
you dress because of something
someone said to you?

RACE & CULTURE
Conversation Cards
—★★★— for kidS!

Do you change how you act
when you're around people who
don't look like you?

RACE & CULTURE
Conversation Cards
—★★★— for kidS!

Has anyone ever told you that
you "act White"? If so, how did
it make you feel?

RACE & CULTURE
Conversation Cards
—★★★— for kidS!

Has anyone ever made fun of
you because of the toys or
games you like to play with?

RACE & CULTURE
Conversation Cards
—★★★— for kidS!

Has anyone ever asked you
"What are you?" If so, how
did that make you feel?

RACE & CULTURE
Conversation Cards
—★★★— for kidS!

Have you ever felt left
out because of the color
of your skin?

RACE & CULTURE
Conversation Cards
—★★★— for kidS!

Has anyone ever said something
mean about how you look? If so,
how did you feel about it?

RACE & CULTURE
Conversation Cards
—★★★— for kidS!

Has anyone ever thought you and
your friends were doing something
wrong, even though you weren't?

RACE & CULTURE
Conversation Cards
— ★★★ — For kids!

Have you ever been out with your
family or friends and someone
thought you didn't belong?

RACE & CULTURE
Conversation Cards
— ★★★ — For kids!

Have you ever had a teacher
that you felt was always
picking on you?

RACE & CULTURE
Conversation Cards
— ★★★ — For kids!

Have you ever been to a
protest or a march? If so,
what was it like?

RACE & CULTURE
Conversation Cards
— ★★★ — For kids!

Has anyone ever made fun of
you for getting free services,
like food, at school?

RACE & CULTURE
Conversation Cards
— ★★★ — For kids!

Has anyone ever thought you
were yelling or going to hurt them
even though you weren't?

RACE & CULTURE
Conversation Cards
— ★★★ — For kids!

Have you ever told someone
you were feeling sick but they
didn't believe you?

RACE & CULTURE
Conversation Cards
— ★★★ — For kids!

Has anyone ever made fun of
your name? If so, how did that
make you feel?

RACE & CULTURE
Conversation Cards
— ★★★ — For kids!

Has anyone ever asked you "Why
did your parents name you that?"
If so, how did it make you feel?

RACE & CULTURE
Conversation Cards
—★★★— For kidS!

Has anyone ever said your
name wrong on purpose? If so,
what did you do?

RACE & CULTURE
Conversation Cards
—★★★— For kidS!

Has someone ever made
fun of the food you eat?

RACE & CULTURE
Conversation Cards
—★★★— For kidS!

Has anyone ever made fun
of the way you or your
family dresses?

RACE & CULTURE
Conversation Cards
—★★★— For kidS!

What is your favorite
thing about your culture?

RACE & CULTURE
Conversation Cards
—★★★— For kidS!

What is your favorite
thing about your hair?

RACE & CULTURE
Conversation Cards
—★★★— For kidS!

What is your favorite thing
about your skin color?

RACE & CULTURE
Conversation Cards
—★★★— For kidS!

Who is a Black person that
you look up to?

RACE & CULTURE
Conversation Cards
—★★★— For kidS!

Who is a Black person that
has the same hair as you?

RACE & CULTURE
Conversation Cards
—★★★— For kidS!

Who is a Black person that has
the same skin color as you?

RACE & CULTURE
Conversation Cards
—★★★— For kidS!

Who is a singer that makes
music that makes you proud
of who you are?

RACE & CULTURE
Conversation Cards
—★★★— For kidS!

What is a T.V. show that you
watch where the
characters look like you?

RACE & CULTURE
Conversation Cards
—★★★— For kidS!

Have you ever wished your
skin was a different color?

RACE & CULTURE
Conversation Cards
—★★★— For kidS!

Have *you* ever made fun of
someone because of how
they look?

RACE & CULTURE
Conversation Cards
—★★★— For kidS!

Have you ever been told to
stay away from a certain
group of people?

RACE & CULTURE
Conversation Cards
—★★★— For kidS!

Do you have the same
skin color as most of
your friends?

RACE & CULTURE
Conversation Cards
—★★★— For kidS!

Do you have the same skin
color as most of your
family members?

RACE & CULTURE
Conversation Cards
For Kids!

RACE & CULTURE
Conversation Cards
For Kids!

RACE & CULTURE
Conversation Cards
For Kids!

RACE & CULTURE
Conversation Cards
For Kids!

RACE & CULTURE
Conversation Cards
For Kids!

RACE & CULTURE
Conversation Cards
For Kids!

RACE & CULTURE
Conversation Cards
For Kids!

RACE & CULTURE
Conversation Cards
For Kids!

56 cards filled with prompting questions to
get the conversation underway!

RACE & CULTURE
Conversation Cards
—★★★—

How to Use

This card deck contains 56 total cards and requires printing and cutting. For best results, it is recommended to print in high quality, on card stock, and laminate, if possible, for prolonged use.

*If you would like the back graphic design on each card, then the card pages should be printed double-sided beginning on page 4. It is recommended to conduct a test print to ensure proper formatting and orientation. Cards are designed to print as traditional playing cards. Due to differences in printer functions, Mylemarks is unable to provide support if there are printing issues. To print cards without the back design, you can print the card pages Even Pages only, single-sided, starting on page 4.

Terms of Use

DEFINITIONS
—★★★—

These definitions are helpful to review with your client(s) prior to use of the cards.

Race
A group of people who have similar physical characteristics like skin color, facial features, type of hair, etc. [1]

•Examples: Black, White, Biracial/Multiracial, Asian, Hawaiian Pacific Islander, American Native

Culture
Certain characteristics or traditions that a group of people have in common. Culture is often passed down through generations.

•Example: Music, food, religion, clothing, holidays, language, and beliefs are all a part of culture.

Discrimination
When someone is treated unfairly because of something that makes them different. This can be their race, the way they dress, age, gender, religion, or other things. [2]

•Example: A school makes a rule that bans common Black hairstyles like braids, cornrows, dreadlocks, etc.

Stereotype
An assumption someone makes about a person or group of people based on how they look or a certain group they belong to. [3]

•Example: Believing that *all* Black boys are aggressive or thinking that *all* Black girls are angry or loud.

Prejudice
Pre – judging. Making a judgment about a person or group without really having a reason to. This can lead to treating them unfairly before getting to know them. [4]

•Example: A teacher thinks a Black student might be a "trouble maker", so they make them sit in the front of the class on the first day of school.

Microaggression
Hurtful things someone says or does that are subtle or something you may not notice right away.

•Example: Someone purposefully mispronouncing your name or asking you "Why did your parents name you that?"

Code Switch
Changing the way you talk, dress or behave to blend into a different (often White) environment.

•Example: Talking "more proper" or not using "slang" when around White people.

1 Kids Encyclopedia Facts. (2020, October, 21). *Race (sociology) facts for kids.* Kiddle. https://kids.kiddle.co/Race_(sociology)
2 Kids Encyclopedia Facts. (2020, October 21). *Discrimination facts for kids.* Kiddle. https://kids.kiddle.co/Discrimination
3 Kids Encyclopedia Facts. (2020, October 21). *Stereotype facts for kids.* Kiddle. https://kids.kiddle.co/Stereotype
4 Kids Encyclopedia Facts. (2020, October 21). *Prejudice facts for kids.* Kiddle. https://kids.kiddle.co/Prejudice

RACE & CULTURE
Conversation Cards
—★★★—

Have you ever experienced
a microaggression? If so,
how did it feel?

RACE & CULTURE
Conversation Cards
—★★★—

Was there ever a time you
felt discriminated against?
If so, how did it feel?

RACE & CULTURE
Conversation Cards
—★★★—

Has anyone ever made a
negative comment about
your hair?

RACE & CULTURE
Conversation Cards
—★★★—

Has anyone ever made a
negative comment about
the way you talk?

RACE & CULTURE
Conversation Cards
—★★★—

Has someone from your race
ever made a negative comment
about your skin tone?

RACE & CULTURE
Conversation Cards
—★★★—

Has anyone ever made a
negative comment about
the way you dress?

RACE & CULTURE
Conversation Cards
—★★★—

Has anyone ever made a
negative assumption about you
before getting to know you?

RACE & CULTURE
Conversation Cards
—★★★—

Name an adult who can help
you deal with a difficult
situation involving racism or
prejudice.

RACE & CULTURE
Conversation Cards
—★★★—
mylemarks · BMH Connect

RACE & CULTURE
Conversation Cards
—★★★—
mylemarks · BMH Connect

RACE & CULTURE
Conversation Cards
—★★★—
mylemarks · BMH Connect

RACE & CULTURE
Conversation Cards
—★★★—
mylemarks · BMH Connect

RACE & CULTURE
Conversation Cards
—★★★—
mylemarks · BMH Connect

RACE & CULTURE
Conversation Cards
—★★★—
mylemarks · BMH Connect

RACE & CULTURE
Conversation Cards
—★★★—
mylemarks · BMH Connect

RACE & CULTURE
Conversation Cards
—★★★—
mylemarks · BMH Connect

RACE & CULTURE
Conversation Cards
—★★★—

Have you ever felt like
your teacher was
prejudiced towards you?

RACE & CULTURE
Conversation Cards
—★★★—

Have you ever experienced
a teacher committing a
microaggression against
you?

RACE & CULTURE
Conversation Cards
—★★★—

What has your family
taught you about how to
behave around the police?

RACE & CULTURE
Conversation Cards
—★★★—

Have you ever had a
negative experience with
a police officer?

RACE & CULTURE
Conversation Cards
—★★★—

Have you ever witnessed
someone having a negative
encounter with a police
officer?

RACE & CULTURE
Conversation Cards
—★★★—

How do you feel when you
watch videos of police
using excessive force with
Black people?

RACE & CULTURE
Conversation Cards
—★★★—

When you're angry, what
do you do?

RACE & CULTURE
Conversation Cards
—★★★—

When you're sad, what
do you do?

RACE & CULTURE
Conversation Cards
—★★★—
my!emarks · BMH Connect

RACE & CULTURE
Conversation Cards
—★★★—
my!emarks · BMH Connect

RACE & CULTURE
Conversation Cards
—★★★—
my!emarks · BMH Connect

RACE & CULTURE
Conversation Cards
—★★★—
my!emarks · BMH Connect

RACE & CULTURE
Conversation Cards
—★★★—
my!emarks · BMH Connect

RACE & CULTURE
Conversation Cards
—★★★—
my!emarks · BMH Connect

RACE & CULTURE
Conversation Cards
—★★★—
my!emarks · BMH Connect

RACE & CULTURE
Conversation Cards
—★★★—
my!emarks · BMH Connect

RACE & CULTURE
Conversation Cards
—★★★—

What's a positive way to deal
with your anger when
dealing with a racial
experience?

RACE & CULTURE
Conversation Cards
—★★★—

What's a positive way to deal
with your sadness when
dealing with a racial
experience?

RACE & CULTURE
Conversation Cards
—★★★—

What's a positive way to deal
with feeling embarrassed
after a racial experience?

RACE & CULTURE
Conversation Cards
—★★★—

Who is an adult you can talk
to if you're feeling confused
after a racial encounter?

RACE & CULTURE
Conversation Cards
—★★★—

Have you ever changed your
hairstyle because of something
someone said to you?

RACE & CULTURE
Conversation Cards
—★★★—

Have you ever changed
the way you talk because
of something someone
said to you?

RACE & CULTURE
Conversation Cards
—★★★—

Have you ever changed
the way you dress because
of something someone
said to you?

RACE & CULTURE
Conversation Cards
—★★★—

Have you ever felt the need
to code switch?
If so, when and why?

RACE & CULTURE
Conversation Cards
—★★★—
mylemarks · BMH Connect

RACE & CULTURE
Conversation Cards
—★★★—
mylemarks · BMH Connect

RACE & CULTURE
Conversation Cards
—★★★—
mylemarks · BMH Connect

RACE & CULTURE
Conversation Cards
—★★★—
mylemarks · BMH Connect

RACE & CULTURE
Conversation Cards
—★★★—
mylemarks · BMH Connect

RACE & CULTURE
Conversation Cards
—★★★—
mylemarks · BMH Connect

RACE & CULTURE
Conversation Cards
—★★★—
mylemarks · BMH Connect

RACE & CULTURE
Conversation Cards
—★★★—
mylemarks · BMH Connect

RACE & CULTURE
Conversation Cards
— ★★★ —

Has anyone ever told you that you're "not Black enough?" If so, how did that make you feel?

RACE & CULTURE
Conversation Cards
— ★★★ —

Has anyone ever used a homophobic insult towards you because of how you acted?

RACE & CULTURE
Conversation Cards
— ★★★ —

Has anyone ever asked you "What are you?" If so, how did that make you feel?

RACE & CULTURE
Conversation Cards
— ★★★ —

Which friends can support you if you have a racial encounter?

RACE & CULTURE
Conversation Cards
— ★★★ —

Have you ever felt left out because of your race?

RACE & CULTURE
Conversation Cards
— ★★★ —

Has anyone ever used the "N-word" towards you? How did you respond?

RACE & CULTURE
Conversation Cards
— ★★★ —

Have you ever been in the community and someone made a negative assumption about you?

RACE & CULTURE
Conversation Cards
— ★★★ —

Has anyone ever questioned if you belonged somewhere?

RACE & CULTURE
Conversation Cards
—★★★—
mylemarks   BMH Connect

RACE & CULTURE
Conversation Cards
—★★★—
mylemarks   BMH Connect

RACE & CULTURE
Conversation Cards
—★★★—
mylemarks   BMH Connect

RACE & CULTURE
Conversation Cards
—★★★—
mylemarks   BMH Connect

RACE & CULTURE
Conversation Cards
—★★★—
mylemarks   BMH Connect

RACE & CULTURE
Conversation Cards
—★★★—
mylemarks   BMH Connect

RACE & CULTURE
Conversation Cards
—★★★—
mylemarks   BMH Connect

RACE & CULTURE
Conversation Cards
—★★★—
mylemarks   BMH Connect

RACE & CULTURE
Conversation Cards
—★★★—

Have you ever felt like you
had a teacher who was
"out to get you"?

RACE & CULTURE
Conversation Cards
—★★★—

Have you ever participated
in a march or protest?
If so, what was it like?

RACE & CULTURE
Conversation Cards
—★★★—

Has anyone ever made fun of
you for receiving free or
reduced services in school or
somewhere else?

RACE & CULTURE
Conversation Cards
—★★★—

Have you ever been told that
you were being "aggressive",
even though you felt you
weren't?

RACE & CULTURE
Conversation Cards
—★★★—

Do you believe that racism is
still an issue for your
generation? Why or why not?

RACE & CULTURE
Conversation Cards
—★★★—

Has anyone ever made fun
of your name? If so, how
did that make you feel?

RACE & CULTURE
Conversation Cards
—★★★—

Has anyone ever asked
you "Why did your
parents name you that?"
How did it make you feel?

RACE & CULTURE
Conversation Cards
—★★★—

How do you feel when
others mispronounce your
name?

RACE & CULTURE
Conversation Cards
—★★★—
mylemarks ⚜ BMH Connect

RACE & CULTURE
Conversation Cards
—★★★—
mylemarks ⚜ BMH Connect

RACE & CULTURE
Conversation Cards
—★★★—
mylemarks ⚜ BMH Connect

RACE & CULTURE
Conversation Cards
—★★★—
mylemarks ⚜ BMH Connect

RACE & CULTURE
Conversation Cards
—★★★—
mylemarks ⚜ BMH Connect

RACE & CULTURE
Conversation Cards
—★★★—
mylemarks ⚜ BMH Connect

RACE & CULTURE
Conversation Cards
—★★★—
mylemarks ⚜ BMH Connect

RACE & CULTURE
Conversation Cards
—★★★—
mylemarks ⚜ BMH Connect

RACE & CULTURE
Conversation Cards
—★★★—

Has someone ever made fun
of something in your
culture? If so, how did that
make you feel?

RACE & CULTURE
Conversation Cards
—★★★—

What is your favorite
thing about your
culture?

RACE & CULTURE
Conversation Cards
—★★★—

What is your
favorite thing about
your hair?

RACE & CULTURE
Conversation Cards
—★★★—

What is your favorite
thing about your skin
tone?

RACE & CULTURE
Conversation Cards
—★★★—

Who is someone in the Black
community that you see as a
positive role model?

RACE & CULTURE
Conversation Cards
—★★★—

Who is someone in the Black
community that has the same
hairstyle/texture as you?

RACE & CULTURE
Conversation Cards
—★★★—

Who is someone in the
Black community that has
the same skin tone as you?

RACE & CULTURE
Conversation Cards
—★★★—

Who is someone in the Black
community that has the
same sense of style as you?

RACE & CULTURE
Conversation Cards
—★★★—
mylemarks · BMH Connect

RACE & CULTURE
Conversation Cards
—★★★—
mylemarks · BMH Connect

RACE & CULTURE
Conversation Cards
—★★★—
mylemarks · BMH Connect

RACE & CULTURE
Conversation Cards
—★★★—
mylemarks · BMH Connect

RACE & CULTURE
Conversation Cards
—★★★—
mylemarks · BMH Connect

RACE & CULTURE
Conversation Cards
—★★★—
mylemarks · BMH Connect

RACE & CULTURE
Conversation Cards
—★★★—
mylemarks · BMH Connect

RACE & CULTURE
Conversation Cards
—★★★—
mylemarks · BMH Connect

RACE & CULTURE
Conversation Cards
—★★★—

Who is a musician that makes you proud of who you are?

RACE & CULTURE
Conversation Cards
—★★★—

When you're embarrassed, what do you do?

RACE & CULTURE
Conversation Cards
—★★★—

What do you do when a friend or family member says something offensive?

RACE & CULTURE
Conversation Cards
—★★★—

Have you ever participated in a social media movement for social justice?

RACE & CULTURE
Conversation Cards
—★★★—

Have you ever felt like an adult didn't hear you or take you seriously?

RACE & CULTURE
Conversation Cards
—★★★—

Has someone outside your race ever made a negative comment about your skin tone?

RACE & CULTURE
Conversation Cards
—★★★—

How do you feel when you are around people who look like you? What about those who don't look like you?

RACE & CULTURE
Conversation Cards
—★★★—

Have you ever wished you were a member of a different race?

Inside

Using words or pictures, describe places where you feel that you can be your true self. What feelings do you experience when you no longer have to *switch* in front of others?

Outside

Using words or pictures, describe places where you feel that you have to switch and act "less Black". What feelings do you experience when you have to wear this mask in front of others?

Code-Switching Mask

Use the coloring utensils to color your mask however you want. The front side of the mask is going to be the places or people you code switch around and your feelings about having to wear that mask. On the inside of the mask, you can decorate it with the feelings, places or people where you feel the most comfortable and authentic.

Required Materials

Craft mask, skin tone paint/markers, colored pencils, markers, paint, crayons, magazines, scissors, and glue. You can cut out words from magazines and/or use the words/phrases below.

SEEN
INVISIBLE
UNSEEN
SCARED
HAPPY
Safe
Valued
UNWORTHY
APPRECIATED
VALUED
IGNORED
Loved

BMH Connect

mylemarks

© 2022 BMH Connect & Mylemarks

3

▚▚▚

Play Therapy as a Solution to Racial Trauma

Historically, Black American children have used play to process the cruel and unusual treatment they have encountered (King, 2011; National Archives, n.d.; Wiggins, 1980). Research on play among Black children during the 19th century (both enslaved and free children) brings light to the use of play to process traumatic experiences. The game "Hide the Switch" was a way for enslaved children to psychologically process the constant fear associated with whippings from their "Master" (National Archives, n.d.). King (2011) highlights imitative play in the reenactment of funerals, church activities, and even slave auctions. Wiggins (1980) furthers this claim by stating "the evidence strongly suggests that slave children attempted to relieve particular anxieties and fears through the medium of imitative play. By reenacting certain events, they attempted to master specific problems which they were not able to resolve realistically" (p. 25). Play is a child's natural way of communicating their awareness of themselves and others (Landreth, 2002). Therefore, utilizing play therapy with Black students is a natural, authentic and fun way to engage students in a way that allows them to be their authentic selves.

Play Therapy Overview

Play therapy is the use of expressive arts such as games, art, music, and toys to help children of all backgrounds address mental health disturbances such as grief and loss, divorce, anger management, and trauma (Association for Play Therapy™ [APT], 2022a). Play therapy with Black youth has been found to be effective in increasing attachment, self-esteem, and self-regulation and in decreasing worry and negative intrusive thoughts (Patterson et. al.,

Black Students Matter. April D. Duncan, Oxford University Press. © Oxford University Press 2024.
DOI: 10.1093/oso/9780197669266.003.0004

2018; Wilson & Ray, 2018). Baggerly and Paker (2005) found play therapy with Black students improved empathy, self-confidence, and responsibility. It is a form of treatment that respects the culture of Black students while also promoting a free place to express emotions. It is key that school social workers create this environment through their verbal and nonverbal communication, tone of voice, and even their selection of toys and art materials.

Behaviors and norms in a person's culture are passed on from different generations through games, storytelling celebrations, music, and festivals (Gill & Drewes, 2005). Children learn about the rules and norms of their specific culture, as well as cultural differences, through play. Play therapy serves as a culturally competent intervention that respects the culture and traditions of Black students. It also allows the social worker to learn about children through the way that they play. This is important for students who are more resistant to verbally communicating their concerns—their play does the talking. Play therapy provides a space in which to honor cultural traditions and customs in the Black community that can serve as important protective factors for Black students. This is important for Black children who are often judged and punished for cultural differences that fall outside of Eurocentric standards of behavior.

Trauma in Play

After a traumatic event, a child may become closed off as a means of self-protection (Parker et al., 2021). Since Black students are constantly exposed to racial trauma, they are dealing with high levels of toxic stress. Without treatment, repeated childhood exposure to traumatic events can affect the brain and nervous system, increasing the probability of engaging in health risk behaviors (e.g., smoking, eating disorders, substance use) (National Childhood Traumatic Stress Network, n.d.). However, early intervention through expressive arts can positively shift long-term health outcomes (Pliske et al., 2021). Play therapy provides a free place for children to process their traumatic experiences under their own terms. The toys in play therapy can help students gain mastery of their trauma, allowing them to use their imagination to rewrite their stories, which can aid in processing and healing from the trauma (Parker et al., 2021). Play therapy with traumatized children can aid in emotional expression, enhancing relationships with caring adults and improving problem behaviors (Haas & Ray, 2020; Pliske et al., 2021). Since play therapy can address trauma in children, it also can be an effective tool to address racial trauma in Black students of all ages.

Earlier in my career I did not have the word "racial trauma" in my vocabulary to name the type of trauma I saw Black children experiencing. I have had the opportunity to integrate play therapy with Black children with trauma in a variety of settings including schools, therapeutic preschools, private practice, and the juvenile justice system. From preschoolers to high schoolers, one thing has been common; Black children are struggling to manage the emotions they experience when dealing with race-related stress and trauma. They also are not encouraged to engage in playful activities as much, as our community often encourages, they "grow up" early to face a world that will treat and judge them as adults. However, Black children are missing out on an essential element needed to jumpstart their development when they have experienced trauma—play. Article 31 of the Convention on the Rights of the Child from the United Nations states (Office of the High Commissioner for Human Rights, 1989):

1. Parties recognize the right of the child to rest and leisure, to engage in play and recreational activities appropriate to the age of the child and to participate freely in cultural life and the arts
2. Parties shall respect and promote the right of the child to participate fully in cultural and artistic life and shall encourage the provision of appropriate and equal opportunities for cultural, artistic, recreational and leisure activity

Since play is a right according to the UN, Black children are often denied their right to play when they are forced into parentified roles because of systemic and institutionalized trauma. They are denied their right to play when their punishment in schools is the removal of recess, art class and music class. They are denied their right to play when mental health professionals shy away from the use of play in their therapy sessions because of their own implicit biases. Black boys are denied their right to play when they are discouraged from playing with toy kitchens and dolls. Black girls are denied their right to play when they are encouraged put down their baby dolls and help raise their younger siblings. And in the long term, they are denied access to what their brains and development need to heal from racial trauma, therefore it is imperative school social workers integrate play therapy in schools, and within the family and community system, to help Black children regain their rights and their childhood.

Play Therapy in Schools
Offering play therapy in schools may be a solution for accessibility issues that many Black students experience in receiving mental health treatment. School

social workers can work with teachers to identify students who need individual or group play therapy or they can push into the classroom with group play sessions on topics like bullying, anxiety, and anger management. Play therapy is an appropriate intervention for students who are at risk of failing (Winburn et al., 2017), therefore it can be a way for school social workers to support Black youth who experience high levels of school discipline that disrupts their education, such as out-of-school suspensions. There are several benefits to integrating play therapy into schools, including the use of teachers and paraprofessionals to provide services to children, the regular attendance of students, and the availability of interdisciplinary services (Davis et al., 2022).

The Association for Play Therapy™ (APT), the credentialing body for certification as a Registered Play Therapist™ (RPT), offers a credential specific for school therapists: School-Based Registered Play Therapist™ (SB-RPT). To become an SB-RPT, applicants must meet the following requirements (APT, 2022b):

- An active and current individual state license or certificate from the state department of education to independently practice as a school psychologist or school counselor
- A school psychologist license/certification or clinical experience as required by the state department of education *plus* 2 years of continuous work in a school setting post certification/licensure
- A master's or higher mental health degree with demonstrated coursework in child and adolescent psychopathology, ethics, child development, theories of personality, and principles of psychotherapy
- 150 hours of play therapy–specific instruction from APT-approved providers or from institutions of higher education (limit 50 noncontact hours)
- The applicant must have received supervision from an RPT Supervisor™ (RPT-S) for a period of no less than 1 school year. Applicant must document a minimum of 600 direct client contact hours using play therapy plus 50 hours of simultaneous play therapy supervision. Supervisors providing 10 or more hours of supervision must observe at least one play therapy session during supervision. No more than 25 of the 50 hours of supervision may be in a group setting. Supervised hours must be completed during or after the applicant has earned their master's degree.

School social workers may need to work with teachers to discuss the benefits of play therapy with students. Teachers may display apprehension at having a student leave class to "play" if the child is not progressing academically or if the child had behavioral issues in the classroom prior to the session (Landreth et al., 2009). Sometimes teachers may see play therapy as a "reward," as opposed to a therapeutic intervention that can assist in addressing problem behaviors. The school social worker should not only offer psychoeducation to educators about play therapy, but they should also work collaboratively with them. That can include monthly consultations or once every 3–5 sessions, during which the school social worker checks on the child's behavioral and emotional progress in the classroom, listening to concerns and providing general updates on the progress shown in play therapy sessions (Landreth et al., 2009). This can allow teachers to feel more involved in the process and may in turn help them buy-in to the intervention. Chapter 9 provides more specifics on using play therapy to support teachers, along with the use of play in the classroom. For additional information on play therapy and how to become an RPT or SB-RPT, please visit the Association for Play Therapy™ website (Appendix A).

Virginia Axline's Eight Basic Principles of Self

Virginia Axline developed standard ways to engage in nondirective play therapy. Nondirective play is when the therapist allows the child to select the toys and activities for the session. The therapist allows the child to lead the play and does not attempt to control the direction of the session. Three of the principles developed by Axline are applicable to the ways that counselors can reduce implicit bias in their clinical work with Black students. First, the therapist needs to accept the child exactly as they are (Axline, 1981). This includes the student's way of talking and dressing. For example, schools will often reprimand Black students for using slang. It is important to recognize that vernacular varies by culture. There is no right or wrong way to talk, even if there is a standard way to write and talk from an educational standpoint. However, when a student comes into a clinical session, the social worker is not the teacher and their goal in that session is to accept the child as they are, rather than correcting the way they talk. Also, from a rapport aspect, the professional should see the use of slang in sessions as the student's way of communicating a level of comfort and connection with them.

The counselor should focus on establishing a feeling of permissiveness (Axline, 1981), which can also include the use of music and profanity in sessions. There can be a lot of debate around the use of profanity and/or playing hip-hop music, however, the amount of profanity and violence in rap lyrics is comparable to that in country music lyrics (Henning, 2021). Therefore, limiting the playing of one genre of music over another is an implicit bias that school social workers should seek to avoid. The final principle to consider is that the therapist should recognize and reflect the student's feelings to help them gain insight into their own behavior (Axline, 1981). For example, if a student is communicating that they are really frustrated with a teacher and the way the teacher has been treating them, the therapist can help them connect their behavior as being caused by their feelings to provide further insight. This can help validate the student's feelings and experiences while also helping them learn more about how they behave whenever they are dealing with conflict. However, many times Black children are not afforded the luxury of sharing their side of the story or their perceptions, so it is even more important for school social workers to advocate for and support them beyond the playroom.

In my clinical work with Black children who have been suspended or disciplined at school, I have always tried to make sure I listen to the whole story, empathize with their emotions and discuss alternative ways to navigate the situation. This is different from the approach "It doesn't matter what the teacher did, you were the one who was wrong" that many Black children hear. Instead, I may say "Tell me the whole story and let's talk through what could have gone different." In that conversation, I also validate their perception, either real or perceived, that they are being singled out or "picked on." Knowing the prevalence of bias towards Black students, I know that their perception may have some truth. However, we also talk about how their behavior may have contributed to, or escalated the incident, and discuss ways to feel empowered to advocate for themselves so their voice and concerns are heard, like talking to their school social worker or principal about the unfair treatment they believe they are receiving. Sometimes I have called or visited the school myself to help them advocate for themselves. Rooted in Axline's principles, then the school social work is promoting permissiveness for the child to be and advocate for themselves, while also helping them gain insight into their behavior.

Toys and Materials to Support Black Students

There are several key items to have at your school to implement play therapy with Black students. However, it is important to remember that cultural inclusivity should be communicated from the moment someone steps into the therapeutic space. This includes diversity in magazines, books, puzzles, and toys. Although this book focuses on play therapy with Black students, the toys and materials in that space should be welcoming for all students and reflective of all races and ethnicities, sexual orientation and gender identities, religions, and even political affiliations. Funding for play materials is often acquired through local businesses or school parent–teacher associations (Landreth et al., 2009).

There are several play therapy websites where social workers can purchase diverse dolls, puppets, and books (Appendix A). Diversity in the art materials in the playroom is also important for creating a space of self-expression for Black students. Companies such as Crayola sell multicultural colored pencils, markers, paint, crayons, and construction paper. School social workers should also invest in additional materials like Colorations multicultural modeling dough (Appendix A). Culturally diverse dolls, puzzles, and grief toys/sand tray miniatures and aggressive toys/sand tray miniatures are important items in a playroom to support Black students experiencing racial trauma.

Dolls

Doll play is utilized a lot by younger girls, so school social workers should have culturally diverse dolls with different skin tones and hair textures. Black students have different skin complexions and hair textures, so this form of representation for Black children can be empowering. Some Black girls and women with darker skin struggle with low-self-esteem and self-worth due to deep-rooted issues of colorism in the Black community. Providing dolls of all complexions, especially those with darker skin, can serve as an assessment tool to offer insight into the clients' perception of themselves. Black dolls with different hair textures may also open the conversation around hair discrimination or other issues around hair that are important to the client. (Issues of colorism and hair discrimination in Black girls are explored in more depth in Chapter 4. Issues of hair discrimination toward Black boys are further discussed in Chapter 5.) Several Black-owned businesses sell dolls that provide this varied representation (Appendix A) and these can also be beneficial for displaying cultural humility in the playroom. School social workers should also include Black action figures and superheroes in the playroom like Black Adam, Storm from X-Men, Luke Cage, and characters from *Black Panther* to name a few.

Puzzles

School social workers should also provide puzzles and books that reflect Black students, their culture, and their unique experiences. Puzzle Huddle (Appendix A) sells puzzles that depict Black people in different professions and careers. They also have free coloring sheets for immediate download that can be printed and made available for students to color in the playroom during nondirective play, especially elementary-age students. Additionally, Bevy & Dave (Appendix A) has several puzzles featuring historical Black figures. Another puzzle, "A Day at the Barbershop" (Appendix A) can be used to evoke conversations around hair culture and discrimination. For students struggling with low self-esteem and self-worth, affirmation cards and coloring sheets created for Black children, such as those by Darlying & Co. (Appendix A) can assist in empowerment and self-esteem building in Black students.

Grief Toys

Black youth have higher rates of negative interactions with systems such as schools and law enforcement. These incidents can be seen as grief events as they may often illicit the emotions of the grief cycle (e.g., confusion, anger, denial, bargaining, and depression) (Stanaway, 2020). Therefore, it is important to have toys available to help them process and communicate their experiences. Toys like a miniature police station, handcuffs, a doctor's kit, and community helpers (e.g., doctors, police officers, and firemen), their vehicles (e.g., fire truck, police car, and ambulance), and costumes are recommended to help students process grief events such as community violence or adverse police contact. These toys can also provide a space to discuss the student's sense of safety around police officers, especially if there are police officers in the school. This could provide insight into problem behaviors that are often misinterpreted as defiance or opposition but are instead rooted in trauma responses to law enforcement. Those same toys can be used to support child welfare–involved youth and students with incarcerated family members, along with other toys, such as a courthouse toy set, to help them communicate their feelings and concerns about their life experiences.

Aggressive Toys

Black students are exposed to higher levels of violence in their communities and in the media. This can include gang violence, mass shootings, and police brutality. Exposure to these events means these students could benefit from aggressive toys to help release their emotions and communicate their experiences. Aggressive toys such as toy guns and swords are healthy outlets for children to express aggressive and angry feelings. The inclusion of aggressive toys into school-based therapy can provide a safe way for students to express frustration, hostility, anger, and fear through supportive and symbolic means (Davis et al., 2022). However, schools that have adopted a zero-tolerance policy for students may mean that any weapon—or anything resembling a weapon—can result in immediate expulsion (Brady, 2002). It is recommended that school social workers educate their district on the importance of play to process trauma and the benefits of aggressive play for children.

There are negative consequences from restricting children from using aggressive toys in schools, such as feeling unequipped to process experiences or repressing anger, which may lead to guilt and shame, an inability to control aggression in social settings, and difficulty effectively balancing conflict and cooperation (Davis et al., 2022). If school social workers receive approval from their school district or any of their administrative staff to have toys guns and swords in the playroom, it is important that the counselor documents that approval. Another toy that is recommended for aggression release is a "bop bag," an inflatable punching bag that students can use to release aggression. However, this can be controversial as well.

> I was working with Marcus, a 10-year-old Black boy who struggled with aggression. When he was upset, he would often hit things or destroy property. So, I brought in a bop bag to the school as a healthy outlet for his aggression. One day, as I'm walking down the hall, an administrator stopped me and said, "Hey, I heard in a meeting that you gave Marcus a bop bag. I'm confused. If we're trying to stop him from hitting stuff, why would you give him something to hit?!"
>
> This is a valid question that required patience and empathy. The staff member needed to be educated on the benefits of aggressive-release toys, rather than me being offended that she would question my decision. I thanked the administrator for wanting to learn more about my decision and explained that the goal was to redirect Marcus's anger into a healthy outlet until the source of his anger was identified and resolved. In that instance, the administrator understood and thanked me for taking the time to explain the intervention. However, other educators may require additional psychoeducation on how Black students with high levels of racial stressors may struggle with anger management and need healthier outlets to express that emotion.

Play Therapy Approaches to Address Racial Trauma in Black Youth

APT has several seminal and historical play theories that provide the foundation for various expressive therapy modalities that can be used to work with clients from all backgrounds. Several approaches serve as a roadmap to utilize play therapy interventions to address racial trauma in Black students. This book explores the use of the following seminal theories: Adlerian Play Therapy (AdPT), Filial Therapy (FT), Theraplay, Cognitive Behavioral Play Therapy (CBPT), Child-Centered Play Therapy (CCPT), Ecosystemic Play Therapy (EPT), Psychoanalytic Play Therapy, and Jungian Analytical Play Therapy (JAPT). Determining the most appropriate theory to use with a student will be based on the child's presenting problem, developmental age, level of engagement in the playroom, and rapport with the counselor. Nondirective approaches are helpful for building rapport with Black students, especially younger students, whereas game play therapy may be a more appropriate rapport-building activity with older Black students. Social workers should rely on their professional judgment on which play therapy seminal theory to utilize with a student while recognizing the need to adjust their approach based on the measurable success or failure of the selected theory.

Ecosystemic Play Therapy

EPT is a seminal theory that should be used by all school social workers when working with Black students. The theory focuses on a conceptualization of the child's presenting problems in an environmental context while also creating interventions that ensure the child's needs are appropriately and consistently met (O'Connor & Braverman, 2009). Providing ethically and culturally competent clinical therapy with Black students will require identifying the key systems interacting with the child, acknowledging the impact of those systems, and working with individuals within the system to ensure that the child's needs are being met. Some key tenets in EPT include using information gathered from an ecosystemic intake, along with developmental information, to inform case conceptualization and treatment (O'Connor & Vega, 2019). This is essential when taking into account the role adultification bias plays in the lives of Black children. School social workers should be mindful of this bias when creating treatment goals and selecting interventions that are based on the child's developmental age opposed to their perceived chronological age. Another important tenet of EPT is for the therapist to assume an advocacy role (O'Connor & Vega, 2019), another key skill school social workers should utilize when working with Black students. The work to heal racial trauma in Black students will extend beyond individual play therapy sessions and should include advocating for the needs and rights of Black children in their schools and communities. EPT can aid the therapist in developing a racial trauma lens that can help to effectively identify and treat the symptoms of racial trauma in Black children, which in turn can allow for more appropriate diagnosis, treatment planning and positive long-term outcomes.

Cognitive Behavioral Play Therapy

CBPT focuses on the client's thoughts, feelings, fantasies, and environment while offering play-based strategies to help the client develop more adaptive behaviors and thoughts (Drewes & Cavett, 2019). This can be an effective approach with Black students for increasing self-esteem; learning self-regulation, anxiety, anger management, and coping skills; and assisting in gaining better control over their thoughts and feelings as they pertain to race-based stress and trauma. CBPT incorporates techniques like role-playing and modeling, using play therapy materials such as puppets (Drewes & Cavett, 2019). A useful cognitive behavioral therapy (CBT) technique is called "Play the script to the end," which is meant to treat fears and anxiety (Ackerman, 2017). Black students can be encouraged to use this technique to process any anxiety around potential race-based events (e.g., being harmed by a police officer) or any hypervigilance/anxiety they may have about a past event that is being retriggered. The student can be encouraged to think about a scenario that causes anxiety and use dolls or puppets to play the scene out until the end to help them process the worst-case scenario they may be internalizing. This technique can also be implemented in sand tray therapy, where the student can create the anxiety-inducing scene, then play the scene out in role-play until the end. CBPT can serve as an useful tool for adolescents and teens dealing with negative self-talk and distorted cognitions related to racial trauma.

Adlerian Play Therapy

In AdPT, the therapist believes that everyone is born with a capacity for self-interest, which is a measurement of their mental health (Meany-Walen & Kottman, 2019). This approach can be beneficial for Black students because it believes in the inherent worth of the child and their ability to overcome their circumstances. It can also be a tool for empowerment in Black students, as Adlerian play therapists believe that people are creative and unique, following their own life trajectories (Meany-Walen & Kottman, 2019). Because Black children are often labeled early in their life, AdPT provides a space for students to explore those labels and gain insight into how those labels have shaped their relationships with individuals outside of their family.

There are four phases of treatment in AdPT (Kottman, 2011):

- Building an egalitarian relationship: In this phase, the focus is on the relationship, with the therapist using both directive and non-directive play therapy interventions to deepen the connection with the child.
- Exploring the child's lifestyle: The therapist in this phase observes the client's behaviors and consider things like the child's family constellation, strengths, goals of misbehavior, functioning at life tasks, and personality priorities (ways the child seeks to belong).
- Helping the child gain insight into their lifestyle: In this phase, the focus of the therapist is using mostly directive techniques to help clients gain insight into their patterns of thinking, feeling and behaving.
- Reorientation & re-education: In this final phase, the therapist uses mainly directive activities focused on problem solving, communication, anger management, metacommunication, communication and anxiety management.

The patterns of cognitions, emotions, and behaviors that children develop comprise their lifestyle, which helps children predict and control life (Meany-Walen & Kottman, 2015). AdPT can be a way for Black students to identify and change destructive thoughts, feelings, and behaviors into more positive ones while finding more appropriate ways to belong in their classrooms, families, and communities. Children are often egocentric and have a limited ability to interpret relationships and events, which may lead to mistaken beliefs and destructive lifestyle patterns (Meany-Walen & Kottman, 2019). For Black students, this may be the root of disruptive behaviors because they may start to engage in self-fulfilling negative prophecies that have been communicated to them from an early age. AdPT can be used in individual, group, and family play therapy with Black students to address feelings of inferiority and mistaken beliefs while improving connections and confidence. (Chapter 10 explores the use of AdPT in group therapy sessions.)

Theraplay

Theraplay is an attachment-based play therapy approach that seeks to enhance emotional regulation and attachment (Booth & Jernberg, 2010). This approach can be most appropriate with students who have experienced some form of attachment trauma that has led to impaired adult relationships. Theraplay activities are based on four categories: nurture, challenge, structure, and engagement (Booth & Jernberg, 2010). Theraplay can be used with students of all backgrounds, especially child welfare–involved youth and children with incarcerated parents. Theraplay can be used in individual, group, and family play therapy sessions with young children and adolescents who have difficulty socializing with others like peers, parents, and teachers (Booth & Lindaman, 2019). (Chapter 9 explores the use of Theraplay in schools.)

Child-Centered Play Therapy

CCPT is a nondirective approach to working with children ages 3–10 years with social, emotional, behavioral, and relational disorders (Ray & Landreth, 2019). Students are encouraged to lead the play using toys and materials in the playroom at their leisure, with no direction from the school social worker. This approach will be used most with students in kindergarten through 4th grade. CCPT is appropriate for kids with sibling conflict, peer conflict, and other emotional and behavioral problems (Ray & Landreth, 2019). The Center for Play Therapy (2022) offers a list of preferred toys to use in CCPT sessions. This is an important approach to address racial trauma because a lot of Black children are not afforded the same freedoms and independence as White children. For safety reasons, many Black children are not encouraged to explore their environments or play freely with the toys they like. CCPT allows Black children a break from their controlled environment and allows them the freedom to make their own choices and establish independence within the playroom.

Child-Centered Group Play Therapy

Although Child-centered group play therapy (CCGPT) is not a seminal play therapy theory, it is an approach that can be beneficial for younger students, pre-kindergarten up to 3rd grade. In CCGPT, it is recommended that there are no more than 2–3 children in the group at once so the therapist can be attuned to each group member individually and collectively (Blalock et al., 2019). There are several benefits for students participating in CCGPT. Black students who are more resistant to individual therapy could benefit from

CCGPT because it can be viewed as a less threatening entrance into the therapeutic environment when there are other children seen engaging in play. A group setting can diminish tension and stimulate participation, as seeing the level of permissiveness granted by the therapist in a group setting can help encourage spontaneity that may not occur in an individual CCPT session (DeMaria & Crowden, 1992). For younger Black boys, this may include the use of doll play or play that is seen as more feminine because seeing their peers engaging the play, along with the therapists' encouragement, may allow the child to feel more comfortable engaging in play that they may not have necessarily engaged in during individual CCPT sessions. Therefore, CCGPT could be a hidden gem for school social workers in unlocking in Black student's new behaviors or emotions that may not appear in CCPT sessions.

Filial Therapy

Since Black caregivers struggle to find mental health support for their children, the social worker could benefit from teaching them how to conduct play therapy sessions at home with their child. FT was developed by Bernard and Lewis Gurney in the 1960s, and it is closely related to CCPT (Scuka & Guerney, 2019). It involves the caregivers directly as the agents of therapeutic change, with the social worker supervising and training caregivers to conduct non-directive play sessions with their kids at home (Scuka & Guerney, 2019). This model will not be effective for caregivers of older students, but social workers working in preschool and elementary schools may benefit from this intervention, which is most appropriate for children 3–12 years old (Scuka & Guerney, 2019).

In FT sessions, the social worker teaches the caregiver to follow the child's lead, with the caregiver often initiating and leading the session themselves (Scuka & Guerney, 2019). These sessions at the school are meant to help the caregiver take those skills and implement them in the home environment of the child. These home sessions should be done daily, during what is called "special time," where the caregiver and the child spend one-on-one time engaging in non-directive play sessions (Scuka & Guerney, 2019). After the caregiver learns how to implement FT in their environment, they are encouraged to continue the home sessions, along with monthly parent consultations to review the child's progress and discuss any themes the caregiver notices in their play (Scuka & Guerney, 2019). This short-term therapy model may be appealing to caregivers who are unable to give a long-term commitment to therapy. (Chapter 11 explores the use of FT with caregivers of Black children.)

Psychoanalytic Play Therapy

Psychoanalytic play therapy focuses on the child's anxieties, defenses, and fantasies that are communicated unconsciously (Punnett & Green, 2019). During play therapy sessions, the school social worker will look for play themes that develop within the student's play which can help communicate the child's unconscious desires. This theory can serve as an assessment tool for identifying racial trauma in Black children along with creating treatment goals that address the identified need and/or issue. A main goal of psychoanalytic play therapy is to help children develop their unique identities and experiences so they can persevere despite their life circumstances (Punnett & Green, 2019). This seminal theory can serve as tool of empowerment for Black children as they continually navigate racial trauma triggers in their lives. Play themes associated with racial trauma using a psychoanalytic play therapy framework are explored in further detail later in the chapter.

Jungian Analytical Play Therapy

JAPT is focuses on increasing the client's awareness of their inner world through the facilitation and interpretation of symbolic expression in fantasy play (Lilly & Heiko, 2019). This seminal theory is similar to Psychoanalytic Play Therapy using symbolism to interpret the play of children. This is especially important when addressing racial trauma in Black children, who may not be willing or able to verbalize the feelings they have around race-based stressors. Goals for JAPT include maintaining an analytical attitude, grounding the child in reality, and blocking self-destructive processes (Lilly & Heiko, 2019). JAPT may be useful for clints of all ages, as it uses a variety of Techniques including sandplay, mandalas and drawings (Lilly & Heiko, 2019). Sand tray therapy, which is discussed in more detail later in the chapter, is one of my favorite interventions to use with children, especially older Black children, as it allows them to engage in a modality that promotes emotional safety and self-expression.

Additional Play and Expressive Therapies with Black Students

Art Therapy

The use of art-based activities can be an effective tool to support Black students of all ages. Art therapy uses art media, the creative process, and the resulting artwork as a therapeutic and healing process (Art Therapy Credentials Board, 2021). Art therapy is an effective modality by which to help clients explore their feelings, foster self-awareness, reconcile emotional conflicts, reduce anxiety, manage behavior, develop social skills, improve reality orientation, and increase self-esteem (Art Therapy Credentials Board, 2021). It should be noted that all school social workers are able to use expressive arts in play therapy sessions, but they should receive some training to ensure it is being done with as much competence as possible. Therapists who wish to utilize this approach should not refer to themselves as art therapists; instead, they should communicate that they use art-based approaches in treatment with students.

The use of art-based interventions with Black students is another way to create an environment where they are encouraged and supported in processing their experiences and identifying their needs for healing, Art-based therapy techniques are also helpful tools for older students who are less likely to engage in play activities that involves toys. It also provides visual reminders that students can take with them to remind them of lessons learned in their clinical sessions. Finally, art-based play therapy interventions can provide an avenue by which to tackle tough subjects in group therapy settings while also allowing students to work individually within a group setting.

Music Therapy

Music therapy is the clinical and evidence-based use of music interventions to accomplish individualized goals within a therapeutic relationship (Halverson-Ramos et al., 2019). Music therapy seeks to promote wellness, manage stress, alleviate pain, enhance memory, improve communication, and express feelings (Halverson-Ramos et al., 2019). Like art therapy and play therapy, clinicians should receive some training in music therapy and avoid referring to themselves as a "music therapist," a term designating a credentialed professional who has completed an approved music therapy program (Halverson-Ramos et al., 2019). Music therapists utilize music as a therapeutic tool; all styles of music are believed to be useful to effectively change the lives of clients, and the genre and type of instrument is tailored to the individual (Halverson-Ramos et al., 2019). This is helpful for Black students who are often discouraged from listening to certain genres of music, either from the perception of the genre being "too violent" or being "too White" in the eyes of their peers, family, and community members.

When integrating music-based play therapy interventions into sessions, there a few things to consider. First, the students' developmental age is important when deciding what music to play or that is deemed appropriate for their age. This requires the clinician to eliminate any of their own opinions on which music is tasteful or distasteful. For example, a 1st-grader listening to or asking to play music with profanity is highly inappropriate, but allowing a junior in high school to play the same song may be a way to build rapport and help the student develop trust in the therapeutic relationship. Younger students can use more age-appropriate channels like *Kidz Bop* on YouTube to play versions of current songs that are more appropriate for their age. Also, the therapist should be mindful about the schools' policy on technology use to determine the best outlet for playing music (e.g., laptop, student's phone, etc.). Finally, the therapist should consider the different ways that music can be used in sessions, including playing music in the background during game play or art activities or hosting a dance party at the beginning and/or end of sessions.

Game Play

Game play is a play-based intervention that uses board games, video games, card games, or other game forms to address problem behaviors in children and adolescents (Stone & Schaefer, 2019). There are three different therapeutic applications of game play therapy. First, some therapeutic games are created to specifically address a problem behavior such as anger or bullying. Second are traditional games that are adapted by clinicians to utilize in clinical sessions. For example, Feelings Candyland assigns a feeling to each color, and the child must identify a time when they felt that feeling associated with the color on their card. The third application of games in sessions with students simply plays traditional games with no pressure to talk or teach a skill.

Games are powerful motivational tools for students to engage in therapy (Stone & Schaefer, 2019). Game play serves as a useful rapport-building tool, especially with older students who will not typically engage in play. In those sessions, it is important for the counselor to respect any silence and embrace the connection made through the game. For Black students with high levels of mistrust, providing a place to play with no pressure will be key to developing trust and rapport. Game play offers a safe place for kids to progress through therapy at their own pace. Even more, it can serve as a rapport-building activity for Black youth who may struggle with mistrust.

Sand Tray Therapy

Sand tray therapy was developed by Margaret Lowenstein in 1939, with adaptations that integrate evidence-based practices such as CBT, solution-focused therapy, and mindfulness-based stress reduction (Homeyer & Sweeny, 2017). This can serve as an effective tool for Black students who can be given the ability to use the sand tray to unlock unconscious feelings and behaviors, which can help provide further insight into students' therapeutic needs. This approach allows students to express nonverbalized emotions, serves as a form of self-expression, and provides a safe place for the student explore and learn new things about themselves and their world (Homeyer & Sweeney, 2017). It is highly recommended that clinicians receive training in sand tray therapy from play therapy professionals, such as the World Association of Sand Therapy Professionals (WASTP), before implementing sand tray therapy. For clinicians with experience in the modality, sand tray prompts are presented throughout the book to help aid Black students work through race-based experiences using a sand tray. When using sand tray therapy with Black students, some sand tray miniatures are key to integrate into the sand tray miniature collection. Sand tray miniatures that explore racial stressors include the following:

Sand tray miniatures for racial trauma: Superheroes, wishing well, wizard, angry birds, or other miniatures that reflect emotions (e.g., Inside Out characters), multicultural people, school building, school bus, backpack, books

Sand tray miniatures for community violence/grief: Community helpers and their vehicles, aggressive miniatures (e.g., toy guns, swords), army men, tombstones, coffin, ghosts, skeletons, church, preacher, substance use (e.g., wine bottles), fake blood

Sand tray miniatures for child welfare–involved students and students with incarcerated family members: Gavel, judge, court bench, jail, prison bus, inmate, police officers, two houses, handcuffs, luggage, cell phone

It is important to note that clinicians should be deliberate and intentional when creating their sand tray miniature collection (Homeyer & Sweeney, 2017). Some things to consider when building a collection is geographic location, student demographics, the background experiences of students, and, of course, diversity in the skin tones and hair textures of sand tray miniatures. When working with Black students, it is important to consider the backgrounds of many of the students. For example, if a social worker works in a school with high levels of community violence, there should be sand tray miniatures that reflect that experience.

Play Themes Associated with Racial Trauma in Black Students

Play themes are inferences made about a students' emotional issues based on their patterns of play with materials and/or their patterns, both nonverbal and verbal, with the school social worker (Ryan & Edge, 2012). Play themes develop in several ways. One way is that the theme is present several times across several sessions. For example, a student who does not talk to the therapist or plays in a session on their own is showing an independent play theme. If the student continues to display this theme in several sessions, this theme can be accurately identified. However, it is important to note that some students new to therapy or struggling with levels of mistrust may show themes of chaos or independence in the first sessions due to their uncertainty about therapy.

Another way a play theme develops is when a student displays the same theme in one session while using different toys or engaging in different activities. For example, in a play therapy session, the student plays with superheroes and acts out scenes of dying. Then they play with puppets and act out death scenes. This can be a client displaying the grief theme. These themes will help guide the school social worker to determine the appropriate course of treatment for that child. It can also assist with advocating for appropriate services for the child, such for Individual Education Plan (IEP) meetings. Although additional play themes exist, we will focus on examples in the playroom that could signal distress in Black students experiencing racial trauma. Using a psychoanalytic play therapy framework, the following play themes could be used to identify signs of racial trauma in play therapy sessions with Black students.

Grief

The grief theme is often used in the playroom by Black children who have experienced some type of grief event such as bullying, death of a loved one, or having a family member being incarcerated. The grief theme appears through scenes of death and dying in the child's play. In the sand tray, it can include the use of miniatures associated with death like coffins, headstones, or other cemetery-related items. If the grief theme is present in a child's play, the counselor should work to address the grief symptoms that are shown in the child's presenting problem, targeting interventions to address the untreated grief in the child. This may include seminal play theories such as CBPT, trauma-focused CBPT (TF-CBT), and expressive modalities such as art therapy, music therapy, and sand tray therapy. (Play therapy for students experiencing grief and bereavement is covered in more detail in Chapter 8.)

Connection

The connection theme is exhibited when the child is constantly saying "Watch this" or "Look." This should alert the counselor to address any attachment issues through modalities that can work with teachers or caregivers to strengthen their relationship. Theraplay and FT can be appropriate seminal play theories to enhance attachment between Black students and important adults in their lives, including their teachers. The connection theme may also be shown in a student who is struggling with isolation due to thoughts of suicide or struggling with depression. Art therapy, music therapy, sand tray therapy, CBPT, and AdPT would all be appropriate play therapy approaches to support older students exhibiting this theme in sessions.

Self-Esteem

The self-esteem theme is shown when a student asks your opinion about them or about their work. For example, they may ask questions like "Is this pretty?" or "Do you like my picture?" This is often a sign of confidence or self-esteem issues in a child. Although it seems natural to respond "yes" to these questions, it is important that the social worker commend the effort opposed to the final product. In those situations, the social worker may say "I like how hard you worked on your picture" or "I like how you used different colors on your picture." It is important to remember that a Black child may be struggling with self-esteem issues due to racial trauma. CBPT, AdPT, EPT, or mindfulness activities like affirmations can be used to improve self-esteem for Black students struggling with racial trauma.

Aggression

The next play theme, aggression, does not necessarily mean that a child is becoming aggressive toward the therapist in the session, but they may engage in some type of aggressive play. Aggressive play could include using aggressive toys, such as toy guns or swords. Aggressive play can present in the energy level or way in which the child interacts with the toys. For example, a student may want to engage in a toy sword fight with the therapist, which is an aggressive type of play, but they are not harming the therapist. This may represent a student struggling with some anger, especially in relation to race-based stress and trauma. Play therapy interventions using approaches like art and music therapy can be an appropriate way to identify the source of their aggression and teach them healthier coping skills to manage those feelings. Seminal theories like JAPT, CBPT, and AdPT may also be effective in identifying and addressing the source of anger in Black students experiencing racial trauma.

Independent Play

The theme of independent play is displayed when students play quietly on their own and does not engage with the therapist. The social worker should have respect for silence and identify silence as a sign that the child may not be comfortable talking or engaging in the therapeutic relationship. Silent play also could reflect the child's personality, which we are not aiming to change. Instead, the social worker should provide a space of permissiveness by not forcing the student to talk. Another way the independent theme is shown occurs when a student plays with toys and talks with the therapist but does not invite the therapist into their play. In this situation, the therapist should not invite themselves into the student's play. Instead, they should continue to use tracking statements to describe the child's behavior and only enter the child's play when invited.

For Black students, experience with race-based stress and trauma may lead to a level of independence that they have developed to protect themselves. They may also engage in independent play because of they have been parentified and placed into adult roles, or even a result of adultificiation bias. CCPT and CCGPT will be appropriate play therapy approaches that will respect the student's therapeutic progress as they move at their own pace while also respecting the students' need for independence.

Fear

Many times, Black children, especially boys, may struggle with communicating fear. This may be due to being told in their family and community systems not to show fear or be afraid. However, this emotion is often evident in their behavior in the playroom. Those behaviors include a child asking the therapist to hide certain toys or avoiding certain areas of a playroom because they are fearful of something. It may also be communicated in their role-play. For example, a student who has experienced adverse police contact may communicate fear through the actions of toy police officers. The use of *safety language* with the student is important; the social worker communicates that the playroom is a free place and talks to the child about people or places where they feel safe. The use of CBPT and AdPT are seminal play theories the therapist can use to support students communicating this theme.

Anger

Like the aggressive play theme, the anger theme may be present in a Black student's play as an emotion related to constant interactions with people and environments that contribute to their racial stress. This theme will often be communicated through the child's role-play with toys like dolls, superheroes, or toys. It can also include the student verbalizing the emotion during their session. The social worker should validate their emotions and help them understand that anger is an appropriate emotion that everyone experiences. Play therapy approaches that aid in identifying the source of the emotion, along with learning appropriate coping skills, include sand tray play therapy, music therapy, CBPT, and CCPT.

Mistrust

The play theme of mistrust may be communicated in a student who does not feel comfortable talking about things with the therapist or who avoids answering questions. This play theme is shown in the play of Black students experiencing racial trauma through interactions they have had with adults in their lives. Using a racial trauma lens, the social worker communicates to the child that they do not have to talk about anything that makes them feel uncomfortable. This is another way that the social worker displays a place of permissiveness, by not forcing the student to talk. This can aid in rapport-building, as the student may appreciate the therapist respecting their desire to not talk since many Black children are scolded or reprimanded for not talking about things with adults. CCPT is the best approach to developing rapport with younger students, while music therapy, sand tray play therapy, and game play therapy can be effective expressive interventions for developing rapport with older students (5th graders and older).

Protection and Safety

The play theme of protection and safety can be shown when a student uses toys like handcuffs and toy swords. This theme is also shown when the child uses community helpers, including their vehicles and costume play. Costume items associated with the protection and safety theme include helmets and body armor. Additionally, the student may communicate this theme by using items like a net or blanket to cover toys. This play theme can be a student's way of communicating feelings of helplessness, which is a risk factor for suicidal thoughts and behaviors. CBPT and AdPT, along with safety language will be effective ways to support students exhibiting this theme in therapy sessions. Additionally, game play therapy and music therapy can provide a space for Black students to connect with the therapist at their own pace and comfort level.

Chaos

A student who engages in multiple activities and uses many toys in the session may show the chaos play theme. The chaos theme also appears with students who dump toys during their play. The student may also struggle with engaging in any play activity for a sustained amount of time. This theme is often associated with anxiety and can be supported with play therapy interventions that encourage self-regulation and address any cognitive distortions that may be contributing to anxious thoughts and behaviors. Suggested seminal play theories to utilize with these students are CBPT, CCPT, and AdPT, along with sand tray therapy, music therapy, and art therapy.

Conclusion

Black students can benefit from the use of play therapy to express their emotions appropriately while learning new skills to manage their thoughts and feelings associated with racial stressors and negative race-based experiences. There are several seminal play theories and expressive play and art interventions that the school social worker can use to build rapport with Black students and create a place for healthy emotional expression around racial trauma. More than ever, Black students need an avenue to process events that directly affect their mental health. Play therapy can be used in individual, group, and family play therapy sessions to effectively address racial stressors from preschool to high school. The reminder of the book will discuss the use of historical and seminal play therapy theories to support Black students of all ages, including culturally inclusive play therapy interventions that can address the unique needs of Black students of all ages.

References

Ackerman, C. E. (2017). CBT techniques: 25 cognitive behavioral therapy worksheets. *Positive Psychology*. https://positivepsychology.com/cbt-cognitive-behavioral-therapy-techniques-worksheets/ -:~:text=Play the script until the end of the worst-case scenario.

Art Therapy Credentials Board, Inc. (2021). What is art therapy? https://atcb.org/what-is-art-therapy/

Association for Play Therapy™. (2022). Credentialing guide: School-Based Registered Play Therapist™ (SB-RPT). https://cdn.ymaws.com/www.a4pt.org/resource/resmgr/credentials/sb-rpt_guide_master.pdf

Association for Play Therapy™. (2022). Why play therapy? https://www.a4pt.org/page/WhyPlayTherapy

Axline, V. (1981). *Play therapy*. Random House.

Baggerly, J., & Parker, M. (2005). Child-centered group play therapy with African American boys at the elementary school level. *Journal of Counseling & Development, 83*(4), 387–396. https://doi.org/10.1002/j.1556-6678.2005.tb00360.x

Blalock, S. M., Lindo, N. A., Haiyasoso, M., & Morman, M. K. (2019). Child-centered play therapists' experiences of conducting group play therapy in elementary schools. *Journal for Specialists in Group Work, 44*(3), 184–203. https://doi.org/10.1080/01933922.2019.1637985

Brady, K. P. (2002). Zero tolerance or (in)tolerance policies? Weaponless school violence, due process, and the law of student suspensions and expulsions: An examination of Fuller v. Decatur Public School Board of Education School District. *Brigham Young University Education and Law Journal*. https://digitalcommons.law.byu.edu/cgi/viewcontent.cgi?referer=&httpsredir=1&article=1141&context=elj

Booth, P. B., & Jernberg, A. M. (2010). *Theraplay: Helping parents and children build better relationships through attachment-based play therapy*. Wiley.

Booth, P. B., & Lindaman, S. (2019). Attachment theory and theraplay. *Play Therapy, 14*(3), 14–16. https://cdn.ymaws.com/www.a4pt.org/resource/resmgr/publications/pt_theories/Attachment_Sept2019_FINAL.pdf

Center for Play Therapy. (2022). Recommended toy list. University of North Texas. https://cpt.unt.edu/recommended-toy-list

Davis, E. S., Babel, K. H., Davis, A. P., O'Bryan, T., & Ritz, J. (2022). The use of aggressive toys in schools: Insights and experiences of school-based play therapists. *International Journal of Play Therapy™, 31*(3), 184–195. https://doi.org/10.1037/pla0000174

DeMaria, M. B., & Cowden, S. T. (1992). The effects of client-centered group play therapy on self concept. *International Journal of Play Therapy™, 1*(1), 53–67. https://doi.org/10.1037/h0090235

Drewes, A., & Cavett, A. (2019). Cognitive behavioral play therapy. *Play Therapy, 14*(3), 24–26. https://cdn.ymaws.com/www.a4pt.org/resource/resmgr/publications/pt_theories/CognitiveBehavioral__Sept201.pdf

Gill, E., & Drewes, A. (2005). *Cultural issues in play therapy* (1st ed.). Guilford.

Haas, S. C., & Ray, D. C. (2020). Child-centered play therapy with children affected by adverse childhood experiences: A single-case design. *International Journal of Play Therapy™, 29*(4), 223–236. https:// doi.org/10.1037/pla0000135

Halverson-Ramos, F., Breyfogle, S., Brinkman, T., Hannan, A., Hyatt, C., Horowitz, S., Martin, T., Masko, M., Newman, J., & Sehr, A. (2019). Music therapy in child and adolescent behavioral health. American Music Therapy Association, Inc. https://www.

musictherapy.org/assets/1/7/FactSheet_Music_Therapy_Child_Adolescent_Behavior al_2019.pdf

Henning, K. (2021). *The rage of innocence: How America criminalizes Black youth.* Vintage Books.

Homeyer, L. E., & Sweeney, D. S. (2017). *Sandtray therapy: A practical manual* (3rd ed.) Routledge.

King, W. (2011). *Stolen childhood. Slave youth in nineteenth-century America* (2nd ed.) Indiana University Press.

Kottman, T. (2011). Adlerian play therapy [Book chapter]. Foundations of Play Therapy. 87–104. 2nd Edition. John Wiley and Sons, Inc.

Landreth, G. L. (2002). *Play therapy: The art of the relationship* (2nd ed.). Brunner-Routledge.

Landreth, G. L., Ray, D. C., & Bratton, S. C. (2009). Play therapy in elementary schools. *Psychology in the Schools, 46*(3), 281–289. https://doi.org/10.1002/pits.20374

Lilly, J. P., & Heiko, R. (2019). Jungian analytical play therapy. *Play Therapy, 14*(3), 40–42. https://cdn.ymaws.com/www.a4pt.org/resource/resmgr/publications/pt_theories/Jun gian_Sept2019_FINAL.pdf

Meany-Walen, K. K., & Kottman, T. (2019). Group Adlerian play therapy. *International Journal of Play Therapy™, 28*(1), 1–12. https://doi.org/10.1037/pla0000079

National Archives. (n.d.). What was it like to be a child slave in America in the nineteenth century? https://www.nationalarchives.gov.uk/documents/education/childhood-slav ery-contextual-essay.pdf

National Child Traumatic Stress Network. (n.d.). What is a traumatic event? https://www. nctsn.org/what-is-child-trauma/about-child-trauma

O'Connor, K. J., & Braverman, L. D. (2009). *Play therapy theory and practice: Comparing theories and techniques* (2nd ed.). Wiley.

O'Connor, K., & Vega, C. (2019). Ecosystemic play therapy. *Play Therapy, 14*(3), 32–34 https://cdn.ymaws.com/www.a4pt.org/resource/resmgr/publications/pt_theories/Eco systemic_Sept2019_FINAL.pdf

Office of the High Commissioner for Human Rights. (1989). Convention on the rights of the child. United Nations. https://www.ohchr.org/sites/default/files/crc.pdf

Parker, M. M., Hergenrather, K., Smelser, Q., & Kelly, C. T. (2021). Exploring child-centereplay therapy and trauma: A systematic review of literature. *International Journal of Play Therapy™, 30*(1), 2–13. https://doi.org/10.1037/pla0000136.supp

Patterson, L., Stutey, D., & Dorsey, B. (2018). Play therapy with African American children exposed to adverse childhood experiences. *International Journal of Play Therapy™, 27*(4), 215–226. https://doi.org/10.1037/pla0000080

Pliske, M. M., Stauffer, S. D., & Werner-Lin, A. (2021). Healing from adverse childhood experiences through therapeutic powers of play: "I can do it with my hands." *International Journal of Play Therapy™, 30*(4), 244–258. https://doi.org/10.1037/pla 0000166

Punnett, A., & Green, E. J. (2019). Psychoanalytic play therapy. *Play Therapy, 14*(3), 46–48. https://cdn.ymaws.com/www.a4pt.org/resource/resmgr/publications/pt_theories/Psych oanalytic_Sept2019_FINA.pdf

Ray, D. C., & Landreth, G. L. (2019). Child-centered play therapy. *Play Therapy, 14*(3), 46–48. https://cdn.ymaws.com/www.apt.org/resource/resmgr/publications/pt_theories/ChildCentered_Sept2019_FINAL.pdf

Ryan, V., & Edge, A. (2012). The role of play themes in non-directive play therapy. *Clinical Child Psychology and Psychiatry. 17*(3), 354–369. doi:10.1177/1359104511414265

Scuka, R. F., & Guerney, L. (2019). Filial therapy. *Play Therapy, 14*(3). https://cdn.ymaws.com/www.a4pt.org/resource/resmgr/publications/pt_theories/Filial_Sept2019_FINAL.pdf

Stanaway, C. (2020). The stages of grief: Accepting the unacceptable. University of Washington, Counseling Center. https://www.washington.edu/counseling/2020/06/08/the-stages-of-grief-accepting-the-unacceptable/

Stone, J., & Schaefer, C. E. (2019). *Game play: Therapeutic use of games with children and adolescents* (3rd ed.). Wiley.

Wiggins, D. (1980). The play of slave children in the plantation communities of the Old South, 1820–1860. *Journal of Sport History, 7*(2). https://pdfs.semanticscholar.org/3d34/2134a22af139207aa1a6d3538b1a490bc10d.pdf

Wilson, B., & Ray, D. (2018). Child-centered play therapy: Aggression, empathy, and self-regulation. *Journal of Counseling & Development, 96*(4), 399–409. https://doi.org/10.1002/jcad.12222

Winburn, A., Gilstrap, D., & Perryman, M. (2017). Treating the tiers: Play therapy responds to intervention in the schools. *International Journal of Play Therapy™, 26*(1), 1–11. https://doi.org/10.1037/pla0000041

Appendix A
Important Websites

Association for Play Therapy™ (www.a4pt.org)

Websites for play therapy toys and materials:

- Child Therapy Toys (https://www.childtherapytoys.com/)
- Play Therapy Supply (https://www.playtherapysupply.com/)

Diversity in play therapy toys and materials:

- Colorations (https://colorations.com/molding/)
- HarperIman (https://www.harperiman.com/)
- Healthy Roots dolls (https://healthyrootsdolls.com/)
- Nana dolls (https://kidsswag.ca/collections/nana-dolls)
- Sugar Island dolls (https://blacktoystore.com/product/sugar-island-dolls/)
- Ikuzu dolls (https://www.ikuzidolls.com/)
- Malaville dolls (https://www.malavilletoys.com/)
- Fresh dolls (https://freshdolls.com/)

- Queens of Africa dolls (https://queensofafricadolls.com/index.html)
- Puzzle Huddle (https://puzzlehuddle.com/)
- Bevy & Dave (https://www.bevyanddave.com/shop)
- "A day at the barbershop" puzzle (https://blacktoystore.com/product/a-day-at-the-barbershop-puzzle/)
- Darlying & Co. affirmation cards (https://blacktoystore.com/product/alphabet-affirmation-flashcards/)

4

■■■

Play Therapy to Address Bullying Among Black Students

Not only do Black children have to endure systemic racism in schools, but they also bear the brunt of racism and prejudice from their peers. Race and ethnicity are an additional risk factor for Black students that increases the likelihood that they will be bullied or bully someone else as means of self-protection. Bullying is another racial stressor that school social workers should account for when working with Black students. For Black LGBTQ+ students, gender identity and/or sexual orientation provides an additional intersection that leaves this population vulnerable to bullying. *Cyberbullying*, harassment on social media or through other forms of electronic communication, is another form of bullying that school social workers should consider as well. When considering mental health treatment, it is important to consider everyone involved and affected by bullying: the students who are the victim of bullying, the students who bully others, and the students who witness others being bullied (also known as bystanders).

Empowering Black students to manage their own thoughts and feelings when experiencing race-based bullying can serve as an important tool to help combat potential negative mental health effects. School social workers can use play therapy to support both Black heterosexual and LGBTQ+ students who have experienced race-based bullying. Empowerment can also serve as a useful tool for students who bully others, because bullying may be a sign of their own inability to process their traumatic experiences that are being projected onto others as a means of self-protection. Racial socialization messages can also be used to empower Black students to persevere through incidents of bullying both in school and online.

Black Students Matter. April D. Duncan, Oxford University Press. © Oxford University Press 2024.
DOI: 10.1093/oso/9780197669266.003.0005

National Trends in Bullying

The term "bullying" is sometimes loosely used when there are disagreements between peers in a social environment. *Bullying* is defined as the unwanted use of repetitive psychological or physical aggression against a person, group, or community (Lee et al., 2019). This issue affects children of all socioeconomic backgrounds, race/ethnicities, gender, and sexual orientation. The 2018–2019 National Survey of Children's Health, which surveys parents and guardians, found approximately 33% of students nationwide were bullied, excluded by, or picked on by other children 1–2 times in the 12 months prior to the survey being conducted (Child and Adolescent Health Measurement Initiative (2022).Gender identity and sexual orientation become an additional obstacle to navigate for Black students who identify as LGBTQ+ . Socioeconomic status and geographic locations become additional risk factors for these students. Across the country, LGBTQ+ students who come from higher-poverty communities and those who live in the South experience higher levels of victimization in school and are less likely to have access to LGBTQ+ resources (Craig et al., 2018). School social workers working with students' who experience higher levels of poverty and/or those in Southern states will require additional skills and interventions to support students with less access to community resources.

There are often three parties involved in a bullying event: the student who has been bullied, the student who has bullied others and, if someone was there to witness the event, the bystander.[1] Students who are bullied are more likely to experience increased feelings of sadness and loneliness, changes in sleeping and eating patterns, loss of interest in pleasurable activities, elevated levels of anxiety and depression and have more health issues and skip or drop out of school (Irwin et al., 2022; Stop Bullying, 2021). This puts students who are experiencing bullying at a higher risk for self-harm and/or suicidality, an issue often overlooked in Black students. School social workers working with students who have been bullied should focus on addressing any anxiety or depression stemming from the event, decreasing self-harm behaviors and/or suicidal thoughts, and increasing self-esteem.

---

[1] Please note that the literature may refer to the student who have bullied others as the "perpetrator." However, due to the heavy use of criminalizing and stereotypical language with Black students, that term is not used in this chapter.

For students who bully others, there are long-term effects that persist into adulthood. As adolescents, these students are more likely to get into physical fights, vandalize property, and engage in early sexual activity (Stop Bullying, 2021). Treatment planning for students who bully others should focus on decreasing aggression, anger, and impulsivity while learning important social, coping, and anger management skills. Learning those skills at an early age could help change the trajectory of their life as adults, as studies have shown that children who bully others are more likely to abuse alcohol and drugs, be involved with the criminal justice system, and be abusive in their interpersonal relationships as adults (Stop Bullying, 2021).

Often the well-being of students who witness bullying incidents is overlooked. This is important to remember because it relates to racial trauma in Black youth. Witnessing someone else being bullied or hurt because of their race meets criterion A for posttraumatic stress disorder (PTSD) in the *Diagnostic and Statistical Manual of Mental Disorders* (DSM-5; American Psychiatric Association, 2013) and therefore should be considered an adverse childhood event (ACE), especially if those students witness these events consistently. Students who witness bullying are also at an increased risk for negative outcomes. These students are more likely to miss or skip school; have an increased use of substances like tobacco, alcohol, and illicit drugs; and have increased mental health problems like depression and anxiety (Stop Bullying, 2021). When working with students who have witnessed bullying, school social workers can focus on treatment goals that address any anxiety and depression or helplessness they may experience because of witnessing these events.

Bullying in Schools

Bullying is a pervasive problem in schools across the United States. In the 2019–2020 school year, 14.6% of all public schools reported student bullying and 15.9% of public schools reported their students were victims of cyberbullying (Wang et al., 2022). According to the 2021 Report of Indicators of School Crime and Safety, students who are at the highest risk for being bullied are female students, students of two or more races, students in rural schools, and students in 6th–8th grades (Irwin et al., 2022). Additionally, students who identify as LGBTQ+ are at an increased risk for bullying, with 1.5% of public schools reporting harassment of students based on sexual orientation or gender identity (Green et al., 2020; Wang et al., 2022). The most recent Youth Risk Behavior Surveillance System (YRBSS) report found approximately 15,000 of high school students were threatened or injured with a weapon (like a gun, knife, or club) on school property (2022).

The lack of safety that students feel in their schools and sometimes their communities impacts their school attendance and has dire consequences for Black students. The 2019 YRBSS report found that more than 12,000 students did not go to school because they felt unsafe at school or on their way to or from school (Centers for Disease and Prevention [CDC], 2020). It is important that educators be more aware of the prevalence and symptoms of bullying, especially since Black children are often referred to juvenile courts for not attending school. In 2019, 54% of status offense cases for Black children were for truancy (Hockenberry & Puzzanchera, 2021). Safety factors should be assessed in Black students to determine if bullying is the contributing factor for truancy, as opposed to deviant behavior that could result in confinement. If the student is not attending school because of a safety issue, the school social worker can advocate for the student—and empower them to advocate for themselves—for alternative support such as virtual learning or moving the student to another class.

Cyberbullying

Since technology provides unlimited ways to harass and bully children, it increases the potential that Black students are being bullied outside of school, which can make it more difficult to detect. 24/7 access to technology and electronics has extended the arm of bullying beyond the walls of the school, which makes bullying harder to track and trace. It also may make it more difficult for school social workers to identify students experiencing bullying as it may not always occur on school grounds. The 2019 YRBSS report found that instances of bullying were more likely to happen at school, with 19% of respondents reporting being bullied on school property and 14.9% electronically bullied through social media and/or texting (Centers for Disease Control, 2020). Public schools are more likely to experience cyberbullying than private schools, with 16% of public schools reporting cyberbullying among students once a week in the 2019–2020 school year (Irwin et al., 2022). Bullying via electronic means has the same lasting effects on children as in-person bullying. Tynes and colleagues (2019) found that Black children who experienced high levels of vicarious and direct online racial discrimination were likely to experience anxiety and depressive symptoms. Assessing the electronic usage among Black students can be one way that school social workers can screen for cyberbullying.

Bullying and Black Children

Approximately 37% of Black children were reported to have experienced bullying 1–2 times in the past year (Office for Civil Rights, 2017–2018). Although this is lower than the rates of White and multiracial children, it is important to note that bullying experiences are more frequent for this population. Black children are more likely to report being bullied almost every day compared to other children (Child and Adolescent Health Measurement Initiative (2022):

- Multiracial and Black girls and boys were more likely to be threatened with or injured by a weapon on school property. The same is true for biracial LGBTQ+ youth.
- Black and multiracial girls, boys, and LGBTQ+ youth were more likely to get in a physical fight on and off school property.
- Multiracial girls, boys, and LGBTQ+ youth were more likely to report being electronically bullied.

Bullying for Black children in school is experienced physically, verbally, and visually. In the 2019–2020 school year, 9% of students reported a gang presence, 7% reported being called hate-related words, and 23% reported seeing hate-related graffiti (Irwin et al., 2022). The same study found multiracial and Black students were more likely to report being called hate-related words. In the 2019–2020 school year, 3.8% of public schools reported student racial/ethnic tensions (Wang et al., 2022). This highlights the need for schoolwide support to decrease race-based bullying in schools for students of color.

When working with Black students, it is important to understand cultural concepts like the importance around hair and hair maintenance, "joinin'," and issues around disrespect as these are often precipitating events that could incite bullying among Black students. In the Black community, looking nice is valued and there is a high emphasis on both hair and clothes. In 2020, the Black haircare industry market was $2.5 billion, with Black Americans spending 35% of their income on hair products (Prinzi, 2021). Black Americans also account for $60 million of the $385 million annual spending on luxury items (Hale, 2021). Fifty percent of Black consumers report their hair is central to their identity, Black Americans are more likely to experience hair anxiety than White Americans, and Black Americans are more likely to buy services or products that are in line with their self-image (Griffiths, 2022; Hale, 2022; Prinzi, 2021). Therefore, if a Black student does not keep up with their hair or if they do not have the latest brands in clothes, they may be more susceptible to bullying from peers in their community. This type of social bullying may negatively impact that student's mental health and self-esteem, as well as negatively affect their socialization.

"Joinin'" is a cultural way of bonding in the Black community. Originally referred to as "playing the dozens," it involves making fun of each other in a way that is playful and unifying (DeGruy, 2017). On one end, a Black student joinin' on another student could be misperceived as bullying by school officials and result in a suspension or expulsion, even though this could have been friendly banter that was misunderstood by educators as harmful or harassing. However, sometimes these friendly exchanges of jokes could go too far and venture into the territory of bullying. This is especially true if the playful joking leads to something that is deemed disrespectful by the student on the receiving end. In the Black community, Black children, especially boys, are often told not to let someone disrespect them and to defend themselves if someone is disrespectful. So a joke that has gone too far could easily lead to a physical altercation or continued teasing that is no longer playful and is harmful emotionally and socially to that student.

Black Students as Initiators of Bullying

Black youth experience high rates of bullying; however, they are at times the ones who bully others. This places the school social worker in a precarious place as Black youth have an increased risk of both being bullied and bullying others. Although White children are more likely to bully others, Black children are more likely to bully a peer almost every day (Child and Adolescent Health Measurement Initiative, 2022). Studies have found Black youth are more likely to be initiators of verbal, physical, and cyberbullying and less likely to experience bullying victimization and that these incidents are often perpetrated by peers from their own community, especially for Black girls (Patton et al., 2013). There is an important opportunity to connect and engage with Black caregivers to support Black youth who bully others. Risk factors for Black youth engaging in bullying behavior include low parental warmth, low family cohesion, low involvement with parents, single-parent family structures, and parental abuse (Patton et al., 2013). Therefore, it is imperative that school social workers work with caregivers of Black students who have bullied others to address any attachment trauma that may be occurring within the family system. (Chapter 11 explores the use of play therapy to engage caregivers of Black students.)

It is important to note how bias may play a role in how bullying behaviors in Black students may be perceived. One may argue that behaviors that are labeled as bullying among Black children may be defensive responses to societal, structural, and peer threats (Lee et al., 2019). If Black students feel unsafe at school or during their journey to and from the building, they could be hypervigilant to threats and may be responding from a place of self-protection rather than harm to others. Some Black students may be at a higher risk for bullying others due to their environments and circumstances. For example, children who experiencing family disruptions and lack adequate parental monitoring and support may be at a higher risk to being recruited into peer networks that endorse delinquent and negative norms (Lee et al., 2019). However, these same networks may be a source of connection and/or protection for the Black child. In Tupac Shakur's song, "Dear Mama," he raps about how his mother's drug addiction and father's absence pushed him toward the affection of gangs as he states, "They say I'm wrong and I'm heartless, but all along I was lookin' for a father, he was gone/ I hung around with the thugs and even though they sold drugs, they showed a young brother love" (Tupac Shakur, 1995). It can be easy to judge a child for their decision to join a gang, yet it is also important to acknowledge and explore the societal factors that may cause a child to seek comfort in a group that may engage in illegal activities and behavior.

The bullying behaviors of Black students should be explored in more depth by mental health professionals to determine what is at the root of the behavior before it is labeled as deviant or aggressive. Equally important is the acknowledgment of how being a bully is perceived in the peer relations of Black youth. Although Black children are more likely to bully others, 81% of Black children were reported to have no difficulty making or keeping friends (DHHS, 2022). This may be due to the acceptance of aggression among peers, their families, and their communities. Many Black children are encouraged to fight and "don't back down" when someone is bothering them, which then becomes a source of push and pull between the child's home rules and the school rules that preach zero tolerance. This disconnection between what the child is taught culturally puts them at a disadvantage as they often have to make decisions that will inevitably result in punishment. If the child fights at school so they do not get in trouble at home, they are punished at school. If the child does not fight back at school, they might be in trouble when they get home, especially if another family member was fighting and the child did not join in to defend them. Unfortunately, there is no clear solution, which is why school social workers should seek to be the bridge between cultural/familial beliefs and school policies.

There are gender differences in the bullying behaviors of Black students that should be explored in more depth as it may require different play therapy approaches for their clinical treatment. Black males often find validation and acceptance from their peers when they engage in bullying behaviors. Cassidy and Stevenson (2005) found Black males may receive more acceptance from their peers when they engage in physical and verbal aggression. The endorsement of gender role socialization, like hypermasculinity and relational aggression (e.g., engaging in rumors, gossip, and threatening to ruin friendships), may lead Black males to put on a facade of aggression when they really are experiencing feelings of vulnerability, which is associated with depression, fear of safety, and sensitivity to peer rejection (Patton et al., 2013). Perceived relationships from teachers also affect the behaviors Black boys may exhibit in the classroom. Black boys, when perceived as being failures and troublemakers, were more likely to engage in stereotyped behaviors of the hypermasculine male to gain respect and self-esteem (Ferguson, 2000). Bullying behaviors for Black girls vary slightly from Black boys. Although Black girls are more likely to engage in physical fights than are girls of other races, relational aggression is more prevalent in this population (Talbott et al., 2002). A study found that Black girls who were identified as engaging in relational aggression were more popular than girls who were not (Leff et al., 2009).

None of these facts offers an excuse to students who bully, but instead encourages school social workers to practice cultural humility when exploring the behaviors of Black students who bully others. Like any other behavior, if a student is harming others, either verbally or physically, it is communicating a symptom of a bigger issue that needs to be addressed in a clinical setting. Black students who engage in bullying behaviors require a social worker who can be patient in learning their backgrounds and exploring their resources and connections with family, all while providing them with the skills to manage their feelings more appropriately and without harm to others.

Bullying Among Black LGBTQ Youth

Already facing high levels of race-based discrimination and prejudice, Black LGBTQ youth have the extra layer of sexuality and/or gender identity that makes them vulnerable to bullying victimization. As a result, these students are often socially rejected by peers, their family members, and even within the LGBTQ+ community. It is important for social workers to be mindful of how the intersectionality of race and gender/sexual orientation provides added stress to LGBTQ students of color who experience bullying victimization.

In schools, Black LGBTQ+ students are subjected to rejection from both school officials and peers. Among Black gay, lesbian, and bisexual high schoolers, approximately 14% reported being threatened or injured with a weapon on school property, 20.5% reported being electronically bullied, and 18.2% reported being bullied on school property (Centers for Disease Control and Prevention [CDC], 2020). Although Black LGBTQ+ students reported fewer incidents of bullying compared to other racial groups, they had the highest rate of physical fights on and off school campus (32.6% and 19.3%, respectively) (CDC, 2020). Further research is required to identify the difference in reported bullying in this population when these students get into more physical altercations than other racial groups. It could be a lack of reporting on the part of these students, as research has found Black LGBTQ+ students experience higher rates of exclusionary forms of school discipline for violating gender norms and often retaliate toward their aggressors when experiencing bullying (McCarter, 2017).

LGBTQ+ students often experience victimization in schools, online, and from within their own communities. Black LGBTQ+ youth face racism, homophobia, and transphobia from their families, society, and within the LGBTQ+ community that can take the form of psychological or physical abuse perpetrated by a friend, stranger, or even a loved one (Hailey et al., 2020). This attachment trauma places Black LGBTQ+ youth at a higher risk for experiencing social isolation and impaired relationships as they may often avoid social situations out of fear of repeated transphobic or homophobic attacks (Hailey et al., 2020; Johnson & Amella, 2014).

Black LGBTQ+ youth may experience rejection within their community and their own families. I was working with a 15-year Black girl who identified as lesbian. In the intake with her parent, the mother shared the child was engaging in behaviors like running into traffic. As the conversation continued, the mother shared she made the child stop hanging out with her friends because they were "making her gay." She even made them quit their favorite sports team. Although your first thought may be "Why would the mother do that?," it is important to acknowledge some caregivers of Black children worry about the extra target placed on their child due to their gender identify and/or sexual orientation. There worry comes from a place of protection but ultimately could be harmful to the child's development, self-esteem and the parent-child relationship.

In a study conducted by the Trevor Project, 35% of Black LGBTQ+ youth experienced homelessness after being kicked out of home or they ran away from home (Price-Feeney et al., 2020). Although religion is a protective factor for a lot of Black students, for LGTBQ+ youth of color it is more correlated with higher levels of suicidality and increased alcohol use as adults (Hong et al., 2021). LGBTQ+ youth often are exposed to *conversion therapy*, a treatment modality meant to "rid" an individual of their sexual orientation (Watson Coleman, 2020). A reported 9% of Black LGBTQ+ youth were found have undergone conversion therapy, with 82% of those who underwent conversion therapy experiencing it before the age of 18 (Price-Feeney et al., 2020). The use of conversion therapy communicates that there is something wrong with the child that can be "fixed" which can negatively affect a child's self-esteem and sense of self-worth.

Black LGTBQ+ youth have an additional stressor that is associated with their gender identity and/or sexual orientation and that places them at a higher risk for victimization. Experiences with racism provide another path of harassment and bullying for Black LGBTQ students. The 2018 LGBTQ+ youth report conducted by the Human Rights Campaign found that 4 in 5 LGBTQ+ youth of color have personally experienced racism and 1 in 5 think about racism every day. The same report found 94% of LGBTQ+ youth of color say racism affects the lives of people of their same ethnic/racial group and 86% reported racism has impacted the life experiences of people close to them (Human Rights Campaign, 2018). Black LGBTQ+ youth also experience direct acts of discrimination in relation to their race, gender identity, and/or sexual orientation. Another study found 38% of Black LGBTQ+ youth reported discrimination based on their gender identity or sexual orientation, and 52% reported discrimination based on their race or ethnicity (Price-Feeney et al., 2020). The mental health of these students should be considered, as these high levels of exposure to victimization places them at a higher risk of pervasive mental health issues that further threaten their safety.

Increased contact with harassment, discrimination, and prejudice based on their race, gender identity, and sexual orientation, coupled with the lack of support provided in their environments, is depleting the mental health of Black LGBTQ+ youth. Victimization based on race and gender identity/sexual orientation in LGBTQ+ youth of color compromises their mental health and is associated with higher rates of depression than in youth who solely experience LGBTQ+ discrimination (Mallory & Russell, 2021). A 2020 report

(Price-Feeney et al., 2020) conducted by the Trevor Project, "All Black Lives Matter: Mental Health of Black LGBTQ Youth," found that

- 63% of Black LGBTQ+ youth and 61% Black transgender and nonbinary youth reported major depressive order.
- 55% of Black LGBTQ+ youth and 70% of Black transgender and nonbinary youth reported generalized anxiety disorder.
- 44% of Black LGBTQ+ youth and 59% of Black transgender and nonbinary youth reported seriously considering suicide in the past 12 months.
- 44% of Black LGBTQ+ youth and 61% Black transgender youth reported self-harming behaviors.

Despite these outcomes, Black LGBTQ youth encounter mental health accessibility issues that prevent them from receiving the services they desperately require. In the same study, 60% of Black LGBTQ youth who wanted mental health care were unable to receive it due to issues of being able to afford treatment, unable to receive care because of difficulty obtaining parental permission, and difficulty finding an LGBTQ-competent provider (Price-Feeny et al., 2020). Overall, Black LGBTQ+ youth are 30% more likely to have unmet mental health needs (Green et al., 2020). Schools are in a unique position to fill the void of mental health services for these students in need.

School social workers are tasked with leading the charge to provide free, safe and affirming spaces for all LGBTQ+ students, especially those of color. Multiracial and Black LGBTQ+ students are more likely to report missing school because they felt unsafe at school or on their way to or from school (CDC, 2020). Black transgender and nonbinary youth who report high family support have lower rates of attempted suicide, and Black youth who have access to at least one LGBTQ-affirmed space had suicide attempt rates 50% lower than Black LGBTQ youth without access to those spaces (Price-Feeney et al., 2020). Support for safe environments for LGBTQ+ students extends beyond school and can serve as a protective factor for students. Craig et al. found LGBTQ+ high school students expressed the need for safe housing; inclusivity and belonging in school; safe, school-based adults; freedom from violence and harassment in schools; and LGBTQ+-affirming resources that aid in the development of family support (2018).

Signs of Bullying

School social workers should be mindful of signs that a student is being bullied or that they are bullying others. The following signs of a student being bullied should be considered (Stop Bullying, 2021):

- Lost or destroyed clothing, books, jewelry, or electronics
- Unexplained injuries
- Changes in eating habits
- Difficulty sleeping or frequent nightmares
- Frequent somatic complaints like headaches or stomachaches, or faking illness
- Declining grades, loss of interest in schoolwork, or not wanting to go to school
- Self-destructive behavior like running away from home, self-harm, or suicidal thoughts
- Sudden loss of friends or avoidance of social situations

On the other hand, signs that a student may be bullying others include:

- Having friends who bully others
- Increase in aggression
- Getting into verbal or physical fights
- Frequent disciplinary referrals to the office or detention
- Having unexplained new belongings or extra money
- Being highly competitive and worried about popularity or their reputation
- Blaming others for their problems
- Lack of accountability and responsibility for their actions

There are also key signs in the playroom that may communicate a child is a victim or instigator of bullying behaviors. For students experiencing bullying, they may show play themes of fear, mistrust, perfectionism, chaos, protection and safety, and rescue. These students may engage in more independent play and may be more silent in play therapy sessions. For students who are bullying others, play themes may include anger, limits and boundaries, aggression, connection, mistrust, chaos, and guilt. These students may also use more aggressive toys in the playroom and require more redirection and limit setting.

Black Student Empowerment

Supporting Black students will require an emphasis on empowerment and tapping into protective factors that can mitigate the negative effects of race-based bullying. From their first introduction into the world, Black youth are pitted against untenable odds that prevent them the luxury of a childhood. Well-intentioned parenting practices within the Black community put Black caregivers in a precarious place where they must think of the extra layers of mental and emotional protection their children need to survive their daily interactions with negative race-based experiences. Despite the odds, Black youth possess a level of resilience that should be tapped into, to help them have both a childhood and an awareness of their unjust realities. This book focuses on the deficits left in Black children due to race-based stress and trauma, but there should also be an acknowledgment of all the strengths Black youth possess in the face of adversity. These protective factors will be key when engaging Black youth in mental health services to deal with both bullying and race-based experiences.

Protective Factors in the Black Community

Several protective factors within the Black community warrant attention. These cultural concepts within the community help shape how Black youth perceive and treat people inside and outside their community, as well as themselves. Protective factors will be important when determining the best course of treatment for a Black student experiencing racial trauma as these factors may be the buffer needed to curtail any negative feelings, thoughts, or behaviors that may arise after a negative race-based experience.

First, there are strong kinship bonds within the Black community that are attributed to the African tribal heritage of the importance of maintaining family and community cohesion in the face of adversities (Gil & Drewes, 2005). These bonds are rooted in practices that developed in enslaved times, along with an emphasis on extended family. It is important to understand that Black students will often have a source of support within their community that includes biological family members and family through friendship. School social workers working with Black students may hear them reference "play cousins" or talk about aunts, uncles, and cousins who have no blood relation to them but are instrumental in caregiving and child-rearing for that student. This provides a unique resource for Black students because these "village members" may be able to help with issues that immediate family caregivers may not be able to manage or deal with for any number of reasons.

Another protective factor in the Black community is possessing a humanistic orientation, in which members of the community show genuine concern for each other and deal with each other in a spontaneous, natural, and authentic way (Gil & Drewes, 2005). This is further evidenced through the village concept, as the community often rallies around each other even if they do not personally know that individual. Mentorship has been identified as a protective factor against racial discrimination in both Black boys and girls (Cooper et al., 2013). Therefore, school social workers can also consider connecting Black students with mentors to combat bullying. These mentors may be available through community organizations like the Boys & Girls club, or through Black sororities and fraternities.

The next protective factor to explore is role flexibility. Systems theory recognizes that a change in one person affects the entire system, and its application to Black families considers how structural racism can affect the functioning of individual and family systems (Kelly et al., 2013). Mass incarceration, high rates of child-welfare involvement, and other instances of systemic racism change family composition. As a result, there are different roles that family members may need to navigate to help the family adjust to change. For example, if one caregiver is incarcerated, the other caregiver may need to take on extra work. Then the older child may have to take on more parental roles to help with taking care of their younger siblings. Although this is not the most ideal situation, this highlights a high level of resilience, to step in and fill whatever role is necessary to help the system continue functioning.

Another way resilience is exhibited as a protective factor is in the endurance of suffering. Black Americans have developed a great tolerance for conflict, stress, ambiguity, and ambivalence (Gil & Drewes, 2005). This has allowed them to survive decades of racism, physical and emotional abuse, and violence in their community. Some individuals are highly suspicious of others who are different from them, which can serve as a protective factor for Black students. This paranoia may push them toward environments that are more inclusive for them and provide a sense of community and support that is not offered in mainstream environments. Student clubs that are exclusively for children of color are an example of how students find a free space with students that look like them and have similar experiences. This can help in connecting and validating of their experiences while also affirming their identities.

There also is a strong work, education, and achievement orientation in the Black community (Gil & Drewes, 2005). Education is valued in the community and often seen as a necessity to success. Black caregivers are often highly invested in their children's education and that investment often serves as a protective factor, especially for Black students transitioning to middle school (Burchinal et al., 2008). It is also important to acknowledge how protective factors against racial discrimination vary based on the child's gender. Research has found maternal and neighborhood support and religious connection as protective factors for Black boys, while protective factors for Black girls are parental support (both mother and father) and mentor presence (Cooper et al., 2013). School social workers could benefit from using attachment-based play therapy to help Black students enhance their relationships with adults who can help serve as a buffer to race-based stress and trauma.

Religion as a Protective Factor

Another protective factor in the Black community is a strong commitment to religious values and church orientation (Gil & Drewes, 2005). Historically, churches were an escape for Black Americans from the oppression of slavery, so religion and social services in church are often used in times of crisis (DeGruy, 2017). Church is a place where Black children learn to have reliance on and understanding of a higher power that can help guide them through difficulties. The Black church also provides an important source of community, healing, and hope (Butler-Barnes et al., 2018). Black children are often introduced to church early on, with regular attendance for Sunday services as well as involvement in additional church activities such as the children's choir and Sunday School.

A connection to this community also provides an additional source for members in their village to provide support and comfort during difficult times. School social workers could benefit from assessing the family's spiritual and religious beliefs and community as this can be an additional resource if other resources for mental health or community support are limited. This may also be helpful for some children and caregivers who struggle with mistrust of the mental health and/or school systems. They can be encouraged to talk to their pastors or other church leaders/members, where they can have a safe place to express and process their emotions around the mental and emotional toll of racial trauma. I have a rule, "You don't have to talk to me, but you do need to talk to someone." Church members can serve as that "someone" until the child develops more trust with the therapist and the therapeutic process. The emotional and spiritual support provided by Black clergy and the church community fills a void in mental health support in the Black community that the school social worker cannot ignore.

Racial Socialization Messages

Since Black children are dealing with high levels of racial trauma, Black caregivers have adopted *racial socialization*, the practice of protecting the emotional, physical, and mental well-being of their children (Jones & Neblett Jr., 2019). To help foster their child's ethnic and racial identity, Black caregivers transfer messages about their cultural heritage and history, promote positive racial identity and pride, and teach children how to cope with discrimination while negotiating in- and out-group relationships (McWayne et al., 2020). Common racial socialization messages include cultural socialization (e.g., an emphasis on pride, history, or heritage), promotion of mistrust (e.g., being suspicious of other cultures), preparation for bias (e.g., teaching discrimination awareness and coping), and egalitarianism (e.g., highlighting racial equality or individual traits) (Jones & Neblett Jr., 2019). These messages are also communicated through another practice used by Black caregivers called *positive parenting*, which focuses on building the child's spiritual, socioemotional, and academic well-being as well as their ethnic and racial identity (McWayne et al., 2020). Some examples of racial socialization messages include "Black Lives Matter," "Black Boy Joy," and "Black Girls Rock" to name a few. School social workers could benefit from exploring the racial socialization messages that are impactful for Black students and integrating those messages into play therapy sessions.

Using racial socialization messages to empower Black students experiencing race-based bullying can be an important tool to improve mental health outcomes. Placing importance on being Black and having positive feelings of group belongingness or membership is associated with positive self-esteem, decreased internalizing and externalizing behaviors, decreased risky sexual behavior, and decreased aggression (Jones & Neblett Jr., 2019). The use of affirmations is helpful in addressing negative mental health issues stemming from racial trauma. Black youth who use affirmations have better self-esteem, well-being, social functioning, academic achievement, and attitudes and fewer depressive symptoms, internalizing behaviors, and externalizing behaviors (Zapolski et al., 2019). Naturally, play therapy can be used to help school social workers integrate racial socialization messages into the playroom for Black students.

Play Therapy to Empower Black Students

Empowering Black students through play therapy can be undertaken in a variety of ways. First, child-centered play therapy (CCPT) in individual play therapy sessions with students who have been bullied and bystanders may be helpful. When children experience and/or witness a traumatic event like bullying, it can leave them feeling helpless. CCPT can be an effective tool to help students regain a sense of control after dealing with a bullying event. Additionally, child-centered group play therapy (CCGPT) may be helpful for children who have been bullied and those who bully others. The small group setting of nondirective play provides a natural environment for students to work through social issues and build healthier relationships. Depending on the nature of the bullying event, school social workers can also consider having the victim and the student who did the bullying participate in group sessions together to build more positive interactions between them. It is not recommended that these sessions occur if there is physical violence involved because the bullied student may not feel safe and could possibly be triggered by being in the presence of the student who bullied them. Next we will explore two play therapy activities help empower Black youth: One Mic and I Matter cards.

One Mic

One Mic is an art therapy activity that can be used with students in the 3rd through 12th grades in individual and group play therapy. The materials for this activity include the One Mic handout (Appendix A), scissors, glue, a Styrofoam ball, and a paper towel roll. Alternative materials can be magazines so the student can find their own words/pictures outside of the handout, or a plastic microphone. When introducing the activity, you can share with the student that it is based on the song by hip-hop artist Nas, "One Mic," where he talks about how he would use his voice to tell his story with one microphone. It may be developmentally appropriate to play the song for junior high and high school students. The student is then encouraged to decorate their microphone with words, phrases, and pictures that communicate things that they want to say or the feelings that they have. This tangible item can be used to express their feelings aloud in a safe place. The student can also be encouraged to create positive affirmations and use the microphone to verbalize them. The student may also be encouraged to repeat these affirmations daily outside of play sessions, which may also assist in encouraging empowerment and self-esteem.

I Matter Cards

I Matter cards are a way for school social workers to integrate racial social-ization messages into positive affirmations for Black students. The activity contains cards and posters with positive affirmations associated with Black culture. There is a digital version where students can type in their own affirmations, or they can be printed for them to write their affirmations. The I Matter cards (Appendix B) can be used with students as young as kinder-garten all the way up to high school. This activity is best for students who are suffering from self-esteem issues due to race-based bullying. The school social worker can encourage students to think of racial socialization messages they have heard in their family or community or make up their own to add to their cards. They can also be encouraged to keep the cards at school in places like their bookbag, desk, or locker or at home, as well as saying the affirmations out loud daily.

Play Therapy to Support Black LGBTQ Youth

Play therapy interventions for LGBTQ+ youth should focus on decreasing anxiety and depression, increasing self-esteem and connections with peers, and affirming their identities. This can be achieved using art therapy approaches, affirmations, and sand tray therapy techniques. The use of sand tray can be effective in supporting LGBTQ+ youth with prompts specific to their experience (Appendix C). Social workers should also have some key sand tray miniatures for Black LGBTQ such as rainbows, caterpillars, and butterflies (representing transformation), and miniatures that communi-cate dual identities like a minotaur. It is important to remember that some students may not have come out to their peers and families, so they may be reluctant to take their finished products outside of the playroom. The school social worker should consider a confidential space to store their artwork that can be referenced in future sessions or used as a tool to assess the student's progress in treatment.[2]

---

[2] I understand some school social workers may be in states or school districts that restrict or prohibit the promotion of gender identity/sexual orientation in students. The school social worker should always adhere to their state and school policies, or contact the National Association of Social Workers for consultation on the most ap-propriate ways to support LGBTQ+ students that honors our code but does not cause legal trouble for the social worker.

Mirror Affirmations

The activity Mirror Affirmations combines art therapy, Cognitive Behavioral Play Therapy, and affirmations to help Black LGBTQ+ youth struggling with their identity and/or sexual orientation. This activity promotes empowerment in LGBTQ+ youth by using affirmations that can address any self-esteem issues or negative thoughts. The materials for the activity includes small mirrors, decoupage glue, foam brush, paper plate, scissors, the Mirror Affirmations handout (Appendix D), and paint markers. This activity can be used with students in 3rd through 12th grades. First, talk to the student about any negative things they have heard directly or indirectly about the LGBTQ community. Then have them practice turning those negative statements into positive ones to create their own affirmations. Then provide them with materials and encourage them to write those affirmations, or any other ones they would like, on their mirror. Finally, the student should be encouraged to look into the mirror and practice saying those affirmations to help improve self-esteem and decrease negative thoughts.

My Support Systems

The next activity, My Support Systems, is helpful to explore support systems for clients who are members of the LGBTQ+ community. The materials required for this activity are the My Support System handout (Appendix E), something to write with, and sand tray miniatures. This activity is most appropriate for students in 3rd through 12th grades. For each circle, they will identify people that fit the prompt. For the circle in the center, they will identify someone who they would consider their closest support people. These should be people who are aware of their gender identity/sexual orientation or people they would feel comfortable sharing that information with first if they haven't come out yet. For the middle circle, they will identify people who are part of their support system but who may not be as close to them as the people in the center. The outermost circle will be people who are part of their support system who they may not disclose their gender identity/sexual orientation to for a while, if at all. Then, have the child select a sand tray miniature to represent each person they identified on their circles. After the activity, the school social worker can ask some follow-up question, such as

1. Tell me about the people and miniatures you chose who are your closest support people. Why did you choose them?

2. Tell me about the people in your middle circle and the miniatures you chose for them. What keeps them from entering into the center circle of support?
3. Tell me about the people and miniatures you chose for your outside circle. What makes them stay in that outside circle?
4. Are there any people in middle or outside circles that you would like to move closer to the center circle? What prevents you from doing that?
5. What would you need to see or hear from the people in your middle or outer circle to feel comfortable to move them closer to the center circle?

Representin' Scavenger Hunt

Representin' Scavenger Hunt is an art activity where students are encouraged to find images of people who represent their gender identity and sexual orientation. This is another activity that may need to stay with the social worker after completion. The materials required are the Representin' Scavenger Hunt poster activity (Appendix F), Afrocentric magazines, scissors, and glue. Again, the student can search for images online if the social worker has that an option. The student is encouraged to "hunt" for the images that match the activity prompts. Afterward, the social worker may ask the client to describe the images they selected and provide an explanation for their selection. They can also ask the student to name people in their lives that they feel comfortable sharing their poster with, if anyone.

Say My Name

The Say My Name activity is appropriate for students who identify as transgender or have a gender identity that is different from their biological sex. The materials required for this activity are the Say My Name poster activity (Appendix G), the Say My Name handout (Appendix H), scissors, glue, posterboard, and crayons, colored pencils, or markers. The student is encouraged to create a posterboard using their preferred name and explore the journey of selecting and using that name. This activity can help open conversation around gender identity and provide the social worker with a better assessment of the child's support system. Follow-up questions may include, "What type of feelings do you have looking at this poster?" "Who is aware of your preferred name?" "Do you have anyone in your life who knows your preferred name but does not use it? How does that make you feel?"

Conclusion

Black youth of all backgrounds experience high rates of daily incidents with race-based bullying. For Black LGBTQ+ youth there is an additional intersection with gender identity and/or sexual orientation that places them at a higher risk of experiencing bullying. For Black children, this bullying happens in almost all the environments they frequent, including schools, online, and within their own communities. This places Black students at a higher risk for negative mental health issues that are often mislabeled or overlooked as disrespect, anger, or noncompliance. Understanding the factors contributing to children who bully and those who have been bullied is an important step to supporting the whole Black student in an empathic, compassionate, and nonjudgmental manner.

References

American Psychiatric Association. (2013). *Diagnostic and statistical manual of mental disorders* (5th ed.). American Psychiatric Publishing.

Burchinal, M. R., Roberts, J. E., Zeisel, S. A., & Rowley, S. J. (2008). Social risk and protective factors for African American children's academic achievement and adjustment during the transition to middle school. *Developmental Psychology, 44*(1), 286–292. https://doi.org/10.1037/0012-1649.44.1.286

Butler-Barnes, S. T., Martin, P. P., Copeland-Linder, N., Seaton, E. K., Matusko, N., Caldwell, C. H., & Jackson, J. S. (2018). The protective role of religious involvement in African American and Caribbean Black adolescents' experiences of racial discrimination. *Youth & Society, 50*(5), 659–687. https://doi.org/10.1177/0044118X15626063

Cassidy, E. F., & Stevenson, H. C., Jr. (2005). They wear the mask: Hypervulnerability and hypermasculine aggression among African American males in an urban remedial disciplinary school. *Journal of Aggression, Maltreatment, & Trauma, 11*, 53–74.

Centers for Disease Control and Prevention (CDC). (2020). Youth Risk Behavior Surveillance: United States 2019. *Morbidity and Mortality Weekly Report, 69*(1). https://www.cdc.gov/mmwr/volumes/69/su/pdfs/su6901-H.pdf

Child and Adolescent Health Measurement Initiative. (2022). National survey of children's health 2018–2019. Data Resource Center for Child and Adolescent Health supported by the U.S. Department of Health and Human Services, Health Resources and Services Administration (HRSA), Maternal and Child Health Bureau (MCHB). www.childhealthdata.org

Cooper, S. M., Brown, C., Metzger, I., Clinton, Y., & Guthrie, B. (2013). Racial discrimination and African American adolescents' adjustment: Gender variation in family and community social support, promotive and protective factors. *Journal of Child and Family Studies, 22*(1), 15–29. https://doi.org/10.1007/s10826-012-9608-y

Craig, S. L., McInroy, L. B., & Austin, A. (2018). "Someone to have my back": Exploring the needs of racially and ethnically diverse lesbian, gay, bisexual, and transgender high school students. *Children & Schools, 40*(4), 231–239. https://doi.org/10.1093/cs/cdy016

Degruy. J. (2017). *Post traumatic slave syndrome: America's legacy of enduring injury & healing.* Uptown Press.

Ferguson, A. (2000). *Bad boys: Public schools in the making of Black masculinity.* University of Michigan Press.

Gil, E., & Drewes, A. (2005). *Cultural issues in play therapy.* (1st ed.). Guilford.

Green, A. E., Price-Feeney, M., & Dorison, S. (2020). Breaking barriers to quality mental health care for LGBTQ youth. The Trevor Project. https://www.thetrevorproject.org/wp-content/uploads/2020/08/Breaking-Barriers-to-Quality-Mental-Health-Care-for-LGBTQ-Youth-Updated-7-28-2020.pdf

Griffiths, J. (2022). 70+ Key Black hair industry statistics & facts in 2022. *Afro Lovely.* https://afrolovely.com/black-hair-industry-statistics/

Hailey, J., Burton, W., & Arscott, J. (2020). We are family: Chosen and created families as a protective factor against racialized trauma and anti-LGBTQ oppression among African American sexual and gender minority youth. *Journal of GLBT Family Studies, 16*(2), 176–191. https://doi.org/10.1080/1550428X.2020.1724133

Hale, K. (2021). The $300 billion Black American consumerism bag breeds big business opportunities. *Forbes.* https://www.forbes.com/sites/korihale/2021/09/17/the-300-billion-black-american-consumerism-bag-breeds-big-business-opportunities/?sh=46782baf34fc

Hockenberry, S., & Puzzanchera, C. (2021). Juvenile court statistics 2019. National Center for Juvenile Justice. https://www.ojjdp.gov/ojstatbb/njcda/pdf/jcs2019.pdf

Hong, J. S., Valido, A., Rivas, K. M. M., Wade, R. M., Espelage, D. L., & Voisin, D. R. (2021). Bullying victimization, psychosocial functioning, and protective factors: Comparing African American heterosexual and sexual minority adolescents in Chicago's southside. *Journal of Community Psychology.* https://doi.org/10.1002/jcop.22521

Human Rights Campaign. (2018). 2018 LGBTQ youth report. https://www.hrc.org/resources/2018-lgbtq-youth-report

Johnson, M. J., & Amella, E. J. (2014). Isolation of lesbian, gay, bisexual and transgender youth: A dimensional concept analysis. *Journal of Advanced Nursing, 70*(3), 523–532. https://doi.org/10.1111/jan.12212

Jones, S., & Neblett Jr, E. (2019). Black parenting couples' discussions of the racial socialization process: Occurrence and effectiveness. *Journal of Child and Family Studies, 28*(1), 218–232. https://doi.org/10.1007/s10826-018-1248-4

Kelly, S., Maynigo, P., Wesley, K., & Durham, J. (2013). African American communities and family systems: Relevance and challenges. *Couple and Family Psychology: Research and Practice, 2*(4), 264–277. https://doi.org/10.1037/cfp0000014

Irwin, V., Wang, K., Cui, J., & Thompson, A. (2022). Report of indicators of school crime and safety: 2021. National Center for Education for Education Statistics at IES. https://nces.ed.gov/pubs2022/2022092.pdf

Lee, J. M., Johns, S., Smith-Darden, J. P., Hong, J. S., & Voisin, D. R. (2019). Family incarceration and bullying among urban African American adolescents: The mediating roles of exposure to delinquent peer norms, trauma, and externalizing behaviors. *Families in Society, 100*(4), 422–432. https://doi.org/10.1177/1044389419852017

Leff, S. S., Gullan, R. L., Paskewich, B. S., Abdul-Kabir, S., Jawad, A. F., Grossman, M., et al. (2009). An initial evaluation of a culturally adapted social problem-solving and relational aggression prevention program for urban African-American relationally aggressive girls. *Journal of Prevention & Intervention in the Community*, 37, 260–274.

Mallory, A. B., & Russell, S. T. (2021). Intersections of racial discrimination and LGB victimization for mental health: A prospective study of sexual minority youth of color. *Journal of Youth and Adolescence*, 50(7), 1353–1368. https://doi.org/10.1007/s10964-021-01443-x

McCarter, S. (2017). The school-to-prison pipeline: A primer for social workers. *Social Work*, 62(1), 53–61. https://doi.org/10.1093/sw/sww078

McWayne, C., Mattis, J., & Li, L. (2020). Parenting together: Understanding the shared context of positive parenting among low-income Black families. *Journal of Black Psychology*, Article e9579842093165. https://doi.org/10.1177/0095798420931653

Office for Civil Rights. (2017–2018). 2017–2018 State and national estimations. U.S. Department of Education. https://ocrdata.ed.gov/estimations/2017-2018

Patton, D. U., Hong, J. S., Williams, A. B., & Allen-Meares, P. (2013). A review of research on school bullying among African American youth: An ecological systems analysis. *Educational Psychology Review*, 25(2), 245–260. https://doi.org/10.1007/s10648-013-9221-7

Price-Feeney, M, Green, A. E., & Dorison, S. (2020). All Black lives matter: Mental health of Black LGBTQ youth. The Trevor Project. https://www.thetrevorproject.org/research-briefs/all-black-lives-matter-mental-health-of-black-lgbtq-youth/

Prinzy, L. (2021). Hair facts: 50 Impressive Black hair industry facts. *All Things Hair*. https://www.allthingshair.com/en-us/all-things-natural-hair/black-hair-industry-statistics/

Roberts, D. (1997). *Killing the Black body: Race, reproduction, and the meaning of liberty*. Vintage Books.

Shakur, T. (1995). Dear Mama [Song]. *On Me Against the World*. Interscope; Jive.

Stop Bullying. (2021). Effects of bullying. U.S. Department of Health and Human Services. https://www.stopbullying.gov/bullying/effects

Talbott, E., Celinska, D., Simpson, J., & Coe, M. (2002). "Somebody else making somebody else fight": Aggression and the social context among urban adolescent girls. *Exceptionality*, 10, 203–220.

Tynes, B., Willis, H., Stewart, A., & Hamilton, M. (2019). Race-Related traumatic events online and mental health among adolescents of color. *Journal of Adolescent Health*, 65(3), 371–377. https://doi.org/10.1016/j.jadohealth.2019.03.00

Wang, K., Kemp, J., Burr, R., & Swan, D. (2022). Crime, violence, discipline, and safety in U.S. public schools in 2019–2020. Findings from the school survey on crime and safety. U.S. Department of Education. Institute of Education Sciences.

Watson Coleman, B. (2020). Ring the alarm: The crisis of Black youth suicide in America. [Report]. Congressional Black Caucus. https://watsoncoleman.house.gov/imo/media/doc/full_taskforce_report.pdf

Zapolski, T. C. B., Beutlich, M. R., Fisher, S., & Barnes-Najor, J. (2019). Collective ethnic–racial identity and health outcomes among African American youth: Examination of promotive and protective effects. *Cultural Diversity and Ethnic Minority Psychology*, 25(3), 388–396. https://doi.org/10.1037/cdp0000258

One Mic Activity

Required Materials

Paper towel roll, Styrofoam ball, hot glue gun, Afrocentric magazines, scissors and glue

Directions

Use the hot glue gun to glue the Styrofoam ball to the paper towel. Then use the magazines or the pictures/words provided below to decorate the "microphone" to show the things you want to say or want the world to know about you if you had "one mic" to use that voice.

I MATTER CARDS

Black kids and teens often receive direct or indirect messages regarding their worth. These messages can be found in many forms of media including movies, television, and music. They can also develop through interactions and experiences with friends, family, or others outside of the home. *I Matter Cards* were created to combat these negative messages and empower Black kids and teens through the use of positive affirmations.

Positive affirmations are useful for moments when clients are feeling unsure, anxious, depressed, angry, or experiencing moments of low self-esteem. These affirmations are a reminder to clients that they matter in a world that may tell them otherwise.

In this download, you will find the following 12 positive affirmations:

1. I Matter no matter what color my skin is!
2. I Matter because Black is beautiful!
3. I Matter because I am loved!
4. I Matter no matter what people think of me!
5. I Matter because my voice is important and needs to be heard!
6. I Matter even when people say mean things about me!
7. I Matter to those who know the real me!
8. I Matter and deserve to be treated with respect!
9. I Matter and have an important gift to share with the world!
10. I Matter and have Black girl magic!
11. I Matter because there is no one else in the world like me!
12. I Matter and have Black boy joy!

Additional blank cards are included in this download for customized *I Matter Cards*. Copies are allowed to be made as needed. Clients can develop their own positive affirmations about why they believe they matter.

Also within this download are 12 full page (8.5x11) posters corresponding with each of the *I Matter Cards!*

Sand Tray Prompts to Promote Empowerment

Create a sand tray that highlights your sexual orientation

Pick a miniature for each person in your support system

Create a sand tray that highlights your gender identity

Create a scene showing your safe place

Create a scene that represents your coming out experience

Create a scene that shows you before you came out and after you came out

BMH Connect

mylemarks

Mirror Affirmations

This activity is to promote empowerment in LGBTQ+ youth. They will use this to practice affirmations that can address any self-esteem issues or negative thoughts.

Required Materials

Small mirrors, Mod podge, foam brush, paper plate, scissors, images from worksheet, paint markers

My Support Systems

As a member of the LGBTQ+ community, it may be hard to find support in your gender identify/sexual orientation. This activity helps you identity people in your circle who affirm and encourage your gender identify/sexual orientation. .

BMH Connect

© 2022 BMH Connect & mylemarks

mylemarks

Directions

This activity is helpful to explore the support systems for our clients who are members of the LGBTQ+ community. For each circle, they will identify people that fit the prompt.

For the circle in the center, they will identify someone who they would consider their closest support people. These are people who are fully aware of their gender identity/sexual orientation or people they would feel comfortable sharing that information first, if they haven't come out yet.

For the middle circle, they will identify people who are part of their support system, but they may not be as close to them as the people in the center.

The most outer circle will be people who are part of their support system who they may not disclose their gender identity/sexual orientation to for a while, if at all. Then, have the child select a sand tray miniature to represent each person they identified on their circles.

Processing Questions

1. Tell me about the people and miniatures you chose are your closest support people. Why did you choose them?
2. Tell me about the people in your middle circle and the miniatures you chose for them. What keeps them from entering into the center circle of support?
3. Tell me about the people and miniatures you chose for your outside circle. What makes them stay in that outside circle?
4. Are there any people in middle or outside circles that you would like to move closer to the center circle? What prevents you from doing that?
5. What would you need to see or hear from the people in your middle or outer circle to feel comfortable to move them closer to the center circle?

 BMH Connect

© 2022 BMH Connect & Mylemarks

Black Students Matter

Appendix F   Representin' Scavenger Hunt Poster Activity

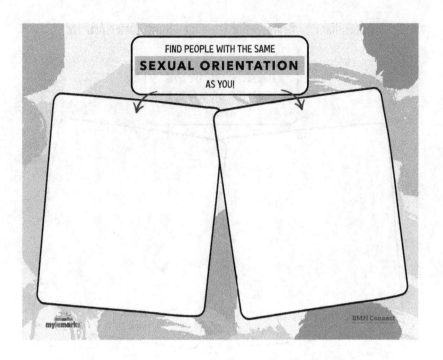

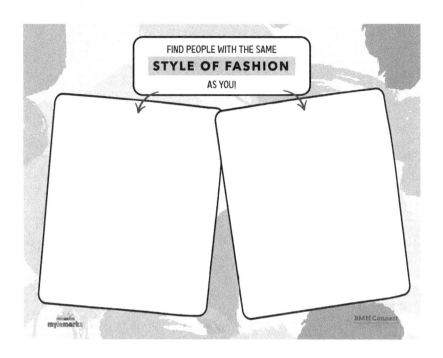

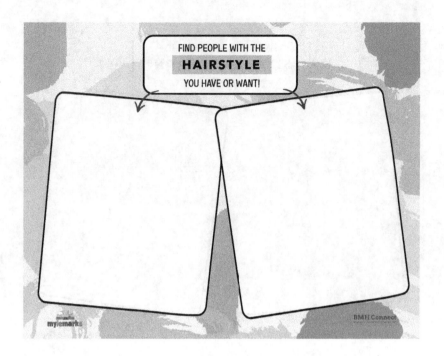

How to Use

Say My Name is an activity designed to allow the client to color in the letters that make up their name. In this download, you will find 26 letters (uppercase and lowercase) each with a unique design. These letters can be printed as needed. Also included are name-related writing prompts such as "I prefer to be called.." and "My given name is...", as well as other design elements that can be used for decorative purposes.

Clients can use a poster board to display their names and decorate their board as they please. Clients could also use cut-out words or images taken from magazines.

Terms of Use

MY given naME IS

I PREFER TO be CALLED

My Family Calls Me

IM PROUD OF MY naME

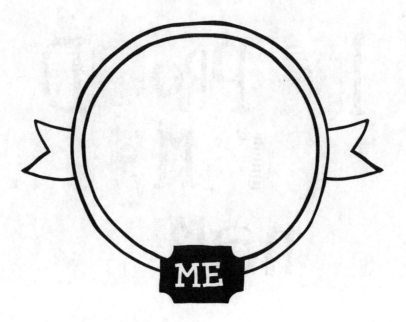

ME

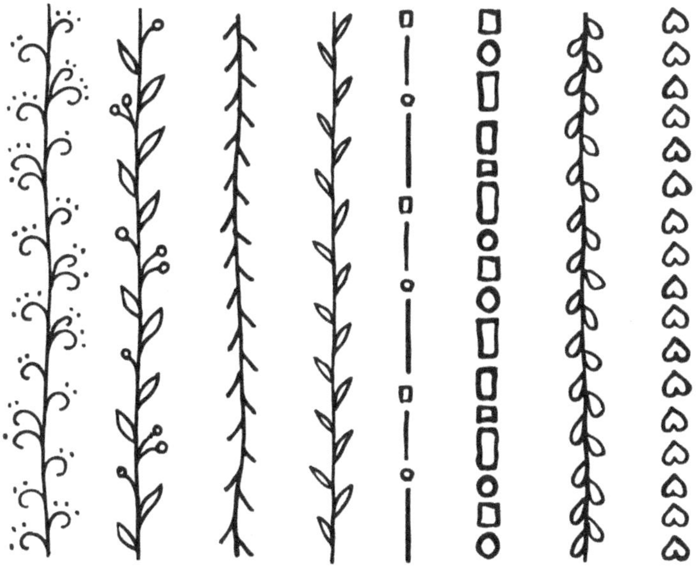

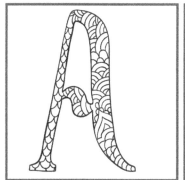

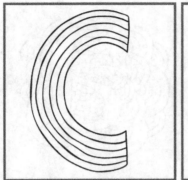 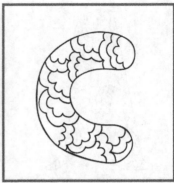

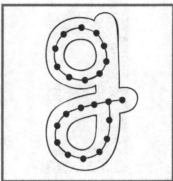

Black Students Matter

 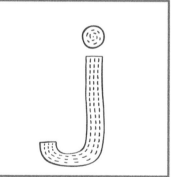

 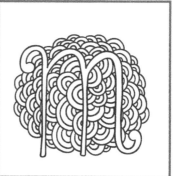

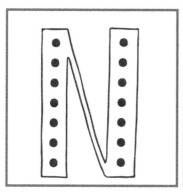 

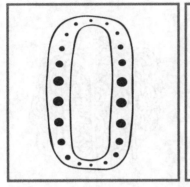
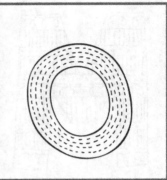

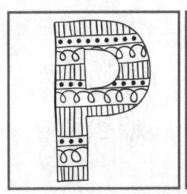

Black Students Matter

 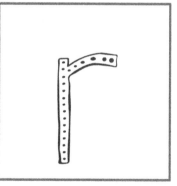

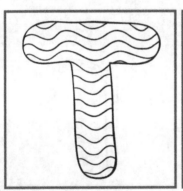
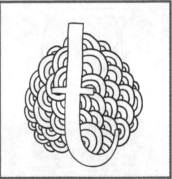

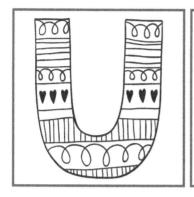 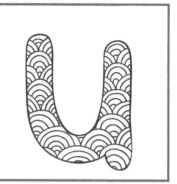

 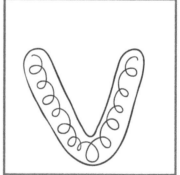

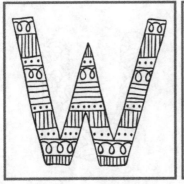

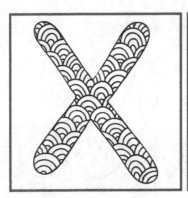

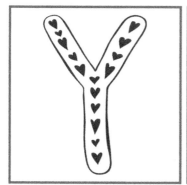

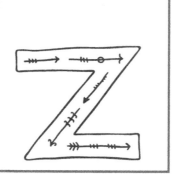

5

Play Therapy to Empower Black Girls

Black girls in America are dealing with unique racial trauma stressors that negatively impact their mental health. *Adultification bias* causes adults to see and treat Black girls as adults, which leads to harsher discipline in systems such as schools and the juvenile justice system. Additionally, Black girls must deal with an intersectionality of gender and sex, which, combined with adultification bias, leaves them vulnerable to sexual exploitation and violence. Disproportionality of support and services within the child welfare system also contributes to high rates of domestic sex trafficking among Black girls. Just like any other child, Black girls deserve safety from physical, emotional, and sexual harm yet they are denied that luxury simply because of the color of their skin.

To effectively support Black girls, it is imperative that social workers educate themselves on disparities in the systems that leave these girls unprotected and punished. That includes more closely examining stereotypes and how they correlate with the unjust treatment of Black girls. Issues of colorism and hair discrimination are also important stressors to examine in the lives of Black girls to understand how these may negatively affect their mental health. This chapter will explore how play therapy can serve as an empowerment tool to help address issues of self-esteem, anxiety, depression, and thoughts of self-harm that may result from untreated race-based stress and trauma in Black girls.

Mental Health Among Black Girls

The mental health of American Black girls is directly connected to their race-based stressors and experiences throughout their childhood. High levels of

Black Students Matter. April D. Duncan, Oxford University Press. © Oxford University Press 2024.
DOI: 10.1093/oso/9780197669266.003.0006

race-based stress and trauma in Black girls are correlated with negative mental health outcomes. Racial discrimination has been found to place Black girls at an increased risk for both anxiety and depressive disorders (Walker et al., 2016). Black girls who are dealing with mental health issues often are not given the support they need. Studies have found that adults tend to view Black girls with depression or mental health issues as troublemakers or problems (Physicians for a National Health Program, 2021). Rather than providing affirmation or mental health support, Black girls are punished, especially in schools. If a Black girl is having a bad day, she is seen as having an attitude, which may then result in a school referral for detention for "being disrespectful."

School social workers should be aware of the messages Black girls are routinely exposed to via the media, social media, and even in their own communities. Exposure to oppressive messages about Black women is correlated with depressive symptoms in Black girls (Stokes et al., 2020). In a study conducted by the Dove personal care products company, 32% of their participants shared that hearing negative comments about their hair made them feel bad about themselves (JOY Collective, 2021). Despite a high prevalence of anxiety and depression, Black girls may be resistant to receiving mental health services. Black girls may be less receptive to engage in mental health services because of distrust of providers, social stigma, apprehension about the efficacy of treatment, and accessibility issues (Givens, 2020). A high incidence of mental distress as a result of racial stressors, left untreated, increases suicidal risk in Black girls. However, the symptoms of suicidal thoughts and behaviors may be overlooked because of bias toward Black girls.

A recent study found Black girls are more likely to report suicide ideation than Black males (Hooper et al., 2015). Black girls are also at a higher risk for suicidality compared to their peers of other racial and ethnic backgrounds. Recent trends for suicidality among adolescent girls have decreased for all ethnic groups, except for Black girls, where there has been an increase in suicide attempts (Lindsey et al., 2019). This risk is most evident among high schoolers. Approximately 41% of Black girls in high school reported feeling some type of sadness or hopelessness in the past year, 23% seriously considered suicide, 20% of black girls reported planning for suicide, and 15% reported attempting suicide (Centers for Disease and Control [CDC], 2020). However, this demographic is often overlooked as a high risk for suicidality because of the systemic and individual bias that drives school discipline regarding Black girls.

Black Girls and Adultification Bias

Black girls are subjected to adultification bias, which is the catalyst for systemic and direct racial trauma stressors. This bias views and treats Black girls as being older than their actual age (Epstein et al., n.d). There are two ways adultification bias appears among Black girls. First is through the process of socialization, where a child may function at a more mature developmental stage because of necessity and situational circumstances (Epstein et al., n.d). As previously explained, various systemic issues contribute to Black children having a higher probability of having an incarcerated family member and/or entering into the child welfare system. As a result, Black girls may be socialized to be older due to the demands placed on the family, where that child must help take care of younger siblings by getting a job or assisting with caretaking. Even in two-parent homes in high socioeconomic neighborhoods, Black girls are often socialized to help assist in child-rearing. This phenomenon is connected to the "Mammie" stereotype in Black women, where they are seen as caretakers (Epstein et al., n.d.) and, conversely, is also reflected in the stereotype of a "Strong Black Girl," where they are expected to forfeit their childhood to fill parental roles.

Another way adultification bias presents towards Black girls is through social or cultural stereotypes (Epstein et al., n.d). Statements within the Black community and families like "Lil mama" or "Miss thang" are innocent yet reaffirm the perceived maturity of Black girls. This can also include referring to a child as "grown," which is an effort to encourage independence as a protective factor but also aids in perpetuating the aging of Black children in a way that prohibits them from making the same mistakes as other children. This form of bias can cause a mental health professional to misinterpret the behaviors and feelings of Black girls as immature or inappropriate for their age and thus not requiring the same level of empathy as White girls. This bias often leaves Black girls punished, vulnerable, and unprotected.

Black girls are not disciplined at higher rates because they have worse behaviors than other students, but because of bias in school discipline practices and rules. Adultification bias is the foundation of how behaviors are perceived and treated in Black girls. For Black girls, adultification provides an additional layer of bias and racial stress that can contribute to racial trauma. There are real-life consequences to this bias because it also places Black girls at a higher risk of being victims of sexual abuse and violence. Several stereotypes among Black girls are rooted in adultification bias and contribute to racial trauma and driving exclusionary discipline in schools. Those stereotypes include Sapphire, Jezebel, and Mammie.

Why Are Black Girls So Loud?

The first stereotype, Sapphire, is displayed when Black girls are seen as being emasculating and aggressive and often stereotyped as being loud, unfeminine, and stubborn (Epstein et al., n.d). As Chapter 4 explored, Black girls may be dealing with bullying around their hair, skin tone, or other racial factors that can contribute to levels of aggression or defiant behaviors. There is no evidence showing that Black girls are more aggressive than other girls. However, they receive higher rates of suspensions and expulsions for the same behavior exhibited by their peers. The Sapphire stereotype is reflected in schools where Black girls are more likely to be penalized for more subjective issues, like being loud, using profanity, exhibiting defiance, or having "attitude" (Blake et al., 2011). Black girls are penalized more harshly because they do not meet the Eurocentric standard of behavior. Behaviors that are seen as being loud, stubborn, or challenging authority are also seen as being unladylike, and this contributes to punishment in Black girls (Killeen, 2019). The result is that Black girls are being told that they are not good enough just as they are, which could further worsen their self-esteem.

She's "Fast"

The next stereotype, Jezebel, is a woman depicted as being hypersexualized, seductive, and sexually exploitative (Thompson, 2022). This is shown through the higher levels of sexual abuse and exploitation found in Black girls. This stereotype and adultification bias serve as pointed excuses, and Black girls are often blamed for their own abuse. A narrative that says a teenaged girl can serve as a vixen who places men under her spell is particularly problematic for the adultified Black girl (Thompson, 2022). Black girls who are abused are often blamed for the clothes they were wearing or for "looking older." These excuses further victimizes Black girls. And this often stems from stereotypes about Black girls and their sexual activity: Black girls are often stereotyped as being sexually advanced, even though the numbers tell a different story.

The Youth Risk Behavior Surveillance Survey (YRBSS) found that Black girls are having sex at rates comparable to Latinx and White girls (CDC, 2020). However, Black girls are more likely to have sex earlier, as 3% of Black girls in high school reported having sex before the age of 13 (CDC, 2020).

It should be noted that 17 years is the age of consent in most states, and if a child under the age of 13 cannot legally consent to sex, then that child is being abused. So, in essence, one could theorize that approximately 3% of Black girls were sexually abused before the age of 13. Additionally, 11% of Black high school girls have reported being raped (CDC, 2020).

In many cases, however, if that girl is Black, she's not a victim, she's just "fast." This moves the child from the survivor/victim space to that of offender/ perpetrator and leaves these girls further vulnerable to abuse and exploitation. This is also reflected in school discipline, where many of the behaviors of Black girls, such as inappropriate dress, are correlated with an Eurocentric ideal of femininity that views some clothing as "inappropriate" or "unlady-like" (Blake et al., 2011). Multicultural feminism argues that the concept of "sameness" could counterintuitively be used as an instrument of oppression rather than liberation (Tong, 2001), which is evidence when Black girls are prohibited from wearing clothing that expresses their culture and identity. Furthermore, it again places Black girls into the roles of offender/perpetrator, labeling their clothing and bodies as sexualized and inappropriate. In turn, this may widen the gap for mental health services because sexual abuse is being overlooked due to the child being seen as more sexually advanced, therefore, more culpable for the abuse they have experienced.

Strong Black Girl

The final stereotype, Mammie, perpetuates the belief that Black women and girls are self-sacrificing, nurturing, loving, or asexual (Epstein et al., n.d). These stereotypes contribute to hidden biases that exist across systems and are contributing factors to racial trauma in Black girls. By 5 years old, many Black girls are robbed of their childhood and left to fend for themselves both mentally and emotionally. Studies found that adults view Black girls as less innocent and more adult-like, especially between the ages of 5 and 14 years (Epstein, n.d). Georgetown Law Center on Poverty and Inequality conducted a study that found Black girls were perceived as needing less protection, support, nurturance, and comfort; as being more independent; and as being more knowledgeable about adult topics and sex (Epstein, n.d.). This is also reflected in the way Black girls are treated in the criminal and juvenile justice system.

"The age of mistake defense" currently exists in at least 20 states, like Illinois, where a defendant charged with having sex with a minor can use the defense that they reasonably believed that the person was 17 years of age or older (Thompson, 2022). In a society that already views Black girls as older, this law further leaves Black girls unprotected because it increases the likelihood that an older offender might take sexual advantage of a Black girl and face no legal consequences. This was evident in the trial of R. Kelly, a notorious child molester whose lawyers used this defense and were able to paint the children involved as promiscuous and sexually advanced for their age (Thompson, 2022), even though decades of accusations of sexual exploitation came from young Black girls since the mid 1990s. Finally, in 2022, Kelly was found guilty of his crimes but not before leaving hundreds of child victims in his wake.

Direct Racial Stressors in Black Girls

Black girls are at an increased risk for racial trauma due to stereotypes and biases that villainize them and further remove them from the childhood they deserve. There are several unique racial stressors to consider when working with Black girls: colorism, hair discrimination, sexual violence, domestic sex trafficking, and adverse police contact. School social workers should consider these stressors when providing assessment and treatment planning with Black girls.

Colorism

Colorism is the practice of discrimination in which individuals with lighter complexions are treated more favorably than those with darker skin (National Conference for Community and Justice, 2022). This is an international issue that affects all minority populations. The differential treatment for women and girls with lighter complexion is observed in all systems, including the criminal justice system and schools. Researchers found light-skinned women were sentenced to 12% less time in jail and served 11% less time in jail than women with darker complexions (National Conference for Community and Justice, 2022).

This same bias is shown in school discipline in students of color. Studies found Black female students with darker complexions were more than twice as likely than White females to receive an out-of-school suspension (Blake et al., 2017). Black girls are likely to mirror the same colorist beliefs as Black women. Abrams et al. (2020) found Black girls often saw light skin as beautiful and associated with higher socioeconomic class, while darker skin was seen as unattractive and associated with low social standing. This may have negative effects on Black girls, especially when they start becoming interested in romantic relationships. I remember vividly an 11-year old Black girl telling me in session, "Ms. April, the guys only like the light-skinned girls with good hair." However, a lot of Black girls are pushing back against this discriminatory concept that pits individuals from the same community against each other. Rosario and colleagues (2021) found that 74% of discussions among Black girls in their study were focused on resistance to colorism as a denouncement of the ideologies of White patriarchy, supremacy, and anti-Blackness. This highlights the resilience that Black girls possess to buffer racial trauma stressors along with the importance of empowerment to resist society's standards of beauty and acceptance.

Hair Discrimination

Black girls experience bias toward their hair that is reflected in school discipline and contributes to racial trauma and negative mental health outcomes. The CROWN Act (which stands for "Creating a Respectful and Open World for Natural Hair") prohibits race-based hair discrimination in employment and education (The Crown Act, n.d.). This policy is currently law in 19 states, and its proponents hope to make it nationwide (The Crown Act, n.d.). In 2022, the House of Representatives passed the bill, but it stalled in the Senate (Stracqualursi, 2022). Hair discrimination in Black girls is associated with their self-esteem and school engagement. In a study conducted by Dove, 53% of Black mothers reported hair discrimination against their children as young as 5 years old, and 45% of Black girls in the study, ages 5–18, reported experiencing hair discrimination and bias (JOY Collective, 2021). The same study found Black girls are more likely to be punished in school for hairstyle and dress (National Black Women's Justice Initiative, 2020). Both implicit bias and lack of cultural competence leads to the policing of Black hair and contributes to the "preschool-to-prison pipeline."

Black students, particularly girls, are expected to conform to the Eurocentric standards of beauty, yet they are punished if they do and punished when they do not. Ignorance of cultural norms in the Black community could have contributed to a Black family being separated, as studies have shown Black caregivers are more likely to be investigated and have their children removed and their parental rights terminated (Child Welfare Information Gateway, 2021). In the Black community, mothers often use harsh hair treatments such as hot combs and perms at an early age due to high levels of hair discrimination or from the pressures of European standards of beauty that encourage long, straight hair. The reward for adhering to these standards is the scrutinization of the methods to achieve such standards. It is a double-edged hot comb; you get burned either way.

This highlights the way in which the racial demographics of a Black girl's school and community contributes to disparate treatment. A study found that Black, Latinx, and White children living in diverse neighborhoods are more likely to be reported to child protective services than children of their same race or ethnicity living in homogeneous neighborhoods (Klein & Merritt, 2014). This disparity in reporting reveals that individuals who are less understanding of the cultural differences of other communities can lead to an increase in suspected maltreatment calls for children of color. This is important to explore within the context of school systems as well. If Black students are attending more diverse schools, this may increase the probability that their parents will be reported for suspected maltreatment than would the parents of a Black student who attends a school where Black children are in the majority. The school social worker plays an integral part in advocating for the understanding of cultural differences in parenting that may lead to a school official wanting to make a hotline call on a caregiver. Making hotline calls without cultural understanding of Black traditions and behaviors can be detrimental to any established rapport with the child and/or, which could be difficult for the school social worker to regain, if at all.

Black Hair in School

The racial demographics of a school also has an impact on the exposure a Black girl may have to hair discrimination. Black girls in majority White schools experience higher rates of hair discrimination than do their peers in majority Black schools. Young Black girls in majority White schools are 50% more likely to experience discrimination, and 100% of those girls reported experiencing hair discrimination before the age of 10 (JOY Collective, 2021). As it relates to school, Black girls also are known to miss school because of their hair. Teenage Black girls are missing a week of school because they are dissatisfied with their hair (JOY Collective, 2021). It is important to know that Black girls will sometimes skip school or activities because their hair is not done or unkempt.

Personally, when I was a child I was kicked out of gym several times because I refused to run after just receiving a perm. The teacher did not understand how running could ruin my hair and leave me feeling embarrassed for the rest of the school day. It was seen as an act of defiance that often landed me in detention. This may result in discipline for missing school or even truancy charges. Some Black girls will miss school or be tired at school because they were up late getting their hair done. This may contribute to them having a bad day at school because they're more irritable or have trouble paying attention because they are tired. This could result in discipline for "being disrespectful." A Black girl who will not remove her hood or headwrap may not being defiant: it is because her hair is not done and she does not want to be embarrassed in front of her peers.

Cultural competence on Black cultural practices and norms is imperative when working with Black students. Unfortunately, girls of color are more likely to attend under resourced schools that lack cultural competence and are not personalized to their needs/interests, which negatively affects their educational opportunities and future earnings as adults (Onyeka-Crawford et al., 2017). Additionally, a lack of knowledge about how culture correlates to behavior contributes to racial trauma and can rob Black girls of their education and their freedom.

Black Girls and Sexual Violence

Sexual violence is an issue that plagues American girls of all backgrounds. The 2019 Youth Risk Behavior Surveillance Survey found 56% of girls in grades 7–12 reported some form of sexual violence victimization by a peer (e.g., unwelcome touching, comments or being forced to do something sexual) (Basile et al., 2019). The most recent data for the 2018–2019 school year found that 11% of Black high school girls reported sexual violence (2022). Black girls have a higher risk of being exposed to sexual violence while also receiving lower levels of protection from their communities, families, and the criminal and child welfare systems. To respond to the misbehaviors of Black girls effectively and appropriately, it is important that school social workers understand how the intersection of race and gender, including inadequate protection from educators and sexual harassment from male students, contribute to those behaviors (Haight et al., 2016).

This blind eye to abuse in Black girls is shown in the statistics. One in four black girls will experience sexual abuse before the age of 18 (The National Center on Violence Against Women in the Black Community, 2022). The same study found that between 40% and 60% of black women reported experiencing sexual coercion by the age of 18 (The National Center on Violence Against Women in the Black Community, n.d.). Research has been able to highlight that girls who experience gender-based violence, including sexual harassment, tend to have an elevated risk of sexual harm, suicidal thoughts, and feeling unsafe at school (Chiodo, 2009). Therefore, it is key that school social workers working with Black girls are aware of how sexual violence correlates with poor mental health. It is also important to possess an awareness of the prevalence of domestic sex trafficking, especially among Black girls.

Black Girls and Domestic Sex Trafficking

Black girls account for 43% of minors who are victims of sex trafficking (Hershberger, 2021). Yet again, these girls are treated as criminals as opposed to victims. Black girls are often charged as "juvenile prostitutes," which is an oxymoron because a child cannot legally consent to sex. However, according to the FBI, 57.5% of all juvenile prostitution arrests are Black children (Davey, n.d.). Again we see the consequences when Black girls are oversexualized as a result of the "Sapphire" stereotype. Black adolescent girls have disadvantages that place them in the path of harm more than their peers. Black girls are more likely to experience family instability, poverty, and disconnection from important systems like schools that place them at a higher risk of entering the child welfare system. The rejection that Black girls face in these systems pushes them into the hands of predators who sexually exploit these young girls. Traffickers also tend to target Black girls and women of lower socioeconomic status, and studies have shown that traffickers admittedly believe that trafficking Black girls and women will land less jail time than if they were to traffic White women and girls (Davey, n.d). Since Black girls are more likely to be trafficked, this also increases their chances of experiencing adverse police contact.

Black Girls and Adverse Police Contact

Black girls, like Black boys, have higher interactions with police officers that are often negative and traumatizing. Many of those incidents for Black girls occur within schools. Although Black girls only account for 16% of the female student population, they account for 39% of school arrests and are five times more likely to be arrested than White female students (Whitaker et al., 2019). It is important to remember that the most common school disciplinary infractions among Black girls are inappropriate dress and disrespect. One can draw a correlation between these infractions and deduce that Black girls are being arrested not for things like fighting, but because bias in both educators and police officers escalates situations of perceived disrespect or not adhering to the status quo. Biased discipline toward Black girls pushes them out of schools and into the streets or juvenile justice system.

In her book, "Pushout: The Criminalization of Black Girls in Schools," Morris (2016) states:

> From coast to coast, Black girls tell stories of being pushed out of school and criminalized for falling asleep, standing up for themselves, asking questions, wearing natural hair, wearing revealing clothing, and in some cases engaging in unruly (although not criminal or delinquent) acts in school—mostly because what constitutes a threat to safety is dangerously subjective when Black children are involved. (p. 57)

This sobering statement brings light to lack of freedom and independence Black girls have in self-expression in communication, dress, and behavior. It also is important to consider how that child may be mentally and emotionally affected from the shame and embarrassment after a police encounter. Then, the emotional safety they may lack when they have to return to school and see the same police officer from the incident. So, school social workers should be attuned to incidents involving adverse police contact among Black girls, especially when those encounters happen at school.

Systemic Racial Stressors in Black Girls

Disparities in school discipline, the juvenile justice system, and child welfare system serve as additional racial stressors for Black girls. As previously explored, adultification bias is often the root of these disparities. Therefore, school social workers should be tasked with finding ways to support Black girls interacting with these systems and advocate for fair and equal treatment for Black girls.

Black Girls and School Discipline

Within the school system, Black girls experience disparities in the ways they are disciplined, with glaring differences appearing in early childhood. Black preschool girls specifically account for about 9% of the total preschool enrollment, but they receive out-of-school suspensions at a rate comparable to their population (Office for Civil Rights, 2021). In elementary school and beyond, Black girls represent 11.2% of in-school suspensions and 13% of out-of-school suspensions but they only account for about 7% of school enrollment (Office for Civil Rights, 2021). These disparities highlight the differential treatment of Black girls that pushes them out of schools and into environments that further victimize, neglect, and abuse them such as the juvenile justice and child welfare systems.

Black Girls in the Juvenile Justice System

Disparities within the juvenile justice system are often connected to school disciplinary practices toward Black girls. Compared to White girls, Black girls are three times more likely to be incarcerated (National Black Women's Justice Initiative, 2021). The only demographic that outpaces Black girl arrests are arrests of Indigenous girls, who are four times as likely to be incarcerated (Whitaker et al., 2019). As in schools, in the juvenile justice system, many Black girls are not being punished for violent behaviors but rather for subjective behaviors. One-third of girls who are incarcerated are there for status offenses such as truancy and curfew violations or for violating the terms of their probation (Sentencing Project, 2022). Considering school disciplinary tactics toward Black girls, it is entirely possible that schools are pushing Black girls out of the education system and into the streets by making them feel unheard, unseen, and unprotected and thus exposing them to high levels of sexual violence that leave Black girls victimized in their homes and their communities. If Black girls feel unprotected in schools and in their homes, they may be more likely to skip school or run away from home, further exposing them to the risk of entering the juvenile justice system or becoming a victim of domestic sex trafficking. This is especially true for Black girls in the child welfare system, who are often left with less services and support than their White peers.

Black Girls and the Child Welfare System

Overall, child welfare–involved youth are 10 times more likely to be sexual abused (Davey. n.d). Black children are at an even greater increased risk for sexual abuse in this system. Black children are sexually abused twice as often as their White counterparts in the child welfare system (Davey, n.d.). And studies found that Black girls are more likely to run away from foster care (Davey, n.d.). These factors place Black girls at a higher risk for being victims of domestic sex trafficking because Black girls who are runaways are more likely to be targeted by sex traffickers (Davey, n.d.). The child welfare system has unintentionally become a pipeline to the world of sex trafficking in the United States. A staggering 86% of sex trafficking victims were in the care of social services when they went missing (Davey, n.d.). These statistics highlight the need for more psychoeducation on the risks of Black girls within the child welfare system, along with solutions to help decrease their vulnerability to the juvenile system and/or domestic sex trafficking, and increasing the protection and services they desperately require.

Maladaptive Coping Skills in Black Girls

The lack of mental health support for Black girls can lead to a search for a quick fix to erase the pain, which can also serve as an avoidant coping mechanism. For Black girls, this can be the abuse of alcohol and drugs as maladaptive coping skills. Approximately 45% of Black girls in high school reported trying marijuana at least once in their lifetime; 7% of Black girls have tried marijuana before the age of 13, and about a quarter of Black girls report currently using marijuana (CDC, 2020). Both Black girls and Black boys use marijuana at higher rates than Latinx and White youth (CDC, 2020), and the abuse of other substances has been found in this population at alarming rates. Black girls in high school reported using inhalants, like sniffing glue or breathing the contents of aerosol spray cans, once in their lifetime, which is comparable to usage rates in Latinx girls (CDC, 2020) Also, 1–2% of Black girls in high school reported using heroin, meth, and steroids (CDC, 2020). These are drugs not typically associated with Black children, so it can be easy to miss usage among this demographic. These statistics communicate a lack of healthy coping skills in dealing with stressors, which can also include racial trauma stressors.

Engaging Black Girls in the Playroom

In the playroom, Black girls need activities that affirm their culture and identity as well as provide a space in which to openly express their emotions about how they are treated in the settings they encounter. However, there may be layers of mistrust that the social worker will have to navigate to build a strong, therapeutic relationship with the student. Play therapy interventions that focus on self-esteem, anxiety reduction, and empowering Black girls provide vital ways to engage these students. Racial socialization messages that encourage pride in being Black and being a woman result in more positive attitudes about being Black (Stokes et al., 2020). Exploring the history of play and leisure for Black girls will provide the social worker with ways to build rapport with these students through the implementation of traditional games and activities from their communities.

There are some key things to know about the play of Black girls that can help the school social worker engage them in play therapy sessions.

Historically, Black girls played with toys that are still relevant today: in the 19th century, Black girls participated in games, played with dolls, and enjoyed playing dress up, keeping house, preparing food, serving meals, caring for babies, and washing dishes (King, 2011). Jumping rope is another common activity among Black girls, so the social worker could benefit from integrating jumping rope into individual sessions or try double-Dutch rope jumping in group settings. It also is important to have baby dolls and Barbie dolls with different skin tones and hair textures because this can provide an opportunity for the social worker to identify any issues around colorism, hair discrimination, or other racial trauma stressors that the child may be experiencing.

Doll Play

Piaget believed that play is inherently social and provides a place where kids can rehearse social interactions and social perspective-taking (Seow, 2019). The playroom provides a natural environment for this play to occur for Black girls. Studies have shown that when children engage in doll play, there was an increase of engagement in the posterior superior temporal sulcus (pSTS) region, the part of the brain involved in developing emotional and social processing skills (Hashmi et al., 2020). Therefore, doll play provides a space for Black girls to process and develop empathy. Reviewing the history of dolls in the Black community, the first African American Barbie with Afro hair was released in 1980 (Seow, 2019). Since then, a steady stream of Black dolls have been produced in response to an increasingly discerning market. Studies have shown that a girl's self-esteem and confidence are increased when they see themselves represented in toys and dolls (Seow, 2019). Doll play mimics larger social relationships so they can be an effective tool for Black girls to navigate the stereotypes and roles placed on them.

Sand Tray Therapy

Sand tray therapy can be an effective tool to supporting Black girls through racial trauma stressors. Directive sand tray prompts specific to Black girls (Appendix A) can help start the conversation around race-based stress and trauma. There are some key miniatures to have for sand tray therapy with Black girls. First, substance abuse kits that have miniatures for marijuana, cigarettes, and other substances of abuse can help the social worker identify substance use and abuse in the student. Next, self-harm miniatures, like fake blood and bandages, will be useful for Black girls who are struggling with suicidal thoughts and behaviors. It will also be important to have grief miniatures to help express any feelings around grief events they may have experienced. Finally, it will be beneficial to have miniatures with different skin tones and hair textures to help communicate and address any issues around self-esteem, especially colorism.

Barbie Dolls for Role Play

Doll play can be beneficial for younger Black girls but may not be as successful with older students. The use of Barbie dolls can be helpful for role-playing instances of discrimination, racism, and prejudice that the child has encountered. Older students in junior and high school can use these dolls to help explain and problem-solve any issues they are dealing with, which may assist in developing empathy and healthier coping skills. It will be important to use dolls that are consistent with the student's culture, such as Fresh Dolls, which are manufactured by a company whose dolls sport current hair styles and clothing that is reflective of Black culture.

Role-play with Barbie dolls for older students may also help Black girls navigate the barriers that they encounter when they seek support or help that is withheld because of bias. Role-play can also be used to provide homework where the student can practice things they want to say or do in racially charged situations. It may also serve as a form of exposure therapy, a way to help students who are avoiding certain people or environments because of their racial trauma.

Hand Games

Hand games, like Miss Mary Mack, are traditional games used by Black girls in socializing with their peers. Using popular childhood hand games can be helpful to instill joy, sisterhood, and safe touch for Black girls through music and education (Varlas, 2019). Additionally, hand games help Black girls learn the rules of social identity and provide musical practice, as hand games often have some type of accompanying melodic tune or chanted lyrics that resemble an approach to rapping (Varlas, 2019). In play therapy sessions, the social worker can encourage the student to teach them a hand game from their childhood, or they can work together to create their own. And in group play therapy, the girls can work together to create a unique hand game or a variation of an existing one. Providing an activity rooted in both their culture and their childhood can be an effective way to build a therapeutic relationship with Black girls.

Play Themes Signaling Racial Trauma in Black Girls

There are several themes that may appear in the play of Black girls in the playroom. First, a theme of nurturance may be displayed in doll play and other nurturing activities. Anger may be another presenting theme in the playroom, given the high level of stressors Black girls experience daily. The rescue and protection theme may arise as a way to communicate their need to be protected by others. Additionally, the limits and boundaries theme may present when a child has learned to set boundaries to protect themselves as a result of a lack of protection from adults. Black girls may also exhibit the connection theme in the playroom, communicating a need to connect with others. These students could benefit from attachment-based play interventions to strengthen their attachments with adults. Given the high levels of sexual violence involving exploitation of Black girls, they may have issues with mistrust, which may be evident through the theme of trust and betrayal.

Several themes may communicate anxiety in Black girls, and the school social worker should be alert for these. The theme of perfectionism may show up because of the need to please others or out of worry of "messing up" and being disciplined. Another important play theme, self-esteem, can be present in the play of Black girls and communicate the need to increase confidence. If they are exhibiting the self-esteem theme, they may be anxious about how other people perceive them or in how they are dealing with stereotypes and/or bias in their environments. The chaos theme may also be present in their inability to settle into an activity or by engaging in very disorganized play. Also, because of the lack of protection from adults, the student may also play out themes of guilt.

These themes will be central to identifying the mental health needs of Black girls, especially as they pertain to racial trauma. Black girls may not be open to talking about their experiences given the high level of rejection they may have already experienced with other adults and professionals. The school social worker should display patience and understanding to the unique needs of this population, along with providing play therapy supports to help with encouraging emotional expression, increasing confidence, and building stronger relationships with Black girls.

Play Therapy to Empower Black Girls

Play therapy interventions that emphasize empowerment and self-esteem should be the focus of school social workers working with Black girls. It is also important to remember Black girls are often adultified, so they may be less engaged in activities that are seen as "kiddie," or they may be drawn to them because of a lack of childhood due to the parentified roles they have stepped in. Nondirective play therapy can be powerful to provide young Black girls with a space in which to control their narrative. For older students, art therapy activities can be a way to help empower and heal.

My Beautiful Crown

This art therapy activity is for students in 4th grade and older and explores issues around hair discrimination. My Beautiful Crown is an art-based intervention to explore hair-based experiences in Black girls. For the activity, the student will need the poster activity handout (Appendix B), poster board, scissors, and art materials like pom-pom balls and pipe cleaners. The student is directed to pick a face that resembles their skin tone and use their choice of art materials to create a self-portrait. The activity comes with discussion cards that the therapist can use while the student works on the activity, or the cards can be something students can read and respond to after completing the activity. This can also jumpstart the conversation around other acts of discrimination the child has experienced, thus opening the door for additional conversations around race-based issues.

Zentangle Affirmations

Affirmations are a way to help empower children, and Black girls are no different. Sayings like "Black Girl Magic" and other racial socialization messages can be used in play therapy settings with students of all ages. This art activity can be used with students as young as 2nd grade. The materials required for this activity are something to color with (crayons, markers, and/or colored pencils) and the Zentangle Affirmation handout (Appendix C). Zentangle is an art form that can help individuals enter a mediative state in an untraditional way (Zentangle, n.d.). Using the materials, the student is encouraged to create their own Zentangle, then create an affirmation based on the symbols integrated into their Zentangle. For example, if they have five different symbols, they must make five different affirmations that go along with those symbols. The student can also be encouraged to use these affirmations daily to assist with self-esteem and confidence-building.

Beaded Mosaics

The next art activity, Beaded Mosaics, honors hair culture in the Black community. Beads are used a lot in black culture, especially in younger Black girls. For many Black girls, caring for their hair is a time-consuming and important ritual. This activity can be helpful in communicating any hair discrimination the child has experienced. Since this activity requires the use of a hot glue gun, it is recommended only for junior high and high school girls. Other materials required are hair beads, canvas, scissors, tweezers, regular glue, and the Beaded Mosaics handout (Appendix D). Using the beads and handout, the student is prompted to create a mosaic picture. The student may also be encouraged to write affirmations that are centered around hair and standards of beauty as an additional support for empowerment and self-esteem building in Black girls.

Slap Out of It

The final art activity, Slap Out of It, is a CBPT intervention that can help address any cognitive distortions the student may be experiencing. This is an activity that can be used with students as young as 1st grade through high school. The materials required are a blank slap bracelet, fabric markers, and the Slap Out of It handout (Appendix E). The student is encouraged to pick a slap bracelet and think of a negative statement someone has made toward them. Then the student is encouraged to turn that negative thought into a positive one. For example, someone may have said the student was dumb. They would be encouraged to turn that negative remark into a positive statement like "I am smart." Next, they would be prompted to decorate the front of the bracelet however they want; then, on the inside, they will write their positive statement "I am smart." They can then be encouraged to use their bracelet to "slap out" of any negative thoughts they may have associated with those thoughts, and they can slap the bracelet back on as a reminder to replace negative thoughts with positive ones.

Resources for Black Girls

There are some important resources that can be beneficial to address the unique needs of Black girls outside of the school and playroom. The website Black Girl Yoga can be used to encourage the use of healthy coping skills outside of sessions. For Black girls in need of additional therapeutic support outside of the school, Therapy for Black Girls and Therapy for Black Kids can be helpful for them and their families. The Loveland Foundation provides financial support for mental health services for Black girls (Loveland Foundation, 2022). Black Girls Smile (2022) also provides conflict mediation support, suicide prevention training, coaching, workshops, and therapy assistance for Black girls. School social workers also can benefit from learning about community programs and services in their area that can assist Black girls with safe places for healing. Black sororities and clubs/organizations such as Jack and Jill are other community resources that can assist in Black female empowerment and support for Black girls.

Conclusion

Adultified perceptions of Black girls leave them vulnerable in every facet of their lives. Black girls are subjected to higher levels of abuse and exploitation that contribute to racial trauma stressors. Bias within systems such as schools, juvenile justice, and child welfare put the Black girl at a further disadvantage to receive the love and care they so desperately deserve. School social workers are in a unique position to develop real and authentic relationships with Black girls and provide a healing space where they can be seen, heard, and valued. The attention and nurturance provided in these spaces can help minimize the risk of untreated mental health disorders that are caused by racial trauma and punished by laws and policies that degrade the worth of Black girls.

References

Abrams, J. A., Belgrave, F. Z., Williams, C. D., & Maxwell, M. L. (2020). African American adolescent girls' beliefs about skin tone and colorism. *Journal of Black Psychology*, *46*(2-3), 169–194. https://doi.org/10.1177/0095798420928194

Basile, K. C., Clayton, H. B., DeGue S., et al. (2019). Interpersonal Violence Victimization Among High School Students — Youth Risk Behavior Survey, United States, 2019. *Morbidity and Mortality Weekly Report*, 2020;69(Suppl-1):28–37. doi:http://dx.doi.org/10.15585/mmwr.su6901a4

Black Girls Smile. (2022). https://www.blackgirlssmile.org/

Blake, J., Butler, B., Lewis, C., & Darensbourg, A. (2011). Unmasking the inequitable discipline experiences of urban Black girls: Implications for urban educational stakeholders. (Report). *Urban Review*, *43*(1), 90–106. https://doi.org/10.1007/s11256-009-0148-8

Blake, J. J., Keith, V. M., Luo, W., Le, H., & Salter, P. (2017). The role of colorism in explaining African American females' suspension risk. *School Psychology Quarterly*, *32*(1), 118–130. https://doi.org/10.1037/spq0000173

Centers for Disease Control and Prevention (CDC). (2020). Youth Risk Behavior Surveillance: United States, 2019. *Morbidity and Mortality Weekly Report*, *69*(1). https://www.cdc.gov/mmwr/ind2020_su.html

Child Welfare Information Gateway. (2021). Child welfare practices to address racial dispro-portionality and disparity. Office of the Administration for Children & Families, Children's Bureau. https://www.childwelfare.gov/pubPDFs/racial_disproportionality.pdf

Chiodo, D., Wolfe, D. A., Crooks, C., Hughes, R., & Jaffe, P. (2009). Impact of sexual harassment victimization by peers on subsequent adolescent victimization and adjust-ment: A longitudinal study. *Journal of Adolescent Health*,*45*(3), 246–252. https://doi.org/10.1016/j.jadohealth.2009.01.006.

Crown Act. (n.d). About us. https://www.thecrownact.com/

Davey, S. (n.d.) Snapshot on the state of Black women and girls: Sex trafficking in the U.S. Congressional Black Caucus Foundation. https://www.cbcfinc.org/wp-content/uploads/2020/05/SexTraffickingReport3.pdf

Epstein, R., Blake, J. J., & Gonzalez, T. (n.d.). Girlhood interrupted: The erasure of Black girls' childhood. Center on Poverty and Inequality, Georgetown Law. https://genderjusticeandopportunity.georgetown.edu/wp-content/uploads/2020/06/girlhood-interrupted.pdf

Givens, D. (2020). The extra stigma of mental illness for African-Americans. *New York Times*. https://www.nytimes.com/2020/08/25/well/mind/ black-mental-health.html.

Haight, W., Kayama, M., & Gibson, P. (2016). Out-of-school suspensions of Black youths: Culture, ability, disability, gender, and perspective. *Social Work, 61*(3), 235–243. https://doi.org/10.1093/sw/sww021

Hashmi, S., Vanderwert, R. E., Price, H. A., & Gerson, S. A. (2020). Exploring the benefits of doll play through neuroscience. *Frontiers in Human Neuroscience, 14*. https://doi.org/10.3389/fnhum.2020.560176

Hershberger, J. M. (2021). A relational-cultural theory approach to work with survivors of sex trafficking. *Journal of Creativity in Mental Health, 16*(4), 456–466. https://doi.org/10.1080/15401383.2020.1790457

Hooper, L., Tomek, S., Bolland, K., Church, W., Wilcox, K., & Bolland, J. (2015). The impact of previous suicide ideations, traumatic stress, and gender on future su-icide ideation trajectories among Black American adolescents: A longitudinal inves-tigation. *Journal of Loss and Trauma, 20*(4), 354–373. https://doi.org/10.1080/15325024.2014.897573

JOY Collective. (2021). Dove CROWN research study for girls. Dove. https://static1.squarespace.com/static/5edc69fd622c36173f56651f/t/623369f7477914438ee18c9b/1647536634602/2021_DOVE_CROWN_girls_study.pdf

Killeen, E. (2019). The increased criminalization of African American girls. Georgetown Law. https://www.law.georgetown.edu/poverty-journal/blog/the-increased-criminalization-of-african-american-girls/

King, W. (2011). *Stolen childhood. Slave youth in nineteenth-century America* (2nd ed.) Indiana University Press.

Klein, S., & Merritt, D. H. (2014). Neighborhood racial and ethnic diversity as a predictor of child welfare system involvement. *Children and Youth Services Review, 41*, 95–105. https://doi.org/10.1016/j.childyouth.2014.03.009

Lindsey, M., Sheftall, A., Xiao, Y., & Joe, S. (2019). Trends of suicidal behaviors among high school students in the United States: 1991–2017. *Pediatrics, 144*(5), Article e20191912. https://doi-org.libproxy1.usc.edu/10.1542/peds.2019-1912

Loveland Foundation. (2022). https://thelovelandfoundation.org/

National Black Women's Justice Initiative. (2020). The CROWN Act and the link between Black hair, school discipline and criminalization of Black girls. https://www.nbwji.org/post/the-crown-act-and-the-link-between-black-hair-school-discipline-and-criminalization

National Black Women's Justice Initiative. (2021). Mental health of Black girls. The case for gender-specific and culturally affirming services. https://www.nbwji.org/_files/ugd/0c71ee_4d42be28ce5b4d3d913115fa165be6e3.pdf

National Conference for Community and Justice. (2022). Colorism. https://www.nccj.org/colorism-0

Office for Civil Rights. (2021). An overview of exclusionary discipline practices in public schools for the 2017–2018 school year. U.S. Department of Education, 2017–2018 Civil Rights Data Collection (CRDC). https://ocrdata.ed.gov/assets/downloads/crdc-exclusionary-school-discipline.pdf

Office for Civil Rights. (2022). 2017–2018 Civil rights data collection. Sexual violence in k-12 schools. U.S. Department of Education. https://ocrdata.ed.gov/assets/downloads/sexual-violence_updated-December-2022.pdf

Onyeka-Crawford, A., Patrick, K., & Chaudry, N. (2017). Let her learn: Stopping school pushout for girls of color. National Women's Law Center. https://nwlc.org/wp-content/uploads/2017/04/final_nwlc_Gates_GirlsofColor.pdf

Physicians for a National Health Program. (2021). Black, Hispanic children, youth rarely get help for mental health problems. www.sciencedaily.com/ releases/2016/08/160812132708.htm

Rosario, R. J., Minor, I., & Rogers, L. O. (2021). "Oh, you're pretty for a dark-skinned girl": Black adolescent girls' identities and resistance to colorism. *Journal of Adolescent Research*, 36(5), 501–534. https://doi.org/10.1177/07435584211028218

Sentencing Project. (2022). Incarcerated women and girls. https://www.sentencingproject.org/wp-content/uploads/2016/02/Incarcerated-Women-and-Girls.pdf

Seow, J. (2019). Black girls and dolls navigating race, class, and gender in Toronto. *Girlhood Studies*, 12(2), 48–64. https://doi.org/10.3167/ghs.2019.120205

Stokes, M., Hope, E., Cryer-Coupet, Q., & Elliot, E. (2020). Black girl blues: The roles of racial socialization, gendered racial socialization, and racial identity on depressive symptoms among Black girls. *Journal of Youth and Adolescence*, 49(11), 2175–2189. https://doi.org/10.1007/s10964-020-01317-8

Stracqualursi, V. (2022). US House passes CROWN Act that would ban race-based hair discrimination. CNN. https://www.cnn.com/2022/03/18/politics/house-vote-crown-act/index.html

The National Center on Violence Against Women in the Black Community. (2022). Black women and sexual assault. https://ujimacommunity.org/wp-content/uploads/2022/12/Black-Women-and-Sexual-Assault-Fact-Sheet-Ujima-2021.pdf

Thompson, M. K. (2022). Sexual exploitation and the adultified Black girl. *St. John's Law Review*, 94(4), 971–988. https://scholarship.law.stjohns.edu/cgi/viewcontent.cgi?article=7184&context=lawreview

Tong, R. (2001). Feminist theory. *International Encyclopedia of the Social & Behavioral Sciences*, 5484–5491. doi.org/10.1016/B0-08-043076-7/03945-0

Varlas, L. (2019). Reclaiming Black girlhood with hand games. Association for Supervision and Curriculum Development (ASCD). https://www.ascd.org/el/articles/reclaiming-black-girlhood-with-hand-games

Walker, R., Francis, D., Brody, G., Simons, R., Cutrona, C., & Gibbons, F. (2016, May 3). A longitudinal study of racial discrimination and risk for death ideation in African American youth. *Suicide and Life-Threatening Behavior*, 47(1), 86–102. https://doi-org.libproxy1.usc.edu/10.1111/sltb.12251

Whitaker, A., Torres-Guillen, S., Morton, M., Jordan, H., Coyle, S., Mann, A., & Sun, W. L. (2019). Cops and no counselors: How the lack of school mental health is harming students. American Civil Liberties Union. https://www.aclu.org/sites/default/files/field_document/030419-acluschooldisciplinereport.pdf

Zentangle. (n.d.). https://zentangle.com/pages/what-is-the-zentangle-method

Sand Tray Prompts for Black Girls

Create a sand tray showing a time you felt empowered. Create another tray that shows a time you felt disempowered.

Show a time you felt someone treated you differently because of how you look

Create a sand tray showing what empowerment means to you

Create a scene showing a difficult situation you had with a peer at school

Create a scene showing a difficult situation you had with a teacher or other school official

Create a sand tray that shows how you feel about your racial identity

Create a sand tray that shows a time you dealt with racism, prejudice or discrimination

BMH Connect

mylemarks

Terms of Use

<u>Thank you for your purchase! Please read the Terms of Use before you proceed.</u>

By purchasing this resource, you are agreeing that the contents are the property of Mylemarks LLC and BMH Connect licensed to you as a single user. To learn more about Mylemarks' licensing options, please visit: https://www.mylemarks.com/mylemarks-licensing-options.html. Mylemarks LLC and BMH Connect retain the copyright and reserve all rights to this product.

YOU MAY:

- Use this item with clients/students/small groups or for your own personal use and clients on your caseload only.
- Reference this product in blog posts, social media posts, at seminars, professional development workshops, or other such venues PROVIDED there is both credit given to Mylemarks LLC and BMH Connect and links provided to www.mylemarks.com and https://www.bmhconnect.com/.

YOU MAY NOT:

- Claim this work as your own, alter the files in any way, or remove/attempt to remove the copyright/watermarks.
- Extract any images from this file. All images are copyrighted by Mylemarks LLC.
- Post this document for sale or free elsewhere on the internet or in person including making the document accessible on social media platforms, shared drives, or additional places in which printed or digital copies can be accessed by unlicensed parties.
- Make copies of this item to share physically or electronically with others without the purchase of an additional license. This is strictly forbidden and is a violation of the Terms of Use, along with copyright law. Please direct interested parties to www.mylemarks.com to purchase a copy of their own.
- Obtain this product through any of the channels listed above.

If you encounter an issue with your file, notice an error, or are in any way experiencing a problem, please contact hello@mylemarks.com and we will be more than happy to help you out!

My Beautiful Crown

Hair is very important in the Black community, with a lot of time and money being invested in hairstyles and hair maintenance. However, the prevalence of hair discrimination in schools and in public places prevents Black children from fully embracing their crowns. All around the world, Black children have been expelled and disciplined for hairstyles like afros, braids, and dreadlocks. They have also experienced microaggressions and damaging comments from others related to their hair texture or style often continuing into adolescence and adulthood. This activity and discussion is designed to help Black children embrace their hair choices while acknowledging the discrimination and prejudice that might occur for doing so.

Set Up

This card deck contains 4 full page characters with varying skin tones. Prior to printing, the child can identify the skin tone that best represents them to use for this activity. 36 *My Beautiful Crown* discussion cards are included, requiring printing and cutting. For best results, it is recommended to print in high quality, on card stock, and laminate, if possible, for prolonged use. *If you would like the back graphic design on each card, then the card pages should be printed double-sided starting on page 8. It is recommended to conduct a test print to ensure proper formatting and orientation. Cards are designed to print as traditional playing cards. Due to differences in printer functions, Mylemarks is unable to provide support if there are printing issues. To print cards without the back design, you can print the card pages Even Pages only, single-sided, starting on page 8.

How To Use

The *My Beautiful Crown* activity is designed to be used to create a poster board collage. Once the child chooses a character, the image is cut out and posted onto the board. The child is then able to design a hairstyle that best represents them. They are able to use pencils, crayons, markers, or paint to draw their hair or use objects and other materials to design their hair on the board. Some suggested materials include yarn, buttons, cotton balls, pom pom balls, macaroni, and construction paper.

For the rest of the collage, the client will surround their image with positive words they feel best describes themselves and their hair (texture, color, etc.). It is recommended to provide a diverse collection of magazines for client use in developing their collage. Clients can extract words or images to add to their collage. Below is a list of additional hair descriptor words that they might use:

Luxurious, Kinky, Curly, Coily, Bouncy, Shiny, Soft, Healthy, Beautiful, Natural, Unique, Exciting, Free, Full, Fabulous, Wavy, Fine, Coarse, Short, Long, Wild, Thick, Sleek

The discussion cards are designed to be a supplemental tool while the activity is being completed. The child is able to answer questions and share about their unique experiences with their hair.

My Beautiful Crown

Have you ever heard of
the term "good hair"?
If so, where?

My Beautiful Crown

What does
"good hair"
mean to you?

My Beautiful Crown

Have you ever been
upset or disappointed
about how your hair
turned out?

My Beautiful Crown

Has anyone ever made fun
of you because of how your
hair was styled?

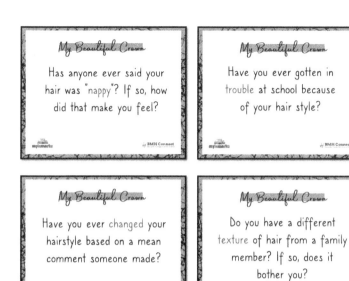

My Beautiful Crown

Has anyone ever said your hair was "nappy"? If so, how did that make you feel?

mylemarks — BMH Connect

My Beautiful Crown

Have you ever gotten in trouble at school because of your hair style?

mylemarks — BMH Connect

My Beautiful Crown

Have you ever changed your hairstyle based on a mean comment someone made?

mylemarks — BMH Connect

My Beautiful Crown

Do you have a different texture of hair from a family member? If so, does it bother you?

mylemarks — BMH Connect

My Beautiful Crown

What's the longest time you've had to sit to get your hair done?

My Beautiful Crown

Have you ever gotten a relaxer? If so, how old were you?

My Beautiful Crown

Has anyone ever made fun of you for wearing your natural hair?

My Beautiful Crown

Has anyone ever made fun of you for wearing hair extensions or "weave"?

My Beautiful Crown

Has anyone ever touched your
hair without your permission?
How did you feel?
How did you respond?

mylemarks · BMH Connect

My Beautiful Crown

Have you ever been accidentally
burned while getting your hair
done? Either from a perm, curling
iron, or something else?

mylemarks · BMH Connect

My Beautiful Crown

Has anyone ever said
something mean about
your edges?

mylemarks · BMH Connect

My Beautiful Crown

Have you ever had a hairstyle
that damaged your hair or
caused it to fall out?

mylemarks · BMH Connect

My Beautiful Crown

Have you ever changed your
hairstyle to cover up or fix a hair
accident (e.g. bald spot, edges
missing, etc.)?

mylemarks   BMH Connect

My Beautiful Crown

Have you ever changed the
way you wore your hair to
be more accepted?

mylemarks   BMH Connect

My Beautiful Crown

Have you ever changed
the way you wore your hair
to feel prettier?

mylemarks   BMH Connect

My Beautiful Crown

Who typically does your
hair, and where do you
usually get it done?

mylemarks   BMH Connect

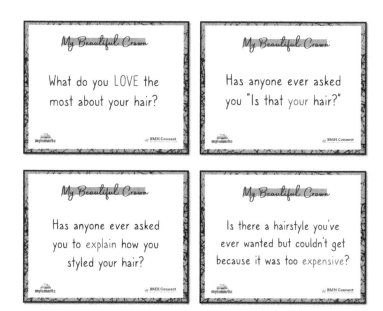

My Beautiful Crown

What do you LOVE the
most about your hair?

mylemarks   BMH Connect

My Beautiful Crown

Has anyone ever asked
you "Is that your hair?"

mylemarks   BMH Connect

My Beautiful Crown

Has anyone ever asked
you to explain how you
styled your hair?

mylemarks   BMH Connect

My Beautiful Crown

Is there a hairstyle you've
ever wanted but couldn't get
because it was too expensive?

mylemarks   BMH Connect

My Beautiful Crown

What are some of your favorite hair accessories?

My Beautiful Crown

Would you change the way you wore your hair for an important meeting?
If so, why?

My Beautiful Crown

Have you ever avoided doing something because of your hair style (e.g. swimming, working out, etc.)?

My Beautiful Crown

Have you ever avoided going somewhere because your hair wasn't done?

My Beautiful Crown

Have you ever avoided or tried to avoid going somewhere because you didn't like how your hair looked?

My Beautiful Crown

Have you ever had to sleep in an uncomfortable position because of the way your hair was styled?

My Beautiful Crown

Have you ever wished you had different type of hair? Color, texture, length, etc.?

My Beautiful Crown

What's the nicest compliment you've received about your hair?

My Beautiful Crown

What's the meanest comment you've received about your hair?

My Beautiful Crown

Is your hair an important part of your identity?

My Beautiful Crown

What three words would you use to describe your hair?

My Beautiful Crown

Is there a hairstyle you've ever wanted but didn't get because of what others would say?

Zentangle Affirmations

Use the area below to create a zentangle with 3-4 sections. Use a different pattern/symbol in each section. Then, use the next page to pick an affirmation for each symbol!

Symbol	Affirmation

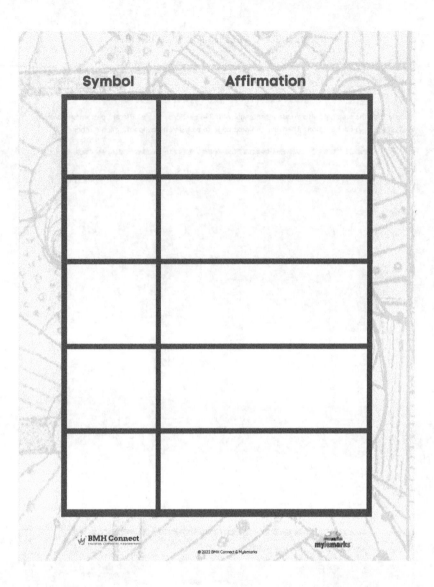

Black Students Matter

Appendix D   Beaded Mosaics

Beaded Mosaics

This art activity uses beads to create a mosaic picture to empower Black girls. Beads in the African culture have historically been used in ceremonies to communicate wealth and social status and for fashion (Durosomo, n.d.). It has even been seen as an act of resistance to the status quo of Europeanized values of beauty (Durosomo, n.d.). Use the following materials to create your mosaic:

Required Materials:

An assortment of hair beads, medium-sized canvas, craft glue (hot glue gun if child is older), and mosaic handout

Instructions:

Pick a mosaic handout and glue it onto the canvas. Then use the beads of your choosing to glue onto the handout to create a mosaic. You are welcome to add a quote or affirmation to your mosaic if you'd like.

BMH Connect   mylemarks

Reference: Durosomo, D. (n.d.). Reclaiming tradition: How hair beads connect us to our future. OkayAfrica.
https://www.okayafrica.com/hair-beads-history-african-black-beauty-hair-jewelry-fulani-braids-twists-solange-floella-benjamin/

Black Students Matter

Appendix E   Slap Out of It

This is a cognitive behavioral play therapy and art therapy activity to help manage negative thoughts. You will make slap bracelets that have positive thoughts or statements that can help you with thought replacing.

Required Materials:

Blank slap bracelets, markers

Instructions:

Pick a slap bracelet and think of a negative thought you have about yourself or that someone has said about you. Then turn that negative thought into a positive one!

For example, someone may have said you were dumb. You can turn that into a positive statement like "I am smart". Decorate the front of the bracelet however you want, then on the inside, write that positive statement "I am smart".

When you wear your bracelet, if you start to think you are dumb, you can take off your bracelet and remind yourself you are smart. Then remember to slap the bracelet back on as a reminder to replace negative thoughts with positive ones.

6

Play Therapy to Encourage Social-Emotional Expression in Black Boys

Black boys, like a lot of American boys, are socialized to be tough and sup-press their emotions. As a result, Black boys often struggle with expressing their emotions and needs. In turn, this results in an explosion of emotions that are often exhibited as hyperactivity, aggression, and defiance. A lack of understanding of the cultural factors that condition Black boys to act tough in the face of adversity has resulted in the overuse of diagnoses such as oppo-sitional defiant disorder (ODD), conduct disorder, and attention deficit hy-peractivity disorder (ADHD), as well as an overuse of medication to suppress behaviors that caregivers and teachers struggle to manage. Additionally, Black boys are dying from suicide at alarming rates, which drives home the impor-tance of accurately assessing and identifying mental distress in Black boys. The recent suicide of entertainer tWitch showed that even successful Black men with assumed accessibility to mental health services, still are struggling in silence. His unfortunate death highlights the need for adults to help Black boys learn the importance of emotional expression and aid in eliminating toxic masculinity among Black boys.

School social workers are in the perfect position to build strong ther-apeutic relationships with Black boys to help them address mental health issues stemming from race-based stress and trauma. The use of game play, sand tray, and music therapy interventions is helpful to engage Black boys in individual and group play therapy so they can learn healthy emotional expression and regulation. As a result, school social workers can offer Black boys a safe place to explore, be themselves, and discover new ways to deal with racial stressors.

Black Students Matter. April D. Duncan, Oxford University Press. © Oxford University Press 2024.
DOI: 10.1093/oso/9780197669266.003.0007

Mental Health and Black Boys

Black boys are silently experiencing a mental health crisis, as their moods and behaviors are often misdiagnosed. Black boys are more likely to be diagnosed with conduct disorder than are boys of other racial backgrounds (Barbarin et al., 2019). Additionally, low-income Black boys have lower levels of self-regulation (Barbarin et al., 2019). Black boys are over diagnosed with externalizing disorders like conduct and attention deficit disorders, when these could be signs of depression instead (Holliday-Moore, 2019). There are several factors to consider when discussing mental health among Black boys. An important factor to consider when assessing the overall self-image of Black boys is how they are depicted in the media. The media tend to project negative images of Black males, who are often depicted as ignorant, violent, and criminal (Hewitt, 2017). Other boxes Black boys are placed in, both in the media and within their own communities, are being athletes or rappers, which limits the full range of opportunities Black boys can explore as careers when they are older. In addition to these stereotypical societal images, Black boys are faced with constant reminders that their identity is perceived as a threat. It could be the nonverbal behaviors that teachers show whenever a Black child reacts, such as thinking that a child will become aggressive toward them even though they have no history of aggressive or violent behaviors. This communicates to Black boys that they are a threat. In turn, this can cause Black boys to feel invisible. This invalidation can lead to them feeling that their identity is not important or nonexistent, placing them at a higher risk for suicidal thoughts and behaviors.

Black Boys and Suicide

Black boys who believe they are unimportant or unseen are at a higher risk for suicidality. Across their lifespans, Black boys are experiencing an alarming rise in suicidal thoughts and behaviors. Black Boys, particularly between the ages of 5 and 11 years have experienced an increase in the rate of suicide deaths (Lindsey et al., 2019). From 1991 to 2017, injuries from a suicide attempt increased almost 122% for Black boys, which may suggest that Black males are engaging in more lethal means when they are attempting suicide (Congressional Black Caucus, 2019). Self- reported attempts have increased 73% for Black males over the past 25 years (Congressional Black Caucus, 2019). And while self-reported suicidal thoughts and plans have decreased for Black children, we need to examine why Black boys may be going straight to attempts without an expression of intent. One theory to explore is the lack of self-regulation skills in Black boy. If a child does not have self-regulation skills, it is likely they will impulsively hurt themselves when dealing with high levels of race-based stress.

Another theory to explore in examining the rising rates of suicide in Black boys is the cultural act of emotional suppression. Black boys are often encouraged not to cry, to be tough and to "be a big boy." High rates of toxic masculinity may also contribute to Black boys jumping to lethal means of suicide in such large numbers. Also, a lack of healthy coping skills to deal with high levels of racial discrimination may result in Black boys engaging in lethal means of suicide as an alternative means for coping. Black boys endure stressors of gender biases and racial biases that are associated with their identity, which may result in poor interpersonal relationships and can hinder healthy development and self-regulation.

Socialization and Black Boys

Black boys are socialized differently than Black girls. In the Black community, Black boys are often given more information about ways to behave and respond in society due to negative stereotypes that view them as threatening. As a result, the racial socialization messages employed by Black caregivers are less positive and more focused on the reality of the negative experiences Black boys will encounter. Likewise, parenting practices may be less nurturing toward Black boys to toughen them up to deal with the harsh treatment they will undoubtedly encounter. These decisions to prepare Black boys for their reality are important, but they also reinforce toxic masculinity early, which prevents the encouragement of explorative play and emotional expression.

Racial Socialization Messages

Gender differences exist in how racial socialization messages are communicated to Black children. *Racial socialization messages* are the ideas and beliefs communicated to Black children from within their families (Stokes et al., 2020). Black boys are often told more about racial barriers, egalitarianism, and negative stereotypes (Arshanapally et al., 2018). In contrast, Black girls tend to get more messages about racial pride, like "Black Girl Magic." Attempts have been made to instill racial pride in Black boys with terms like "Black Boy Joy," yet they do not have the same marketing effect as the "Black Girl Magic" movement that includes merchandise, books, and conferences. Black boys have been found to have higher racial socialization scores than Black girls while also reporting more frequent sad moods and greater levels of hopelessness (Arshanapally et al., 2018). This communicates that Black boys who are more socialized to the realities of racial stressors are less equipped to cognitively process and developmentally cope with this information. Additionally, it highlights how racial socialization in Black boys can also be a risk factor for suicidality. Therefore, school social workers should be cognizant of the mental effects of racial stressors on Black boys and equip them with healthy coping skills.

Parenting Practices

Working with caregivers to teach them ways that they can show nurturance to their sons will be a key part of promoting social-emotional expression in Black boys. In the Black community, Black boys are often denied as much nurturance and affection as Black girls, to keep from "babying them." Studies found that low-income mothers are more likely to show nurturance to girls than boys (McWayne et al., 2020). Even Black teachers may exhibit implicit bias in their treatment of Black boys in connection with the belief that Black boys need "tough love." A study conducted at the Yale Child Study Center found Black teachers held Black students to a higher standard than White students and rated their behavior as more severe (Turner, 2016). As a result, Black boys are constantly in environments that are tough on them, with very few providing nurturing spaces to allow Black boys to be soft and vulnerable. If Black boys are being raised without physical affection, verbal affirmation, and encouragement, it could have negative consequences on their social-emotional, cognitive, and social development.

Toxic Masculinity

"Masculinity" refers to the attitudes, behaviors, beliefs, and roles that are associated with and created by our society about what it means to male (Hewitt, 2017). It is important to note that masculinity is defined by the culture in which it exists. Cultures define the norms about how males should act and these norms can vary. In the United States, boys of all races are socialized to be independent, strive for high status, display toughness, and hide emotions (Hewitt, 2017). When we add the additional layer of race, it creates an intersection for Black boys that serves as an additional barrier to emotional expression. Because of stereotypes, Black boys are conditioned to be tough and suppress their emotions. This socialization process handicaps Black boys because they tend to struggle with how they express, label, or identify their feelings. As a result, Black boys exhibit higher restrictive emotionality, which often presents as a containment of emotions, limited emotional expression or the lack of acknowledgment of emotions.

In clinical practice, Black boys may often state that nothing scares them or struggle with identifying things that make them feel sad. Research has found an association of high emotional restrictions with more depressive symptoms in Black men 20–30 years old (Hammond, 2012). Therefore, it is key to encourage emotional expression in Black boys at an early age. Black boys and men often cope with experiences of oppression by adopting an exaggerated form of masculinity, or something that we would call a "cool pose." A cool pose is often manifested by a tough mannerisms or postures to show that you're in control despite the daily navigation of racial trauma stressors (Hewitt, 2017). I remember a 4-year old boy walking around the therapeutic preschool with his chest puffed out and arms held out to his side. He walked around the room in this manner saying, "I'm a thug." This coping mechanism can directly affect the outcomes of healthy relationships as Black boys and men have with their partners. If they do not learn the skill of social-emotional expression at an early age, it could hinder their ability to effectively communicate their wants and needs in interpersonal and romantic relationships throughout their lifespan.

In Black boys, this block of emotional expression often occurs at an early age, controlled through the toys they can and cannot play with. In the Black community, Black boys are often discouraged from engaging in play that may be deemed as feminine, such as playing with dolls and dollhouses or using toy kitchen sets. Homosexuality is still a difficult thing to accept in the Black community. These "feminine" toys are often stereotyped as only being appropriate for girls, and if Black boys are using them, they are often perceived as gay by their family members and other members in the community. There are no correlations between the toys used by children and their sexual orientation or gender identity. However, it is important to be aware of this misconception because it restricts Black boys from the therapeutic benefits of play to help them express themselves in healthy ways. Black boys are constantly interacting with environments and systems that reject them, both physically and emotionally. Therefore, Black boys, more than any other demographic, need play to heal in a safe and natural way.

Tyrese is a 6-year-old Black boy who likes to play with the dolls in the playroom. One day after session, the child's father asks to speak to me. He expresses that he doesn't like his son playing with dolls and would like me to stop allowing the child to play with dolls in their session. I communicated a respect for the father's opinion, then explained the benefits of doll play for the child. However, the father was adamant about the child discontinuing the play. I validated their concern but ultimately shared that I try not to allow parents to dictate what toys are used in session. Allowing parents to control the toys used in the playroom, especially in CCPT, signals to the child that their parent is in control, even when they are not physically present.

In this scenario, where a caregiver is still strongly against the toys the child plays in session, the school social worker is encouraged to explain that the playroom is a safe place for all kids to explore and play with any toys they are naturally drawn toward. It is also important to communicate respect for the parent's opinion and the cultural norms around certain toys for Black boys. The counselor should then follow-up by explaining the importance of protecting that space from outside influence, including the therapist's own values and beliefs, so the child can benefit from an environment where they are not judged or told what to do. The therapist can also explain they will not use any directive activities that involve dolls or the dollhouse, but if the child chooses to play with dolls during any nondirective play, they will not place any limits on that play. The therapist can also explain how Tyrese playing with a kitchen set or dolls is effective in teaching important life skills he will need when he is older and has his own family.

Stereotypes in Black Boys

Adultification bias in Black boys foists Black adult stereotypes onto Black boys and drives the disciplinary actions utilized by teachers and school administrators. Like Black girls, Black boys are often disciplined for subjective behaviors like disrespect, defiance, or noisiness, while White boys are more likely to be disciplined for observable and concrete violations such as fighting, smoking, or obscenity (McGill Johnson & Godsil, n.d.). This can lead administrators to issue harsher discipline to Black boys who are perceived as disruptive, dangerous, and difficult (Haight et al., 2014). These adjectives to describe the behaviors of Black boys are open for interpretation, drive disciplinary actions for Black boys, and further reinforce the preschool-to-prison pipeline. Many of these subjective interpretations of behavior are rooted in stereotypes of Black boys and men.

Sambo

The Sambo stereotype depicts a docile, simple-minded Black man who is lazy and reliant on his master for direction (Green, 2023). School officials often form invalid assumptions about a Black child, such as believing them unable to obtain certain resources or thinking that they may not have a father in their life. And although a teacher may not realize the biases they are presenting through their language and behavior, a student notices. Black boys in schools also experience lower expectations from teachers, shown through giving Black males less direct instruction, paying less personal attention to them in academic situations, calling on Black boys less often, failing to give feedback, and demanding less work and effort from Black boys compared to other students (Bailey, 2003). In teachers, "White stereotype threat," or the fear of being seen as racist, is another way that the Sambo stereotype is reinforced in schools. This threat is exhibited when White teachers undermine their students' educational advancement because of their fear in being seen as racist (McGill Johnson & Godsil, n.d.). For example, they may recognize that a Black child is more successful with a Black teacher, but may refrain from moving that child so they do not appear to be racist. As a result, Black boys are often afforded less opportunities to excel academically.

Savage

The Savage stereotype was introduced in early silent movies during the 1900s, which painted Black men as violent, mentally inferior, and ape-like (Green, 2023). Black boys are often stereotyped as violent, pitiable, ignorant, and criminal in the media, which contributes to poor self-image (DeGruy, 2017). Teachers often see Black males as intimidating and treat them worse than they do other students (Hernadez Sheets, 1996). When school officials unconsciously react negatively to Black boys or show discomfort through nonverbal behaviors, this can lead to actual or misconstrued behavioral problems in that student. This behavior may be misconstrued because the bias that the school official has developed about that child stems from the stereotypes of Black boys being "savages," which may cause teachers to misperceive and mislabel

Black boys' behaviors as violent or aggressive. This fear could cause teachers to distance themselves emotionally or even withhold affirmations and affection from Black boys. Poor relationships with teachers deprive Black boys of the opportunity to learn self-regulation skills, which is necessary to decrease impulsive reactions to racial stressors that lead to school disciplinary actions.

Jim Crow

The Jim Crow stereotype is based on the blackface minstrel shows of the early 19th century, which depicts the Black man as an entertaining, wisecracking, and dancing buffoon (Green, 2023). This stereotype is reinforced in Black boys when people assume they will pursue careers that entertain others, such as athletes and rappers. It perpetuates the idea that Black boys are not smart and that their paths to success are only through the entertainment industry or sports. With a lack of cultural competence, it is possibly teachers may also subconsciously rely on stereotypical ideas of Black males to interpret and manage behavior (Blake et al., 2011). If a Black boy is goofing off with peers, that behavior may be labeled as the child being a "class clown" or "disruptive," again leading to high rates of unjustified, subjective discipline in Black boys. Black boys are often expected to have behaviors beyond their developmental age, with less affordance of mistakes for being a child. Studies have found that Black boys can be seen as five times older than their age and are often misperceived as being older in relation to peers, less innocent, and hence more culpable for their actions (Goff et al., 2014). Adultification bias results in viewing Black boys as more mature, so their behaviors are often judged as being "immature" and punished more severely than they are in White boys.

Adultification Bias and Black Boys

For Black boys, adultification bias can result in violent reactions to their perceived behaviors. Police officers were found to consistently overestimate the age of Black adolescent felony suspects by approximately 4.5 years (Epstein et al., n.d.). This is evident in the behaviors of police officers towards Black boys. The death of Tamir Rice, a 12-year-old boy killed by police in Cleveland, Ohio, for playing with a toy gun, highlights this reality that many Black students and families across the country face. As a result, Black boys have a heightened level of hypervigilance and awareness when they are outside of their homes. Racial socialization plays a key role in how Black boys present as paranoid or overreactive. At an early age, Black boys are informed

Black Students Matter

about how others may perceive them and are told of the possible harm that could come to them. They also see it for themselves, which is evident in the poem written by a young boy named Antwon Rose in 2016. He was 15 years old when he wrote "I Am Not What You Think" (Barjas, 2018).

I am confused and afraid
I wonder what path I will take
I hear that there's only two ways out
I see mothers bury their sons
I want my mom to never feel that pain
I am confused and afraid
I pretend all is fine
I feel like I'm suffocating
I touch nothing so I believe all is fine
I worry that it isn't, though
I cry no more
I am confused and afraid
I understand people believe I'm just a statistic
I say to them I'm different
I dream of life getting easier
I try my best to make my dream true
I hope that it does
I am confused and afraid

Two years later, on June 19th 2018, 17-year-old Antwon died from three gunshots from a police officer when he was pulled over in a car he was riding in with friends. This child's biggest fear came true. Although Black boys may struggle with communicating fear or sadness, it exists and is often related to their safety as they navigate different environments. This is important to re-member when working with Black boys who may not always have the words to express their feelings, like dear Antwon did. That does not mean they do not have those feelings; it means they do not have a safe outlet to express them as they navigate systems that continue to oppress them.

Systemic Racial Stressors in Black Boys

Racial trauma effects appear to affect Black boys in ways that also leave them void of healthy coping skills for the management of these events. Studies have found that Black boys who experience perceived racial discrimination show significant harmful effects on their mental health decades later, including anxiety and depression (Assari et al., 2017). Some risk factors for racial trauma in Black boys include being younger, being male, and having a lower socioeconomic status (SES). Studies show that young Black males and youth with lower SES also are at a higher risk of receiving or experiencing racial discrimination, specifically in middle and high school (McNeil Smith & Fincham, 2016). There are many factors to consider that contribute to racial trauma stressors in Black males. These include community violence, the juvenile justice system, adverse police contact, and racial disparities in school discipline. These *adverse childhood events* (ACEs) are often overlooked when assessing the mental health needs of Black boys. Black boys are dealing with layers of racial stressors as they navigate stereotypes that exist in the community, and these stereotypes taint the lens that is used to view the behaviors of Black boys in schools, their communities, and sometimes within their own families.

Community Violence

In 2019, 77% of Black homicides were Black males (Violence Policy Center, 2022). Therefore, school social workers have a high probability of working with Black boys who have lost someone that they know to some type of community violence. In working with Black boys, it is likely that they may have lost a loved one to violence and that their grief probably isn't even acknowledged or treated. Add in levels of mistrust, and school social workers and educators may not be privy to the student either being a victim of violence or losing a loved one to violence. Recognizing a change in the students' behavior, as well as identifying shifts in their play behavior in play sessions, can provide alternative ways to identifying signs of grief in students. Being aware of this is important because untreated grief may be the root cause of mental and behavioral disturbances in Black boys.

Also, community violence exposure is related to maladaptive coping skills. Youth who are exposed to community violence are at an increased risk for abusing alcohol, marijuana, and tobacco (Tache et al., 2020). It will be important for school social workers to acknowledge this racial stressor in Black boys that may impact their mental health and to equip them with healthy coping skills that also help them process their grief respectfully and in ways that relate to their culture. (Chapter 7 explores ways to support grieving Black youth in more detail.) There are long-term effects of childhood exposure to high levels of violence. Community violence, financial hardships, and familial stress have been found to serve as barriers to emergence into adulthood for low-poverty Black youth (Patton et al., 2016). School social workers can benefit from being mindful of any violence happening to that student or a loved one or their exposure to violence in the media that may contribute to higher levels of hypervigilance, anxiety, and depression in Black boys. Another way to identify community violence as a risk factor for suicidality in a Black student is to include a suicide risk assessment in intake as a way to be proactive in addressing suicidality risk in Black boys.

School Discipline

As we explore factors contributing to racial stressors in Black boys, it is important to acknowledge the racial disparities that exist within school discipline rates. Unfortunately, these disparities begin in early childhood. Black preschoolers accounted for 9.6% of the preschool population in the 2017–2018 school year (Office for Civil Rights, 2021). However, Black preschool boys received suspensions and expulsions at rates that were more than three times their share of total preschool enrollment (Office for Civil Rights, 2021). In that same school year, approximately 34% of preschool Black boys were suspended and 31% were expelled in preschool. In comparison, White preschool boys account for roughly 24% of the preschool enrollment and received about 32% of one or more out-of-school suspensions (Office for Civil Rights, 2021). From an early age, Black boys are shown through discipline that they are not welcome in educational spaces. This may contribute to low self-esteem and self-worth in young Black boys. Biased perceptions of Black boys also place them at risk for not receiving the educational support services needed to be successful in grade and high school.

In my professional experience working in therapeutic preschool, Black boys were often denied Individual Education Plans (IEP) despite being provided documentation of their trauma and aggressive behavior. Earlier in the book, I shared two examples of Black boys who were denied IEP's, despite documented trauma, mental health diagnoses and enrollment in a therapeutic setting. Luckily, both of those children had someone to advocate—and empower their caregivers to also advocate—for the school's incompetence and prevent further harm. However, across the country, young Black boys are being arrested and pushed into the juvenile justice system, sometimes before even starting elementary school.

Unfortunately, these disparities continue throughout the educational lifespan for Black boys. In elementary through high school, Black boys comprise 7% of the school population, but they account for 20% of students who have had one or more in-school suspensions (Office for Civil Rights, 2021). About a quarter of Black boys have had one or more out-of-school suspension and 30% of them have been arrested in schools (Office for Civil Rights, 2021). Middle and high school Black males have been found to have a higher risk of experiencing racial discrimination from their peers and their teachers (McNeil Smith & Fincham, 2016). This may contribute to negative thoughts and feelings that then feed into negative behaviors. Another concern is the social disconnection that Black students with high rates of school discipline may experience. If a student is labeled as "bad" or "disruptive," it can cause them to be removed from the classroom or, at times, from social activities and clubs where Black boys can form interpersonal relationships. The denial of this opportunity may cause the Black boy to disconnect from others as they may start to buy into the labels placed on them and further engage in behaviors that could impair interpersonal relationships.

Adverse Police Contact

Eight years old. This is the earliest age at which Black youth have been found to have contact with law enforcement (Jindal et al., 2022). Adverse police contact is defined by the physical and emotional harm resulting from a young person's interaction with law enforcement or having an incarcerated loved one (St. John et al., 2022). The high levels of law enforcement in schools with Black students increase the probability that they will have a negative and traumatizing experience with a police officer. Grills et al. (2019) stated the following in the 2019 American Civil Liberties Union Report "Cops Not Counselors: How the Lack of School Mental Health Is Harming Students":

> Students of color are more likely to go to a school with a law enforcement officer, more likely to be referred to law enforcement, and more likely to be arrested at school. Research also demonstrates that students who attend schools with high percentages of Black students and students from low-income families are more likely to attend schools with tough security measures like metal detectors, random "contraband" sweeps, security guards, and security cameras, even when controlling for the level of serious misconduct in schools or violence in school neighborhoods. (p. 7)

By time a Black male is 24 years old, it is estimated he will have nine times as many police encounters as an age-matched White youth (Jindal et al.,

2022). Youth report feeling dehumanized and helpless when the police stop, verbally abuse, harass, or physically abuse them or other people (St. John et al., 2022).

In relation to the savage stereotype, Black males are disproportionately stopped and searched by police based on the perceived notion of wrong-doing, which can lead to the development of anxiety and posttraumatic stress disorder (PTSD) (Alves-Bradford et al., 2019). Additionally, a study found a correlation between Black boys and Black people being seen as apes and excessive force against young Black males (McGill Johnson & Godsil, n.d.). Although school resource officers were placed in schools under the guise of protection, that is not true for Black boys. Negative interactions with law enforcement, on and off school grounds, can possibly lead to negative thoughts such as "I'm not good enough," "I'm just criminal," or "I'm a thug." An internalization of these thoughts could cause a child to disengage from school or even drop out before graduation. Black males who have been exposed to police killings through the media have expressed fear of police and concern for their personal safety and mortality around police officers (Smith Lee & Robinson, 2019). Therefore, one can theorize that police officers are harmful to the emotional safety of Black students and are a contributing factor to perceived misbehaviors in Black students who may be exhibiting trauma stressors when around police.

Juvenile Justice System
Police officers assign greater culpability to Black male felony suspects compared to White male suspects (Epstein et al., n.d.); this is an example of how adultification bias presents in the juvenile justice system. Black youth are four times more likely to be detained or committed in juvenile facilities compared to White youth (Sentencing Project, 2021). Another example of adultification bias in the juvenile justice system is the way juvenile offenders are treated in courts. In 2014, Black youth accounted for more than half of the youth transferred to adult court (Thomas, 2018). Black youth, especially males, are not given the same empathy for their actions as White youth, and this discrimination further raises levels of mistrust in Black boys toward schools and the criminal justice system.

Black Boys and Maladaptive Coping Strategies
As a means of coping, Black boys and men use their voices to appear powerful or to demand respect (Assari et al., 2017). You may wonder why

this happens. When anyone, but especially people of color, are put into situations where they're constantly disrespected, then disrespect can often trigger a trauma response. With Black boys, being disrespected is often the trigger for anger and violent behaviors (DeGruy, 2017). If a student is dealing with daily discrimination, racism, and prejudice, they are constantly interacting with environments that are riddled with disrespect. In applying a racial trauma lens, when a Black student is triggered by something like disrespect, their behaviors operate from their brainstems: the student is using his survival brain, which may cause him to either freeze up, fight, or run. This may also be why some children elope from their environment: they are trying to escape that environment because it's too much for them. Therefore, it is essential that school social workers understand how deep of a trigger disrespect can be for a Black child, especially a Black male.

What's even scarier is that approximately 2% of the Black male American population is missing (McGill Johnson & Godsil, n.d.). These boys aren't in school. They're not in the criminal justice system. They're not in the child welfare system. These boys may be living in the streets; most likely, they are alive, but they are disenfranchised from society (McGill Johnson & Godsil, n.d.). We do not know where they are, but we do know that racial trauma contributes to Black boys disengaging with society. Mental health and school professionals must do a better job of identifying signs of distress and providing the appropriate level of support.

Play Therapy with Black Boys

Directive and nondirective play therapy can be used to support social emotional expression in Black boys and ultimately help improve their mental health. This includes the use of sand tray, music play therapy, and game play therapy to encourage social emotional development. This chapter has explored the unique events Black boys experience that contribute to race-based stress and trauma. School social workers have a unique opportunity to use play therapy to provide a safe outlet for Black boys to fully express emotions they may be ashamed of or dissuaded from sharing outside of your playroom. It is important to provide a nonjudgmental stance when applying a racial trauma lens to the behaviors and emotions that may arise in play therapy sessions.

There are several toys and items that school social workers should have in their playroom when working with Black boys. Although it is controversial, baby dolls, toy kitchens, and toy foods are recommended to help Black boys explore nurturance and learn self-help skills in relation to becoming fathers later in life. Another thing to consider are aggressive toys such as a punching bag, nun chucks, toy guns, and toy swords as a way for boys to express and release anger in healthy ways. Music also can be a helpful tool to create a comfortable environment for the student. This also can serve as a tool for rapport-building, along with board and card games such as Uno, Connect 4, and checkers.

When working with Black boys, several play themes may signal emotional distress. The anger and aggression theme may be present through the use of aggressive toys or anger shown in role plays. The school social worker should focus treatment on addressing the root of the anger and helping the student learn healthy coping skills for managing anger and aggression. The grief theme may be present in Black boys who have experienced violence (directly and/or indirectly), who have an incarcerated family member, or who are in the child welfare system. The grief theme may also be present when dealing with high levels of racial stressors, especially if those stressors are within the school walls themselves. School social workers should focus interventions on identifying the grief event to find the best way to effectively address the student's grief. Play-based interventions can then be used to help the student preserve the memories of their loved ones and/or process their grief in safe ways.

A mistrust theme in the playroom may be exhibited through silence or the student refusing to answer questions. The school social worker should display patience and concentrate on building the therapeutic relationship so the child can express themselves openly when they are comfortable. Protection and safety may also be present in play sessions, signaled by using superheroes or community workers. The school social worker should use safety language and play-based activities to help Black boys identify safe places and people in their support system. Last, the student may display the limit and boundaries play theme by testing the limits placed by the therapist. The school social worker should refrain from immediately labeling these behaviors as defiant or oppositional. The student may be testing the therapist to see if they are just another adult who is going to think the worst of them. Again, patience is key. As is communicating to the student that they can make the appropriate decision and praising them when they do so.

Play Therapy Interventions to Support Social-Emotional Expression

Counselors can utilize several play therapy approaches to support Black boys including child-centered play therapy (CCPT), child-centered group play therapy (CCGPT), game play therapy, art therapy, and sand tray therapy. This chapter has explored the unique challenges of Black boys that encourage emotional suppression. These play therapy activities have been created to help promote healthy emotional expression with art, music, and sand tray techniques used to support Black students of all ages. Remember, there is no right or wrong way for students to engage in these interventions; this should be communicated to the student as well. Our goal is to facilitate their emotional expression in a nonjudgmental manner.

Child-Centered Play Therapy and Child-Centered Group Play Therapy

Almost every encounter that Black boys experience limits their freedom and controls them. CCPT and CCGPT with younger Black boys can help provide a safe place where they are in control of their play. The permissiveness allotted through both individual and group nondirective approaches allows Black boys to explore toys that are usually prohibited due to toxic masculinity. The playroom also can present a nonjudgmental, free place for their play to communicate their needs and wants without the pressure of verbalizing them until they are comfortable. School social workers should consider using CCGPT with Black boys with similar experiences to prevent feelings of isolation in the boy's feelings and circumstances. It also can provide a safe place for Black boys to enhance their socialization skills and strengthen interpersonal relationships.

In My Feelings

The In My Feelings activity can be utilized in individual and group play therapy sessions. It is appropriate for students from kindergarten to high school. The materials needed for this activity are the In My Feelings worksheet (Appendix A) and something to color with (crayons, colored pencils, and/or markers). When introducing the activity, talk about how people can have several feelings at the same time. Providing examples may be helpful, especially with younger children. Next, encourage the student to identify a feeling they have and write it on the first line. Then ask them to pick a color to represent that feeling. The student is encouraged to pick as many feelings as they would like. After they identify their feelings, ask the student to pick the feeling they have the most and color that amount on their sneaker. Some students may choose to place colors on a specific part of the shoe, and that is okay. The following questions can be used to promote additional discussion with the student:

1. Which feeling is the strongest? Which one is the smallest?
2. Which feeling do you feel the most often?
3. How do you express each feeling?
4. Are there any feelings that relate to a negative experience at school?
5. Who is someone you feel comfortable sharing these feelings with the most?

My Magnificent Crown

My Magnificent Crown is a poster board art activity appropriate for both individual and group therapy sessions with kindergarten through 6th-grade students. This activity seeks to encourage racial pride and hair pride in Black boys. The materials required are poster board, art materials that can resemble hair (e.g., yarn, pom-pom balls, etc.), scissors, glue, and the Magnificent Crown poster handout (Appendix B). When introducing the activity to the student, explain that it is helpful to explore times when they were treated differently because of their hair and the emotions they experienced at that time. The student is prompted to pick the picture of the boy with the complexion they prefer, then cut and glue that person onto the posterboard. Then the student is encouraged to pick art materials to create the hair texture and style that most resembles their hair. The packet includes discussion cards to help guide the conversation during or after the activity.

My Coping Playlist

My Coping Playlist is a music therapy activity that is appropriate for individual therapy for students in 2nd grade and beyond. The student is given the My Coping Playlist handout (Appendix C) that has categories relating to Black culture. The categories include *entertainment, revival, strong sensation, racial pride*, and *it's a vibe*. Each category has several prompts for students to identify songs that assist in emotional expression. The student is encouraged to find songs that affirm them or remind them of their culture and write them on the handout. After completing the handout, they can also select a few songs they would like to play in session. The student may even start dancing—if so, be sure to join in on the fun!

For younger students, be mindful that the songs they are selecting to play should be censored. Kidz Bop on Youtube is an appropriate outlet for those younger students to play their songs. Allowing older students to play music that features profanity is up to the discretion of the mental health professional. Be mindful that profanity for older students (e.g., junior high and high school) may be a way for the therapist to bond with the student and show how your space is a free place for their emotional expression. They are also encouraged to take the songs from the worksheet to create playlists on their phones and/or tablets, to utilize at times when they may be feeling inadequate, invisible, or not good enough. Follow-up questions for this activity include:

1. Which songs are your favorite?
2. Which songs have happy memories with them? Which songs have sad memories with them?
3. What are sometimes you may need to play one of these playlists?
4. Do you have a favorite artist that helps you feel better when you're feeling down? If so, what makes you feel connected to their music?

Goin' with Tha Flow

Another music play therapy intervention, Goin' with Tha Flow, can be used in individual and group play therapy sessions with students in 4th through 12th grades. This activity can help Black boys expand their emotional vocabulary and learn new coping skills. All that is needed for this activity is the Goin' with Tha Flow handout (Appendix D), which contains a set of emotions and a set of coping skills. The student is then encouraged to select 1–2 words from each list to create a rap. They can use other words outside of those provided on the worksheet, but the list can be used as a starting point for students who may struggle with identifying both feelings and coping skills. Some suggested follow-up questions for the activity include:

1. What other feelings can you think of that you could incorporate into your rap?
2. What other coping skills can you think of that you could incorporate into your rap?
3. Can you think of some scenarios where these lyrics would be helpful for you?

Sand Tray Therapy for Social-Emotional Expression

There are several benefits to implementing sand tray therapy as a play therapy approach for Black boys to encourage social-emotional expression. First, a sand tray can be helpful for Black boys who struggle with feelings of safety or who may display hypervigilance or anxiety around safety. Sand tray therapy is helpful for clients who have experienced trauma because it can unlock the conscious and unconscious (Homeyer & Sweeney, 2017). Therefore, this can be an especially effective tool for Black boys who struggle with emotional expression because the sand tray can allow them to communicate their feelings, perceptions, and experiences unconsciously. Also, the sand provides a kinesthetic experience and can serve as a self-regulation tool for Black boys. Another benefit to utilizing sand tray play therapy with Black boys is that it creates a necessary therapeutic distance. Students may be dealing with some mistrust in the session. They may be thinking "How do I know that you're a safe person?" "How do I know that I can trust you?" or "How do I know that you're somebody that's not going to judge me like everyone else?" Black boys may benefit from having that distance to help them feel more comfortable in the therapeutic relationships and openly share their feelings.

Additionally, sand tray is good for clients who have poor verbal skills because the miniatures they select and scenes they create become their voice. Finally, this form of therapy with Black boys can help with social-emotional expression because the sand tray cuts through verbalization as a defense because it "confronts the maker" (Homeyer & Sweeney, 2017): the student may be saying one thing, but their sand tray communicates something different. For example, they may say they do not have feelings of sadness, but the creation of sand trays with empty worlds communicates some level of emptiness or depression the student may be knowingly or unknowingly experiencing. Sand tray therapy prompts for Black boys (Appendix E) can be used as a starting point for school counselors to explore race-based experiences by these students. (Be sure to refer to Chapter 2 for recommended sand tray miniatures for implementing the approach with Black students.)

Conclusion

School social workers are in a unique position to develop healthy relationships with Black boys who may experience higher levels of sadness, withdrawal, and perceived burdensome due to high levels of race-based stress and trauma. Play therapy approaches such as music, art, games, and sand trays can be used with Black boys across the lifespan to aid in social-emotional expression. It is important to have patience when working with Black boys. As this chapter highlighted, historical and cultural factors hinder Black boys from feeling safe to openly express their feelings. There may be a lot of sessions where there is minimal to no talking. The therapist should learn to feel comfortable with that silence. The value in the interaction lies in the student being present and connected with the activity, with less of an emphasis on talking. That can go a long way in creating that important therapeutic bond and space to help Black boys feel safe to be and express their authentic selves.

References

Alves-Bradford, J. M., Bailey, R., Durham, M. P., Comer Frolov, L., Gordon-Achebe, K., Malone, P., Nzodom, C., Wallace, A., & Wilson, W. (2019). Stress & trauma toolkit for treating African Americans in a changing political and social environment. American Psychiatric Association. https://www.psychiatry.org/psychiatrists/cultural-competency/education/stress-and-trauma/african-americans

Arshanapally, S., Werner, K., Sartor, C., & Bucholz, K. (2018). The association between racial discrimination and suicidality among African-American adolescents and young adults. *Archives of Suicide Research*, 22(4), 584–595. https://doi-org.libproxy1.usc.edu/10.1080/13811118.2017.1387207

Assari, S., Moazen-Zadeh, E., Caldwell, C., & Zimmerman, M. (2017). Racial discrimination during adolescence predicts mental health deterioration in adulthood: Gender differences among Blacks. *Frontiers in Public Health*, 5, 104–104. https://doi.org/10.3389/fpubh.2017.00104

Bailey, D. F. (2003). Preparing African-American males for postsecondary options. *Journal of Men's Studies*, 12(1), 15–24. https://doi.org/10.3149/jms.1201.15

Barbarin, O. A., Hitti, A., & Copeland-Linder, N. (2019). Behavioral and emotional development of African American boys growing up in risky environments. *Child Development Perspectives*, 13(4), 215–220. https://doi.org/10.1111/cdep.12341

Barjas, J. (2018). Antwon Rose's mother wants everyone to hear this poem. PBS News Hour. https://www.pbs.org/newshour/arts/poetry/antwon-roses-mother-wants-everybody-to-hear-this-poem

Blake, J., Butler, B., Lewis, C., & Darensbourg, A. (2011). Unmasking the inequitable discipline experiences of urban Black girls: Implications for urban educational stakeholders. (Report). *Urban Review*, 43(1), 90–106. https://doi.org/10.1007/s11256-009-0148-8

Congressional Black Caucus. Emergency Task Force on Black Youth Suicide and Mental Health (2019). Ring the alarm: The crisis of Black youth suicide in America. https://watsoncoleman.house.gov/uploadedfiles/full_taskforce_report.pdf

Degruy. J. (2017). *Post traumatic slave syndrome: America's legacy of enduring injury & healing*. Uptown Press.

Epstein, R., Blake, J. J., & Gonzalez, T. (n.d.). Girlhood interrupted: The erasure of Black girls' childhood. Center on Poverty and Inequality, Georgetown Law. https://genderjusticeandopportunity.georgetown.edu/wp-content/uploads/2020/06/girlhood-interrupted.pdf

Goff, P. A., Jackson, M. C., Di Leone, B. A., Culotta, C. M., & DiTomasso, N. A. (2014). The essence of innocence: Consequences of dehumanizing Black children. *Journal of Personality and Social Psychology, 106*(4), 526–545. https://doi.org/10.1037/a0035663

Green, L. (2023). Stereotypes: Negative racial stereotypes and their effect on attitudes towards African Americans. Ferris State University. https://www.ferris.edu/HTMLS/news/jimcrow/links/essays/vcu.htm

Grills, C., Banks, J., Norrington-Sands, K., Jackson, T. R., Steve, S. L., & Clark, M. (2019, October 15). Black child suicide: A report. National Cares Mentoring Movement & the Association of Black Psychologists. https://www.caresmentoring.org/black_child_suicide_report.pdf

Haight, W., Gibson, P., Kayama, M., Marshall, J., & Wilson, R. (2014). An ecological-systems inquiry into racial disproportionalities in out-of-school suspensions from youth, caregiver and educator perspectives. *Children and Youth Services Review, 46*, 128–138. https://doi.org/10.1016/j.childyouth.2014.08.003

Hammond W. P. (2012). Taking it like a man: Masculine role norms as moderators of the racial discrimination-depressive symptoms association among African American men. *American Journal of Public Health, 102*(Suppl 2), S232–S241. https://doi.org/10.2105/AJPH.2011.300485

Hernández Sheets, R. (1996). Urban classroom conflict: Student-teacher perception: Ethnic integrity, solidarity, and resistance. *Urban Review, 28*(2), 165–183. https://doi.org/10.1007/BF02354383

Hewitt, A. A. (2017). Giving voice to the feelings of Black boys. Psychology Today. https://www.psychologytoday.com/us/blog/you-empowered/201705/giving-voice-the-feelings-black-boys

Holliday-Moore, R. (2019). Alarming suicide trends in African American children: An urgent issue. Substance Abuse and Mental Health Services. https://blog.samhsa.gov/2019/07/23/alarming-suicide-trends-in-african-american-children-an-urgent-issue

Jindal, M., Mistry, K. B., Trent, M., McRae, A., & Thornton, R. L. J. (2022). Police exposures and the health and well-being of Black youth in the US: A systematic review. *JAMA Pediatrics,176*(1),78–88. doi:10.1001/jamapediatrics.2021.2929

Lindsey, M., Sheftall, A., Xiao, Y., & Joe, S. (2019). Trends of suicidal behaviors among high school students in the United States: 1991–2017. *Pediatrics, 144*(5), Article e20191912. https://doi-org.libproxy1.usc.edu/10.1542/peds.2019-1912

McGill Johnson, A., & Godsil, R. D. (n.d.). Transforming perception: Black men and boys. American Values Institute. https://equity.ucla.edu/wp-content/uploads/2016/11/Transforming-Perception.pdf

McNeil Smith, S., & Fincham, F. (2016). Racial discrimination experiences among Black youth: A person-centered approach. *Journal of Black Psychology, 42*(4), 300–319. doi.org/10.1177/0095798415573315

McWayne, C., Mattis, J., & Li, L. (2020). Parenting together: Understanding the shared context of positive parenting among low-income Black families. *Journal of Black Psychology*, Article e9579842093165. https://doi.org/10.1177/0095798420931653

Office for Civil Rights. (2021). An overview of exclusionary discipline practices in public schools for the 2017–2018 school year. U.S. Department of Education, 2017–2018

Civil Rights Data Collection (CRDC). https://ocrdata.ed.gov/assets/downloads/crdc-exclusionary-school-discipline.pdf

Patton, D. U., Miller, R. J., Garbarino, J., Gale, A., & Kornfeld, E. (2016). Hardiness scripts: High-achieving African American boys in a Chicago charter school navigating community violence and school. *Journal of Community Psychology, 44*(5), 638–655. https://doi.org/10.1002/jcop.21791

Sentencing Project. (2021). Black disparities in youth incarceration. https://www.sentencingproject.org/wp-content/uploads/2017/09/Black-Disparities-in-Youth-Incarceration.pdf

Smith Lee, J. R., & Robinson, M. A. (2019). "That's my number one fear in life. It's the police": Examining young Black men's exposures to trauma and loss resulting from police violence and police killings. *Journal of Black Psychology, 45*(3), 143–184. https://doi.org/10.1177/0095798419865152

St. John, V. J., Headley, A. M., & Harper, K. (2022). *Reducing adverse police contact would heal wounds for children and their communities.* Child Trends. https://www.childtrends.org/publications/reducing-adverse-police-contact-would-heal-wounds-for-children-and-their-communities

Stokes, M., Hope, E., Cryer-Coupet, Q., & Elliot, E. (2020). Black girl blues: The roles of racial socialization, gendered racial socialization, and racial identity on depressive symptoms among Black girls. *Journal of Youth and Adolescence, 49*(11), 2175–2189. https://doi.org/10.1007/s10964-020-01317-8

Tache, R. M., Lambert, S. F., & Ialongo, N. S. (2020). The role of depressive symptoms in substance use among African American boys exposed to community violence. *Journal of Traumatic Stress, 33*(6), 1039–1047. https://doi.org/10.1002/jts.22566

Thomas, J. (2018). The prosecution of Black youth as adults. Campaign for Youth Justice. https://www.campaignforyouthjustice.org/voices/item/the-prosecution-of-black-youth-as-adults

Turner, C. (2016). Bias isn't a just a police problem, it's a preschool problem. NPR. https://www.npr.org/sections/ed/2016/09/28/495488716/bias-isnt-just-a-police-problem-its-a-preschool-problem

Violence Policy Center. (2022). Black homicide victimization in the United States. An analysis of 2019 homicide data. https://vpc.org/studies/blackhomicide22.pdf

In My Feelings

We can have a lot of feelings at the same time, and sometimes we may not show them because we have been taught they are not good to show. But this is a safe place to explore those feelings! Pick a feeling you're having at the moment and pick a color you feel best represents that feeling. Once you're done, color on the shoe just how much of that feeling you're experiencing right now. Then you can identify another feeling and do the same thing. Repeat until the shoe is colored just the way you like it!

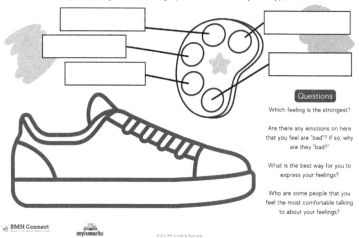

Questions

Which feeling is the strongest?

Are there any emotions on here that you feel are "bad"? If so, why are they "bad?"

What is the best way for you to express your feelings?

Who are some people that you feel the most comfortable talking to about your feelings?

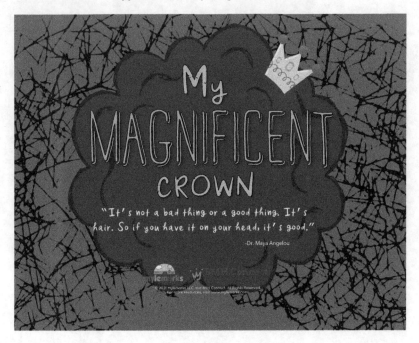

MY MAGNIFICENT CROWN

Terms of Use

Social-Emotional Expression

MY MAGNIFICENT CROWN

Hair is very important in the Black community, with a lot of time and money being invested in hairstyles and hair maintenance. However, the prevalence of hair discrimination in schools and in public places prevents Black children from fully embracing their *crowns*. All around the world, Black children have been expelled and disciplined for hairstyles like afros, braids, and dreadlocks. They have also experienced microaggressions and damaging comments from others related to their hair texture or style, often continuing into adolescence and adulthood. This activity and discussion is designed to help Black children embrace their hair choices while acknowledging the discrimination and prejudice that might occur for doing so.

Set Up

This download contains 4 full page characters with varying skin tones. Prior to printing, the child can identify the skin tone that best represents them to use for this activity. 36 *My Magnificent Crown* discussion cards are included, requiring printing and cutting. For best results, it is recommended to print in high quality, on card stock, and laminate, if possible, for prolonged use. *If you would like the back graphic design on each card, then the card pages should be printed double-sided starting on page 8. It is recommended to conduct a test print to ensure proper formatting and orientation. Cards are designed to print as traditional playing cards. Due to differences in printer functions, Mylemarks is unable to provide support if there are printing issues. To print cards without the back design, you can print the card pages Even Pages only, single-sided, starting on page 8.

How To Use

The *My Magnificent Crown* activity is designed to be used to create a poster-board collage. Once the child chooses a character, the image is cut out and posted onto the board. The child is then able to design a hairstyle that best represents them. They are able to use pencils, crayons, markers, or paint to draw their hair or use objects and other materials to design their hair on the board. Some suggested materials include yarn, buttons, cotton balls, pom pom balls, macaroni, and construction paper.

For the rest of the collage, the client will surround their image with positive words they feel best describes themselves and their hair (texture, color, etc.). It is recommended to provide a diverse collection of magazines for client use in developing their collage. Clients can extract words or images to add to their collage. Below is a list of additional hair descriptor words and styles that they might use:

Fresh, Curly, Short, Waves, Locks, Healthy, Magnificent, Natural, Unique, Exciting, Tight, Messy, Fade, Brushed, Coarse, Short, Long, Wild, Thick, Clean

The discussion cards are designed to be a supplemental tool while the activity is being completed. The child is able to answer questions and share about their unique experiences with their hair.

BMH Connect

MY MAGNIFICENT CROWN

Do you think the term
"good hair" applies to
boys?

 BMH Connect

MY MAGNIFICENT CROWN

Have you ever been upset
or disappointed about how
your hairstyle or cut
turned out?

BMH Connect

MY MAGNIFICENT CROWN

Have you ever wished
you had different type
of hair? Color, texture,
length, etc.?

 BMH Connect

MY MAGNIFICENT CROWN

What's the nicest
compliment you've
received about your hair?

 BMH Connect

MY MAGNIFICENT CROWN

Has anyone ever made fun
of you because of how your
hair was styled or cut?

 w/ BMH Connect

MY MAGNIFICENT CROWN

Have you ever gotten in
trouble at school because
of your hair style?

 w/ BMH Connect

MY MAGNIFICENT CROWN

What do you do to your
hair before you leave the
house?

 w/ BMH Connect

MY MAGNIFICENT CROWN

Has anyone ever touched
your hair without your
permission? How did you feel?
How did you respond?

 w/ BMH Connect

MY MAGNIFICENT CROWN

Has anyone ever messed
up while cutting or styling
your hair?

 mylemarks   BMH Connect

MY MAGNIFICENT CROWN

Has anyone ever said your
hair was "nappy"?
If so, how did that make
you feel?

mylemarks   BMH Connect

MY MAGNIFICENT CROWN

Has anyone ever said
something mean about
your hair style or cut?

mylemarks   BMH Connect

MY MAGNIFICENT CROWN

Is your hair an important
part of your identity?

mylemarks   BMH Connect

Social-Emotional Expression

MY MAGNIFICENT CROWN

Have you ever changed
the way you wore your
hair to be more
accepted?

MY MAGNIFICENT CROWN

Who typically cuts your
hair, and where do you
usually get your haircut?

MY MAGNIFICENT CROWN

What's the meanest
comment you've received
about your hair?

MY MAGNIFICENT CROWN

What three words would you
use to describe your hair?

Black Students Matter

MY MAGNIFICENT CROWN

Have you ever changed your hairstyle based on a mean comment someone made?

BMH Connect

MY MAGNIFICENT CROWN

Do you have a different texture of hair from a family member? If so, does it bother you?

BMH Connect

MY MAGNIFICENT CROWN

Have you ever avoided going somewhere because you didn't like how your hair looked?

BMH Connect

MY MAGNIFICENT CROWN

Is there a hair cut or style you've ever wanted but didn't get because of what others would say?

BMH Connect

Do you style or cut your
hair to impress others?

BMH Connect

MY MAGNIFICENT CROWN

Have you ever clowned
someone because of their
hair cut or style?

BMH Connect

MY MAGNIFICENT CROWN

Have you ever tried to
cut your hair yourself?
How did it turn out?

BMH Connect

MY MAGNIFICENT CROWN

What's the longest you've
ever let your hair grow out?

BMH Connect

MY MAGNIFICENT CROWN

Have you ever had an afro, flat top, dreads, twists, waves, cornrows, fro-hawk, fade, or buzz cut? What do you think of each of those styles?

MY MAGNIFICENT CROWN

What is the experience like for you in the barbershop? What was it like the first time?

MY MAGNIFICENT CROWN

What do you ask for at the barbershop?

MY MAGNIFICENT CROWN

Do you think it's important for boys to care how their hair looks? Why or why not?

Have you ever styled or cut
your hair because you were
influenced by a musician or
someone famous?

 BMH Connect

How long does it take you
to get your hair ready
each day?

 BMH Connect

Would you change the way
you wore your hair for an
important meeting?
If so, why?

 BMH Connect

Has any one ever judged
you because of your hair
style/cut?

 BMH Connect

MY MAGNIFICENT CROWN

Are there certain hair styles or cuts that you are not allowed to get? Why?

mylemarks   BMH Connect

MY MAGNIFICENT CROWN

How do you feel when you get a fresh cut or line up?

mylemarks   BMH Connect

MY MAGNIFICENT CROWN

What do you think is the most popular style for boys now?

mylemarks   BMH Connect

MY MAGNIFICENT CROWN

Do you judge others based on how they choose to style or cut their hair?

mylemarks   BMH Connect

Ultimate Coping Playlist

Make the perfect coping playlist to help you with all the emotions
that come along with being Black in America.

ENTERTAINMENT

A song that stays stuck in your head when you hear it

_____

A song you know all the words to

_____

Your favorite song from a movie

_____

REVIVAL

A song that represents empowerment

_____

A song that you'd listen to fall asleep

_____

A song that gets you hype

_____

STRONG SENSATION

A song that reminds you of a good memory

_____

A song that reminds you of someone you care about

_____

A song that reminds you of someone who cares about you

_____

RACIAL PRIDE

A song that makes you feel proud of your race

_____

A song that encourages you to be who you are

_____

A song that reminds you of your heritage

_____

IT'S A VIBE

A song that matches your vibe when you feel anxious or worried

_____

A song that matches your vibe when you feel annoyed or angry

_____

A song that matches your vibe when you feel sad or afraid

_____

Social-Emotional Expression 301

Goin' With Tha Flow

It can be stressful to deal with racism, prejudice, and discrimination on a daily basis. Use the area below to use at least one emotion and one coping skill to create a hip-hop lyric to help you boss back against race-based stress! You can use your own emotions and coping skills or use the examples below to help you.

EMOTIONS		COPING SKILLS	
Happy	Nervous	Take a walk	Watch a funny show
Sad	Ashamed	Take deep breaths	Hang with friends
Mad	Proud	Sing a song	Count to 10
Scared	Hopeful	Dance it out	Take a time out
Frustrated	Concerned	Talk to a friend	Work out
Disgusted	Encouraged	Read a book	Talk to a parent
Embarrassed	Loved	Take a time out	Color a picture

Appendix E   Sand Tray Prompts for Black Boys

Sand Tray Prompts for Emotional Expression

Pick five emotions, then pick five miniatures to show how you communicate those emotions

Create a sand tray showing your biggest fears

Pick a miniature to represent each person you feel comfortable sharing your emotions with

Create a sand tray showing the happiest time in your life

Create a scene that shows a time you were jealous of someone or jealous about something someone had/owned

Create a scene showing a time you felt embarrassed

Create a scene that shows the healthy ways you can express your feelings

Create a scene that shows the triggers to your anger

Create a scene that shows what you think you need to feel happy

Create a sand tray showing the things you are sad about

BMH Connect

mylemarks

2022 BMH Connect & Mylemarks

Social-Emotional Expression

303

7

Supporting Black Youth Through Grief and Bereavement

In 2022, Sesame Place went viral with a video of Black children trying to get the attention of two of their characters who subsequently walk past them and proceed to hug White children (Lawrence, 2022). Many in the media labeled the incident as racism and the family is even pursuing legal action (Carras, 2022). The incident also serves as an example of the unique grief events Black youth experience that trigger the same feelings as loss through death. At a young age, Black children experience race-based events where they see themselves being treated differently, which can lead to feelings of confusion and embarrassment. It can also affect their self-esteem, and self-worth, which is why it is important for school social workers to be versed in the different experiences of Black children and how they are associated with grief and bereavement.

Black students are not all the same and they have diverse experiences. However, among the numerous grief events that Black students can have are exposure to racism, discrimination, economic insecurity, neighborhood violence, and other adverse childhood experiences like the Sesame Place event. For example, students who live and attend schools in urban communities of color may have higher rates of trauma and traumatic grief because of community violence, discrimination, poverty, and negative experiences with law enforcement (Dutil, 2019). Black students who attend predominantly White schools may have higher rates of exclusion from social groups, clubs, and activities; deal with more microaggressions from peers and teachers; and be exposed to violence in the Black community through the media. It is important that school social workers are educated on traumatic grief in Black students, because these children are likely to experience multiple

Black Students Matter. April D. Duncan, Oxford University Press. © Oxford University Press 2024.
DOI: 10.1093/oso/9780197669266.003.0008

grief events that are often overlooked or misdiagnosed as a mental health disorder due to the high level of disruption these event cause in their daily functioning.

Grief often is associated with losing a loved one to death, but grief can also include other childhood events that illicit the same feelings. Grief events also can include having incarcerated caregivers and being involved in the child welfare system. Play therapy can serve as an effective intervention to help support grieving Black youth. When children experience a grief event, they can feel helpless and powerless. Children in the child welfare system and/or those with incarcerated caregivers may struggle with grief as everyone makes decisions about where they go and with whom. The use of child-centered play therapy (CCPT) can help those students have a place where they have some modicum of control. Additionally, the use of art and music therapy techniques can help students navigate the grief cycle while finding a way to preserve memories of their loved ones and, ultimately, find a way of healing from their grief.

Grief Defined

There are several types of grief to explore, including uncomplicated grief, complicated grief, and traumatic grief. First, *uncomplicated grief* is the "normal" grieving process that individuals experience after a grief event (Zisook & Shear, 2009). "Normal" grieving is defined by the individual, as there is no one way or right way to grieve. So, this grieving process does not hinder the child's development or disrupt their daily functioning. *Complicated grief*, in contrast, includes symptoms of trauma and separation distress and is disruptive to the child's daily functioning (Zisook & Shear, 2009). Behaviors associated with complicated grief include disruptive behaviors in school, difficulty paying attention, or tantruming when separating from a caregiver (Zisook & Shear, 2009). When this grief is overlooked as a contributing factor to the child's behavior, it can be misdiagnosed and treated as other mental health disorders such as attention deficit-hyperactivity disorder (ADHD) or oppositional defiant disorder (ODD). Social workers must be educated on grief reactions to best support children dealing with grief and bereavement. When complicated grief goes unresolved, it can develop into *traumatic grief*, which presents with symptoms associated with posttraumatic stress disorder (PTSD) and/or depression (Zisook & Shear, 2009). When considering grief in Black students, one should also consider *disenfranchised grief* and *polyvictimization*.

Disenfranchised Grief

Like most things with Black students, the emotions associated with a grief event are often dismissed. Sometimes this is unintentional, when adults do not recognize the emotions Black students experience with the grief event or the grief is shown in the students' behavior and is thus mislabeled as misbehavior. Disenfranchised grief is unacknowledged, discouraged, or socially invalidated (Dutil, 2019). An example of disenfranchised grief in Black students includes their reactions to the killing of unarmed Black Americans at the hands of police and other citizens. On social media, in their schools, and even in their communities, the student may hear people saying things like, "They should have listened to the police officers" or "Why would they run away if they're not guilty?" Comments like these often invalidate the grief that students may have. It can also cause the student to feel isolated in their feelings or even alter the relationships they have with teachers and peers who disenfranchise their grief. Another example of disenfranchised grief occurs when deaths are related to substance use or suicide, as these events are perceived as self-induced (Dutil, 2019). Finally, Black students with incarcerated family members may experience disenfranchised grief due to the stigma of incarceration and lack of empathy for the "criminal" adult. (I purposely use quotation marks here to recognize the injustice of mass incarceration in the Black community and how many Black people are locked up for petty or nonviolent crimes or have been jailed because of failure to make bail without being charged for a crime.) School social workers can support grieving Black students through these situations by validating their feelings and giving them a safe, nonjudgmental place in which to express their emotions around the event.

Polyvictimization

Another unique factor in the grieving of Black students is the layers of grief events that can occur simultaneously. *Polyvictimization* occurs when an individual experiences multiple forms of traumatic victimization (Dutil, 2019). For example, if a child loses their parent to death involving a domestic violence situation, they are experiencing several losses at once including the death of a parent, the incarceration of the other parent, and their placement into the child welfare system or with other family members. Black students also experienced polyvictimization at the height of the COVID-19 pandemic. Not only were they dealing with the anxiety, fear, confusion, and deaths caused by the pandemic, but, like most Black Americans, they also had to deal with racist, discriminatory, and prejudicial treatment for wearing the required masks during the pandemic: A poll conducted by the Pew Research Center found 42% of Black Americans worried that others would be suspicious of them if they wore a mask in public (Ruiz et al., 2020). In addition to the pandemic and day-to-day racial stressors, Black students also had to deal with heightened racial tensions associated with protests and calls for justice following the murders of Breonna Taylor and George Floyd. The same poll found Black and Asian Americans were more likely to have adverse experiences related to their race and/or ethnicity during the pandemic. Polyvictimization in Black students may make it difficult for adults to know what event is related to the students' behaviors, but simply acknowledging the negative impacts of grief in Black students is a good starting point because it addresses the root of the behavior as opposed to administering discipline for the behavior.

Grieving Black Youth

Due to systemic and structural racism that limits resources and opportunities in communities of color, Black students may be exposed to higher levels of community violence. This can include living in a neighborhood with high levels of murder, domestic violence, assaults, robberies, and gang violence. However, with the internet and social media, Black students are also exposed to the deaths of individuals who look like them such as Tamir Rice, Mike Brown Jr., Antwon Rose, and Trayvon Martin. Although these murdered children might be unknown to the student, their deaths are equally as impactful and traumatic as if they were known associates. Black students also experience grief through the sudden losses of their favorite hip-hop artists. Simply put, every Black student will experience the grief associated with death even if it is someone they have never met. However, several different grief events are common occurrences in the lives of Black students outside the loss of a loved one through death.

Grief events such as losing a parent to incarceration or entering the child welfare system are often overlooked as significant occurrences in the lives of these students. In response, their behaviors are often misinterpreted as deviant or misattributed to mental health issues. It is key that the school social worker increases their awareness of how these various grief events negatively affect Black youth and trigger the same grief cycle and symptoms as losing a loved one through death. In exploring these grief events, the goal is to help the social worker develop a sharper lens through which to view grief and loss in a different way. The first unique grief event to consider is adverse police contact. Although this may not be considered a loss, there is often a loss of dignity due to the possible shame and embarrassment experienced during that encounter. Second, when a child comes into the child welfare system, they are experiencing multiple losses, such as the loss of their home, their environment, community, and family. Another grief event to consider occurs for children with incarcerated family members. If a caregiver enters the criminal justice system, especially in a one-parent household, that child may also enter the child welfare system or be placed into the care of a family member, which is another loss of community, environment, and home. A final grief event to consider in Black students is the loss of their favorite musicians, as many Black youth often are negatively affected by the death of their favorite artists, especially if that death is sudden. Supporting Black youth through grief and bereavement can be difficult, especially when dealing with higher levels of violence exposure in both their community and family.

Multidimensional Grief Theory and Black Students

Multidimensional grief theory posits that grief is a multidimensional construct and that grief reactions fall into three domains: separation distress, identity distress, and circumstance-related distress (Douglas et al., 2021). *Separation distress* is usually characterized by having feelings of despair or sadness over the permanent separation from the deceased person or the caregiver (Douglas et al., 2021). For child welfare–involved youth, this may also include a desire to be reunited with their caregivers. Another documented form of grief reactions is *circumstance-related distress*, where the student may become preoccupied with details of the death or the loss. These students may also blame themselves for the death, or sometimes even have revenge fantasies (Douglas et al., 2021). For Black youth, this type of distress reaction may be a result of the traumatic death of a loved one or someone in their community, or seeing the death of unarmed Black people via media.

On the other hand, *identity distress* consists of disruptions to a person's sense of self (Douglas et al., 2021). It may also include the student feeling like they're stuck or lost without certain important people in their life, which also may have negative implications on their own future or plans. This may often be the grief reactions associated with community violence or even the death of a favorite hip-hop artist. Black youth may engage in fatalistic behaviors, such as planning their funerals, due to their exposure to high levels of death and foreshortened future (DeGruy, 2017). When we consider the murders of hip-hop artists important to Black youth, this may further exacerbate feelings of a foreshortened future. Seeing the murders of successful role models may cause the Black child to feel hopeless and helpless in their own journey to success and could cause them to feel distressed about their own identity.

Grief Event: Violence

There are racial disparities in both community and family violence for Black children and families. On top of that, the loss of several hip-hop artists that are important in the lives of Black youth puts Black students at a higher risk for untreated grief. Higher levels of exposure to violence creates a heavier allostatic load, where a child's brain is constantly stressed and operating in "survival mode," which increases the likelihood the child will experience and display symptoms of PTSD such as hypervigilance and avoidance (Douglas et al., 2021). Chapters 5 and 6 explored adverse police contact in Black girls and boys. However, it is important to also recognize this as a grief event that is disruptive to the students' functioning. Adverse police contact is linked to several negative outcomes including poor physical health, emotional well-being, and social outcomes (St. John et al., 2022). Students residing in communities with high levels of violence are more likely to encounter law enforcement, and those experience are often negative. Constant negative interactions with law enforcement can lead to distrust in police, psychological strain, heighted emotional distress, and even negative education outcomes (St. John et al., 2022).

Several factors contribute to higher rates of untreated grief in Black children including cultural stressors such as racial discrimination, the stigma around mental health problems, and a lack of access to resources. Along with higher levels of violence exposure, Black students may not have access to the resources needed to treat their grief. Additionally, many school social workers find themselves navigating constant death in their students' communities while also feeling helpless in how to support them. Understanding the dynamics of community violence in the lives of Black youth provides a blueprint for how to adequately support students experiencing high levels of death or violence in their families and communities.

Community Violence

Homicide is the second leading cause of death for Black youth ages 1–14 and the leading cause of death for black youth ages 15–24 (National Center for

Injury Prevention and Control, 2020). Additionally, 8% of children have lost a loved one to firearm violence (Martin et al., 2022). These sobering statistics reflect a history of systemic racism and poverty that has led to high levels of violence in Black communities. Black students also experience violence directly. Black youth are at a higher risk for more harmful forms of violence such as fights with injuries, aggravated assaults, and homicides (Sheats et al., 2018). However, it is important to know that Black and White Americans have the same rates of violence (Alliance for Gun Responsibility, 2022), although there tends to be more media attention and a negative focus on violence in communities of color than in White communities.

The high level of interconnectedness in the Black community can result in grief reactions for the loss of community members, either directly or through exposure via social media. The death of people in their community can have a significant impact on a students' sense of self (Douglas et al., 2022). Identity stress can be higher in Black students because they may start to attribute the high numbers of senseless deaths of people who look like them to mean that they are worthless as well. Therefore, the deaths of individuals the child knows intimately or the high-profile deaths of unarmed Black people should be treated the same, as if that person was directly related to the grieving Black student.

Death of Hip-Hop Artists

Another example of disenfranchised grief for Black students occurs with the deaths of their favorite artists, who often die from drug overdoses or have been murdered. In these cases, society may view these victims as people who made decisions contributing to their deaths, so the student's death is often invalidated. Or, because the student did not personally know the artist, their grief may be overlooked without understanding the loss of connection that the child feels, which is like any other grief event. Very little conversation is held around the loss Black youth experience when their favorite artists die. Over the past four years, Black youth and adults have grieved the loss of rappers such as Nipsey Hussle, Mac Miller, JuiceWRLD, XXXTenancion, Pop Smoke, Young Dolph, and, most recently, Takeoff from the Migos. Adults who are not connected to the music or the child may not attribute behavioral and cognitive changes in the child to grief for their role models. Because these artists often talk about controversial things like drugs, gang life, and violence, this grief may be invalidated or ignored. School social workers working with Black youth should be connected to things that are impactful in their world, including these deaths, as they can alter or negatively affect the child's emotional and mental health, just like any other grief event.

Grief Event: An Incarcerated Family Member

Exploring the racial disparities in the criminal justice system and American penal system highlights the probability that school social workers will have Black students on their caseload who have a caregiver who is or has been previously incarcerated. This is not to say that Black parents are all criminals and dangerous, but it is acknowledging the grim reality that mass incarceration has destroyed communities of color due to the biased systems that unfairly judge the actions of Black people more harshly than those of White people. Black children are seven and a half times more likely to have an incarcerated caregiver than are White children (Kautz, 2019). The incarceration of a family member has major impacts on the mental health of children and adolescents due to the traumatic loss and the disruption of attachment relationships (Dutil, 2019). The incarceration of a loved one or even a death that may be connected to illegal activity serves as an example of losses that often are invalidated by society (Dutil, 2019). The focus on the "what" rather than the fact that the child has lost an important attachment may lead to disenfranchised grief. That in turn creates a conflict for those who are grieving because they often do not receive sympathy from others.

Children with incarcerated family members experience several losses when their family member enters the criminal justice system. A loss that often is not considered with these students is a loss of control in their life or even a loss of their identity, especially if the incarcerated adult was the primary or sole caregiver. In these cases, a child may lose their identity as a child because they are forced to step into a parent's role. This is yet another way that Black children are adultified through socialization, by way of institutional and systemic racism. For example, a Black girl may become maternal due to helping with younger siblings, or a Black boy may be told that he must be "the man of the house." Their identities are lost through this adultification process, which further puts them at a disadvantage developmentally. They no longer have control over their life. They cannot be kids anymore and must assume adult roles when they developmentally lack the capacity to do that. There also is an extra layer of shame and stigma related to parental incarceration that puts further strain on these children and increases their level of social isolation

(Dutil, 2019). The role of the school social worker is to validate and support these children's grieving process while also acknowledging social conditions that contribute to its disruption.

Grief Event: Child Welfare–Involved Youth

Many caregivers who are incarcerated also have children who are placed in the child welfare system. Disparities within the child welfare system increase the chances a school social worker may be working with a child who is in foster care. These disparities within the child welfare system add an additional layer of grief that must be explored in Black students. Black children account for 14% of the US population, but they account for almost a quarter of kids in the child welfare system (Davey, n.d.). This is not because Black children are being harmed at higher rates or because Black parents harm their children more than do White parents: it is because of the biases that exist at every point of contact in the child welfare system. Abuse or suspected maltreatment is reported at higher rates for Black children than for any other demographic (Child Welfare Information Gateway, 2021). Overall, Black children are more likely to spend more time in foster care, be removed from their homes, and experience a termination of parental rights, and they are less likely to receive services and reunify with their families (Child Welfare Information Gateway, 2021).

Black children are 77% more likely than White children to be removed from their homes following a substantiated maltreatment investigation (Dettlaff & Boyd, 2020). The problem with the child welfare system is it disproportionately affects families of color while also denying them the same services and support to be reunified with their children. Parents of color have more difficulty reunifying with their children because of a lack of resources available to support them, inaccessible or unavailable services, and barriers to kinship care placements (Child Welfare Information Gateway, 2021). This grief event contributes to separation distress, causing Black students to struggle with forming meaningful relationships and attachments due to the trauma. Additionally, identity distress may be present, especially for Black children placed in homes with White people who are not aware of important cultural factors, such as taking them to get their hair done. Thus, cultural competence in foster care providers is important because understanding these cultural considerations can help resolve a lot of behaviors presented in Black children that are often labeled as oppositional or defiant.

I was working with a five-year old Black girl who was placed in foster care with a White couple. The child was shy and did not talk at all, and when she did speak, it was barely a whisper. She had been given a diagnosis of Selective Mutism due to her limited communication. As a Black therapist, it bothered me that the girl's hair was always unkept when she came to the preschool. I called the foster mother and asked if it would be okay to do the child's hair at school, to which the foster mother agreed. I brought in all of my hair supplies and took her into the kitchen to wash and style her hair. After I was done, the girl had a head full of twists and a huge smile all day. She spent the day running around and laughing with her peers. It was the most, and loudest, we saw her communicate. And all she needed was her hair done. Something so simple yet so powerful.

Foster care providers, case workers, school social workers, and the teachers of Black students in the child welfare system need to understand how separation and other grief events contribute to childhood traumatic grief (CTG) in Black students. This will aid in accurately assessing, and treating, CTG in Black students of all ages.

Symptoms of Childhood Traumatic Grief

There are several signs of complicated and traumatic grief that school social workers must recognize. These symptoms are often misinterpreted as mental health issues, but they are important signs that the student may be struggling with their grief. It will be important to also share this information with teachers and the students' caregivers so they are more aware of the child's needs and how to support them. School social workers should use screening assessments for adverse childhood events, such as the Childhood Trust Events Survey, which can offer more insight into the child's experiences that may be related to an important grief event. The signs to look for include reexperiencing, avoidance, hyperarousal, dysregulation, or maladaptive cognitions and learning problems.

When a child is struggling with focus and attention or having difficulty sleeping, it could be an important sign of CTG. The student may be reexperiencing frightening or distressing memories, including dreams or thoughts that may interfere with their ability or desire to remember happy times with loss event (Cohen & Mannarino, 2011). When this symptom is overlooked in Black students, it can result in school discipline for sleeping in class or not paying attention or lead to a misdiagnosis of attention deficit hyperactivity disorder (ADHD). A student may show signs of CTG through avoidance, as they try to avoid memories of a deceased person (Cohen & Mannarino, 2011). They may avoid certain places in their community or home that remind them of their loved one or use alcohol or substances of abuse to suppress memories and emotions connected with the loved one. School social workers should be aware of any change in the child's normal behavior or patterns that could signal this distress.

As another symptom of CTG, a child may have increased anger, physical symptoms, difficulty sleeping, or increased jumpiness (Cohen & Mannarino, 2011). Black students who are exhibiting aggression and anger because of CTG are often punished and mislabeled as deviant. It is imperative that school social workers stress the importance of recognizing this behavior as a symptom of CTG while using individual and group play therapy to help resolve the grief that is feeding the anger. The child may have also difficulty modulating their feelings and behaviors, especially when they are reminded of the deceased person (Cohen & Mannarino, 2011). In schools, this may look like an explosive outburst that seemingly came out of nowhere. However, an event or a conversation may have triggered uncomfortable and distressing memories that lead to emotional dysregulation in the child that may look like tantrums, arguing, and defiant behavior. School social workers working with students exhibiting these symptoms must focus treatment on emotional regulation, decreasing impulsivity and increasing coping skills to manage distressing memories and emotions more appropriately. Last, the student may have trouble with memory, comprehension, concentration, paying attention in class, and/or falling asleep in class (Cohen & Mannarino, 2011). This student may receive a learning disability or ADHD diagnosis. Again, the school social worker should advocate for time to explore the students' behaviors more thoroughly, along with getting more information from the student and their family on any grief event that could be contributing to learning problems.

Treating Traumatic Grief in Black Youth

The first step to supporting Black students through grief is to understand how they process their grief. It is important to educate students that each person grieves differently and that it is important to understand their own grief process, especially if it includes maladaptive coping mechanisms such as isolating themselves from others or substance use. It is also important to acknowledge that children have the same feelings that adults do around grief events. Those feelings may include anger, insecurity, feeling deserted, and feeling confused. For students with incarcerated family members, there may be feelings of shame due to the stigma associated with incarcerated people. An important factor to consider is the child's developmental stage. Young children may be in the *ego stage*, so they may think that they did something that contributed to the grief event. These students may have feelings of guilt as well as grief because they assume responsibility for what happened.

There are four ways social workers can treat traumatic grief in Black youth. First, grief-focused psychoeducation (Allen et al., 2012) can be provided through books that address grief events for Black students. For example, one of the children who witnessed the murder of George Floyd, Judeah Reynolds, recently published *A Walk to the Store*, which details the day she witnessed Floyd's death. Another key resource for teachers, mental health professionals, and caregivers is Sesame Street in Communities, a website that provides psychoeducation, resources, and play activities covering topics like death, divorce, and incarcerated parents, to name a few. Finally, grief psychoeducation can be achieved through game play therapy with games like The Wilderness Grief Journey, Doggone Grief, and Healing Hearts, which can all be found on play therapy websites. These games can be especially useful in group play therapy with Black students who have all experienced similar grief events.

Next, activities in the playroom should focus on resolving negative or ambivalent feeling (Allen et al., 2012). First, activities should address the loss of the relationship. This may include activities that help the student to identify things that they did with lost deceased person or caregiver. Activities should also address any anticipated loss reminders. Children who have lost a loved one to death may struggle with important rites of passages, like graduations, holidays, or a father-daughter dance, as these events may retrigger feelings of loss. Therefore, attention should be placed on helping that student develop a plan for how they can develop positive coping responses for these loss reminders. This can include writing the narrative of their event, writing their emotions around the event, and then participating in some exposure exercises. It's also important that students know it is okay to have sadness around their grief event, as this gives them an opportunity to express these feelings in a setting where they can be more vulnerable. Likewise, they should feel comfortable acknowledging the imperfections of the loved one, especially where the child may be dealing with some unresolved conflicts or struggling with things they said or did that they now regret. The social worker should seek to understand the child's viewpoint and utilize activities like role-play where they can process and act out those feelings in a safe place.

The next step is to bring in activities that help maintain and consolidate positive memories (Allen et al., 2012). These activities should focus on the positive aspect of the relationship with a absent person or caregiver. These activities are done after the child has begun the grieving process and is able to process or communicate their feelings around their loss. Then, the social worker can address any residual negative memories or feelings the student may have. The goal is to record and preserve memories in a concrete way, to allow students to capture the joy and happiness they had with that individual. This can include the use of technology by having the child make a slideshow or social media reel with different music and pictures of their loved ones.

The final step in treating Black youth experiencing grief and bereavement is the use of interventions that help the student accept the relationship that they may or may not have with loved ones a result of the grief event (Allen et al., 2012). This is where the social worker can address any negative feelings like guilt, anger, or betrayal. For example, the student may feel as if they are betraying their loved one when they accept the reality of their current or future relationship with them. A student may feel guilt because they are in foster care and they are starting to develop a close relationship with their foster parents: they may feel as if they're betraying their biological family or biological caregiver. It can be helpful for the student to learn how to invest in the present relationships they have while still honoring the relationships they may or may not have with their family and/or parents. Helping the child accept their relationship can ultimately enhance the child's adaptive functioning. Interventions should also focus on positive cognitive coping. This can include activities that utilize mindfulness techniques which may help the child appreciate the current relationship.

Grief in the Playroom

There are several signs of grief that may present in play with Black students, and it is important to have toys in the playroom that will support these children in working through their grief. In play, the child may exhibit any of several themes, including anger, aggression, chaos, self-esteem, guilt, perfectionism, power and control, and limits and boundaries. Also, grief themes are exhibited through the use of grief toys, such as a doctor's kit, coffins, tombstones, skeletons, and ghosts. The grief theme also is shown when characters die during role-playing or imaginative play or when a child buries things in the sand tray. The student may communicate confusion about the grief event by playing out scenes of them living with their parents who are incarcerated.

There are several important items to have in the playroom to support grieving Black youth. First, the school social worker should have costumes, especially those for community helpers (e.g., doctors, firefighters, police officers). These community helpers are often correlated with grief events as they are usually present during the grief event in some way. Another costume to consider is a graduation robe to act as a judge's robe for child welfare-involved youth and students with incarcerated family members. Other costume items include handcuffs and superhero capes to act out themes of protection, safety, and/or rescue. Toys to consider include a police station, hospital, a doctor's kit, and toy court set. Also, social workers should consider having various superhero toys, as they often are used to communicate a rescue protection theme. Black Panther is a big hero in the Black community, so having superheroes from the movie series can support empowerment in Black students. When Chadwick Boseman, the actor who played Black Panther, died suddenly in 2020, social media pictures of Black boys using their Avengers superheroes as funerals for Black Panther went viral. To me, this showed the value of play in children of all races and gender in processing difficult emotions.

Sand Tray Therapy

In sand tray therapy with Black students, the counselor must be mindful of signs of grief. Sand tray organizations are categories of sand tray scenes that communicate key diagnosis and assessment information in the same way as play themes. First, an *empty world* is a sand tray that has two-thirds of the sand tray left empty, which could be a possible sign of depression (Homeyer, 2017). Next, a *disorganized* or *chaotic sand tray* scene is disjointed, may be chaotic and seem disorganized, which may be a sign of anxiety. Another category of sand tray organization is the *unpeopled sand tray* that does not have any people in it; these are often created when a client has a high level of mistrust (Homeyer, 2017). These students may also be a victim/survivor of abuse. (Please note that although abused children may create unpeopled worlds, the counselor should not assume that if a student creates this type of scene they are abused. They are not synonymous.)

The social worker can also benefit from specific miniatures that can help students experiencing grief events, such as miniatures related to death such as coffins, headstones, ghosts, and zombies. Next, it will be important to have miniatures of community members and their vehicles. And as previously mentioned, animated characters like Black Panther and other superheroes are highly recommended. Another category of sand tray miniatures to consider are religious symbols, as religion is protective factor in the Black community and for many Black students. Last, the school social worker should consider addiction miniatures because substance use may be prevalent in the student's home and community, or even used personally as a maladaptive coping mechanism to deal with race-based stress and trauma.

Play Therapy Interventions to Support Grieving Black Youth

Play therapy interventions, both group and individual, can be effective tools to identify the feelings around the grief event while also providing an outlet for students to process their grief. Child-Centered Play Therapy (CCPT) is an approach that can be useful for younger students experiencing grief. Additionally, there are play-based interventions that utilize different expressive therapies including art therapy, sand tray therapy, music therapy, and mindfulness. All these interventions are designed to accompany the steps of addressing grief in Black students.

Child-Centered Play Therapy

CCPT has been shown to be effective in supporting students through trauma and violent grief events. Play therapy naturally desensitizes children because it provides a safe environment for them to process their trauma: traumatized children can use toys to work through these emotions and safely distance themselves from their trauma (Hall, 2019). CCPT also offers children a healthy amount of control, predictability, and consistency while also providing the opportunity to alter the outcome of the trauma on their own terms (Hall, 2019). CCPT provides a place where children can process their emotions safely, come up with a resolution that is fitting for them, and decrease negative behaviors that have disrupted their daily functioning. Play allows kids to symbolically deal with emotions related to violence and provides a physical distance from the grief event so that they can reduce their anxiety enough to work through these emotions (Hall, 2019). Therapeutic progress can be observed in the child's play as they manipulate toys and move from a victim role to one that allows them more mastery over the traumatic event. Children exposed to violence need to feel safe and they need to feel supported, but they also must feel understood within the therapeutic environment because this is going to provide a model for healthy relationships they can then have with others in their life.

African Grief Masks

The activity African Grief Mask is an art therapy activity that helps students explore the grief cycle. This activity is most appropriate for 2nd through 12th grade students. The materials for this activity are the African Grief Mask handout (Appendix A) and something to color with, like crayons for younger students and markers or colored pencils for older students. First, explain the different stages of the grief cycle and share that sometimes people go back and forth through the different stages. Also explain that they may have feelings outside of those identified in the grief stages. Then ask them to identify a stage or feeling they have in relation to the grief event. Ask the student to pick a color for that stage and color the amount they feel on their mask. They can also place a feeling on a blank spot provided. Prompt the student to repeat this for any other feelings they are experiencing in relation to the grief event. This can serve as an assessment tool for clinicians to gauge where the child is in the grief cycle and which emotions are the most important to address first.

Memory T-Shirts

This next activity, Memory T-Shirts, relates to a tradition in the Black community, where t-shirts are made with pictures of the deceased person. This activity is most appropriate for students in the 3rd through 12th grade. There are two ways to do this activity. The first way is to use the Memory T-Shirt handout (Appendix B) and use colored pencils or markers to decorate their t-shirt. The other option is more tactile and includes a t-shirt and fabric markers. The student can decorate a t-shirt in memory of their loved one. It does not have to be a literal picture of the person but can also include things that remind them of that person, like their favorite color. Each option provides the opportunity for the student to preserve the memories of their loved one in a way that is honored in their culture.

Memory Shoe Box

Another art activity that honors something important in Black culture is Memory Shoe Box. Shoes are big in Black culture, among Black women,

men, boys, and girls. "Sneakerheads" will often pay a lot of money for new shoes, and often Black children are taught early to take care of their shoes. For this activity, the social worker can ask the child to bring in a shoebox that belonged to their loved one or the social worker can provide one. Other materials required are magazines, scissors, glue, markers, and the Memory Shoe Box handout (Appendix C). Students as young as kindergarten can benefit from this activity that assists in preserving memories. In session, the student decorates the shoe box, then is encouraged to take the box home and fill it with keepsakes like pictures, perfume/cologne, etc. that they want to keep to remind them of their loved one. They can be encouraged to bring their Memory Shoe Box to the next session to share with the clinician. It also an opportunity to get the student's teacher involved and ask for permission for the student to share their box with their classmates, which can further assist them in processing their grief.

Memory Hearts

Memory Hearts is an art-based intervention to help children who are experiencing grief in relation to the death of a loved one. This activity can be used with students as young as kindergarten, up to high school. The materials required include the Memory Hearts handout (Appendix D), scissors, glue, and magazine clippings. The student is encouraged to decorate their heart with positive and negative memories they may of their loved ones. This is an activity that can be used to promote positive memories. However, if the student identifies negative memories about their loved ones, the social worker will validate and process those feelings with the student. Additionally, the social worker can talk about how they can honor the memories they have of their caregiver even if there are negative ones associated, too.

Grief Playlist

This music-based activity is beneficial for helping the child express their emotions around the grief loss. This can be used with students in the 4th through 12th grades and requires the Grief Playlist handout (Appendix E) and access to some device that plays music. This can be the child's phone (if they are allowed to have them), a tablet, or computer, whatever is appropriate for the student to search and play songs. It will also provide something tangible they can use outside of sessions as a positive coping mechanism to manage their feelings about their loss. For children who may be resistant to the activity, the therapist may choose a song that is related to a loss they feel comfortable communicating (e.g., the loss of a pet). Older children may be permitted to pick songs that feature profanity, which can be seen as appropriate because it is the honest and transparent expression of the child. This also can communicate the level of rapport the child has with the therapist, as they feel comfortable playing songs they may not normally listen to around adults. If songs featuring profanity are used, the therapist can use this as an opportunity to talk about the child's connection with songs that are not often deemed "appropriate" for children.

Conclusion

Black students experience high levels of grief and bereavement due to their unique circumstances. This grief, on top of their daily exposure to race-based stress and trauma, places them at a higher risk of misdiagnosis and being improperly medicated due to a lack of knowledge of how grief shows up in their behavior, thoughts, and feelings. School social workers are in a key position to help educate students, teachers, and their caregivers on these grief reactions so they are able to safely process the emotions in loving and supportive environments. That is the true path to healing.

References

Allen, B., Oseni, A., & Allen, K. E. (2012). The evidence-based treatment of chronic posttraumatic stress disorder and traumatic grief in an adolescent: A case study. *Psychological Trauma: Theory, Research, Practice, and Policy, 4*(6), 631–639. https://doi.org/10.1037/a0024930

Alliance for Gun Responsibility. (2022). Gun violence in the Black community: Myths and facts. https://gunresponsibility.org/blog/gun-violence-in-the-black-community-myths-and-facts/

Carras, C. (2022). Sesame Street Place hit with racial discrimination lawsuit after viral video sparked outrage. LA Times. https://www.latimes.com/entertainment-arts/story/2022-07-28/sesame-place-discrimination-lawsuit-viral-video-rosita

Child Welfare Information Gateway. (2021). Child welfare practice to address race disproportionality and disparity. https://www.childwelfare.gov/pubpdfs/racial_disproportionality.pdf

Cohen, J. A., & Mannarino, A. P. (2011). Supporting children with traumatic grief: What educators need to know. *School Psychology, 32*(2), 117-131. https://doi.org.10.1177/0143034311400827

Davey, S. (n.d.). Snapshot on the state of Black women and girls: Sex trafficking in the U.S. Congressional Black Caucus Foundation. https://www.cbcfinc.org/wp-content/uploads/2020/05/SexTraffickingReport3.pdf

Degruy. J. (2017). *Post traumatic slave syndrome: America's legacy of enduring injury & healing.* Uptown Press.

Dettlaff, A. J., & Boyd, R. (2020). Racial disproportionality and disparities in the child welfare system: Why do they exist, and what can be done to address them? *Annals of the American Academy of Political and Social Science, 692*(1), 253–274. https://doi.org/10.1177/0002716220980329

Douglas, R. D., Alvis, L. M., Rooney, E. E., Busby, D. R., & Kaplow, J. B. (2021). Racial, ethnic, and neighborhood income disparities in childhood posttraumatic stress and grief: Exploring indirect effects through trauma exposure and bereavement. *Journal of Traumatic Stress, 34*: 929–942. https://doi.org/10.1002/jts.22732

Dutil, S. (2019). Adolescent traumatic and disenfranchised grief: Adapting an evidence-based intervention for Black and Latinx youths in schools, *Children & Schools, 41*(3), 179–187. https://doi.org/10.1093/cs/cdz009

Hall, J. G. (2019). Child-centered play therapy as a means of healing children exposed to domestic violence. *International Journal of Play Therapy™, 28*(2), 98–106.

Homeyer, L. E., & Sweeney, D. S. (2017). *Sandtray therapy: A practical manual* (3rd ed.). Routledge: New York.

Kautz, S. V. (2019). The emotional experience of parental incarceration from the African-American adolescent perspective. *Journal of Child & Adolescent Trauma, 12*(2), 187–199. https://doi.org/10.1007/s40653-018-0232-x

Lawrence, A. (2022). Theme parks were not meant for Black families: Why racism at Sesame Place is part of a shameful tradition. The Guardian. https://www.theguardian.com/travel/2022/jul/30/sesame-place-theme-parks-black-families-racism

Martin, R., Rajan, S., Shareef, F., Xie, K. C., Allen, K. A., Zimmerman, M., & Jay, J. (2022). Racial disparities in child exposure to firearm violence before and during COVID-19. *American Journal of Preventative Medicine, 63*(2), 204–212. https://www.ajpmonline.org/article/S0749-3797(22)00129-5/fulltext

National Center for Injury Prevention and Control. (2020). 10 leading causes of death, United States. Centers for Disease Control and Prevention (CDC). https://wisqars.cdc.gov/cgi-bin/broker.exe

Ruiz, N. G., Horowitz, J. M., & Tamir, C. (2020). Many Black and Asian Americans say they have experienced discrimination amid the COVID-19 outbreak. Pew Research Center. https://www.pewresearch.org/social-trends/2020/07/01/many-black-and-asian-americans-say-they-have-experienced-discrimination-amid-the-covid-19-outbreak/

Sheats, K. J., Irving, S. M., Mercy, J. A., Simon, T. R., Crosby, A. E., Ford, D. C., Merrick, M. T., Annor, F. B., Morgan, R. E. (2018). Violence-related disparities experienced by Black youth and young adults: Opportunities for prevention. *American Journal of Preventative Medicine, 55*(4), 462–469. https://doi.org/10.1016/j.amepre.2018.05.017

St. John, V. J., Headley, A. M., & Harper, K. (2022). Reducing adverse police contact would heal wounds for children and their communities. Child Trends. https://www.childtrends.org/publications/reducing-adverse-police-contact-would-heal-wounds-for-children-and-their-communities

Zisook, S., & Shear, K. (2009). Grief and bereavement: what psychiatrists need to know. *World Psychiatry: Official Journal of the World Psychiatric Association (WPA), 8*(2), 67–74. https://doi.org/10.1002/j.2051-5545.2009.tb00217.x

Appendix A   African Grief Mask

African Grief Mask Activity

Grief & bereavement can be caused by a
variety of events like:

death of a loved one
incarcerated family members
foster care/adoption
move/relocation
loss of friendships
loss of romantic relationships

This activity uses African masks for kids to color to explore
their journey through the grief cycle. African masks
provide a connection with spirits, divine deities, and the
deceased. They are worn in some cultures during religious
or sacred ceremonies, funerals, and exclusive events.

BMH Connect   mylemarks
©2021 BMH Connect & Mylemarks

Grief Masks

Losing a loved one can be difficult. Use the mask below to process the different levels of grief you are feeling. Pick a color for each grief cycle. Then use that color to show how much you feel that emotion. You can also add your own emotions.

☐ Denial _____

☐ Anger _____

☐ Bargaining _____

☐ Depression _____

☐ Acceptance _____

☐ _____

Grief Masks

Losing a loved one can be difficult. Use the mask below to process the different levels of grief you are feeling. Pick a color for each grief cycle. Then use that color to show how much you feel that emotion. You can also add your own emotions.

	Denial		Depression
	Anger		Acceptance
	Bargaining		

Grief Masks

Losing a loved one can be difficult. Use the mask below to process the different levels of grief you are feeling. Pick a color for each grief cycle. Then use that color to show how much you feel that emotion. You can also add your own emotions.

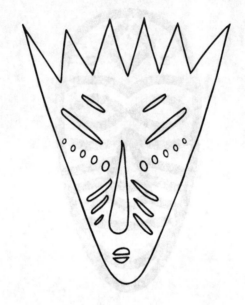

☐   Denial

☐   Anger

☐   Bargaining

☐   Depression

☐   Acceptance

☐   _____

Grief Masks

Losing a loved one can be difficult. Use the mask below to process the different levels of grief you are feeling. Pick a color for each grief cycle. Then use that color to show how much you feel that emotion. You can also add your own emotions.

☐	Denial	☐	Depression
☐	Anger	☐	Acceptance
☐	Bargaining	☐	

Grief Masks

Losing a loved one can be difficult. Use the mask below to process the different levels of grief you are feeling. Pick a color for each grief cycle. Then use that color to show how much you feel that emotion. You can also add your own emotions.

☐ _____ Denial _____   ☐ _____ Depression _____

☐ _____ Anger _____   ☐ _____ Acceptance _____

☐ _____ Bargaining _____   ☐ _____

Grief Masks

Losing a loved one can be difficult. Use the mask below to process the different levels of grief you are feeling. Pick a color for each grief cycle. Then use that color to show how much you feel that emotion. You can also add your own emotions.

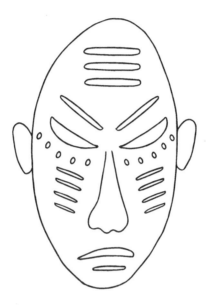

☐	Denial	☐	Depression
☐	Anger	☐	Acceptance
☐	Bargaining	☐	

In Memory Of

Decorate the t-shirt below in honor of your loved one.

Memory Shoe Box

This activity is designed to help you create a box of memories of your loved one. You can use the materials to decorate the shoe box with words and pictures of memories you have of your loved one. When it is complete, you can put things in your shoe box that help you feel close to them like pictures, clothing, cologne/perfume and more! .

Required Materials
Handout, magazines, shoe box, scissors, glue, markers, glitter

BMH Connect

© 2022 BMH Connect & mylemarks

mylemarks

Directions

This activity is designed to help children acknowledge and process memories related to their grief event. In future sessions, you can refer to these memories as a way to help the client think of positive coping strategies when dealing with grief reminders (e.g. If the child had a memory of taking walks in the neighborhood with their parent, encourage them to do that when they are struggling with grief reminders).

First let the client know we will be creating an art project with their memories of their loved one. Let them know they can either use the online sand tray, the whiteboard to draw their memories or a Microsoft word document to use clip art for their activity. Once they chose their way of completing the activity, ask them to share their screen.

Before you begin the activity, ask the client to close their eyes (if they feel comfortable) and think about their loved one. You can have some calming music playing on your phone or from YouTube, or even utilize a calming fish tank video on YouTube for client's who do not want to or do not feel comfortable closing their eyes.

Ask the client to start working on their project when they are ready. Encourage them first to draw a heart (or find a clipart heart they like) on their paper. Then, ask them to find/draw pictures that represent the happy memories they have about their loved one inside their heart. Then inform them they can put any unpleasant or unhappy memories outside their heart. Explain that this helps them acknowledge their full grief story and will ultimately help them with the healing process

Processing Questions

1. Which memory is your favorite?
2. What type of emotions do you have when looking at your heart?
3. What are some coping skills you can use to manage any negative emotions this heart may cause?
4. What are some activities you can do when you're missing your loved one that are related to your memories?
5. Who can you share your heart with that can remind you of your happy memories when you miss your loved one?

GRIEF COPING PLAYLIST

DEATH OF A LOVED ONE

Pick a song that gives you a happy memory about your loved one _____

Pick a song that expresses how you feel about losing your loved one _____

Pick a song that describes your relationship with your loved one _____

DIVORCED/ SEPARATING PARENTS

Pick a song that describes the feeling you have about your parents divorcing _____

Pick a song that describes your relationship with your mom _____

Pick a song that describes your relationship with your dad _____

CHILD-WELFARE INVOLVED -YOUTH

Pick a song that describes how you feel being away from your family _____

Pick a song that reminds you of a happy memory of your family _____

Pick a song that describes how you feel about your relationship with your biological parents _____

INCARCERATED PARENTS

Pick a song that describes how you feel about your family member being in jail _____

Pick a song that reminds you of your family member who is in jail _____

Pick a song that you can listen to when you are missing your family member is in the jail _____

8

Play It Away!
Addressing Suicide Risk in Black Students

The recent suicide of Stephen "tWitch" Boss brought suicide in the Black community back into the spotlight. Many people were left confused and saddened by the death of this person who was always dancing and smiling. He and his family were seemingly happy. This was an individual who had money and access to mental health services, however, they still were not immune to the epidemic of suicide among Black Americans. I believe this highlights a bigger issue in the Black community: the lack of emotional expression and regulation in the lives of Black people. Black women are often trying to fill the role of the "Strong Black Woman" and Black men are also doing the same. As a result, Black children are also socialized to keep their heads down, not complain, and get the work done. This, in my opinion, serves as the foundation of suicide in the Black community. Black children and adults need a free space in which to express their emotions; if they can access mental health treatment, that requires mental health professionals displaying cultural humility and inclusivity, so these individuals can openly express their emotions. For those with accessibility issues, having the confidence to openly share their feelings and thoughts with family members, church leaders, and peers also is key in addressing the epidemic of suicide in the Black community.

There are real consequences to untreated racial trauma in Black children. Studies have found untreated racial trauma in Black youth is linked to a higher prevalence of depression, anxiety, and suicide risk. Considering this information, an increase in suicidal risk in Black youth needs to be addressed in the same vein as racial trauma. There are numerous stories of Black children

Black Students Matter. April D. Duncan, Oxford University Press. © Oxford University Press 2024.
DOI: 10.1093/oso/9780197669266.003.0009

killing themselves, and a lot of times the precipitating factor has been a negative race-based experience.

- 9-year-old McKenzie Nicole Adams died by suicide in 2018 as a result of racist bullying. Students reportedly would call Adams "ugly" and a "Black b----," while also telling her "kill yourself" (Barker, 2018).
- In 2017, a 14-year-old Black student, Deshaun Adderley, died by suicide after enduring racial slurs and physical violence (Andrews, 2019).
- 15-year-old Jo'Vianni Smith reportedly committed suicide after difficulty coping with isolation caused by the COVID-19 pandemic lockdown in 2020 (Black News, 2020).
- Days before they were to enroll at Georgia Tech on an athletic scholarship for football, 17-year-old Bryce Gowdy died by suicide. At the time of his death, his family was struggling with homelessness, financial hardships and Gowdy himself was struggling with mental health issues, including paranoia (Burke, 2020).

Therefore, one can hypothesize that Black children are killing themselves because they don't have the coping skills to deal with the different life stressors, including negative race-based experiences. This makes it even more important for social workers to use a racial trauma lens when observing the behaviors of Black children, especially when race-based bullying is involved. School social workers must provide an empowering space that can help them learn healthy coping skills to deal with negative race-based experiences. It will also require the school social worker to be versed in the signs of suicide and how to support students, of all backgrounds, who are having suicidal thoughts and/or behaviors.

Key Things to Know About Suicide

There are some important terms to know, including *suicidal ideation*, *suicidal self-injurious behaviors*, and *nonsuicidal self-injury* (NSSI). Suicidal ideation occurs when a student is having thoughts of killing themselves (National Strategy for Suicide Prevention, 2001). Suicidal self-injurious behaviors, also known as suicide attempts, are behaviors that are harmful to oneself and can lead to injury, like an attempted overdose (National Strategy for Suicide Prevention, 2001). In suicidal ideation and suicidal self-injurious behavior there is a desire to die. By contrast, NSSI refers to injuries that are caused by a person but without an intention to die, which includes behaviors like skin cutting, burning, scratching, or head banging (Klonsky et al., 2014). Often, these behaviors are used to make a person feel better or to suppress uncomfortable emotions.

There are some key things to know when working with clients who are experiencing any form of suicidality. First, the social worker should use compassionate language and avoid stigmatizing language. An example of compassionate language is using terms like "died by suicide" or "ended their life," whereas stigmatizing language is using terms like "committed suicide" or "successful suicide" (Olson, 2011). Stigmatizing language implies failure or success in suicide attempts. Also, the social worker should develop confidence in using the words "death," "die," and "kill" as this conveys competence. Questions should be direct, such as "Are you having thoughts of killing yourself?" or "Have you ever tried to kill yourself?" Finally, the social worker should take every statement of self-harm or suicide seriously. Even if the child seems to be "joking" when they make a statement of self-harm, the social worker should do a suicide risk assessment, create a safety plan, and inform the school and caregivers.

Suicide Rates in Black Youth

Rates of suicide in Black youth are increasing at alarming rates yet receiving little attention. Even the smallest amount of exposure to racial discrimination can have negative consequences on a Black child's emotional well-being, including depression and anxiety (Lanier et al., 2017; Pachter et al., 2018; Walker et al., 2016). Repeated exposures to acts of racism and discrimination, also known as *microaggressions*, may make Black children feel dismissed, irrelevant, and a burden on others. This, in turn, increases their probability of suicide ideation (Arshanapally et al., 2018; Hollingsworth et al., 2017). Studies have found a direct correlation between racial discrimination and suicidal ideation (Assari et al., 2017). Untreated racial trauma in by Black youth has led to social disconnectedness, and this demands immediate attention. The lack of connection due to racial trauma affects Black youth of all ages negatively. Black children ages 5–12 years old have suicide rates twice as high as their White peers (Lindsey et. al., 2019). Tomek et al. found that younger children are more likely to report suicidal ideation, with reports decreasing for children ages 11–18 (2015).These grim numbers highlight the need for intervention and prevention strategies for Black youth across the lifespan.

The 2018–2019 Youth Risk Behavior Surveillance Survey (YRBSS) report (Centers for Disease Control [CDC], 2020) of suicidality in Black high schoolers provides these statistics:

- Approximately 32% reported feeling sad or hopeless, with Black girls (41%) reporting more sadness than Black boys (22%).
- 17% seriously considered attempting suicide, with Black girls (24%) reporting higher rates of attempts than Black boys (11%).
- 15% plan for how they would attempt suicide, with Black girls (20%) more likely to make a plan than Black boys (10%).
- 12% reported attempting suicide, with Black girls (15%) more likely to report a suicide attempt than Black boys (8.5%).

Although Black female high school students have higher rates of suicidality than Black males, there are still concerning statistics among Black males. Suicide is the third leading cause of death for young Black males (Joe et al., 2018). What is most concerning around Black male suicide is the lack of warning signs that are shown prior to the death. For example, Black males are 20% less likely to have recently carried a gun and 28% less likely to ever consider attempting suicide (Price & Khubchandani, 2019). However, 52% of suicide deaths among Black males included the use of a firearm (Price & Khubchandani, 2019). This highlights the importance of gun laws that require longer waiting times, as it could possibly save the lives of Black males. It also imparts the concern around a lack of emotional regulation, impulse control and coping skills among Black males.

Equally concerning is Black youth suffering in silence rather than reaching out for help. Studies have discovered that a large number of Black youth who die by suicide have no prior suicide attempts and are jumping straight from suicide ideation to lethal means of suicidal behavior (Lee & Wong, 2020). For Black youth, from 1991 to 2017, injuries from suicide attempts among Black boys increased by 122% (Congressional Black Caucus, 2019). Additionally, self-reported suicide attempts have increased for both Black males and females by at least 73% over the past 25 years (Congressional Black Caucus, 2019). Researchers report a 60% increase of serious suicide attempts in Black youth from 2001 to 2017, with 56% of Black females dying by hanging/suffocation (Price & Khubchandani, 2019). This may suggest Black youth lack essential skills and strong connections to caring adults to manage suicidal thoughts and feelings. However, despite these rising trends, little has been done in solutions to resolve the issue among Black youth. One reason may be the misconceptions of the prevalence of suicide in the Black community along with a lack of education of the signs of suicide in Black students.

Suicide Misconceptions in the Black Community

Several misconceptions about suicide in the Black community contribute to missed signs of distress in Black students. One of the misconceptions is "Black folks don't kill themselves." There have been stories in the news about Black people, specifically men, who have been found hanging from a tree and the community, because of historical trauma, immediately dismiss claims of suicide and believe the person was killed via lynching. Some common statements from family members are "He would never do this to himself" or "They did not show any signs of suicide." These statements highlight two possibilities: the person did not exhibit any signs and jumped immediately to lethal means of suicide, or the signs were missed due to this misconception or the lack of education on the signs of suicide. School social workers must work to provide a free place for Black students to share their suicidal thoughts or behaviors, as well as psychoeducation for parents, teachers, and students on the signs of suicide.

Another misconception is that suicidal thoughts can be prayed away. Religion is an important protective factor in the Black community, and Black children and adults are often taught to use prayer and faith in God to resolve problems and persevere through difficult times. Religion for Black children and families is a protective factor that can be utilized as an additional source of support for the family. The social worker may need to work with Black students and families on ways that mental health treatment can supplement their beliefs while still displaying respect and cultural inclusivity towards their beliefs.

The last misconception is "Black people don't get therapy," which is rooted in distrust of medical systems due to historical trauma (Washington, 2007). And although mental health treatment has been more normalized in the Black community, caregivers and children may be apprehensive to enter treatment or lack an understanding of mental health distress signaling the need for services. Psychoeducation on suicide signs and risk is important for both Black children and their caregivers.

Suicide Risk Factors Across the Lifespan

Developmentally, Black students have different risk factors for suicide. Research has identified three different age ranges that have similar behaviors associated with suicide attempts and deaths. The first range includes younger children, ages 5–11 (kindergarten through 6th grade). Students in this developmental range had some type of conflict with family or peers before they killed themselves and were more likely to be male, have a diagnosis of attention deficit hyperactivity disorder (ADHD), and die by hanging, strangulation, or suffocation; only 29% of these children gave an advanced warning before killing themselves (Grills et al., 2019). School social workers working with students in this developmental range should be mindful of younger Black students with impulse control issues because suicide is more of an impulsive act for these students. Also, because students of this age are less likely to leave a note, the school social worker should be more attuned to risk factors, as signs may be more subtle for these students.

The next developmental age group includes Black students 12–14 years old (6th through 9th grades). Black students in this age range were more likely to be male, more likely to have experienced some type of depression or emotional distress prior to the act, and were more likely to experience interpersonal relationship issues prior to the act compared to younger children (Grills et al., 2019). School social workers should be mindful of romantic relationships or conflicts with peers as preceding or triggering events leading to suicidal acts by Black youth. Also, Black students in this age group are less likely to present advanced warning compared to older students, and they are more likely to die by hanging strangulation or suffocation (Grills et al., 2019). School social workers working with students in these grades may focus more on managing social interactions with peers, romantic relationships, and coping skills for managing emotional distress.

The last group are Black students ages 13–17 (7th through 12th grade). Black children who died by suicide in this age group were more likely to have a breakup or interpersonal issue prior to the act, were less likely to have supportive adults in their lives, had a previous suicide attempt, and had lower levels of family closeness (Grills et al., 2019). Studies have found suicide attempts increase threefold for children with fewer supportive adults (Grills et al., 2019). The school social worker should be keenly attuned to the student's support systems to ascertain if they need additional resources to enhance connections in their families and community. Case management for community programs, such as a mentor program with a local organization or fraternities/sororities could be beneficial for students who are at risk of suicide at this age.

Racial Trauma as a Risk Factor for Suicide in Black Youth

Black children who died by suicide may struggle with life changes and transitions because they aren't equipped to cope with emotional strain or adversity. Black youth attending predominately White schools may struggle with fitting in and may deal with feelings of devaluation, rejection, or rebuttal, which may contribute to suicidal thoughts and/or behaviors. Feelings of marginalization, alienation, or interpersonal rejection have also been found to be risk factors for suicide in Black youth (Walker et al., 2016). School social workers should assess for these feelings by utilizing activities that encourage emotional expression as a more effective way to identify these feelings with Black students. Other risk factors for suicide in Black youth to consider are feelings or diagnoses of depression and anxiety.

Another risk factor for suicide in Black youth is the internet and social media. Studies found that the internet was the most frequent context for racial discrimination experiences among Black youth (English et al., 2020). The same study found Black adolescents experienced both individual and vicarious online racial discrimination at high rates, and those experiences were associated with negative mental health outcomes, like depression and anxiety (English et al., 2020). The school social worker could benefit from implementing interventions or questions that assess the student's internet and social media use to provide a space for students to share any negative experiences they have encountered. (See Chapter 10, on group play therapy for the Social Media Scavenger Hunt activity.) Another factor to consider is the vicarious trauma Black youth are experiencing in their exposure to racially motivated incidents that harm the safety of Black children and adults. A student may find themselves self-identifying with these individuals and experiencing trauma symptoms in relation to that exposure, including the same symptoms that put them at risk for suicide.

Conceptually, racism may be used as an antecedent to suicide-related outcomes because it represents societal rejection and a sense of unfulfilled belongingness (Hollingsworth et al., 2017). When Black children deal with this rejection through the everyday experience of verbal and behavioral slights in their environments, they start to believe they are a burden to others; this is known as *perceived burdensome* and is another risk factor for increased thoughts of suicide in Black students (Hollingsworth et al., 2017). Perceived burdensome may also develop if racial slights include comments that make Black people feel incompetent, dismissed, or that they are not equally represented in society (Hollingsworth et al., 2017). This makes exploration questions around the students' internet and social media exposure even more pertinent.

Suicide Risk Among Black LGBTQ+ Youth

Another important risk factor for Black students is gender identity and sexual orientation. A study conducted by the Trevor Project found 35% of Black LGBTQ+ youth reported seriously considering suicide and that they are less likely to receive counseling compared to White LGBTQ+ youth (Green et al., 2020). Trans Black youth are at a higher risk for suicide, as the same report found that one in three black trans youth attempted suicide in the past year (Green et al., 2020). This highlights the lack of support and safety Black trans youth still feel in the 21st century. School social workers working with Black LGBTQ+ youth should also focus on interventions that build their sense of community, empower their identity, and help them maintain a positive sense of self. There should also be a focus on safety planning that includes safe places and people they can talk to when dealing with thoughts of suicide. It will also be beneficial to connect the student to community or national organizations where they can find and build a sense of community among individuals who share their experiences. (See Chapter 4 on bullying and LGBTQ Black youth for more information to support these students.)

Protective Factors for Black Youth

There are several protective factor school social workers can build on to support Black youth who are experiencing suicidality. Besides religion, racial socialization messages, and high levels of resiliency are factors that can assist in developing treatment goals for Black youth. Therefore, it will key to support Black youth who are experiencing suicidality using affirmations or other positive messages related to their culture and identity. Another protective factor to consider is social media. Although social media is a place where Black children are experiencing high rates of racial discrimination, they also reported it as a safe place as well as a place where they can be involved in social justice movements (Auxier, 2020). Black Twitter, Tik Tok, and other platforms were identified by Black youth as a place where they could receive comic relief through jokes while also having a sense of community in spaces where people that look like them and affirm their experiences. Last, all children have high levels of resiliency when compared to adults. When considering the high levels of racial stress and trauma Black children are experiencing, it is important to tap into their resiliency, utilizing a strengths perspective to help them recognize their capabilities and resources to overcome their problems.

Signs of Suicide in Black Students

There are several signs of suicide that the social worker should be privy to. It is important that the social worker stops the session and does a suicide risk assessment if any of these signs show up in clinical sessions or has been communicated from other staff members or students. First, verbal signs of suicide include a student making any type of statements of self-harm, which may include comments like "I should just kill myself," "Everyone would be better off without me," or "My life has no meaning" (Grills et al., 2019). It is imperative that the social worker takes all threats and statements of self-harm seriously, even if they think the student is "joking." Humor may be that student's way of dealing with those feelings and should not be dismissed. Some behavioral signs of suicide in Black youth may include the student seeking a means to kill themselves, giving away prized possessions, isolating from friends and family, withdrawing from activities, increased drug/alcohol use, looking for ways to die, visiting or telling people goodbye, fatigue, and aggression (American Foundation for Suicide Prevention, 2022). Another sign can be making any posts online or sending text messages with threats of self-harm (Grills et al., 2019). This is where the social workers' knowledge of suicidal behavior at different developmental stages will be key, as a teenager seeking to gain access to a gun or a younger student looking for access to pills are going to be red flags that they are engaging in or planning to engage in suicidal behavior.

Another important sign of suicidality in Black youth is engaging in NSSI behaviors, such as nail picking and/or biting, scab picking, and head banging to name a few (Klonsky et al., 2014). It is important to note that a student engaging in NSSI behaviors does not mean they are suicidal, but it does put them at a higher risk for attempting suicide. An increase in violence is another sign of suicide in Black students. This may include behaviors outside of the child's nature, like joining a gang or picking fights with others, including police officers (Grills et al., 2019). The term "suicide by cop" is used when a person with suicidal thoughts provokes a police officer to the point where the officer kills them (Shain, 2019). (Please note that this is not the same as Black students having negative interactions with police officers due to historic and systemic racism.) In schools, this may be a student who is showing a change in their behavior that includes more altercations with school resource officers.

If a school social worker is worried about signs of suicide in a Black student, having the school and/or parents search their internet history may be a good way to identify if the child needs additional support to mitigate feelings and thoughts of suicide.

Signs of Suicide in the Playroom

There are several play themes to be mindful of in identifying and supporting Black youth experiencing suicidality. These themes are important when considering the most appropriate treatment and safety plans for reducing suicidal thoughts and behavior. Students may exhibit play themes of anger and aggression in relation to feelings associated with triggering events to their suicidal thoughts and behaviors. Interventions should be focused on anger management skills and addressing the root of the anger. Other play themes that may be present are the independent play and guilt themes, which are correlated with signs of depression in children and may be a result of perceived burdensome. Therefore, interventions should focus on decreasing depressive symptoms and increasing self-esteem.

The play themes of chaos and perfectionism may also be present, as they are related to feelings of anxiety. School social workers should focus treatment on decreasing anxiety symptoms, increasing self-regulation skills, and addressing the root of the anxiety. As noted earlier, there are different precipitating events to suicidal acts in Black children, such as conflict with peers, family members, or romantic partners, so the student may also be exhibiting the grief theme in play sessions. Interventions focused on addressing grief symptoms and assisting the student through the grief cycle will be beneficial for these students. Another play theme that may signal suicidal risk in Black students is connection, as they may lack strong attachments. Play therapy interventions focused on increasing attachments are important treatment goals for these students. Additionally, students with feelings of helplessness and hopelessness may show signs of the protection and safety theme. The use of safety language, exploring safe places and people for that student, and building a strong therapeutic relationship will be key for students displaying this theme.

Suicide Risk Assessments

Before creating a safety plan, social workers should conduct a suicide risk assessment to determine the threat level and decide the best course of treatment to keep the student safe. It is important to remember that, per the National Association of Social Workers (2023), social workers have an ethical responsibility to break confidentiality when a client expresses harm to themselves or others. School social workers should explain confidentiality and events where confidentiality must be broken, regardless of the student's age. For younger children, it may sound like "I won't tell anyone the things we talk about, except if I'm worried you will hurt yourself or someone else." For older students, the language can more direct. For example, the social worker may say, "What we talk about in session is confidential, however, if you share any thought of hurting or killing yourself or others, I will have to let your parents know so we can come up with a plan to keep you safe."

The suicide threat levels are low, medium, and high risk. All students should continue to receive mental health support and enlist a safety plan until the suicide risk is nonexistent. Low risk is when a child is having thoughts of suicide, but they do not have plan or access to the means (e.g., pills, firearm) to harm themselves (National Institute of Mental Health [NIMH], 2020). These students may require more frequent or longer therapy sessions. The school social worker should also follow-up with the student in 2–3 days to check on their safety plan and conduct another suicide risk assessment. A student at medium risk for suicide may have thoughts of suicide and has either a plan or access to the means to harm themselves (NIMH, 2020). These students may benefit from multiple sessions a week, group therapy, and even additional mental health support from community therapists. The social worker should also follow-up with these students in 1–2 days to assess if the risk has reduced or increased.

The most concerning risk level is high risk, where a client has thoughts of suicide, a plan, and access to the means to harm themselves (NIMH, 2020). These students may also refuse to consent to the details of their safety plan and may be unmoving in their decision to harm themselves. Deploying emergency or crisis services may be necessary for these students or assisting the caregivers in getting the child to the hospital for a higher level of safety assessment. We need to do everything that we can to make sure that we ensure safety. School social workers should continue to conduct suicide risk assessments with the student until they no longer report suicidal thoughts and/or behaviors.

Safety Planning

Safety plans are an important part of documentation that seeks to keep the child safe. It will contain several things including coping skills, resources, and people they can talk to when they are having thoughts of harming themselves. First and foremost, if the child has identified how they will hurt themselves, it is important to determine if they have access to the object/item. If so, it will need to be removed from their environment. Next, the student is encouraged to identify safe people they can talk to if the social worker isn't available. This can include family members, friends, coaches, and teachers. Another important component of the safety plan is the student identifying coping skills or activities that can distract them from suicidal thoughts and/ or behaviors. The safety plan should also provide resources for the student, including suicide hotline numbers and important crisis resources in the community. The school social worker should be knowledgeable of the resources available in the community, including approaches such as Intensive In-Home Services, or wraparound services, that can provide more intense support for both students and their families.

When exploring community resources, the social worker should also be sensitive to cultural factors that may prevent Black caregivers from utilizing emergency services. Due to historical trauma with police interactions in the Black community, caregivers may be resistant to suggestions to call the police if the child is showing a higher risk of harming themselves since the last therapy session. This could also harm the therapeutic relationship, as it could come off as insensitive or tone deaf to the child and their family. It is beneficial to work with the caregiver and student to identify resources they are comfortable utilizing. However, it will still be important to stress that if a child is going to hurt themselves, then more drastic measures may be necessary to keep that child safe.

All safety plans should receive a verbal consent to the plan from the student. If the student is old enough to write their name, you can also have them sign their name as their consent to safety. A copy should go in the student's clinical file, and the student should take a copy home with them. If they are younger, the social worker should ask for permission to put it in the child's bookbag, so it is not misplaced. For older students who are concerned about other people seeing their plan, you can discuss a time when you can meet toward the end of the school day to give them their copy or brainstorm a way to keep their plan private.

Until the student reports no thoughts of suicide, the school social worker should check at each session to make sure the student is utilizing their safety plan and make any changes necessary. For example, a student may have on their safety plan to listen to music when they are having thoughts of harming themselves, but they may have their phone taken away for some other issue. In that situation, the social worker can either talk with the caregiver to find a way to compromise so the student can utilize the phone as part of their plan, help the student come up with other solutions to listening to music, or come up with a different coping skill altogether. Using safety plans like My Chill Plan (Appendix A) can assist school social workers in creating healthy alternatives to self-harm and other suicidal behaviors in students.

Play Therapy to Support Black Youth Experiencing Suicidality

When school social workers are supporting Black youth experiencing suicidality, play activities should focus on several things. Racial socialization messages that teach youth to value positive qualities about their race are important. Activities that value the student's personal attributes have been associated with positive psychological youth outcomes, including higher levels of anger control, fewer internalizing and externalizing behaviors, and higher self-esteem (Cheeks et al., 2020). Activities that focus on racial pride and identity and that encourage self-worth are important as well. There should also be a focus on family and social support. Studies found that on days that adolescents received messages from their parents suggesting that they were special, they reported more positive emotions and fewer negative emotions on that same day (Cheeks et al., 2020). Studies have found that programs that include both individual and group/family components are the most effective in decreasing both suicidal ideation and attempts (Calear et al., 2016). Therefore, after assessing the student's risk level, the school social worker should consider adding group or family play therapy into the student's treatment plan.

There are also some key playroom items to support these students. These include aggressive toys and grief toys/miniatures. Music in the playroom is also a key component to have for students. Music is big in the Black community, especially with adolescents, and is often identified as a coping skill in this population. The school social worker will benefit from having a radio or tablet that allows students to play music during their sessions. This often helps them feel more comfortable and may assist in them opening up more about things contributing to thoughts of suicide. Also, the type of music the child is listening to can alert the social worker to suicidality. For example, if they are listening to songs that are sad or that talk about violence or drug use, it could be an opening for the social worker to more thoroughly explore the client's song/artist selection, which may lead to the student expressing feelings/thoughts of self-harm. There are also several directive activities to help Black students.

Sand tray therapy is modality school social workers can use with Black students who may be at risk for suicide. Directive prompts that also explore race-based experiences (Appendix B) may be useful for students of all ages. School social workers should also consider grief miniatures and self-harm miniatures (e.g., dripping blood, bandages) to help Black students experiencing suicidality. Black students can benefit from engaging in sand tray therapy in individual play therapy, but also in group play therapy because a group setting may help them feel more comfortable talking about their feelings when they see they are not isolated in their thoughts and behaviors.

Adlerian Play Therapy

There are two key concepts in Adlerian Play Therapy that correlate with suicidality in Black youth. First, Adlerian therapists believe that children operate from feelings of inferiority, and their perceptions guide their thoughts, feelings and behaviors (Kottman, 2011). Black students dealing with race-based stress and trauma may start to develop these feelings of inferiority, which often contributes to mistaken beliefs. The idea of *mistaken beliefs*, also known as negative self-perceptions, is that children have subjective interpretations of the way others view them and this guides their behaviors (Kottman, 2011). In addressing Black youth suicide, school social workers could benefit from applying this play therapy seminal theory in individual and therapy, especially in the utilization of the "Crucial C's." The "Crucial C's" state (Kottman, 2011):

- Children need to know they count and are inherently valuable
- Children need the courage to try new things
- Children need positive connections with others
- Children are capable of great things

Play therapy interventions that implement the Crucial C's may be effective in addressing mistaken beliefs in Black children who have developed negative self-perceptions as a result of race-based stress and trauma. The other important piece of AdPT is engaging caregivers and teachers as "partners" (Kottman, 2011). Enhancing the relationships between Black children and the adults in their lives will be essential to address the epidemic of Black youth suicide.

Cognitive Behavioral Play Therapy

Black students exposed to daily acts of race-based stress and trauma may lead to cognitive distortions and negative thoughts, increasing their risk for suicidality. CBPT can be an effective tool to help students experiencing suicidality whose feelings and behaviors are connected to their negative thoughts. Both individual and group play therapy can incorporate CBPT to help students learn more appropriate coping skills like relaxation, mindfulness meditation and guided imagery (Drewes & Cavett, 2019). CBPT may be more appropriate for older students (grades 2nd-12th) whose cognitive development is more established, as younger children usually have not reached that level of development. The following play therapy interventions can be implemented in both CBPT and AdPT sessions.

Major Key Alert

Major Key Alert is an assessment activity that can help identify feelings of helplessness/hopelessness. The activity is most appropriate for students as young as 4th grade. The materials required for the activity are wooden craft keys, permanent markers, and paint markers. Encourage the client to decorate their keys, then write things they want to accomplish in the future. If the child struggles to identify plans for the future, it can help alert the school social worker to suicidal ideation. This activity can also be used in CBPT for students dealing with disparaging remarks that have affected their self-esteem. The student can be encouraged to think about negative things they have heard or have been told, then turn those into positive statements on their keys. Also, the student can be encouraged to have family members or friends write positive and encouraging words on their keys. This can help them with perceived burdensome and be helpful in increasing self-esteem.

Rainbows in the Rain

The next activity is called Rainbows in the Rain and is great activity to help identify mistaken beliefs when using AdPT. This activity is good for clients who struggle with finding the positive things in their lives due to high levels of depression and trauma. It requires colored sand, which can be purchased or students can create their own colored sand. Allowing students to make their own sand provides a sensory experience that can be therapeutically beneficial, and they can control the colors they make. To make their own sand, they will need sand, colored chalk, and a plastic tray. The child is prompted

---

to grind the chalk down into a powder, then mix it in with the sand until it is the color they desire.

For the activity, the materials required are colored sand, a bottle, and a funnel to create sand art. Rainbows in the Rain can be used with students as young as kindergarten. First, the child picks a color to represent each positive thing that they identify in their live. Students may be prone to focusing on the negative things, so if the conversation starts to turn negative, encourage the client to identify something positive that came from that negative situation. You can use the analogy that there are rainbows at the end of storms, so we are acknowledging the positive and beautiful things gained from unpleasant situations. They will use the funnel to pour the different colors into the bottle to create sand art and a visual reminder of the positive things they have gained through negative events. Please note that this activity may not be appropriate for clients who have had a recent grief event or have experienced abuse.

Just Do You Bingo

The next activity, Just Do You Bingo, is a game play therapy activity to help the client identify self-care activities and strategies. This activity can be a part of the client's safety plan and part of their coping skills. The student only needs the Just Do You Bingo handout (Appendix C) and something to write with. This activity is appropriate for clients as young as 2nd grade. The student write their coping skills on their bingo cards. Then they come up with rewards for when they get a bingo for three self-care items and a bigger reward for a blackout. This is a way to help motivate students to utilize their coping skills and follow their safety plan.

Distraction Box

The Distraction Box art therapy activity requires a plastic or cardboard box, the Distraction Box handout (Appendix D), craft materials like stickers and glitter, and pieces of paper. The activity can be used with students as young as 2nd grade. The student is given the materials and encouraged to decorate their box however they'd like. Then they are encouraged to write down coping skills from their safety plan. Next, they are encouraged to put items in their box that remind them of their coping skill or can be used when they are having thoughts of self-harm. Things in their box can include their headphones for listening to music, hard candy to help with regulation, and a jump rope for physical activity. The student should have this box in whatever environment that is the most triggering for them. This may require multiple boxes if suicidal ideation is present in several environments.

Shredded Portraits

The final activity, Shredded Portraits, is another CBPT activity that is appropriate for students as young as 3rd grade. The materials required are the Shredded Portrait handout (Appendix E), construction paper, glue, and markers. The student is encouraged to write negative statements/remarks they've heard or thought about themselves. They are instructed to tear the paper and create a self-portrait, then write positive statements about themselves around their picture. This is a good activity to assess any acts of racial stress or trauma the child may be experiencing while also teaching them important skills to manage those cognitions more appropriately.

Game Play for Social-Emotional Expression

As mentioned previously, Black students often need help learning how to effectively express their emotions, especially in relation to suicidal thoughts and behaviors. Using games in play therapy sessions can be a fun and effective way to help Black students express themselves. School social workers can benefit from keeping a set of playing cards, Uno, Connect Four, and checkers in their offices. These games are often used by older students to engage in talk or quiet therapy. A lot of students will play these games silently or while talking about things that seem unimportant. However, if the school social worker allows the games to serve as the therapeutic vehicle and does not rush the student to talk, students inevitably open up about the important things in their lives, sometimes seemingly out of nowhere. There are some additional games that school social workers can use to encourage emotional expression in Black students experiencing suicidality.

Feelings Dominoes

Feelings Dominoes can be utilized in individual and group play therapy sessions for students in 1st through 12th grades. Materials required for this game are a set of dominoes with different colors on the faces. Both the school counselor and student can work together to come up with 3–4 feelings for each color. For example, the feelings "happy," "scared," and "jealous" may be assigned to the color green. "Mad," "embarrassed," and "lonely" may be assigned to the color blue. Continue to work together to identify feelings for each color. Explain to the student that when they match a color, they must pick a feeling from the list connected to that color. Next, each time a player makes a match, they must name a time when they felt that feeling. If the game is being play in a group play therapy session, other group members can be encouraged to raise their hands when they identify with the feeling and scenario stated by the player. The game can be played with or without keeping score.

Feelings Jenga

Feelings Jenga is a game that can be played in both individual and group play therapy sessions with students in the 3rd through 12th grades. A Jenga game and markers are the only materials required for the game. Prior to the session, the counselor will write questions on the pieces that are as specific to their demographic as possible. For example, if professionals are working with students with high levels of community violence, questions may be more centered on grief. Questions may include "How does it make you feel when you hear about the death of someone you know?" "How do you handle grief?" or "Do you have someone you feel comfortable crying in front of?"

If the professional is working with Black students who are the minority in their school, the questions may be more specific to experiences of discrimination or racism in the school. For example, appropriate questions may include "How does it feel to go to school with a majority of White students?" "Do you think you're treated different at school because you're Black?" And "Have you ever thought a teacher was being tougher on you than a White student?" For younger students, you can use decoupage glue to glue emoji stickers to the pieces. It is recommended that the blocks with questions have two questions per piece so the student can choose which question they want to answer. In session, the game is played in its traditional manner; when a student chooses a block with a question, they have to answer one of the questions before they place it on top of the tower. The younger version with emojis has the student identify a time when they felt that feeling.

Jacked Up Feelings

The next game, Jacked Up Feelings, requires a set of jacks (and its accompanying rubber ball), the Jacked Up Feelings chart (Appendix F), and the Jacked Up Feelings score card (Appendix G). This can be played in individual and group play therapy sessions with 3rd grade students and older. To play the game, players take turns throwing the ball in the air and trying to grab as many jacks as they can. The player picks the number of emotions from the chart provided based on the number of jacks they were able to grab. For example, if they grab two jacks, they will need to pick two emotions from the chart. They are welcome to include emotions that are not listed on the chart. The chart is used as a starting point for those students who may have not the emotional vocabulary to express some emotions on their own. Next, they name a time when they felt the emotion(s) they picked. The student can skip, but they can only receive points for the emotions they share. The first person with 10 points wins the game.

Emoji Connection/Connect Four

The final game for emotional expression is Emoji Connection, which can be played with kindergarten through 5th-grade students in an individual or a group play therapy session. The materials required for the game is a Connect Four game set, scissors, decoupage glue, a brush, a paper plate, and emojis. Prior to playing the game in session, the therapist uses the decoupage glue and brush to secure the emojis to the Connect Four pieces. It is recommended that the decoupage glue be poured onto the paper plate to prevent it from getting too messy. Like the Feelings Jenga game, it is recommended that there are two emojis per piece, to allow the student an option between the two feelings. After the pieces are dry, they can be used in session. The game is played in its traditional fashion, however, when the student gets a connect four, they must pick four of the emojis from their connection and name a time when they felt each feeling to win the game.

Resources

Some key resources are helpful for Black youth experiencing suicidal ideation. The new number for the National Suicide Prevention Hotline is 988. However, generationally, students are more likely to communicate through text messaging, so the Crisis Text Line is a good resource for them. They text the word "home" to 741741 for help 24/7. The Trevor Project is a website that is an important resource for Black LGBTQ+ students. The Suicide Prevention Resource Center is a good resource for professionals who want to provide psychoeducational resources to caregivers and teachers. There also is the Suicide Prevention Lifeline that has a website that provides resources. Resources should be shared with the student, but may also need to be shared with caregivers and school staff members to increase their education around the signs of suicide in Black children.

Conclusion

Black youth are at an increased risk for suicidal ideation and behaviors due to their constant interactions with race-based stress and trauma. The epidemic of Black youth suicide highlights a need for innovative solutions to this complex issue. School social workers have a harder task in identifying suicide risk in this population because the signs are more subtle or overlooked by adults. Play therapy interventions, along with strong therapeutic relationships, can be integral components in saving the lives of Black youth. Therefore, it is imperative that school social workers address the rising trends of suicide in Black youth and help Black children reclaim their childhood.

References

American Foundation for Suicide Prevention. (2022). https://afsp.org/

Andrews, G. (2019, December 17). Bend-La Pine Schools sued for Black student's 2017 suicide. *The Bulletin*. https://www.bendbulletin.com/localstate/bend-la-pine-schools-sued-for-black-students-2017-suicide/article_ed4385a0-2038-11ea-a5e6-33af2d033334.html

Arshanapally, S., Werner, K., Sartor, C., & Bucholz, K. (2018). The association between racial discrimination and suicidality among African-American adolescents and young adults. *Archives of Suicide Research*, 22(4), 584–595. https://doi-org.libproxy1.usc.edu/10.1080/13811118.2017.1387207

Assari, S., Moghani Lankarani, M., & Caldwell, C. (2017). Discrimination increases suicidal ideation in Black adolescents regardless of ethnicity and gender. *Behavioral Sciences*, 7(4), 75. https://doi.org/10.3390/bs7040075

Auxier, B. (2020). Social media continue to be important political outlets for Black Americans. Pew Research Center. https://www.pewresearch.org/fact-tank/2020/12/11/social-media-continue-to-be-important-political-outlets-for-black-americans/

Barker, C. J. (2018, December 11). Black girl commits suicide after racist bullying. *New York Amsterdam News*. http://amsterdamnews.com/news/2018/dec/11/alabama-9-year-old-kills-herself-after-racist-bull/

Black News. (2020, April 17). *15-year old Black teen commits suicide, had mental health issues while self-quarantining*. https://www.blacknews.com/news/jovianni-smith-black-teen-commits-suicide-mental-health-issues-quarantining-california/

Burke, M. (2020, January 5). Florida high school football star's death highlights rising suicide rates among Black youth. *NBC News*. https://www.nbcnews.com/news/us-news/florida-high-school-football-star-s-death-highlights-rising-suicide-n1110436

Calear, A. L., Christensen, H., Freeman, A., Fenton, K., Busby Grant, J., van Spijker, B., & Donker, T. (2016). A systematic review of psychosocial suicide prevention interventions for youth. *European Child & Adolescent Psychiatry*, 25, 467–482. https://doi-org.libproxy1.usc.edu/10.1007/s00787-015-0783-4

Centers for Disease Control and Prevention. (2020). Youth Risk Behavior Surveillance: United States, 2019. [Report]. *Morbidity and Mortality Weekly Report*, 69(1). https://www.cdc.gov/mmwr/ind2020_su.html

Cheeks, B., Chavous, T., & Sellers, R. (2020). A daily examination of African American adolescents' racial discrimination, parental racial socialization, and psychological affect. *Child Development*, 91(6), 2123–2140. https://doi.org/10.1111/cdev.13416

Congressional Black Caucus. Emergency Task Force on Black Youth Suicide and Mental Health. (2019). Ring the alarm: The crisis of Black youth suicide in America. https://watsoncoleman.house.gov/uploadedfiles/full_taskforce_report.pdf

Drewes, A., & Cavett, A. (2019). Cognitive Behavioral Play Therapy. *Play Therapy Magazine*, 14(3), 24–26. https://cdn.ymaws.com/www.a4pt.org/resource/resmgr/publications/pt_theories/CognitiveBehavioral__Sept201.pdf

English, D., Lambert, S., Tynes, B., Bowleg, L., Zea, M., & Howard, L. (2020). Daily multidimensional racial discrimination among Black U.S. American adolescents. *Journal of Applied Developmental Psychology*, 66, 101068. https://doi.org/10.1016/j.appdev.2019.101068

Green, A. E., Price-Feeney, M., & Dorison, S. (2020). Breaking barriers to quality mental health care for LGBTQ youth. The Trevor Project. https://www.thetrevorproject.org/wp-content/uploads/2020/08/Breaking-Barriers-to-Quality-Mental-Health-Care-for-LGBTQ-Youth-Updated-7-28-2020.pdf

Grills, C., Banks, J., Norrington-Sands, K., Jackson, T. R., Steve, S. L., & Clark, M. (2019). Black child suicide: A report. National Cares Mentoring Movement. https://www.caresmentoring.org/black_child_suicide_report.pdf

Hollingsworth, D., Cole, A., O'Keefe, V., Tucker, R., Story, C., & Wingate, L. (2017). Experiencing racial microaggressions influences suicide ideation through perceived burdensomeness in African Americans. *Journal of Counseling Psychology*, 64(1), 104–111. https://doi.org/10.1037/cou0000177

Joe, S., Scott, M., & Banks, A. (2018). What works for adolescent Black males at risk of suicide: A review. *Research on Social Work Practice*, 28(3), 340–345. https://doi-org.libproxy1.usc.edu/10.1177/1049731517702745

Klonsky, E. D., Victor, S. E., & Saffer, B. Y. (2014). Nonsuicidal self-injury: What we know and what we need to know. *Canadian Journal of Psychiatry*, 59(11), 565–568. https://www.ncbi.nlm.nih.gov/pmc/articles/PMC4244874/

Kottman, T. (2011). *Adlerian play therapy [Book chapter]. Foundations of Play Therapy* (2nd ed.). John Wiley and Sons, Inc.

Lanier, Y., Sommers, M., Fletcher, J., Sutton, M., & Roberts, D. (2017). Examining racial discrimination frequency, racial discrimination stress, and psychological well-being among Black early adolescents. *Journal of Black Psychology*, 43(3), 219–229. https://doi.org/10.1177/0095798416638189

Lee, C., & Wong, Y. (2020). Racial/ethnic and gender differences in the antecedents of youth suicide. *Cultural Diversity & Ethnic Minority Psychology*. https://doi.org/10.1037/cdp0000326

Lindsey, M., Sheftall, A., Xiao, Y., & Joe, S. (2019). Trends of suicidal behaviors among high school students in the United States: 1991–2017. *Pediatrics*, 144(5), Article e20191912. https://doi-org.libproxy1.usc.edu/10.1542/peds.2019-1912

National Association of Social Workers. (2023). Read the code of ethics. https://www.social workers.org/About/Ethics/Code-of-Ethics/Code-of-Ethics-English

National Institute of Mental Health (NIMH). (2020). asQ suicide risk screening toolkit. https://www.nimh.nih.gov/sites/default/files/documents/research/research-conducted-at-nimh/asq-toolkit-materials/asq-tool/screening_tool_asq_nimh_toolkit.pdf

National Strategy for Suicide Prevention. (2001). Glossary of suicide prevention terms. U.S. Department of Health and Human Services, Public Health Service. https://www.sprc.org/sites/default/files/migrate/library/glossary.pdf

Olson, R. (2011). Suicide and language. Centre for Suicide Prevention. https://www.suic ideinfo.ca/local_resource/suicideandlanguage/

Pachter, L., Caldwell, C., Jackson, J., & Bernstein, B. (2018). Discrimination and mental health in a representative sample of African-American and Afro-Caribbean Youth. *Journal of Racial and Ethnic Health Disparities*, 5(4), 831–837. https://doi.org/10.1007/s40615-017-0428-z

Price, J., & Khubchandani, J. (2019). The changing characteristics of African-American adolescent suicides, 2001–2017. *Journal of Community Health*, 44(4), 756–763. https://doi-org.libproxy1.usc.edu/10.1007/s10900-019-00678-x

Shain, B. N. (2019). Increases in the rates of suicide and suicide attempts among Black adolescents. *Pediatrics*, 144(5), e20191912. https://doi.org/10.1542/peds.2019-1912

Tomek, S., Hooper, L., Church, W., Bolland, K., Bolland, J., & Wilcox, K. (2015). Relations among suicidality, recent/frequent alcohol use, and gender in a Black American Adolescent sample: A longitudinal investigation. *Journal of Clinical Psychology*, 71(6), 544–560. doi.org/10.1002/jclp.22169

Walker, R., Francis, D., Brody, G., Simons, R., Cutrona, C., & Gibbons, F. (2016). A longitudinal study of racial discrimination and risk for death ideation in African American youth. *Suicide and Life-Threatening Behavior*, 47(1), 86–102. https://doi-org.libproxy1.usc.edu/10.1111/sltb.12251

Washington, E. A. (2007). *Medical apartheid: The dark history of medical experimentation on Black Americans from the colonial times to the present*. Doubleday.

Appendix A   My Chill Plan

My Chill Plan

You may not have control over the racial experiences that happen to you, but you have control over the way you can react to them and manage the stress it may cause. Use the boxes below to create your chill plan of coping skills to help manage racial stress.

Suicide Risk

357

Sand Tray Prompts for Suicidal Behaviors

Create a sand tray showing life if you did not have thoughts of harming yourself

Create a sand tray showing your distraction plan

Create a sand tray showing your safe people

Create a sand tray showing your safe place

Create a sand tray showing your life before and after you started having self-harm thoughts

Create a scene that triggers your thoughts of self-harm. Now create a scene that shows the coping skills you have to manage your triggers

BMH Connect

mylemarks

Appendix C Just Do You Bingo

Distractions

Go for a walk
Talk to a friend
Talk to a parent
Listen to music
Color
Draw
Watch a funny tv show

Watch a funny movie
Cook your favorite food
Take a sip of water
Do yoga
Stretch
Play a board game
Play a video game
Build something with legos

Do a craft
Knit or crochet
Exercise
Go for a jog
Talk to a teacher
Journal
Ask someone for a hug
Give yourself a hug

Do a progressive muscle relaxation exercise
Meditate
Sing your favorite song
Have a dance party
Learn a new tik tok dance
Facetime a friend
Facetime a family member

BMH Connect

mylemarks

© 2022 BMH Connect & Mylemarks

Jacked Up Feelings

Required Materials

A set of jacks, a ball, handout and score card (see folder)

Directions

Use the jacks and ball to play a game of jacks. To do this, you will lightly throw the jacks in the air to have them spread out in front of you. Throw the ball in the air and try to grab as many jacks as you can before catching the ball.

If you do not catch the ball, you lose your turn. If you catch the ball, you have to count the number of jacks you have in your hand. Then using the worksheet, you will pick the amount of feelings to match your jacks in your hand.

For example, if you have two jacks, you will pick two feelings and will have to share about a time you felt that emotion. If you do this, you get 2 points. If you identify a time someone else felt that emotion, you get 1 point. And if you choose to pass, you get 0 points.

The first person to 10 points wins!

BMH Connect

Jacked Up Feelings Faces

happy	awkward	bored	disappointed
excited	miserable	sad	clueless
worried	confused	content	edgy
cranky	deflated	elated	nervous
dizzy	happy	angry	silly

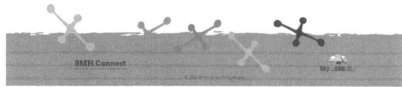

BMH Connect

Jacked Up Feelings
Score Card

Points	Emotion
☐	_____
☐	_____
☐	_____
☐	_____
☐	_____
☐	_____
☐	_____
☐	_____

BMH Connect

Jacked Up Feelings

Score Card

Points   **Emotion**

☐ _____

☐ _____

☐ _____

☐ _____

☐ _____

☐ _____

☐ _____

Total Points _____

BMH Connect

9

■■■

Teachers Play, Too!
Play Therapy to Support Teachers Working with Black Students

Educators are dealing with a variety of variables, including staff shortages as a result of the COVID-19 pandemic. I truly admire the tireless work that teachers provide to educate our children. So, this book is not meant to scold or put down the amazing work done by teachers across the country. However, when teachers are juggling so many roles, it may result in less patience and empathy towards students, especially students of color. Teachers need to education on the unique needs of Black students, as well as patience and empathy from school social workers. This chapter seeks to offer a glimmer of hope of how therapists can build relationships with teachers and offer up solutions that can be used both in and out of the classroom.

School staff members may struggle with understanding the best ways to support Black students. School social workers should dedicate time to educating teachers on the possible racial stressors Black students may experience and how that may guide their moods and behaviors in schools. Consultations, peer support groups, and professional development workshops are ways that school social workers can help teachers learn more about the symptoms and signs of racial trauma in Black students, along with practical skills, tools, and support to manage perceived problem behaviors. However, it is important to consider how overwhelmed educators may feel with their own levels of trauma, including vicarious trauma. Teachers could benefit from school social workers helping them recognize the signs of vicarious trauma and burnout they may experience from working with the overwhelming issues

Black Students Matter. April D. Duncan, Oxford University Press. © Oxford University Press 2024.
DOI: 10.1093/oso/9780197669266.003.0010

plaguing Black students. Additionally, mindfulness activities can be used in teacher support groups and consultations to create self-care plans to address vicarious trauma and aid in learning self-regulation skills.

Using play-based strategies with teachers helps them gain the confidence and skills to build healthier relationships with Black students. Child–Teacher Relationship Therapy (CTRT) is a play-based intervention that utilizes filial therapy to help teachers enhance their attachments with Black students. CTRT could serve as a useful tool to help repair damaged teacher–student relationships with Black students. Additionally, school social workers can work with teachers on how to integrate play into their classrooms to assist with classroom management, increasing on-task behaviors, and emotional regulation.

White Teachers Teaching Black Students

In the 2020–2021 school year, there were 7.7 million teachers for more than 54 million students in both public and private schools in the United State (National Center for Education Statistics [NCES], 2019). The 2019 NCES report found Black students accounted for 14.9% of the public school population (approximately 7.4 million), making them the third largest demographic behind White and Latinx students (22.4 million and 14.1 million students, respectively). It is predicted that students of color will outnumber White students by 2028 (Elmadani et al., 2022). However, the increase of students of color is not reflected in the educators teaching them. The most recent data identify 80% of teachers in public K-12 schools as White, 9% as Latinx, and only 6% as Black (Taie et al., 2022). That same lack of diversity exists in private schools: 83% of private school teachers are White, 8% Latinx, and 4% Black (Taie et al., 2022). The lack of diversity among teachers across the country may make it more difficult to recognize racial trauma symptoms in Black students.

This shortage of teachers of color could put Black students at a higher risk of being disciplined and treated with discrimination due to the implicit biases of White teachers. Individuals who subscribe to norms of whiteness may perceive the cultural expressions of children of color to be deviant, which can result in both teachers and peers treating children of color differently and more harshly (Henderson et al., 2021). As a result, many teachers may not feel equipped to understand the cultural and emotional needs of Black students who constantly navigate minefields of unconscious bias within the school system and sometimes in teachers themselves. Understanding and respecting cultural differences will be a big step in building quality relationships with Black children. When students see that teachers respect their cultural identity, they can then feel safe to explore, share, and learn from other peers' cultures as well (Elmadani et al., 2022).

It is also to acknowledge that there may be times that Black students may have difficulty listening to and interacting with White teachers, but may excel when placed with a Black teacher. While consulting on a case for a Black 6-year-old, the school officials shared that the child "does so much better" with two teachers who are Black, but they were resistant to moving him to the class with those teachers. They were attempting every effort to save a teacher-student relationship that was impaired, however, it was done to the detriment to the child. The child was being suspended for impulsive and aggressive behaviors. Finally, I said "Why don't ya'll put the child with the Black teachers if he does better with them?" Their resistance was due to not wanting to appear to be racist and wanting to make the arrangement work. I told them "I know it shouldn't be that way, but if we know the child does better with the Black teachers, why are we still trying to fit a square peg in a round hole?!". I'm not quite sure what decisions they made after I gave my opinion, but I believe this is an important thing to acknowledge: sometimes Black students are suffering because teachers are trying to avoid the answer that is clear out of fear of how they are perceived, or maybe even ego. Either way, we should not have students suffering because we are afraid to make the hard decisions.

Teachers of all backgrounds often lack the skills to support the mental health needs of their students or de-escalate conflict. A 2019 survey conducted by Education Week Research Center found 29% of teachers received mental health training and less than 40% of teachers received training in conflict de-escalation (Schwartz, 2019). Teachers could benefit from professional development workshops and ongoing support groups on effective ways to de-escalate situations with students, especially incidents with Black students, that may lead to unnecessary disciplinary referrals or intervention from school resource officers/law enforcement. They could also benefit from psychoeducation about the signs of mental distress in relation to race-based stress and trauma. In doing so, teachers may feel more empowered to advocate for more effective disciplinary options for Black students because they have a high level of influence when contributing to the ways in which school discipline policies are shaped.

Impaired Teacher–Student Relationships

Classroom management is another area in which school social workers can support teachers working with Black students. Impaired teacher–student relationships may be an indirect result of school discipline, which may further exacerbate the cycle of discipline among Black students. Sometimes this damage is from previous educational experiences. Since school discipline starts early for Black students, they may be dealing with racial trauma prior to their experience with the teacher. This could lead to high levels of mistrust and apprehension, with the Black student already hypervigilant to labels and mistreatment. That hyperawareness could cause the Black student to be more sensitive to microaggressions or other perceived slights of differential treatment. The student may also feel as if the teacher is "out to get them," which could further damage the teacher–student relationship. If a Black student thinks a teacher does not like them, it may deepen the rift.

The issue of teacher–student relationships among Black children dealing with perceived racial trauma is explored in the book, *Posttraumatic Slave Syndrome: America's Legacy of Enduring Injury & Healing.* DeGruy (2017) states that

> In African American communities, relationship frequently trumps everything else. Consideration of relationship permeates all of our interactions. For example, when Black students feel they have been disrespected by a teacher, they often feel completely justified in rebelling and shutting out the offending teacher, even if it means failing the class and sabotaging academic aspirations. Some students may go so far as to act out and wind up facing disciplinary action of some kind. (19)

Both teachers and students may struggle with breaking this disciplinary cycle. The key to breaking the cycle may lie within the teacher–student relationship. To fix the relationship, the teacher will need to (1) learn how to let go of past incidents and start each day fresh and (2) spend one-on-one time with the student to have more positive interactions in the classroom.

Although a student may have behaviors that the teacher sees as disrespectful or disruptive, it is important that they start each day fresh with the child, regardless of what happened on the prior day. Holding on to previous negative interactions further feeds into the student's mindset of "the teacher is out to get me." Therefore, school social workers should work with teachers on developing a mindfulness mindset, where they are focused on who the student is in the present, not the student from the previous day. It will also include providing teachers with de-escalation strategies and stresses the importance of disengaging from power struggles with students.

Special Time

As mentioned in previous chapters, "special time" is when parents spend five minutes of one-on-one time with their child, regardless of that child's behavior. However, this can also be used with teachers with impaired relationships with Black students. The teacher can be encouraged to identify a child in need of additional attention and engage in five minutes of individual play time with the child. Like special time with caregivers, this should happen regardless of the type of behaviors the student had that day. This can communicate to the student that the teacher is a trusted, nonjudgmental adult who is dedicated to helping them even when they have a tough day or moment. Implicit biases about the child's behaviors may be forming that can impede the way that the teacher interacts with that student or the way they discipline them. The act of "special time" can help the teacher and student participate in more positive interactions, which may then decrease any unconscious biases that have developed in the teacher–student relationship. It may also help the student see the teacher in a better light and heal impaired relationships.

This idea came from a situation with a teacher at a school I was working at a few years ago. The teacher had a student was clingy and would have disruptive and aggressive behaviors when they did not receive attention from the teacher. I educated the teacher on attachment and the use of "special time" with the child in the classroom. The teacher had their apprehensions at first but was open to trying the concept. After three weeks of special time, the teacher shared the child no longer fought for their attention because they had "special time" to look forward to each day. After two full months of "special time," the child no longer needed the one-on-one time and had improved behaviors in the classroom and with peers. I believe this concept can be applicable for students of all ages as an appropriate way to mend impaired student-teacher relationships.

Direct Racial Stressors: School Resource Officers

The fact is that teachers are overburdened and often must wear several hats due to the lack of resources in their schools. Studies have shown that 14 million students in the United States have police officers in their schools, but they do not have any type of school support staff such as nurses, school psychologists, counselors, or social workers (Whitaker et al., 2019). The average classroom size in public schools is 17.9 students per class (Taie et al., 2022) and 4% of public schools report widespread disorder in classrooms (Wang et al., 2022). Almost 10% of public schools reported student verbal abuse toward teachers and 155 of schools reported disrespectful behavior toward teachers in the 2019–2020 school year (Wang et al., 2022). However, "disorder," "verbal abuse," and "disrespectful behavior" are subjective evaluations. This is not to minimize what "disruptive" behaviors teachers deal with, but rather it is to highlight that Black students are being disciplined for subjective behaviors that continue to harm the teacher–student relationship when these issues could be resolved with stronger relationships, cultural humility, and conflict management skills. Teachers also need more support. Some teachers may request help from law enforcement when there are no other behavioral resources available (Whitaker et al., 2019). This has resulted in police becoming de facto disciplinarians and schools becoming a breeding ground for the criminalization of Black children.

Schools with police officers have 3.5 times as many arrests as schools without them (Whitaker et al., 2019). Police officers are being called in for things that normally would be handled by the school, which has aided in sustaining the preschool-to-prison pipeline. Students have been charged with disorderly conduct for cursing, disrupting school for criticizing an officer, assault for throwing baby carrots, petit larceny for taking a milk carton, drug possession for carrying a maple leaf, and indecent exposure for wearing saggy pants (Whitaker et al., 2019). This situation mimics the Convict Lease System, which ran from 1846–1928, where White, southern plantation owners needed cheap labor after the Civil War abolished slavery. They worked to bring trumped up charges against Black people as a way of legally securing large numbers of cheap or free human laborers (DeGruy, 2017). Examples during this dark period included sexual assault charges for looking at a White woman and a charge for disturbing the peace by walking on the wrong side of the street (DeGruy, 2017). One way school social workers can address racial trauma in Black children and help dismantle the preschool-to-prison pipeline is to advocate for more mental health support and less police in schools.

One can argue that the overuse of police officers in school discipline issues, especially with Black students, further exacerbates racial trauma symptoms. This is especially true when we consider the racial messages Black students are given on how to act and/or interact when they encounter law enforcement. "The talk" in the Black community is an important cultural factor to consider when applying a racial trauma lens to view the behaviors of Black students. "The talk" is how Black caregivers discuss with their children how they're supposed to act whenever they are around police officers. Behaviors communicated to Black children at an early age include be respectful, don't talk back, and move slowly when they give a command. Coming from a place of safety, Black parents are consciously protecting their children from perceived harm, but inadvertently they are contributing to racial stressors that may be triggered at schools with school resource officers. In theory, if a child has been conditioned to be fearful or hypervigilant around police officers and they are in a school with officers, this could contribute to behaviors such as impulsivity, problems focusing, anger, and defiance in Black students. These same behaviors are often misdiagnosed as conduct disorder, oppositional defiant disorder, and attention deficit hyperactivity disorder, when instead that student may be dealing with racial trauma triggers that are misinterpreted as other forms of mental distress.

Teacher Advocacy for Black Students

There is an opportunity for teachers to assist in the advocacy for more appropriate disciplinary measures for students of color. Social workers are trained to jumpstart and maintain difficult conversations around race and help individuals be nondefensive and self-reflective, as well as act as mediators between educators and caregivers (Gibson & Haight, 2013). Therefore, school social workers are the bridge to building stronger bonds and healthier relationships between teachers and Black students. Approximately 70% of public school teachers and approximately 80% of private school teachers reported having some influence in setting and shaping discipline policy, while an overwhelming 96% of all teachers report having control over disciplining their students (Taie et al., 2022). These statistics highlight that the first people to help address racial disparities in school discipline toward Black students are the teachers themselves. This will require school social workers to provide psychoeducation on the needs of Black students, along with implicit bias training that can help teachers identify their blind spots in teaching and disciplining Black students. Like both Black students and caregivers, school workers also will need to first build rapport and healthy relationships with teachers to provide the same level of empathy, compassion, and nonjudgmental support they will need to show to Black students and families. Trust can begin by exhibiting empathy for the negative effects on their mental health when working with kids with high levels of trauma.

Vicarious Trauma Risk Factors

Teachers working with students with high levels of trauma may be at an increased risk of developing vicarious trauma. Vicarious trauma, also known as *compassion fatigue*, can occur due to hearing individuals recount their victimization or hearing about or responding to violent or traumatic events daily (Office for Victims of Crime, n.d.). Studies have found 78% of teachers reported feeling physically and mentally exhausted at the end of the workday, and 93% of teachers reported high levels of job stress (Happy Teacher Revolution, 2022). There are some factors that may cause a teacher to experience vicarious trauma. Individuals with prior traumatic experiences, a history of avoidant behaviors, and difficulty expressing their feelings may be at a higher risk for developing vicarious trauma (Office for Victims for Crime, n.d.). Other risk factors include social isolation both on and off the job; lack of preparation, training, and supervision; lack of an effective support process for discussing traumatic incidents; being newer employees; and constant and intense trauma exposure (Office for Victims Crime, n.d.). There are several ways school social workers and administrators can help decrease the probability of teachers experiencing vicarious trauma.

Identifying the signs of vicarious trauma is an important first step in supporting teachers working with students experiencing high levels of trauma. Signs of vicarious trauma in teachers (Office for Victims Crime, n.d.) include:

- Feeling emotionally numb or shut down
- Difficulty managing emotions
- Physical problems or complaints (e.g., pains, aches) and decreased resistance to illness
- Fatigue, sleepiness, or difficulty falling asleep
- Loss of sense of meaning in life or feeling hopeless/helpless about the future
- Easily distracted
- Relationship problems
- Feelings of vulnerability or excessive worrying about potential dangers and the safety of their loved ones
- Increased irritability that may appear as explosive, aggressive, or violent outbursts and behavior
- Destructive coping or addictive behaviors such as over-/undereating, substance use

- Lack of decreased participation in activities that were once pleasurable
- Avoiding work or interactions with students and/or staff
- Experiencing symptoms that meet criteria for posttraumatic stress disorder (PTSD)

Teachers exhibiting these behaviors/symptoms should be assessed for vicarious trauma and given resources and support to help manage them more effectively. This can include referrals for individual therapy in the community or through their Employee Assistance Plan (EAP), if applicable.

Supporting Teachers Through Vicarious Trauma

School social workers possess knowledge in stress management, emotional regulation, and self-care that could benefit teachers and administrators. Providing group therapy support can provide connections for teachers so they do not feel isolated in their experiences and feelings. This can also be a way for school social workers to integrate some play-based strategies that can assist in self-regulation and stress management. Additionally, the use of CTRT can be an effective intervention to help teachers gain skills in classroom management and relationship building with students. Group therapy settings for teachers may also be a place where school social workers can discuss the importance of self-care using self-care plans as well as share resources in the community teachers that can benefit from.

Group Therapy Support

Engaging school administrators will be a crucial step in supporting teachers. School administrators can aid in decreasing rates of vicarious trauma in their teachers by providing more support, training, and supervision to their new teachers. The average years of service of all teachers working at their current school is approximately 8% nationwide; however, 38% of teachers reported working at their schools for 3 years or less, with city schools making up the highest percentage of teachers with 3 years or less at their current school (Taie et al., 2022). This could possibly indicate that teachers feel less equipped to work long-term in schools with higher needs and less accessibility to resources. In turn, this may also contribute to vicarious trauma, burnout, and high turnover in those schools with students who need the most consistency and stable relationships.

Additionally, teachers may benefit from completing a screening of their trauma exposure and their own history of receiving mental health treatment for any past traumatic events. Although teachers may be resistant to sharing this information, which should remain confidential, this may allow school administrators to have a better idea of who has had their own traumatic experiences that may be triggered by students and can further strain teacher–student relationships. Teachers who have not received mental health support may be given community referrals for mental health treatment, directed to available EAP services, or can receive support from monthly or quarterly mental health support groups led by school social workers.

School social workers have an opportunity to provide an innovative prevention tool to address vicarious trauma in teachers. Providing play-based activities in a group setting can create a community for teachers so they do not feel isolated in their experiences. It can also provide a space for emotional expression and a solution for teachers with a history of avoidant behaviors. Additionally, it may provide the opportunity to offer a safe space for teachers to manage their mental distress using play-based activities such as art therapy techniques like Zentangles or sand tray therapy. School social workers can also offer things like game and trivia nights, paint and sip (nonalcoholic drinks), and line dancing classes for teachers to have a safe space to blow off steam. Integrating mindfulness into these groups may also be helpful, using things like yoga, progressive muscle relaxation, and guided meditations in a room featuring calming music and aromatherapy. If the school has the resources, school social workers can advocate for a calming room as a drop-in space where teachers can destress throughout the day as needed. The room could have calming music, jigsaw puzzles, crossword puzzles, fidgets, a massage or rocking chair, coloring books, and aromatherapy to create a place where teachers can decompress before, during, and after the school day. Calmer teachers help create calmer classrooms.

Child—Teacher Relationship Training
The cultural differences between Black students and teachers of other races are a huge barrier to the relationships that can be built. Teachers often feel ill-equipped to manage the layers of issues students experience and that contribute to classroom disruptions and disciplinary issues. Teachers who lack the skills needed to support their students may experience emotional exhaustion, burnout, and secondary stress, which may increase the likelihood that teachers respond to students in ineffective ways that

reinforce negative behaviors and contribute to negative teacher–student relationships (Post et al., 2022). This can also lead to negative mental health effects for teachers. Since teachers may receive inadequate training on responding to the needs of children who have experienced trauma, they may not be trained to manage their own stress responses, which may lead to feelings of powerlessness and hopelessness (Post et al., 2022). The use of teacher training models like CTRT can serve as an effective tool for building stronger skills in teachers and mending damaged relationships with students.

CTRT is a modification of the Child–Parent Relationship Therapy (CPRT) approach that is rooted in the foundations of filial therapy and can be used with teachers in the school environment (Gonzales-Ball & Bratton, 2019). CTRT is a child-centered approach focused on relationship-building skills and attitudes, such as responding to feelings, self-esteem building, tracking, paraphrasing, choice-giving, and limit setting (Landreth, 2012). The limited studies done of this model found teachers to have a better understanding of their students and a higher degree of confidence when dealing with disruptive and problematic behaviors (Gonzales-Ball & Bratton, 2019). A downside to this approach is that it requires a significant amount of time to implement the intervention (Gonzales-Ball & Bratton, 2019). Teachers may already feel overwhelmed and pulled in too many directions, so it may be difficult to gain buy-in for this approach. However, the school social worker should try to help teachers focus on the long-term benefits of their short-term sacrifice, which can lead to better classroom management skills and stronger teacher–student relationships.

Self-Care Plans

Teachers may struggle with identifying their need for self-care or how to engage in the practice. They may also struggle with finding the time to take care of themselves due to the great responsibility they have in taking care of others. The use of a self-care plan could help teachers learn the importance of taking care of themselves and the specific ways that it can be done. I like to say, "You have to be selfish to be selfless." Another phrase used is "You cannot pour from an empty cup." Some important areas of their self-care plan cover the ways they will take care of their mind, body, and spirit. The school social worker should encourage teachers to take time to explore specific things they can do to take care of themselves in each realm (Box 9.1).

Box 9.1 Self-Care Plan Ideas

Mind

- Read a book, go to a museum exhibit, watch a documentary, take a mindful walk, meditate, take a social media break, take a nap

Body

- Try a new exercise class, stretch, take a walk, eat healthier, dance, join a gym, do yoga

Spirit

- Volunteer, attend a religious/spiritual ceremony, practice reiki, practice earthing techniques (e.g., walking barefoot in the grass)

Teachers can also be encouraged to create accountability teams or select accountability partners who can help motivate them and hold them responsible to their plan. Teachers may also be open to a healthy competition that can be school-wide and help promote the overall health of the entire school.

Resources for Teachers

Several resources can be helpful to support the mental health needs of teachers. The app *Calm* from the Calm Schools Initiative offers a self-care guide for teachers and a 30-day guide on implementing mindfulness into the classroom (Calm, 2022b). *Headspace* is another mindfulness app that is free for Teach for America corps members and alumni (Teach.com, 2022). Outside of group support from school social workers, teachers may also be interested in connecting with other educators across the country. Happy Teacher Revolution (2022) is based out of Baltimore and trains "Revolutionaries" to implement their Happy Teacher Revolution support group meetings that focus on the mental health and wellness of teachers around the world. The National Council of Teachers of English (2022) offers informal meetings where members can collaborate, support, and inspire each other.

Teachers can also use social media as a resource of support. The Facebook group Teaching with Mental Health in Mind provides mental health resources and support to educators (Facebook, 2022). For audio learners, the following podcasts provide a community of support and self-care tips: "The Cult of Pedagogy," "HMH Learning Moments," "Passing Notes," "Teach Me, Teacher," "Teachers' Aid," "The Teacher Self-Care Podcast," and "Truth for Teachers" (Teach.com, 2022). Teachers may also be encouraged to start a podcast club to have a space in which to discuss the featured topics and open conversations with their peers on ways to improve the mental wellness of the staff community. Assisting teachers in finding ways to manage their own mental health can give them more tools in their toolkit to share with students and help model self-regulation.

Play in the Classroom

Because of the limitations of funding and staff, many school social workers have difficulty serving all of the students in need. And, as the statistics show, the children most likely to be left behind for mental health treatment are Black students. Therefore, there is an opportunity for teachers to integrate play-based activities into the classroom to aid in classroom management. Teachers can also use play-based interventions to provide sensory experiences that can help create a safe and comfortable environment for all kids to learn and excel. Studies have found most teachers have some form of autonomy over what is taught and how it is taught in their classrooms. For example, 87% of public and private school teachers reported having control over the content, topics, and skills taught in their classrooms, although city public schools report less autonomy than suburban, small-town, and rural public schools (Taie et al., 2022). School social workers have the potential to collaborate with teachers to implement play-based strategies that can assist in classroom management, increase engagement, and build stronger relationships with students. One way this can be achieved is through the use of *solution-focused play therapy* (SFPT) in the classroom.

Solution-Focused Play Therapy

The SFPT approach can help with empowerment in Black students while also helping them work toward goals both in and out of the classroom. SFPT is effective in assisting with classroom management, and it often involves caregivers, teachers, and other important members of the child's system in the process (Hartwig & Taylor, 2022). For younger students, teachers may be encouraged to use puppets each day to have children communicate the goal they have set for themselves. Older students, 3rd grade and beyond, can be encouraged to draw, journal, or play charades to act out their weekly goal, along with their plan to achieve that goal. The goals can be small, like raising their hand before answering a question, or bigger, like turning in their project on time. For younger students, teachers could institute a "store" where students earn points for meeting their daily goal and that they then use to buy things at the end of the week. To account for students who struggle to meet their goals for reasons such as lack of mental health support or a recent traumatic event, teachers could also offer a "good effort" section to choose from for students who did not earn any points that week. This acknowledges their effort, does not isolate them from their peers, and can encourage students to remain positive and motivated to work toward their goals the following week. For older students, teachers could create a classroom goal to work toward a reward that everyone can benefit from like a movie day, free day, or pizza day. This may also encourage peer support and motivation for students who are struggling to meet their goals on their own.

Creating Safe Places in Classrooms with Sensory Supports

Black students need safe places to manage racial stressors in their life. This can include stressors within their school environment such as bullying or impaired teacher–student relationships. Since students spend most of their school days in the classroom, it is a natural environment in which to integrate toys, materials, and sensory materials to provide safe places. There are fun and basic ways teachers can create safe classrooms that include sensory supports, brain break activities, calm-down corners, and fidget boxes. Integrating these suggestions can assist with everyone indirectly addressing their mental health in a more preventative way.

Children who have experienced trauma may have more difficulty with emotional regulation and engaging in appropriate behaviors, therefore interventions should focus on children learning how to regulate their bodies before they are expected to regulate their emotions (Ryan, 2020). Sensory inputs are an effective way to assist with self-regulation. There are several ways teachers can integrate sensory supports into their environment such as weighted toys and blankets, modeling clay, fidget toys, music, and chewable necklaces (Ryan, 2020). Teachers can also implement art-based activities where children can make their own sensory inputs such as making their own chewable necklaces using cut up straws and yarn or making their own stress balls using modeling clay and balloons. These items that also can be implemented into "fidget boxes" that children can have access to throughout the school day. Fidget boxes contain items like stress balls and silly putty that can help children with focus and attention, anxiety, and anger. These are inexpensive ways that teachers can assist in self-regulation while also providing students with the necessary sensory inputs to assist them when they are dysregulated. These are also items that can be integrated into classroom calm-down corners that can be used during times of dysregulation or when students are triggered.

Calm-Down Corners

Calm-down corners are areas of the classroom where students can go when they are having difficulty managing big emotions. It can also be a safe place for students to relax or have a moment to themselves if they are having a difficult day. These corners should have calming items along with sensory inputs to assist with regulation. Teachers can be encouraged to receive input from their students on items to keep in the area, like stuffed animals or bubble blowers for younger students. Some items to include are pillows, regular or weighted blankets, therapy brushes, calm-down jars, and fidget toys (e.g., sensory balls, fidget spinners). There may be concern that this corner will be used as an escape for students who choose not to engage in class. Although that may feel like an inappropriate use of the space, it is the student communicating a need. It could be a need for a mental break, a need for some sensory input to help manage trauma stressors, or even a need for attention from the teacher. Given the difficulty Black students may have in expressing their need for help, the calm-down corner could be used as a nonverbal way for them to communicate when they need help. According to Adlerian play therapy, every misbehavior is communicating a need from the child (Meany-Walen & Kottman, 2016):

- Attention: The child believes they do not belong unless they get attention.

- Power: The child believes their significance & belonging depend on dominating others & making sure others can't control them.
- Revenge: The child believes that others will hurt them & no one will like or love them.
- Proving inadequacy: The child believes they are failures & give up easily.

Therefore, the teacher can see a retreat to the calm-down corner as the student exhibiting positive coping skills because they are choosing alternative ways to handle their feelings. The use of the corner can also communicate that the teacher has successfully created a safe place for the student.

Sensory Plans

Sensory plans are a good way to help students start thinking and talking about their triggers and effective ways to manage them. In a sensory plan, students identify actions or behaviors they could engage in using all five senses. Starting with smell, students are encouraged to pick a pleasant smell that they enjoy. This could be things like an essential oil or a perfume or cologne that is a reminder of a safe person. Then they can discuss some options that could help provide that smell while they are in the classroom. For example, scented markers or scratch-and-sniff stickers are a good way to provide different scents that won't be distracting to their peers. If there is a consensus on a calming smell like lavender, the teacher could use aromatherapy in the classroom, especially during times that may be more stress-inducing, like tests or presentations. Another activity I like to use is called "pocket hearts," where students can cut out two heart shapes from felt, add some calming essential oils to a cotton ball, then enclose the infused cotton ball in between the two hearts, closing the with hot glue (or they can be stitched closed for older students with the fine motor skills to manage a needle and thread).

The next sensory experience to explore is touch. Students are encouraged to come up with a few things that they can touch that help calm them. This could be something like a childhood blanket, a fidget, or a stone. Stones are great tools for grounding, and just holding a stone can help a client with grounding and calming down. Teachers may also consider taking their students on a nature walk to find items like stones that they can use as part of their sensory plan. For the sensory experience of taste, students can be encouraged to identify things that they can taste, drink, or eat that are calming for them. An example may be piece of hard candy or taking a sip of water or tea. Although students may not be allowed to have food in the classroom, they can be encouraged to have those items at home. Another sensory experience to explore for the sensory plan is something that they can watch. Examples may include watching YouTube videos, a fish tank, or a funny movie or television show. Teachers who have access to digital whiteboards in their classroom can consider playing calming fish tanks on YouTube during school.

Sound is the next sensory experience to explore in the sensory plan. Students can be encouraged to identify calming sounds, such as certain musicians and/or songs, autonomous sensory meridian response (ASMR) recordings, and nature sounds. There may also be some discussion on the use of headphones for students to quietly listen to calming music throughout the day. This is also an opportunity to open the discussion on the use of music-based activities in the classroom, such as a classroom playlist. Students can be asked to share appropriate songs or sounds that are calming and that can be played quietly during class through classroom speakers or on the teacher's phone. Teachers can also consider having a "DJ for the Day," where each student can take a turn at creating a playlist for the teacher to play that day. In his interview with Rhythmic Mind (2018), Dr. Bruce Perry talked about the power of combining hip-hop with academic lessons to help students learn easier and faster. Student can consider having student projects include presentations where they turn lessons into hip-hop songs, integrate hip-hop into their lessons, or use lessons that already exist like *Flocabulary*, *Rap Opera for Kids*, or Snoop Dogg's *Doggyland* for younger children that uses hip-hop with nursery rhymes and are available on YouTube.

Brain Break Activities

The final area to explore for the student's sensory plan is movement. Students should be encouraged to engage in some physical activity that can help get their body moving. Perry notes that somatosensory or body movement is best supported by rhythmic actions that can help regulate the system (Rhythmic Mind, 2018). This may include stretching, taking a walk, or dancing. "Brain breaks" are activities that give students a break from learning and are a natural fit for integrating body movement. The use of brain breaks may help increase focus and attention as well as improve on-task behaviors in students. There are a variety of different brain breaks that teachers can use that embrace the culture of Black students. Teachers can consider having breaks where students can stretch, incorporating dance breaks/parties into the school day, or even playing music for children to dance as they enter the classroom to mimic a Soul Train line.

Perry further explained that the combination of sound and movement is optimal for restoring regulatory balance in children with trauma (Rhythmic Mind, 2018). For those with access to a digital whiteboard, using videos from Cosmic Kids Yoga on YouTube is a way to integrate short and long videos with progressive muscle relaxation, guided meditations, and yoga sequences that are connected to animated characters from movies and video games like Frozen, Minecraft, and Spiderman, to name a few. Teachers can also be encouraged to implement Tik-Tok dances and line dances to break up learning and give students—and themselves—a mental break. Encouraging the use of rhythmical regulation is important as this can help repair broken connections in the brain caused by chronic trauma (Rhythmic Mind, 2018). Teachers can be encouraged to use musical instruments like drums or having students drum on their legs as a form of brain breaks or a ritual to start and/or end class. Items that move rhythmically, such as yo-yos, sand pendulums, or balance mobiles are also helpful for healthy brain development. Additional items that can aid in this development are sponge balls and bouncing balls for rhythmic turn-taking.

Implementing Mindfulness in Schools

Implementing mindfulness in schools is an intervention that is starting to garner more attention. Studies have found mindfulness can help with increased focus, attention, self-control, and compassion in the classroom (Zenner et al., 2014). This could be beneficial for both teachers and students who struggle with those issues. Another positive outcome of mindfulness in the classroom is improved academic performance, ability to resolve conflicts, and overall well-being (Zenner et al., 2014). Since Black students are dealing with high levels of stress that may impact their learning, mindfulness can be a tool to help them improve their well-being, grades, and peer relationships. It may also assist with impaired teacher—student relationships because both parties are calmer and have better conflict resolution skills to manage any problematic interactions. Finally, mindfulness activities in the classroom have been shown to decrease depression, stress levels, anxiety, and disruptive behavior (Box 9.2).

Box 9.2 Mindfulness Programs for Schools

- Association for Mindfulness in Education (www.mindfulnessed ucation.org)
- Calmer Choice (www.calmerchoice.org)
- CARE for Teachers (www.careforeducation.org)
- Compassionate Schools Project (www.compassionschools.org)
- Inner Explorer (www.innerexplorer.org)
- Inner Kids Collaborative (www.innerkids.org)
- The Inner Resilience Program (https://lindalantieri.org/the-inner-resilience-program/)
- Inward Bound Mindfulness Education (www.ibme.com)
- Learning to Breathe (www.learning2breathe.org)
- Mindful Life Project (www.mindfullifeproject.org)
- Mindful Moment Program (https://holisticlifefoundation.org/mindfulmoment)
- Mindful Schools (www.mindfulschools.org)
- Mindfulness in Schools Project (www.mindfulnessinschools.org)
- MindUP (www.mindup.org)
- Peace in Schools (www.peaceinschools.org)
- Resilient Kids (https://inspiringmindsri.org/our-programs/resili entkids/)
- Still Quiet Place (www.stillquietplace.com)
- Stressed Teens (www.stressedteens.com)
- The Kindness Curriculum (www.thekindnesscurriculum.com)
- The School Mindfulness Project (www.schoolmindfulness.org)

From (Osten Gerszberg n.d.).

Additionally, Calm offers a free download for teachers to introduce mindfulness activities into their classroom such as breathing exercises, mediations, and relaxation activities (Calm, 2022a). It is recommended that teachers learn how to engage in mindfulness, which includes an explanation of the benefits of mindfulness; engaging stakeholders like faculty, administrators, and parents; and looking for developmentally appropriate practices that best fit the school and classroom environment (Osten Gerszberg n.d.). Other ways that mindfulness can be implemented in schools is through using meditation rooms and mindful moments.

In Philadelphia, the Mindful Moment program was developed to integrate mindfulness throughout the school and school day. It includes a 15-minute meditation and breath work recording that plays every morning at 10:08 am and in the afternoon at 2:09 pm (Holistic Life Foundation, 2021). Another way to implement mindfulness throughout the school is using mindfulness rooms. This requires a Mindfulness instructor, so schools with staff shortages may not be able to fully integrate this intervention. However, schools with the staff and budget can use a mindfulness room in the place of detention or sitting in the principal's office. The same organization integrated the Mindful Moment room where students can self-refer themselves or teachers can send distressed or disruptive students for assistance with emotional self-regulation (Holistic Life Foundation, 2021). In the Mindful Moment room, students then have 5 minutes of discussion followed by 15 minutes of mindfulness practice that can be breathwork or yoga (Holistic Life Foundation, 2021). This can be integrated into the calm-down corner for schools and teachers who lack the support to have a student leave the classroom or do not have the space to dedicate to a full mindfulness room.

Play Therapy Interventions for the Classroom

After providing psychoeducation to teachers on the impact of trauma on the brain, the school social worker can encourage the use of play-based activities to help with brain development inside of the classroom. Using I See You Cards is a way to help teachers motivate their students and communicate to them that they see their efforts. The Worry Monster is an activity the whole class can engage in to address anxiety. Finally, the Dancin' Dice Game is an activity that encourages body movement that can also serve as a brain break.

I See You Cards

I See You Cards provide a way for teachers to communicate the pride they have in their students. Black students, especially ones with frequent disciplinary infractions, are at risk for low self-esteem and classroom disengagement. They may need verbal encouragement from their peers and teachers to motivate them to continue to work toward their goals. Teachers can be encouraged to use index cards or construction paper to make cards that communicate something positive to the student. For example, a card may say

"I see you working hard to get your math grade up" or "I see you trying to get along with your friends." Teachers can then place these cards in the student's bookbag or desk so that they can receive an unexpected compliment. Students can also be encouraged to create and decorate cards for their peers as additional support and to assist in relationship-building.

Worry Monster for Anxiety

A play therapy intervention used in individual play therapy, Worry Monster Box can be implemented in the classroom to help address any issues around anxiety or intrusive, triggering thoughts. Using a shoe box, construction paper, scissors, and other art materials (e.g., googly eyes, pipe cleaners) students can work together as a classroom or in groups to create a Worry Monster. The "monster" should then be kept in the classroom where students can "feed" it their worries. Students should be encouraged to "feed" the monster whenever it is necessary, including during classroom instruction if this is not disruptive to the classroom and their peers. Students may be struggling to pay attention or focus due to their worries, so this is a way for them to process them in the moment and get back to focusing on their work. This may also open the door for conversations with students who frequently "feed the monster," which may be a sign of mental distress or the need for a mental health referral to the school social worker.

Dancing Dice Game

The last play-based activity is the Dancing Dice Game. The only thing required for this activity is a set of dice from a board game. Students should be encouraged to come up with six different dances. These should be dance moves that their peers know or something they can teach them. Then they should assign a dance move to each number. For example, number one may be "The Dab" and number two may be "The Whoa." Students then take turns rolling the dice. Whatever number it lands on is the dance that everyone must do. This can be done as a classroom, or students can use this in small groups. It can also be used as an additional activity for brain breaks. The combination of music, dance, and movement can to jumpstart a child's brain and assist in learning.

Conclusion

School social workers can provide the education and skills teachers need to help with classroom management and improve their impaired relationships with Black students. Since there are not enough mental health professionals in schools to meet the needs of Black students, teachers and school social workers can benefit from extending the use of play into the classroom. However, teachers need play, too! Play can be used by school social workers to help reduce burnout in teachers, assist in classroom self-regulation, and promote the well-being of teachers. Happy and calm teachers will help create healthy, happy, and regulated students. Offering teachers a new way to engage with students through play can provide Black students with life-long coping skills and relationships that they can carry with them into adulthood.

References

Calm. (2022a). https://www.calm.com/schools/resources

Calm. (2022b). 30 days of mindfulness in the classroom. https://static1.squarespace.com/static/57b5ef68c534a5cc06edc769/t/5ff7b753313f4639dd4ef9dd/1610069849460/30+Days+of+Mindfulness+in+the+Classroom.pdf

Degruy. J. (2017). *Post-traumatic slave syndrome: America's legacy of enduring injury & healing.* Uptown Press.

Elmadani, A., Opiola, K. K., Grybush, A. L., & Alston, D. M. (2022). Exploring the experiences of elementary teachers after completing Child Teacher Relationship Training (CTRT): Implications for teaching in diverse school settings. *International Journal of Play Therapy™, 31*(2), 71–81. https://doi.org/10.1037/pla0000163

Facebook. (2022). Teaching with mental health in mind. https://www.facebook.com/twmhnm/?ref=page_internal

Gibson, P., & Haight, W. (2013). Caregivers' moral narratives of their African American children's out-of-school suspensions: Implications for effective family–school collaborations. *Social Work, 58*(3), 263–272. https://doi.org/10.1093/sw/swt017

Gonzales-Ball, T. L., & Bratton, S. C. (2019). Child–teacher relationship training as a Head Start early mental health intervention for children exhibiting disruptive behavior. *International Journal of Play Therapy™, 28*(1), 44–56. https://doi.org/10.1037/pla0000081

Happy Teacher Revolution. (2022). https://www.happyteacherrevolution.com/

Hartwig, E. K., & Taylor, E. R. (2022). Small steps can lead to big changes: Goal setting in schools using solution-focused play therapy. *International Journal of Play Therapy™, 31*(3), 131–142. https://doi.org/10.1037/pla0000179

Henderson, D. X., Jabar Joseph, J., Martin, P., Mburi, M., Stanley, M., McField, A., Irsheid, S., Lee, A., & Corneille, M. (2021). An investigation of coping in response to different race-related stressor experiences in school among racially diverse participants. *American Journal of Orthopsychiatry, 91*(2), 181–192. https://doi.org/10.1037/ort0000529

Holistic Life Foundation. (2021). Mindful moment program. https://hlfinc.org/programs-services/mindful-moment-program/

Landreth, G. (2012). *Play therapy: The art of the relationship.* Routledge.

Meany-Walen, K. K., & Kottman, T. (2016). *An Adlerian approach to play therapy.* American Counseling Association.

National Center for Education Statistics. (2019). Back to school statistics. https://nces.ed.gov/fastfacts/display.asp?id=372

National Council of Teachers of English. (2022). https://ncte.org/rsvp-member-gathering/

Office for Victims of Crime. (n.d). The vicarious trauma toolkit. U.S. Department of Justice. Office of Justice Programs. https://ovc.ojp.gov/program/vtt/what-is-vicarious-trauma

Osten Gerszberg, C. (n.d.). The future of education. Mindful classrooms. *Mindful.* https://www.mindful.org/content/uploads/Mindful-Education-Guide.pdf

Rhythmic Mind (2018). Dr. Bruce Perry interview. https://www.youtube.com/watch?v=a9NtmRj0tm8&t=184s

Post, P. B., Grybush, A. L., García, M. A., & Flowers, C. (2022). Child–teacher relationship training exclusively in the classroom: Impact on teacher attitudes and behaviors. *International Journal of Play Therapy™*, 31(2), 97–106. https://doi.org/10.1037/pla0000173

Ryan, C. (2020). Calming the body before calming the mind: Sensory strategies for children affected by trauma. Australian Institute of Family Studies. https://aifs.gov.au/resources/short-articles/calming-body-calming-mind-sensory-strategies-children-affected-trauma

Schwartz, S. (2019). Teachers support social-emotional learning, but students in distress strain their skills. *Education Week.* https://www.edweek.org/leadership/teachers-support-social-emotional-learning-but-say-students-in-distress-strain-their-skills/2019/07

Taie, S., Lewis, L., & Spiegelman, M. (2022). Characteristics of 2020–2021 public and private k-12 school teachers in the United States. Results from the National Teacher and Principal Survey. U.S. Department of Education. Institute of Education Sciences. https://nces.ed.gov/pubs2022/2022113.pdf

Teach.com. (2022). 50 resources to support the mental health of teachers and school staff. https://teach.com/resources/mental-health-resources-teachers-school-staff/

Wang, K., Kemp, J., Burr, R., & Swan, D. (2022). Crime, violence, discipline, and safety in U.S. public schools in 2019–2020. Findings from the school survey on crime and safety. U.S. Department of Education. Institute of Education Sciences. https://nces.ed.gov/pubs2022/2022029.pdf

Whitaker, A., Torres-Guillen, S., Morton, M., Jordan, H., Coyle, S., Mann, A., & Sun, W. L. (2019). Cops and no counselors: How the lack of school mental health is harming students. American Civil Liberties Union. https://www.aclu.org/sites/default/files/field_document/030419-acluschooldisciplinereport.pdf

Zenner, C., Herrnleben-Kurz, S., & Walach, H. (2014). Mindfulness-based interventions in schools- a systematic review and meta-analysis. *Frontiers Psychology.* https://www.frontiersin.org/articles/10.3389/fpsyg.2014.00603/full

10

Group Play Therapy with Black Students

Racial trauma can leave Black students feeling alone in their experiences. Group play therapy is a modality that can help Black students feel validated in their feelings—and even their responses—to negative race-based experiences. Therefore, it can serve as a solution to addressing racial trauma in Black students. Group play therapy can also provide a safe place where Black students can create a community of individuals with similar backgrounds and experiences. This may then become an effective way to empower Black students to deal with their emotions in healthier ways by learning new coping skills and having fun while doing so. For Black students, group play therapy can integrate their culture through the use of art, music, and sand trays to celebrate who they are and who they can become.

Group play therapy can be an effective tool for school social workers to help meet the increasing demand for mental health services among students of all backgrounds. For Black students, group play therapy can be applied from kindergarten through high school to help students connect with peers and build their own "villages" within school walls. However, the school social worker should institute several practices to increase the probability of a successful group, including having a group with a focused goal and/or topic, using assessment tools to help determine the best group fit, and understanding the different dynamics that can arise in group sessions.

Group Therapy as a Solution to the School Mental Health Crisis

With the increased need for mental health services because of the COVID-19 pandemic, school counselors are dealing with heavy caseloads that will likely continue to explode. Professional standards recommend that schools

Black Students Matter. April D. Duncan, Oxford University Press. © Oxford University Press 2024.
DOI: 10.1093/oso/9780197669266.003.0011

have at least one social worker or counselor for every 250 students, at least one school nurse for every 750 students, and at least one school psychologist for every 700 students, but 90% of public schools fail to meet this standard (Whitaker et al., 2019). School support staff members are one of many victims of school, state, and federal policies that do not prioritize mental health. Studies found school social workers have a caseload that is almost eight times greater than that recommended by professionals (Whitaker et al., 2019). This may result in high turnover and burnout for mental health staff, which is why it is imperative that we help find alternatives to serving high caseloads. Now more than ever, students need mental health support, but the helpers need help, too.

As a result, teachers often must assist in managing mental health issues in their students. However, they are not always given the skills and support needed to understand the best way to support the therapeutic needs of students. Only 39% of school districts in the United States provided professional development to mental health staff on group counseling, and approximately 21% had arrangements with organizations or healthcare professionals to provide group counseling for students (Centers for Disease Control and Prevention [CDC], 2017). So the brunt of mental health services often falls solely on the school social worker, who may be the only mental health professional on staff. Even when schools do have a school social worker, they may be traveling to other schools in the district, adding more to their caseload. And with mental health issues exacerbated by the COVID-19 pandemic, school social workers will continue to see an increased need for mental health services, especially among students of color who will be more likely to be punished for their behaviors than their White peers. Therefore, group play therapy should be a tool that every school social worker has in their toolkit as a means of providing effective therapeutic interventions for a large caseload.

Group Play Therapy Advantages

There are several advantages in implementing group play therapy. First, it helps the school social worker gain insight into students' everyday lives (Sweeney et al., 2014). School social workers are often given subjective reports and interpretations about the student, which for children of color may be accompanied by implicit biases about that child. Group play therapy with Black students will allow school social workers to witness the student's behavior in real-time and may offer a clearer picture of the student's behaviors and/or needs that can be shared with teachers and school administration.

Black students may be guarded in opening emotionally in individual sessions. Group play therapy provides an opportunity for vicarious learning and catharsis, as students can observe the emotional and behavioral expression of other members (Sweeney et al., 2014). For example, Black boys who struggle with hypermasculinity may be motivated to increase their emotional expression if they are around other students who provide a sense of approval and acceptance in doing so. Or a student who was resistant to learning new skills in individual sessions may be encouraged to try those new skills when they see their peers engaging in them.

Having multiple clients in a group play therapy session can assist in the development of therapeutic relationships (Sweeney et al., 2014). Understanding that a level of mistrust may exist in Black students, school social workers may find Black students in a group setting can improve the therapist–student relationship. If a school social worker is deemed "cool" by a student, that may provide the proverbial green light for other students to feel comfortable trusting them. Additionally, group play therapy provides an opportunity for the students to develop interpersonal skills, offer and receive assistance, master new behaviors, and experiment with alternative expressions of behavior and emotion (Sweeney et al., 2014). In essence, Black students can help build a community and village of support among peers with similar backgrounds and experiences, which may assist in decreasing isolation and enhancing peer relationships. As the adage states, "there is strength in numbers," so Black students may also gain a sense of empowerment through this community they have built in a group play therapy setting.

Group Play Therapy Selection

When constructing a group play therapy session, school social workers should have a focused goal that is the intention of the group and a topic that is central to the needs and/or problems of those students and develop a process for selecting the most appropriate students for the group. For example, groups should be constructed based on the child's developmental level. If a student's chronological age is 7 years but their play is more typical of a five-year-old, the school social worker should consider integrating this student into a group with kindergarteners or 1st graders or creating a group with other students of the same developmental age. The use of developmental assessments can help determine the best age group for the student. The school social worker can also engage the student in several child-centered play therapy sessions prior to starting group therapy to allow their play to communicate the child's developmental level and needs.

School social workers should also consider grouping students based on their presenting problems and/or background. Some examples of group play therapy topics for Black students that school social workers should consider include anxiety, coping skills, self-harm/suicidal ideation, bullying, and depression. Groups can also be constructed based on the students' background and trauma history. Group play therapy may be helpful for students who are experiencing the same grief event, including death of a loved one from homicide, victims of violence, child welfare–involved youth, and children with incarcerated parents. Students with incarcerated caregivers often deal with the stigma of incarceration, which can contribute to feelings of shame and humiliation. These students may not feel comfortable even sharing with their peers that they have an incarcerated caregiver. Group play therapy could be a healthy setting for these students to know they are not isolated in their experiences and provide a community of peer support. If the school social worker is considering doing group play therapy with LGBTQ+ students, be mindful of the child's status regarding their gender identity and/or sexual orientation and if it has been shared with teachers, peers, and/or their caregivers to avoid outing a student.

It is important for school social workers to attempt to find the most appropriate fit among group members. Not all clients will be an appropriate fit for group, and these students may need more individual and/or family therapy services to support their needs. For example, students who are hypersensitive to criticism, narcissistic, overly aggressive/dominating, or extremely depressed should be screened out (Corey, 2004). Other students to screen out of group play therapy include (Corey, 2004) the following:

- Siblings with intense rivalry
- Extremely aggressive children
- Sexually acting-out children
- Children with difficulties due to poor infant–mother attachment
- Children with sociopathic tendencies or intent to inflict harm or revenge
- Children with extremely poor self-image

These students may not be appropriate for group play therapy and should be referred for additional, more intensive treatment until their behaviors are decreased to a level at which they can successfully engage in the group play therapy process.

When selecting members for group, it may be helpful to use clinical assessments as they will help provide a subjective account of the child's behavioral needs from a normal, borderline clinical perspective. Clinical assessments such as the PHQ-9 for depression, GAD-7 for anxiety, and the Vanderbilt assessment for attention deficit hyperactivity disorder are all free assessments that both teachers and parents can complete. The Childhood Trust Events Survey is a free screening that can help identify adverse child-hood events (ACEs) the child experienced and serve as a guide for group selection based on ACEs. Additionally, the Child Behavior Checklist-Teacher Form, although it is not free, provides a concise overview of the child's externalizing and internalizing behaviors and can provide a point of reference for the child's most important therapeutic needs.

When creating groups, it is recommended that there are no more than 4–6 children in a group with one facilitator and no more than 6–10 children with two facilitators (Sweeney et al., 2014). Exceptions for this may be for pre-kindergarten and kindergarten students who are able to do group play therapy interventions in the classroom together with a teacher and/or para-professional available to assist with any issues. If the school social worker is taking out pre-kindergarten and kindergarten students to group play therapy with one facilitator, they could benefit from only taking 2–3 students in a group at a time. School social workers may also benefit from advocating for collaborations with local university and colleges to have a practicum student who can help with group play therapy facilitation. Additionally, there should be a balance of personalities, like having a mix of shy and withdrawn children grouped with assertive and outgoing children (Sweeney et al., 2014). This mix may assist in achieving a balance of personalities that is more manageable for the school social worker, as opposed to struggling with a group where all of the students are quiet or a group that is unable to get anything done be-cause everyone is talking too much.

Group Phases and Stages

Four major stages of group therapy should be explored before integrating group play therapy with Black students. The initial stage is orientation and exploration, where group members are getting acquainted and exploring other members' expectations (Yalom & Leszcz, 2020). Students may be re-sistant to participate in group play therapy because of their concern that information they share in the group might be shared with people outside of the group. Unfortunately, school social workers cannot guarantee that group members will maintain the privacy and confidentiality of other group members (Sweeney et al., 2014). This should be communicated to each student prior to them starting the group, especially given the higher levels of mistrust in Black students.

The school social worker should express they can only guarantee their own level of privacy and confidentiality (Sweeney et al., 2014). If the student expresses any additional concern about confidentiality, the school social worker should validate those feelings and discuss individually and in the group setting, appropriate consequences if there is evidence that child has shared confidential information outside the group, like posting something on social media. In that situation, the group may come up with the idea of discussing the harm the broken confidence has caused in the group, with an attempt to repair the rupture. Therapists should be mindful of accusations of broken confidentiality if there is no way to prove the accused student shared information. Although there is no guaranteed way to prevent confidence from being broken among group members, it may help students feel comfortable that they have a voice in how and what is done in the group and may also increase their level of engagement and participation in the group.

The second phase, known as the transition stage, occurs as group members are dealing with issues of resistance, ambivalence, defensiveness, anxiety, and struggle for control (Yalom & Leszcz, 2020). Group members also may be more resistant to sharing, so interventions that focus on building some form of group cohesion is best during this stage. For example, the activity Mic Check is a music-based intervention that can be used to help students connect and build a sense of community within the group setting. Each group member is encouraged to pick their favorite song or a song that describes them. To be fair, the school social worker can allow the first to come to group for that session or the oldest member of the group to pick first. That student is then encouraged to introduce themselves and play their song for approximately 30 seconds.

Group members are encouraged to have some form of response, like the call-to-response experience within the Black religious community (Sale, 1992). This can include saying "Aye!" or dancing to the song. After the student plays their song, they "pass the mic" to the next student of their choosing. This continues until each group member has played their song. While they are playing their song, the school social worker may also choose to create a "group playlist" by writing down the names of each song. That group playlist can be played during the experiential parts of group play therapy sessions and can be added to as the group progresses. Activities such as Mic Check provide the opportunity for group members to find some level of group cohesion and enter the next phase, the working stage.

The working stage of group therapy occurs when school social workers notice an increase in group cohesion and trust that can lead to greater communication and mutual feedback (Yalom & Leszcz, 2020). Within this phase, group members are more open to talking about their thoughts and feelings as well as providing insights to their group members. In turn, they may also have a greater trust in the school social worker and have an enhanced therapeutic relationship with them. If school social workers have been navigating issues of mistrust among Black students, the acceptance of group members may even spread beyond the group, providing some form of "green light" to other students that the school social worker is a trusted adult. This may then increase engagement and participation among current and future students within both individual and group play therapy sessions.

In the final stage, there is a focus on consolidation and termination as group members apply lessons they have learned in group and discover meaning from the group process (Yalom & Leszcz, 2020). School social workers may choose to use terms like "graduation" to signal an important accomplishment achieved by group participants. This may include certificates of completion, having drinks and snacks, and doing a final activity to close out the group. For example, if conducting a group on grief and bereavement, a closing activity can be a collage activity, where group members can bring in pictures of their loved ones and work together to create a group collage. Black Pride Posters is an example that can be used as a closing intervention in group play therapy with Black students.

Black Pride Posters

This art therapy activity can help instill pride in Black students regardless of their gender identity and/or sexual orientation. The materials required for this activity are posterboard, markers, scissors, glue, and Afrocentric magazines. If the school social worker is able to have a laptop or tablet connected to a printer for students to find images online, this can be substituted for magazines. This activity can be used with students as young as kindergarten. The student is encouraged to find images, words, and pictures that represent their culture as a Black person and/or their identity as a member of the LGBTQ+ community. This is an activity where it may be appropriate to play music as students work and reserve questions until the end of the activity. Follow-up questions can include the following:

- Tell me about your poster and why you selected the images/pictures you've added.
- What type of feelings do you have when you observe this poster?
- Which image or word stands out to you?
- Do you have any images or words that you see in yourself?

The student can be encouraged to take their poster home to display, or they can decide to hang it up in the therapist's office. Having these posters displayed contributes to the cultural integrity of the playroom and may also serve as an empowerment tool for other students who see it.

Group Play Therapy Approaches with Black Students

Several group play therapy approaches could be beneficial in addressing racial trauma stressors experienced by Black students. The students' developmental age is important when determining the best play therapy approach to implement in the group setting. Pre-kindergarten through 3rd-graders could benefit from CCGPT and Theraplay, whereas 4th-grade students through high school could benefit from sand tray group therapy, Adlerian group play therapy, and cognitive behavioral group play therapy. It is recommended that students be grouped based on the following ages/grades: pre-kindergarten (3- to 5-year-olds), 1st and 2nd graders (6- to 8-year-olds), 4th and 5th graders (9- to 11-year-olds) or 5th and 6th graders (based on the school setting), 6th through 8th graders (12- to 14-year-olds) or 7th and 8th graders if the junior high has only those two grades, and 9th and 10th graders and 11th and 12th graders if working in a high school.

Child-Centered Group Play Therapy

Child-centered group play therapy (CCGPT) is the use of nondirected play therapy with kids in a group setting. This can be especially helpful for Black boys who struggle with engaging in imaginative play. The session should include three or four students who are encouraged to engage in nondirective play. This modality has been found to be culturally sensitive because it honors the African worldview (emotional vitality, interdependence, collective survival, and harmonious blending) (Baggerly & Parker, 2005). It has also been found to help build self-confidence around culture as well. In CCGPT, the play therapist focuses on the content of the student's play and reflects their individual feelings (Baggerly & Parker, 2005). Another skill in CCGPT is to reflect the group dynamics. For example, the therapist would comment, "I noticed that you guys are working together to resolve this problem." This synergy reflected in their interactions helps facilitate self-confidence.

CCGPT can be an effective way to support all Black students experiencing racial stressors. Five important components of self-confidence include them seeing themselves as being capable, experiencing a sense of belonging, being optimistic about the future, being able to cope with failure, and having positive role models (Baggerly & Parker, 2005). CCGPT helps return responsibility to Black students by building an egalitarian relationship. Additionally, CCGPT suspends judgment, provides encouragement, and displays trust in the child's self-direction and capability to resolve things on their own. For example, students may become upset that something in the group is not "fair." Since Black students must navigate unfair situations from an early age, CCGPT becomes a safe and natural way for them to learn how to manage those situations in healthy ways. Finally, CCGPT provides a safe place where students can enhance their self-concept because it provides the necessary factors for natural self-growth (DeMaria & Crowden, 1992).

CCGPT has been found to be effective for a variety of populations and presenting problems. More specifically, it is related to an improvement in childhood functioning in areas such as depression, negative self-esteem, anxiety, and complex trauma (Blalock et al., 2019). CCGPT has also been found effective in decreasing children's problematic classroom behaviors (Swan et al., 2019) which can be useful for younger children experiencing disciplinary issues early in their school careers. Among Black boys, CCGPT may be an effective intervention because it has been found to be a culturally sensitive approach that honors their culture and builds self-confidence (Baggerly & Parker, 2005). In a study conducted by Baggerly and Parker (2005), they found Black boys exhibiting positive self-concept and internal strength by responding appropriately to racist behaviors and comments, which shows the ability also to respond to race-based stress and trauma.

However, there are some limitations in implementing the intervention in schools. Reported challenges include limited time with children, inconsistent or limited space, missing relevant information from parent assessments and/ or reports, and noise level concerns (Blalock et al., 2019). Therefore, the school social worker may have to dedicate more time to confirming a consistent space large enough for students to play but still have privacy, while also leaning into the children's play to communicate their needs as opposed to relying on subjective reports from their parents and/or teachers. School social workers can also consider combining nondirective art into CCGPT as a solution for space or noise issues. It can also be beneficial in providing a group setting with less directives for older students. The combination of art and CCGPT can assist in improving self-regulation, self-responsibility, self-direction, and self-discovery in students (Perryman et al., 2015).

Theraplay

Theraplay in a group setting includes the school social worker picking three to four activities from those categories focused on the essential qualities of a parent–child relationship: nurture, challenge, structure, and engagement (Booth & Jernberg, 2010). This intervention has been found to increase social skills and a willingness for teachers to implement the intervention (Weaver et al., 2021). Sunshine Circles is a Theraplay group intervention for preschoolers that focuses on developing healthy peer relationships using playful and nurturing activities (Theraplay, 2023). Teachers can implement this group in their classrooms because it has been shown to enhance social-emotional competence (Weaver et al., 2021). Sessions are typically held once or more per week with groups lasting 20–30 minutes (Tucker et al., 2017). This approach may be particularly helpful for teachers who are overwhelmed with the behaviors and needs of Black students experiencing race-based stress and trauma. Sunshine Circles are found to be helpful for early child-hood classrooms containing students with high levels of toxic stress (Tucker et al., 2017). This simple, low-cost intervention can be something that si-multaneously builds the skills of the teacher in classroom management and builds healthier relationships with Black students.

Sand Tray in Group Play Therapy

Sand tray play therapy is another modality that school social workers can use in a group setting. Studies have found that sand tray therapy in school group sessions can assist in improving language and social skills, self-esteem, and a willingness to be vulnerable, let their guards down, and be more authentic (Homeyer & Sweeney, 2017). Group sand tray therapy can also be viewed as more productive because it allows the child to participate and observe simul-taneously, involves peer motivation for change, provides nonintrusive posi-tive adult attention, may prevent chronic problem behaviors in the future, and enhances brain functioning (Kestly, 2001). Sand tray group therapy in schools has its own advantages. School social workers may find it beneficial to serve more students at the same time which may allow them to use their time more efficiently (Wang Flahive & Ray, 2007).

Black students could also benefit from utilizing sand tray therapy in a group setting. Although the research is limited on its effectiveness in Black youth, the advantages of group play therapy are still applicable and valuable. Sand tray therapy in group play therapy may help Black students learn coping behaviors and alternative means of self-expression, assist in strengthening the therapeutic therapist–student relationship, and help students gain more self-reflection and insight into their own behavior (Homeyer & Sweeney, 2017). As a modality to process negative race-based experiences, sand tray therapy may also assist Black students by giving them the opportunity to master new behaviors, develop interpersonal skills, receive and offer assistance, and experiment with alternative expressions of behavior and emotion (Homeyer & Sweeney, 2017). Black students may feel isolated in their feelings and experiences with race-based stress and trauma. Group sand tray therapy can help students experience emotional closeness with their peers and improve the quality of intimate relationships (Wang Flahive & Ray, 2007).

Black students experiencing perceived burdensome or who have disengaged due to negative self-worth and self-concept may also find a community through group sand tray therapy. Group sand tray therapy provides an opportunity for participants to learn how to share ideas and materials and, in turn, learn that their contributions are welcomed and appreciated (Wang Flahive & Ray, 2007). Sand tray in group play therapy also becomes a place where Black students can explore and experience control they may not have in other environments. The choices offered within the group setting allow them the opportunity to make decisions and assert their independence while also exerting control over what they choose to share (Draper et al., 2003). Therefore, group sand tray therapy with Black students can serve as tool to assist with empowerment, building a sense of community and a safe place for verbal and nonverbal emotional expression.

Group Sand Tray Therapy Process

Ethically, school social workers should exhibit competence in sand tray therapy before they implement it into a group setting. To obtain competence, the school social worker should receive training in sand tray, consultation in sand tray therapy, and/or review the literature (Draper et al., 2003). Sand tray groups may have 3–5 students at a time, but school social workers new to sand tray therapy should start by integrating sand tray into an individual play therapy session then build up to 3–4 students in a group setting (Draper et al., 2003; Wang Flahive & Ray, 2007). When setting up for group sand tray, the school social worker should find space that allows physical movement for group members and should provide a standard amount of sand tray miniatures that can allow group members to learn how to share resources (Homeyer & Sweeney, 2017).

There are three basic components in sand tray group therapy. During the building time, the facilitator may allow two students to select up to six miniatures at a time. They then are encouraged to create their own sand worlds (Draper et al., 2003). The facilitator may also play music or offer coloring sheets and/or fidgets for other group members to use while they wait their turn. After a five-minute warning, the student is encouraged to put the final touches on their worlds before they are photographed (Draper et al., 2003). Then students are encouraged to share their sand tray while the facilitator models empathic listening (Draper et al., 2003). Group members may show reluctance to share their trays until a form of group cohesion and trust has been established, so the facilitator should not force students to talk about their sand trays until they are comfortable.

Adlerian Group Play Therapy

Adlerian group play therapy may be an acceptable approach with Black students due to the high levels of behaviors that are labeled deviant and disruptive and that contribute to racial disparities in school discipline for children of color. Black students often engage in behaviors that teachers and peers may label as disruptive. These are called *off-task behaviors*. Off-task behaviors disrupt the learning process and can be precursors to additional risks such as depression, anxiety, school dropout, substance abuse, and teenage pregnancy (Meany-Walen et al., 2015). Off-task behaviors include externalizing issues like hyperactivity, outbursts, aggression, and refusal to comply with teacher expectations (Meany-Walen et al., 2015). Adlerian group play therapy has demonstrated effectiveness in decreasing off-task and disruptive behaviors (Dillman Taylor et al., 2019; Meany-Walen et al., 2015). The phases of Adlerian group play therapy are outlined in Chapter 3.

Given the degree of stereotypes placed on Black students that box them into certain professions/categories (e.g., rapper, thug, teenage mom), Adlerian group play therapy may allow Black students to explore life careers and paths that they thought were unreachable due to the negative feedback they may have received from schools, family members, or members of their community. From this perspective, children gain significance in their family by being "the dramatic child," "the troublemaker," or other stereotyped labels, which they then use to gain a sense of belonging with peers in other social interactions such as school, friendships, and romantic relationships (Meany-Walen & Kottman, 2015). Adlerian group play therapy can provide a space for Black students to explore those labels and alter the ways they gain significance in their environments.

The Adlerian play therapist uses the information gathered from phase one to determine if the child is appropriate for the group, which can include evaluating information provided by teachers or parents or from behaviors witnessed by the therapist (Meany-Walen et al., 2015). To decrease the probability of receiving biased feedback on the child, school workers using this intervention with Black students may benefit from using the nondirective portion of phase one to infer behaviors from the play themes shown in individual sessions. The therapist should meet with the child for at least one to three individual play therapy sessions prior to their start in group (Meany-Walen & Kottman, 2019). In a group setting, Adlerian play therapists work to understand the child within the context of the group, create opportunities to help group members gain insight into their behaviors, teach the group members new skills, and evaluate their readiness for termination (Meany-Walen et al., 2015). For the implementation of this approach in a group school setting, school therapists may benefit from having the group meet twice a week with sessions 30–50 minutes long (Meany-Walen & Kottman, 2019). This may include offering group therapy after school, to avoid any disruptions to the school day.

The use of the *Crucial C's* from Adlerian play therapy, combined with game play therapy, is a way to help address mistaken beliefs in group play therapy setting. AdPT believes that there are four psychological goals of children's misbehavior: to gain attention, to gain power or control, to get revenge, or display inadequacy (Kottman, 2011). The Crucial C's of Adlerian play therapy serve to help children who have been labeled mischievous. The Adlerian play therapist believes there is a goal behind every act of misbehavior and that children can find more acceptable ways to have their needs met with the appropriate support (Kottman, 2011). To determine the goal of the child's misbehavior, the therapist should consider the child's behaviors, their feelings and beliefs, other people's reactions to the child's behavior and the child's reaction when they are punished or corrected (Kottman, 2011). Once the therapist can determine the goal of the child's behaviors, they can employ the use of the Crucial C's as a method to help the child find better ways to achieve a sense of belonging. The Crucial C's encourage connecting with others through cooperation, feeling capable through self-reliance, believing they count and are valuable by finding ways to contribute to society and their community, and being courageous through resiliency (Kottman, 2011).

Black Kids Count Game

The Black Kids Count game helps Black students navigate the use of the Crucial C's in a group game play therapy activity. The game is best for kids ages 8 and up and can be played with 2–4 players. The materials required for this activity are a set of dice, the Black Kids Count printable board game (Appendix A), a file folder or canvas, glue or decoupage glue, and sand tray miniatures for the player pieces. Prior to using the game in a group session, the school social worker will need to print out the board game and glue it onto the file folder or canvas. Allow it to fully dry before using, then cut out the cards and place them in piles based on their colors. There should be one board game and set of dice for each group of four students. It is also recommended that the school social worker use multicultural sand tray miniatures that will be utilized as the group members game piece.

To start the game, each player selects a miniature as their game piece, then takes a roll of the dice. The player with the highest number will start the game. The next player will be the player sitting to their left. The player will roll the dice and move their game piece the amount reflected on the dice. Then they will select a card from the color pile based on the color they land on (e.g., if they land on a purple board piece, they pull a question from the purple question card). The player can either answer the question or pass. If they pass on the question, they must stay where they are. If they answer the question, they can advance to the next board piece without having to answer another question. The first player to the finish line wins.

Let Me Be Great Chips

The next activity, Let Me Be Great Chips, can be used as a termination activity in Adlerian group play therapy. This group therapy activity is designed to help group members identify positive qualities in each other. It can help students gain insight into the positive ways they belong that can extend beyond group termination. The materials required for the activity are wooden craft chips, paper plates, foam brushes, decoupage glue, paint markers, and the Let Me Be Great handout. The school social worker should distribute 2–3 wooden craft chips for each group member. For example, if there four kids in the group each should get 8–12 chips, so each player can make 2–3 chips for each group member and themselves. The therapist can then have each student make a chip for each group member that has a positive quality they see in them. Group members are then encouraged to pass their chips to their peers, and time can be spent processing the chips they received and how they align with the ways they view themselves and their behaviors with others.

Case Study: The Heritage Youth Connection Program

BMH Connect is an organization I began in an effort to use play therapy to support Black children and families. We have identified the need for mental health services to address race-based stress and trauma in Black students, while tapping into the use of play activities rooted in the Black culture and experience. As a result, a group play therapy program was specifically designed to focus on empowerment and skill building in Black teens. The Heritage Youth Connection Program is an 8-week group play therapy program for Black students ages 12–17 years. This empowerment group uses various play approaches, including art techniques, musical interventions, and game play therapy to help Black students gain more positive coping skills to manage race-based stress and trauma. Facilitators for this program are known as Heritage Ambassadors, and they receive 24 hours of APT-approved play therapy training on how to implement the free program in their communities for Black youth. There are currently 25 facilitators trained to implement this program in Richmond, Virginia; Chicago, Illinois; East St. Louis, Illinois; Charlotte, North Carolina; and New York City (Brooklyn), New York. The program session outline is as follows:

- Session 1: Introduction to Racial Trauma
- Session 2: Emotional Expression
- Session 3: Managing Cognitive Distortions
- Session 4: Coping Skills
- Session 5: Social Support Systems
- Session 6: Grief & Bereavement
- Session 7: Empowerment part 1
- Session 8: Empowerment part 2

Youth who complete the program can also be trained to become a Heritage Youth Ambassador and co-facilitate the program in the future with a Heritage Ambassador.

Although there are some promising signs of success of the program, there are also some limitations. The program was originally launched at the height of the COVID-19 pandemic, so there were issues with the implementation of the program in a virtual setting with the initial Heritage Ambassadors in Richmond, Virginia. In a group with five Black teenagers (3 Black males and 2 Black females), there were instances of group members identifying the group as a safe place and offering and receiving assistance from other peers. One of the teens even expressed interest in being trained as a Heritage Youth Ambassador. However, some of the limitations included individuals participating off-screen and a desire for more Black male representation. Additionally, the Ambassador implementing the program in the residential setting has had good participation but has experienced some loss of group members due to them transition from the program. The preliminary information gathered from these two iterations of the program have been key in making changes to the program that honor the need for more Black representation, such as inviting a mentor to the group and abandoning the virtual version and sticking to face-to-face contact groups instead. Two examples of activities that are implemented in the program are "Social Media Scavenger Hunt" and the "Talk Me Up!" card game.

Social Media Scavenger Hunt

The Social Media Scavenger Hunt activity is an ice-breaker used in Session 1 to help open the discussion around race-based experiences while helping group members interact with each other. The only thing required for the activity is the Social Media Scavenger Hunt handout (Appendix B). The participants are encouraged to find group members who have had the online experiences outlined in the handout. After they speak to each group member, the facilitator can use processing questions to help the students process their experience in the activity. Questions can include "What are some ways you cope with these negative experiences?" or "Where are some safe spaces you have found online?" This activity can help students recognize that they are not isolated in their experiences while opening up the floor for peers to offer alternative ways to deal with these behaviors that the school social worker may not be privy to.

Talk Me Up! Card Game

The Talk Me Up! card game is a game play therapy activity in Session 7 that seeks to empower Black students by using positive affirmations. Played like Uno, the only things needed are the Talk Me Up! cards (Appendix C). Prior to using them in group, the school social worker will need to print, laminate, and cut the cards. There should be one deck of cards per four students. As the player matches the card based on the color or number, they must say the positive affirmation displayed on the card played. If they forget to say the affirmation, they have to draw two cards from the deck if they are called out by an opponent. If not, they are not required to draw.

The wildcard in the deck can be played at any moment, particularly if the player does not have a matching card. When the wildcard is laid down, everyone must go around clockwise and say something positive about each person. Once this is complete, the player can lay down any card they would like. The game continues until someone is completely out of cards. This card game can also be used with students outside of the group to build positive self-esteem and self-worth.

Conclusion

Black students may feel isolated in their experiences with race-based stress and trauma. This may be especially true of Black students who attend predominantly White schools. Group play therapy is an effective intervention to help Black students build healthy relationships and a sense of community while addressing problem behaviors. School social workers also can serve more children using group play therapy, which is going to be needed as mental health symptoms for all children, especially children of color, continue to skyrocket. This modality may also provide the buy-in and therapeutic relationship that can help other Black students feel safe in working with and disclosing information to the school social worker. Group play therapy is a tool that every school social worker can benefit from having in their toolbox to help build community and connections among Black students of all ages.

References

Baggerly, J., & Parker, M. (2005). Child-centered group play therapy with African American boys at the elementary school level. *Journal of Counseling & Development*, 83(4), 387–396. https://doi.org/10.1002/j.1556-6678.2005.tb00360.x

Blalock, S. M., Lindo, N. A., Haiyasoso, M., & Morman, M. K. (2019). Child-centered play therapists' experiences of conducting group play therapy in elementary schools. *Journal for Specialists in Group Work*, 44(3), 184–203. https://doi.org/10.1080/01933 922.2019.1637985

Booth, P. B., & Jernberg, A. M. (2010). *Theraplay: Helping parents and children build better relationships through attachment-based play* (3rd ed.). Jossey-Bass.

Centers for Disease Control and Prevention (CDC). (2017, August). Full report: Results from the school health policies and practices study 2016. U.S. Department of Health and Human Services. https://www.cdc.gov/healthyyouth/data/shpps/pdf/shpps-results_2016.pdf

Corey, G. (2004). *Theory and practice of group counseling*. Thomson, Brooks, Cole.

Dillman Taylor, D., Meany-Walen, K. K., Nelson, K. M., & Gungor, A. (2019). Investigating group Adlerian play therapy for children with disruptive behaviors: A single-case research design. *International Journal of Play Therapy™*, 28(3), 168–182. https://doi.org/10.1037/pla0000094

Draper, K., Ritter, K. B., & Willingham, E. U. (2003). Sand tray group counseling with adolescents. *Journal for Specialists in Group Work*, 28(3), 244–260. https://doi.org/10.1177/0193392203252030

Homeyer, L. E., & Sweeney, D. S. (2017). *Sandtray therapy: A practical manual* (3rd ed.). Routledge.

Kestley, T. (2001). Group sandplay in elementary schools. In A. Drewes, L. Carey, & C. E. Schaefer (Eds.), *School-based play therapy*. Wiley.

Kottman, T. (2011). *Adlerian play therapy [Book chapter]. Foundations of Play Therapy* (pp. 87–104, 2nd ed.). John Wiley and Sons, Inc.

Meany-Walen, K. K., Bullis, Q., Kottman, T., & Dillman Taylor, D. (2015). Group Adlerian play therapy with children with off-task behaviors. *Journal for Specialists in Group Work*, 40(3), 294–314. https://doi.org/10.1080/01933922.2015.1056569

Meany-Walen, K. K., & Kottman, T. (2019). Group Adlerian play therapy. *International Journal of Play Therapy™*, 28(1), 1–12. https://doi.org/10.1037/pla0000079

Perryman, K. L., Moss, R., & Cochran, K. (2015). Child-centered expressive arts and play therapy: School groups for at-risk adolescent girls. *International Journal of Play Therapy™*, 24(4), 205–220. https://doi.org/10.1037/a0039764

Sale, M. (1992). Call and Response as Critical Method: African-American Oral Traditions and Beloved. *African American Review*, 26(1), 41–50. https://doi.org/10.2307/3042075

Swan, K. L., Kaff, M., & Haas, S. (2019). Effectiveness of group play therapy on problematic behaviors and symptoms of anxiety of preschool children. *Journal for Specialists in Group Work*, 44(2), 82–98. https://doi.org/10.1080/01933922.2019.1599478

Sweeney, D. S., Baggerly, J., & Ray, D. C. (2014). *Group play therapy: A dynamic approach.* Routledge.

Theraplay. (2023). Sunshine circles. https://theraplay.org/training/training-programs/sunshine-circles/

Tucker, C., Schieffer, K., Wills, T. J., Hull, C., & Murphy, Q. (2017). Enhancing social-emotional skills in at-risk preschool students through Theraplay based groups: The Sunshine Circle Model. *International Journal of Play Therapy™*, *26*(4), 185–195. https://doi.org/10.1037/pla0000054

Wang Flahive, M.-H., & Ray, D. (2007). Effect of group sandtray therapy with preadolescents. *Journal for Specialists in Group Work*, *32*(4), 362–382. https://doi.org/10.1080/01933920701476706

Weaver, J. L., Medyk, N. V., Swank, J. M., Daniels, P. F., & Smith-Adcock, S. (2021). A phenomenological study of Theraplay groups within a middle school. *International Journal of Play Therapy™*, *30*(2), 125–135. https://doi.org/10.1037/pla0000139

Whitaker, A., Torres-Guillen, S., Morton, M., Jordan, H., Coyle, S., Mann, A., & Sun, W. L. (2019). Cops and no counselors: How the lack of school mental health is harming students. American Civil Liberties Union. https://www.aclu.org/sites/default/files/field_document/030419-acluschooldisciplinereport.pdf

Yalom, I. D., & Leszcz, M. (2020). *The theory and practice of group psychotherapy* (6th ed.). Basic Books.

Appendix A   Black Kids Count Game

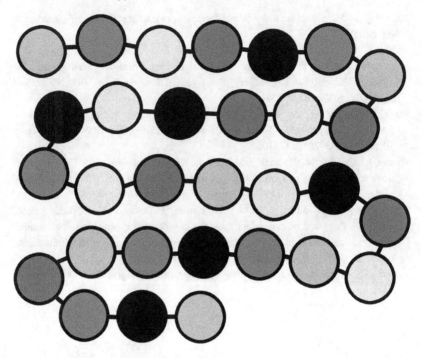

CONNECT	CONNECT	CONNECT	CONNECT
Name a caring adult in your life	Name a game you can play with a trusted adult	Name an activity you'd like a caring adult to do/play with you	Name an important loved one in your life

CONNECT	CONNECT	CONNECT	CONNECT
Name a nice thing you can do for a loved one	Name a nice thing you can do for a loved one	10 second dance party!	10 second dance party!

Black Students Matter

CAPABLE	CAPABLE	CAPABLE	CAPABLE
Repeat the affirmation: "I am capable of anything"	Repeat the affirmation: "I can do anything I put my mind to"	Pick a new skill to learn	Name a time you did something someone thought you couldn't do

CAPABLE	CAPABLE	CAPABLE	CAPABLE
What is something an adult does for you that you'd like to do yourself?	Name a time you accomplished something that you thought you couldn't	Name someone you look up to because of their strength	What's your best quality?

COUNT	COUNT	COUNT	COUNT
Repeat the affirmation: "I am valued"	Repeat the affirmation: "I am important"	Name a positive quality about yourself	Name a positive quality about yourself

COUNT	COUNT	COUNT	COUNT
Create your own affirmation	Create your own affirmation	How would you like someone to show their love to you?	Name someone you look up to because of their confidence

COURAGE	COURAGE	COURAGE	COURAGE
Name a time you tried something really scary	Name a feeling you have difficulty expressing. Why?	Name someone you look up to because of their courage	Name a person that looks up to you because of your courage

COURAGE	COURAGE	COURAGE	COURAGE
Name a time your fear kept you from trying something new	What is a new skill you'd like to try?	Name a time you helped stick up for someone else.	Name a fear you'd like to overcome

OOPING	COPING	COPING	COPING
What is an unhealthy coping skill you use?	Who can help remind you to use your coping skills?	Name a time you were successful in using a coping skill	Name a time you were unsuccessful in using a coping skill

COPING	COPING	COPING	COPING
Stretch your body for 10 seconds	Hum a song you like for 10 seconds	Take 3 deep breaths	Squeeze your fists for 5 seconds, then release

COPING COPING COPING COPING

COPING COPING COPING COPING

Social Media Scavenger Hunt

Racism happens everywhere, especially online. Social media, YouTube, and gaming are all areas where you may be exposed to racism and discrimination. Go on a scavenger hunt, and see if you can find others that have experienced any of the social media interactions below.

Direct Experiences	Appearance	Vicarious Experiences	Feelings	Coping Skills
I've been called a racial slur	I've used a filter to make my skin look lighter	I've seen a racist post	I've felt anxious after seeing something traumatic online	I engage in social justice campaigns
Someone has made fun of my name	Someone made a rude comment about my body	I've seen a video of someone shot or hurt by police	I have felt angry after seeing something traumatic online	Black Twitter helps me feel better
Someone has called me the "n"-word	Someone has made a rude comment about my facial feature(s)	I've seen someone delete their account because of racism	I have had trouble sleeping after seeing something traumatic	I take social media breaks
Someone has threatened me	Someone has made a rude comment about my skin tone	I've seen someone being attacked because of being Black	I have felt sad/depressed after a racist experience	I block/unfollow unhealthy people
I've been told to "Go back to Africa"	Someone has made fun of my hair	I've seen someone being threatened because of being Black	I have felt angry after a racist experience	I speak up for myself

Have you had any other racist experiences online?
Are there other ways you cope with these experiences?
Are there other safe spaces you have found online?
Are there any influencers whom you look up to help you through these experiences?

BMH Connect mylemarks

Thank you for your purchase!

Set Up

This card deck contains 48 *Talk Me Up!* cards and requires printing and cutting. For best results, it is recommended to print in high quality, on card stock, and laminate, if possible, for prolonged use.

*If you would like the back graphic design on each card, then the card pages should be printed double-sided starting on page 4. It is recommended to conduct a test print to ensure proper formatting and orientation. Cards are designed to print as traditional playing cards. *Due to differences in printer functions, Mylemarks is unable to provide support if there are printing issues.* To print cards without the back design, you can print the card pages Even Pages only, single-sided, starting on page 4.

How To Play

Six cards are dealt to each player and the top card in the remaining deck is flipped over. The person with the next closest birthday goes first, and play continues clockwise after that. Players take turns discarding a card from their hand if it matches the number or color of the previously played card.

As a player lays down a card, they *must* say the positive affirmation displayed on the card that is being played. If they forget to say the affirmation and the next person takes their turn, then that player must draw two cards from the deck. This is *only* if they are called out by an opponent. If it is unnoticed, they are not required to draw.

If a player does not have a matching number or color, then they draw one card from the deck. If they are able to play the card, then they can lay it on the discard pile. If they are not able to play it, the card remains in their hand, and then it is the next person's turn.

The *Talk Me Up* card in the deck is a "Wild" and can be played at any moment during the game, particularly if a player does not have a matching card. When a player lays down the *Talk Me Up* card, everyone must go around clockwise and say something positive about that player. Once this is done, the player can then lay down any card that they would like. The *You've Been Skipped* card, when played, skips the next person's turn.

The game continues until a player is completely out of cards. The first player to do so is the winner of the game!

"I am IMPORTANT!"

"I love my body just the way it is!"

"I'm in charge of MY happiness!"

"Good things are going to happen to me!"

Talk Me Up!

Everyone must go around and say something positive about you, and then you can play any card you'd like!

BMH Connect

Talk Me Up!

Everyone must go around and say something positive about you, and then you can play any card you'd like!

BMH Connect

Talk Me Up!

Everyone must go around and say something positive about you, and then you can play any card you'd like!

BMH Connect

Talk Me Up!

Everyone must go around and say something positive about you, and then you can play any card you'd like!

BMH Connect

11

It Takes a Village
Engaging Black Families and Community Members in Play Therapy

Although school social workers may not provide family therapy as much as social workers in other settings, working with Black students requires an ability to also build strong rapport and therapeutic relationships with their caregivers. Culturally, Black children receive direction from their caregivers about who is safe and who to trust. Therefore, it is imperative that school social workers understand the unique needs and pressures plaguing Black caregivers to successfully join with them in supporting their child's mental and social-emotional needs. This chapter explores cultural considerations in working within the Black family system, including the understanding of the "village concept" as a protective factor in this community.

The Village Concept

In the Black community, there are important adults who contribute to child-rearing outside of the child's biological parents. This can include aunts, uncles, grandparents, and family friends who are referred to as "aunts" and "uncles." Black students may also mention "play cousins," who are often the children of the family friends titled as aunts and uncles. Black children are more likely to have family and nonrelatives participate in raising them, providing emotional support, caretaking, discipline, and rules (Hunter et al., 2019). Therefore, the use of "caregivers" will be used instead of "parents" with the understanding that school social workers may also be working with members of the child's village to provide mental health support. These

Black Students Matter. April D. Duncan, Oxford University Press. © Oxford University Press 2024.
DOI: 10.1093/oso/9780197669266.003.0012

kinship-based social networks are sources of bonding social capital that can provide important social competences the child can utilize outside of the family system (Hunter et al., 2019). This will require the assessment of key family members through activities like a play genogram (using toys to identify different family members), which can help the social worker be more cognizant of other adults to engage if the parents are unable or unavailable to do so. Given the numbers of Black parents who are incarcerated and Black children in the child welfare system, other members of the child's village become even more important.

Exploring Intergenerational Trauma Impacts on Black Parenting Practices

Maladaptive parenting practices among Black caregivers are directly rooted in slavery and intergenerational trauma. "Intergenerational trauma" refers to traumatic responses and stress that are passed between generations (Ryder & White, 2022). For example, during the 19th century, enslaved fathers and mothers would belittle their children to protect them; today, however, that same practice can lead to Black children internalizing those criticisms (DeGruy, 2017) which may contribute to depression, low self-esteem, and suicidal thoughts and behaviors. Several negative impacts of intergenerational trauma appear in modern-day Black parenting. Some families may be disconnected, distance themselves from one another, or detach (Ryder & White, 2022). These types of parenting behaviors often stem from the caregiver's inability to connect with and communicate their own feelings, so distancing becomes the normal way of dealing with issues in the family.

Another way intergenerational trauma negatively impacts parenting is through minimization, where the caregiver minimizes the child's trauma compared to their own (Ryder & White, 2022). School social workers may have to work with caregivers employing these practices to obtain their own mental health treatment while also learning the importance of validation and listening to prevent an impaired parent–child relationship. For Black parents, intergenerational trauma shapes the parenting practices that seek to equip Black children with the survival skills needed to navigate a world full of racial stressors. First, "the talk" is used with Black children at an early age as a way for Black parents to help keep them safe. This is an example of socialization practices in the Black community meant to protect children. Next, there is the act of "tough love" that is often shown through physical or harsh discipline to prevent the same behavior outside the home. Working with Black caregivers requires an understanding of the historical trauma that has shaped their parenting while maintaining a nonjudgmental stance.

"The Talk"

Trayvon Martin. Tamir Rice. Mike Brown Jr. Emmitt Till. Black caregivers live with a constant fear that their child will become another hashtag or center of a national protest. These fears govern the way Black caregivers talk to their children about their encounters with the outside world. For example, Black children are not encouraged to explore in the same way as White children are, out of fear that they can be harmed (DeGruy, 2017). "The Talk" is meant to tell Black children how they should interact with police officers so they are not harmed (Whitaker & Snell, 2016). However, this racial socialization practice may cause more harm than help. "The talk" often occurs during early adolescence, at a time when children are developmentally incapable of exhibiting appropriate levels of control and rational decision-making (Whitaker & Snell, 2016) in a scary and traumatizing encounter. Also, the conversation often gives Black children a step-by-step procedure on how to act around police officers, yet it usually does not provide a space to help Black children process their feelings around this scary reality that has been communicated. Black adults and children are often left feeling humiliated, ashamed, angry, and powerless after the discussion (Whitaker & Snell, 2016). I believe "the talk" is important, but caregivers should also create a space for children to process their feelings around the topic, including addressing any fear and/or anxieties the child may have. School social workers should work with caregivers to process these feelings and explain the importance of modeling healthy emotional expression for their children, which can be done through racial socialization messages.

Racial Socialization Messages

Black parents often pass down messages about Black culture and history while also teaching children how to cope with discrimination or negotiate in- and out-group relationships (McWayne et al., 2020). This is often displayed through racial socialization messages, which can promote psychological well-being and reduce risk in Black children (Stokes et al., 2020). Next, many Black children are socialized early to defend themselves, to keep them physiologically and physically safe in dangerous situations, which often becomes problematic in schools (Haight et al., 2014). This becomes a battle of "home rules" versus "school rules" as Black children are often encouraged to fight when someone threatens or disrespects them, which, of course, will result in suspension or expulsion. In some cases, siblings and other family members are also encouraged to fight with the student and may even get in trouble at home for not defending their sibling or family member. Some Black caregivers may not see the problem with their child fighting, especially if it is because of self-defense. However, it is important for them to understand that zero-tolerance policies do not provide flexibility for Black students when it comes to physical altercations in the same way as for White students, and ultimately fighting only harms the Black child more, rather than protecting them.

Authoritative Discipline

Black caregivers are very aware, often from their own childhood experiences, that Black children are treated differently and that they are not given the same latitude as White children. In her book, *Spare the Kids: Why Whupping Children Won't Save Black America*, Patton (2017) states

> Black children are exempt from the protections young people should be granted—to play, run, get dirty, and make mistakes. Their innocence is denied and negated, as they are viewed as stereotyped Black adults. And they are treated accordingly in schools, in public spaces, and sadly, within their own families. (p. 35)

This leads to the belief that Black parents need to be tough on their children to prepare them for the world they will encounter. This may lead to caregivers believing that physical punishment is the best option, or they may advocate for harsh punishment for their child's behavior. Abuse, neglect, and violence are responses to intergenerational trauma in Black caregivers (Ryder & White, 2022). Acts of aggression toward Black children often comes a place of love and trauma. In the Black community, it is often accepted and even encouraged to physically harm Black children when they are disrespectful so they do not make the mistake of standing their ground against a White person in authority (DeGruy, 2017). And although the use of physical punishment in the Black community is not always to the level that defines physical abuse, ultimately, it reflects the caregivers' inability to regulate their own emotions and trauma stressors. It is important to note that although physical punishment may be used among Black caregivers, it is often used as a last resort or for more serious behaviors like blatant disrespect (Adkison-Bradley et al., 2014).

Black caregivers want to see their children to succeed and they believe "tough love" and an authoritative parenting style is the best way to support that dream. Authoritative parents communicate through reason, recognize their children as individuals, and set standards while exerting rational control (Cross-Barnet & McDonald, 2015). Although physical punishment is used in Black families, it is not the only form of punishment used. Studies found Black parents will often discuss problematic behaviors with their children then use clear commands and remove privileges or assign extra work to address misbehavior (Adkison-Bradley et al., 2014). Personally, my parents never used physical punishment towards me, they would "put me to work" with extra tasks and chores around the house (You don't know how many times I've cleaned out garages and organized laundry rooms!). Helping Black caregivers find a balance between affirming their children while preparing them for their harsh reality is a tricky one, but not impossible. Researchers found that on days when adolescents received messages from their parents suggesting they were special, they also reported fewer negative emotions and more positive emotions (Cheeks et al., 2020). One way to help Black caregivers improve the emotional well-being of their children while also guiding them toward safety is to use both authoritative discipline and compassionate parenting.

Compassionate Parenting

The new wave in parenting is "gentle parenting," which focuses on using empathy, respect, boundaries, and understanding (Plant, 2022). However, there is some debate in the Black community on the effectiveness of this practice, with many believing it doesn't work on their children (Johnson, 2022). I believe the issue may be in the term "gentle." Black parents often use strict and harsh discipline with Black children to protect them. Too many Black children have been killed for simply being in the wrong place and encountering the wrong racist. Therefore, the term "gentle" may be off-putting when Black caregivers know there is nothing gentle about the world their children will encounter. I proposition the term "compassionate parenting" as an alternative. This form of parenting still focuses on communicating empathy and respect for the child's feelings in combination with an authoritative discipline tone and style that directs and holds the child responsible for their behavior.

For example, if the child is suspended from school, compassionate parenting would have the caregiver ask the child for their side of the story while also exploring how they felt in the situation. They would talk to the child about what they may have done differently in the situation. Caregivers would then express how the situation made them feel, too. Maybe they felt embarrassed that they had to leave work to pick them up or worried when they got the call that the child was in a fight. This mutual space of emotional expression reinforces the importance of communicating feelings in a respectful way. Finally, the parent would communicate the punishment, if any, such as a removal of privileges. In compassionate parenting, the caregiver is also encouraged to avoid dragging out the punishment. If a child talked back to their teacher, it does not warrant being grounded for a month. It is important for Black caregivers to communicate that they see the best in their children and give them the opportunity to move on from the indiscretion.

Black children are already dealing with teachers and peers who may still be directly or indirectly punishing them for previous incidents. For some Black children, it may discourage them from making the effort to change their behavior. In my clinical experience, I have had Black children say, "I'm already in trouble for the whole semester so there's no point in trying to do good." School social workers should help Black caregivers recognize the confidence they can provide Black children in giving them another chance to succeed, chances they often do not receive in school and within the legal system.

Therapeutic Limit Setting

Another key step in authoritative discipline is teaching Black caregivers how to set limits and guidelines for appropriate behaviors while also encouraging emotional expression. This may include normalizing emotions that are often scolded in the Black community like anger, boredom, or sadness. The goal is for social workers to help Black caregivers understand the importance of emotional expression, especially as it pertains to negative race-based experiences. It is also important to explore the childhood of that caregiver, as it may guide the way they parent their child. The school social worker should exhibit compassion and empathy when working with caregivers and help them identify the positive and negative things that came from their childhood to discuss what parenting tactics are helpful and which ones could be abandoned for the sake of the student's mental health.

School social workers need to work with some caregivers on appropriate ways to set limits and boundaries with their children. First, is it important for caregivers to provide children with choices. This helps them take responsibility for their decisions and the consequences of those decisions. For example, the parent may tell a student, "If you choose to talk back to the teacher, then you choose to lose your tablet for a week." However, Landreth (n.d.)

notes "You give little choices to little kids and big choices to big kids." This also promotes self-responsibility and pride when children make safe choices. It also moves the responsibility of punishment from the parent to the child because the child's action led to the loss of privileges opposed to the parent removing the privilege (Landreth, n.d.). Another way choices can be used is to eliminate refusal to adhere to a command. For example, rather than telling the child to clean their room, they can choose to clean their room while listening to music or while having their favorite television show playing in the background. This eliminates the number of commands the caregiver has to give while providing the child freedom to make age-appropriate decisions.

Another parenting skill to assist Black caregivers comes from parent–child interaction therapy (PCIT). In this attachment-based modality, caregivers are taught not to give a command unless they have time to follow through with a punishment if the child does not adhere to the command. For example, before an outing, parents may say "Put your shoes on or else you're not going!" Which is not true. The child is going to go and must go with the parent in most cases. The child sees that this is an empty threat and may not comply right away. Then the parent gets upset and may react with anger or physical aggression. Again, this is more reflective of the caregiver's inability to follow through with their words. Instead, the parent may say "If you don't get your shoes on in 20 seconds, then you choose not to watch your tablet in the car."

Also, I teach caregivers not to ask a child a "yes-no" question then get upset when the child says "no." For example, the caregiver may ask, "Are you ready to go?" and when the child says "No," the parent is upset and/or punishes the child for their response. The child is not being obstinate or disrespectful. They were giving their honest answer when asked a question. This is another example of how choices can be given. The caregiver instead can say, "It is time to go. Do you want to skip to the car or hop on one leg to the car?" It is important to remember the loss of control that Black students feel when interacting with direct and systemic racial stressors. Providing a place for children to respectfully communicate their feelings while also providing age-appropriate control is vital and can be empowering at any age.

Mental Health in Black Americans

Black caregivers are navigating their own racial stressors that are negatively affecting their mental health on top of trying to be the best parents possible.

But when caregivers are struggling, it can be difficult for them to operate at their best, which may inadvertently cause attachment issues in the parent–child relationship. Life stressors, psychological resources, and the parents' own attachment experiences often impact how sensitive and responsive parents are to their children (Ewing et al., 2015). Therefore, to effectively help Black students, school social workers will also have to acknowledge mental health issues in their caregivers.

Black Americans account for 13.4% of the United States population (approximately 46 million people) (US Census Bureau, 2022). However, many Black Americans are suffering from mental illness that often goes untreated. The 2018 National Survey on Drug Use and Health conducted by the Substance Abuse and Mental Health Services Administration (SAMHSA, 2018) found 4.8 million Black Americans reported having a mental illness and 1.1 million of those individuals identified having a serious mental illness over the previous year. The same study found smoking (cigarettes and marijuana), binge drinking, illicit drug use, and prescription pain reliver misuses is more frequent among Black adults with mental illness. These maladaptive coping skills are often used to deal with racial stressors. Black adults are more likely to experience feelings of hopelessness, worthlessness, and sadness compared to White adults (Mental Health America, 2022). In theory, engaging Black caregivers in family play therapy may also help them address their own mental health needs while equipping them with both the parenting and coping skills need to enhance their bonds in the parent-child relationship.

Barriers to Mental Health Treatment

When working with Black students, it is important to be mindful of the barriers to treatment for mental health. First, there is a history of maltreatment in the medical community, from the Tuskegee experiments to the forced sterilization of Black women (Roberts, 2000). This includes the historical mistreatment of enslaved women and children, most notably by Dr. James Sims, also known as the father of gynecology, who performed experiments on Black women, children, and babies without anesthesia (DeGruy, 2017). This historical trauma has caused apprehension in many Black Americans when dealing with the medical system. However, for those who are willing to brave the system, accessibility is another hurdle to jump. Only one in three Black Americans who need mental health services can obtain them (American Psychiatric Association [APA], 2017). Insurance may be one barrier, as 11%

of Black Americans are still without insurance even after the implementation of the Affordable Care Act (ACA) compared to 8% of White Americans (Argita et al., 2022).

Like Black children, Black adults are often misdiagnosed because of a lack of cultural competence and understanding of how racial stressors drive the emotions, decisions, and behaviors of Black people. Black Americans are more likely to be diagnosed with schizophrenia and less likely to be diagnosed with mood disorders compared to White people with the same symptoms (Mental Health America, 2022). Also, Black adults are offered medication and therapy at lower rates than any other race (APA, 2017). As a result of historical trauma, racial stressors, and systemic racism, Black Americans may be resistant to mental health services. First, they may worry that the therapist is not culturally competent enough to treat their issues, especially since only 2% of American Psychological Association (APA) members are Black or African American (Mental Health America, 2022; no data available on the racial makeup of mental health professionals such as social workers, counselors, and psychiatrists). Then, stigma around mental health still exists in the Black community. There used to be an adage "Black folk don't get therapy," which is evident in research with Black Americans who still communicate resistance to treatment for mild depression or anxiety out of fear they will be seen as "crazy" in their social circles (Mental Health America, 2022). However, the numbers also show that there are a lot of Black people who want treatment for themselves and a lot of caregivers who want their children in mental health treatment yet accessibility still blocks them from receiving these important services. School social workers are in an unique position to engage caregivers in mental health services, but it all starts with a strong therapeutic relationship with these caregivers.

Building Relationships with Black Caregivers

In my career, I have found building rapport with Black caregivers just as important as building rapport with Black children because caregivers often hold the key to offering the green light that the outside person is trustworthy. It is important to remember that Black caregivers come with their own layers of racial stressors and experiences that may cause them to feel suspicious of the intentions of the school and the school social worker. Caregivers may have had their own negative experiences in schools that prevent them from feeling comfortable with the school system. They also may have negative experiences with previous school officials that fuel this distrust. Patience is key. This may include talking about things that are not therapy related, calling to check on them, and making small talk when you see them at the school. This may help caregivers feel more trusting of the social worker and can help with the relationship.

It is important to always be sensitive to the systemic issues that plague the caregivers of Black students. The race-based stress and trauma experienced by Black students also happens to their caregivers, leaving them in need of their own mental health treatment. However, finding mental health treatment for themselves or their child can prove to be a difficult task. Black caregivers are five times more likely to have difficulty finding mental health services for their child (Child and Adolescent Health Measure Initiative, 2018–2019). Therefore, their child may only have access to mental health services through their school, which puts the school social worker in a key place to fill a huge gap in mental health treatment of Black children. That difficulty also extends into therapy services for Black caregivers as well.

The social worker must be mindful of racial mistrust. For non-Black clinicians, there may be layers of historical trauma that have led to levels of racial mistrust that can prevent the caregiver from developing trust immediately. In that case, building rapport and the therapeutic relationship may take longer. Although Black caregivers prefer their child work with a Black clinician, at the end of the day, they just want a competent clinician. Black clinicians have their own implicit biases that can appear as countertransference when working with Black clients. In some cases, clinicians may never establish trust with the caregiver because of their own historical trauma. The social worker should employ empathy toward that caregiver, respect their boundaries, and communicate with them in a manner that feels most comfortable for them, such as email.

Play Therapy with Black Caregivers and Village Members

When building therapeutic alliances with Black caregivers, it will be paramount to assist them in finding a middle ground that prepares Black children for the world they will encounter while also providing nurturance and empathy. If everyone is tough on Black children, who nurtures them? Who provides a safe environment where they can make mistakes and explore their emotions around their realities? School social workers have a unique opportunity to be that person and provide that environment while also building a bridge for their caregivers to do the same. That will require patience while building rapport with both the caregiver and student and providing a free place for them to express their emotions when dealing with race-based or school-based issues. It will also require encouraging racial socialization as a parenting skill for Black caregivers to best support their child's social-emotional needs.

The stress of negative race-based experiences in the school and beyond may be damaging to the parent–child relationship. If the student is constantly in trouble at school, then the caregiver may be expressing frustration, anger, or annoyance with the child, which could negatively affect their relationship. If that is the case, the caregiver could benefit from engaging in play-based family clinical services. Several play therapy approaches can benefit caregivers of Black students: filial play therapy, CPRT, and Adlerian play therapy. Also, parent consultations are a good way to connect with caregivers that requires a short-term commitment during which the social worker can implement sand tray therapy to help activate the therapeutic powers of play for that caregiver.

Gaining Play Therapy Buy-In with Black Caregivers

As mentioned previously, Black children are not afforded the same childhood as their peers due to race-based stress and trauma and parenting within the community that devalues play and emphasizes the need to grow up fast due to societal treatment. Therefore, the social worker may run into issues with gaining buy-in to use play therapy with Black children. A study found Black caregivers were open to their children receiving play therapy if they had an awareness of play therapy interventions, knowledge of where to find a qualified professional to provide services, and had perceived family, community, or social support (Brumfield & Christensen, 2011). Caregivers may not understand the therapeutic value of play and may require psychoeducation and resources for them to truly grasp the benefits of play. The Association for Play Therapy™ (APT) provides free brochures that explain play therapy, and the social worker can share these during parent consultations. It will also be a good idea to place these brochures in the front office so other caregivers have access to the information.

Black caregivers may be resistant to mental health services due to fears of being judged as a "failure" as a parent, cultural perceptions of counseling, negative past experiences in counseling, worries about the counselor's ability to maintain confidentiality, and negative or inaccurate media portrayals of counseling and those who seek counseling (Brumfield & Christensen, 2011). The social worker should also take time to clear up any misunderstandings about playing in therapy sessions. The caregiver may not believe the child should be "rewarded" with play when they misbehave, so it will be important to explain that play is the best medicine for a child struggling emotionally and behaviorally because it provides an appropriate outlet to explore those behaviors and feelings while also learning new ways to cope. The social worker can use the analogy that play is the vehicle that drives the learning of new skills, so it is not something that is used as a reward or a consequence for misbehavior.

Parent Consultations

If school social workers want to make lasting change in Black students, they need to consistently engage with their caregivers. One way to engage with the caregivers of Black students is through conducting parent consultations. These are meetings that are held between the caregiver and school social worker. This is time to build rapport, listen and validate any concerns from the caregiver, review treatment goals, and discuss any progress or setbacks the student has shown in the playroom. This will also be the time to align with the caregiver to hear about their struggles and provide parenting skills when the time is appropriate and the relationship is established. Parent consultations are also a good time to provide psychoeducation on racial trauma and how it may be specifically presenting in their child.

At the minimum, these consultations should happen when the child first starts working with the school social worker, leaving and returning from any school breaks, and when they terminate from services. At most, these consultations should occur monthly, so both the caregiver and the social worker are closely monitoring—and adjusting—the therapeutic plan to support that student. It may also be effective to invite teachers into the consultations. If you are working with child welfare–involved youth or youth with an incarcerated caregiver, it may include the case manager, court-appointed special advocate (CASA) worker, or Deputy Juvenile Officer (DJO). This provides an opportunity to all parties involved with the child to discuss their concerns, report any progress, and keep everyone on the same page for that child's treatment plan.

Sand tray therapy is a fun way to engage parents into consultations while also providing an intervention that does not put pressure on them to talk. The social worker should let the caregiver know the intervention is used with clients of all ages and that it is also an intervention that you may use with their child sometimes. This helps provide a window into what play therapy is and how it is implemented into mental health sessions. The social worker can use prompts like "Create a sand tray showing your concerns about your child" or "Create a sand tray showing how your family world looks at the moment." Solution-focused therapy prompts can include "Create a sand tray that shows how your world would like if the problem was no longer there" or "If you woke up and the problem was gone, what would your child's world look like? Can you create a sand tray showing that world?" A CBPT prompt can be "Think of your biggest fear for your child. Now create a sand tray showing that fear and play the script until the end." This will allow the caregiver to work through their biggest fears and discuss coping skills with the social worker to help alleviate those fears. Integrating sand tray therapy into parent consultations is also a good way to gain play therapy buy-in with Black caregivers.

Filial Therapy

Filial therapy can be an effective solution to addressing mental health accessibility issues for Black children. In this seminal theory, closely related to CCPT, caregivers learn how to engage in child-directed sessions with their children, with the therapist teaching them same skills we use in CCPT sessions (Scuka & Guerney, 2019). It also can help provide caregivers with the skills they need to adequately assist their children during difficult times. Also, these skills can help Black caregivers repair any damaged parent–child relationships because of school discipline. Although this is a flexible model, it is important that the caregiver is present at every session because they are often leading the session themselves (Scuka & Guerney, 2019). If this is not possible due to scheduling or the caregiver is inaccessible during school times, these skills can be taught in parent consultations via role-playing. It may also be worth exploring if other members of the student's village are able to participate in filial therapy play sessions if the caregiver is unavailable. School social workers should get a signed Authorization to Release Information form for that "village member" to participate in sessions, along with coordinating with school officials to find the most appropriate and effective way to have that adult on campus and in session with the child.

Child–Parent Relationship Therapy

CPRT is a group play therapy modality that focuses on enhancing attachments with caregivers (Center for Play Therapy, 2022). It is another filial play therapy

---

model because it teaches caregivers how to lead child-centered sessions at home with their children. This modality could be appropriate if the social worker has several caregivers interested in participating in a group setting. Ten weekly group sessions are used to teach caregivers how to focus on the parent–child relationship and the strengths of both the caregiver and child, rather than focusing on the problem (Center for Play Therapy, 2022). This could be an appropriate modality for caregivers who struggle with identifying strengths in their children.

A study found that CPRT may be effective for Black caregivers, especially low-income families. Sheely-Moore and Bratton (2010) found the model reduced parent–child relationship stress and help decrease child behavior problems in low-income Black families. There also is an emphasis on empathizing with the child and using reflective responding to explore the child's behaviors, needs and wishes, feelings and thoughts without asking questions (Center for Play Therapy, 2022). For caregivers, CPRT can help increase resiliency, confidence, and capability while children learn self-responsibility, effective problem-solving and decision-making skills, self-control, and self-esteem (Sheely-Moore & Bratton, 2010). This could be an effective intervention for caregivers who struggle with allowing their children to express their feelings and needs. Social workers are encouraged to obtain certification in this modality before implementing it. Additional information and training on this approach are available at the Center for Play Therapy at the University of North Texas.

Adlerian Play Therapy

The final modality to engage Black caregivers in family play therapy is Adlerian play therapy. Adlerian therapists believe that people are socially embedded, and that parents and children are locked into negative and reciprocal interactions (Meaney et al., 2015). This is an appropriate intervention for school social workers because it provides the opportunity to engage both teachers and caregivers in the child's treatment needs. Adlerian play therapists consult with both parents and teachers on a consistent bases to receive feedback, and they work as a team to create treatment goals (Meany-Walen et al., 2015). Adlerian play therapy is effective in decreasing problem behaviors in schools and increasing on-task behaviors (Meany-Walen et al., 2015).

There are four phases to the modality: building an egalitarian relationship with the family, exploring the family's lifestyles, helping family members gain insight into their behavior, and reorienting and reeducating the family (Kottman, 2001). In phase one, the therapist uses a nondirective approach to help the adults feel comfortable playing with their child while also observing the behavior in the parent–child or teacher–student relationship (Kottman, 2001). In the second phase, the social worker uses strategies such as family art assessments, puppet shows, or sand trays to gather information about the family atmosphere, assets, mistaken goals of behavior, private logic, personality priorities, and the Crucial C's (Kottman, 2001). During the second phase, the team works collaboratively to create treatment plans (Kottman, 2001). The third phase helps adults form a hypothesis about the goals for their behavior and lifestyles through role-plays, expressive art techniques, humor, confrontation, immediacy, and metaphors (Kottman, 2001). The final phase helps family members learn and practice new ways to view themselves, their family, and their world, while the social worker encourages family members to make appropriate changes in behaviors, attitudes, and beliefs (Kottman, 2001). Social workers can receive additional training and certification on this modality through the League of Extraordinary Adlerian Play Therapists (LEAPT) at https://adlerianplaytherapy.com/.

Play Therapy to Enhance Parent–Child Attachments

Although these modalities are appropriate for caregivers and children, there may still be barriers to getting the parents engaged in therapy sessions. There are some additional ways that social workers can support these caregivers without a weekly or monthly time commitment. The goal is to enhance the parent–child attachment so Black children have more emotional support in their village while caregivers gain better insight into their child's needs. There are several activities that social workers can encourage caregivers to do with their children. For example, family dance parties, movie nights, game nights, and cooking competitions are fun and inexpensive ways to get parents engaged in play with their child. They can also be encouraged to write notes of encouragement to their child and hide them where the child can find them (like the "I see you" activity shared in Chapter 10). Social workers can also talk to caregivers about their favorite childhood games and encourage them to share those memories with their children. Another important way to enhance attachments is through "special time."

"Special time" is when caregivers spend one-on-one time with their child, allowing the child to lead the play. Students of all ages can benefit from special time, although it will look different based on their developmental age. This individual time between the child and their caregiver can help increase attachment and serve as a safe place for emotional expression. Although caregivers are discouraged from asking questions during this time, they may find that the individual attention, combined with play, allows their children to open up without any prompting. If so, caregivers should be encouraged to validate the emotions the child is sharing in that space while still refraining from asking questions and simply enjoying the time together instead. For children in kindergarten through 3rd grade, caregivers are encouraged to spend five minutes of this quality time every day engaging in special time, regardless of that child's behavior that day. If the child was in trouble at school that day, they would still receive special time because it teaches the child that their parent's love is unconditional and that they will be present in their lives even when they are upset or disappointed.

I have encouraged the use of "special time" for children of all ages, although it looks different when used with older children. For students in 4th through 6th grade, 10 minutes of special time twice a week is appropriate, and, for junior high and high school students, once a week for 30 minutes is ideal. I once had a 15-year-old Black girl and her mother participate in special time and at the end of treatment, the mother told me "I feel like I got my little girl back." Special time can help caregivers increase their attachment and the connections that they have with their kids while also allowing them to have fun and receive their own kind of therapy at the same time.

Conclusion

The most effective way to help Black students is to also help their caregivers learn the facts and symptoms of race-based stress while also teaching them learn practical skills they can use to help their child. Not all Black caregivers are able to be physically present in their children's lives due to systemic issues, but the utilization of members of the child's village provides an extra system of support that can help build healthy and strong attachments with that student and important adults in their lives. School social workers should maintain a balance of case manager, teacher, and confidante while using compassion, empathy, and patience to support caregivers of Black students. In doing so, they may be welcomed into the child's village and strengthen their bonds with important and caring adults.

References

Adkison-Bradley, C., Terpstra, J., & Dormitorio, B. (2014). Child discipline in African American families: A study of patterns and context. *Family Journal, 22*(2), 198–205. https://doi.org/10.1177/1066480713513553

American Psychiatric Association [APA]. (2017). Mental health disparities: African Americans. https://www.psychiatry.org/File Library/Psychiatrists/Cultural-Competency/Mental-Health-Disparities/Mental-Health-Facts-for-African-Americans.pdf

Argita, S., Hill, L., & Damico, A. (2022). Health coverage by race and ethnicity, 2010–2021. Kaiser Family Foundation. https://www.kff.org/racial-equity-and-health-policy/issue-brief/health-coverage-by-race-and-ethnicity/

Brumfield, K., & Christensen, T. (2011). Discovering African American parents' perceptions of play therapy: A phenomenological approach. *International Journal of Play Therapy™, 20*(4), 208–223. https://doi.org/10.1037/a0025748

Center for Play Therapy. (2022). Child-parent relationship therapy. University of North Texas. https://cpt.unt.edu/child-parent-relationship-therapy

Cheeks, B., Chavous, T., & Sellers, R. (2020). A daily examination of African American adolescents' racial discrimination, parental racial socialization, and psychological affect. *Child Development, 91*(6), 2123–2140. https://doi.org/10.1111/cdev.13416

Child and Adolescent Health Measure Initiative. (2018–2019). National survey of children's health. U.S. Department of Health and Human Services, Health Resources and Services Administration (HRSA), Maternal and Child Health Bureau (MCHB). https://www.childhealthdata.org/browse/survey?s=2&y=32&r=1

Cross-Barnet, C., & McDonald, K. (2015). It's all about the children: An intersectional perspective on parenting values among Black married couples in the United States. *Societies, 5*(4), 855–871. https://doi.org/10.3390/soc5040855

DeGruy, J. (2017). *Post traumatic slave syndrome: America's legacy of enduring injury & healing.* Uptown Press.

Ewing, E., Diamond, G., & Levy, S. (2015). Attachment-based family therapy for depressed and suicidal adolescents: Theory, clinical model and empirical support. *Attachment & Human Development: Attachment-Based Treatments For Adolescents, 17*(2), 136–156. https://doi.org/10.1080/14616734.2015.1006384

Haight, W., Gibson, P., Kayama, M., Marshall, J., & Wilson, R. (2014). An ecological-systems inquiry into racial disproportionalities in out-of-school suspensions from youth, caregiver and educator perspectives. *Children and Youth Services Review, 46*, 128–138. https://doi.org/10.1016/j.childyouth.2014.08.003

Hunter, A., Chipenda-Dansokho, S., Tarver, S., Herring, M., & Fletcher, A. (2019). Social capital, parenting, and African American families. *Journal of Child and Family Studies, 28*(2), 547–559. https://doi.org/10.1007/s10826-018-1282-2

Jones, S., & Neblett Jr, E. (2019). Black parenting couples' discussions of the racial socialization process: Occurrence and effectiveness. *Journal of Child and Family Studies, 28*(1), 218–232. https://doi.org/10.1007/s10826-018-1248-4

Kottman, T. (2001). Adlerian play therapy. *International Journal of Play Therapy™, 10*(2), 1–12. https://doi.org/10.1037/h0089476

Landreth, G. L. (n.d.). *Choices, cookies and kids. A creative approach to discipline*. [DVD]. University of North Texas.

McWayne, C., Mattis, J., & Li, L. (2020). Parenting together: Understanding the shared context of positive parenting among low-income Black families. *Journal of Black Psychology*, Article e9579842093165. https://doi.org/10.1177/0095798420931653

Meany-Walen, K., Kottman, T., Bullis, Q., & Dillman Taylor, D. (2015). Effects of Adlerian play therapy on children's externalizing behavior. *Journal of Counseling & Development*, *93*(4), 418–428. https://doi.org/10.1002/jcad.12040

Mental Health America. (2022). Black and African American communities and mental health. https://www.mhanational.org/issues/black-and-african-american-communities-and-mental-health

Patton, S. (2017). *Spare the kids: Why whupping children won't save Black America*. Beacon Press.

Plant, R. (2022). Benefits and challenges of gentle parenting. Very Well Family. https://www.verywellfamily.com/what-is-gentle-parenting-5189566

Roberts, D. (2000). *Killing the black body*. Vintage Books.

Ryder, G., & White, T. (2022). How intergenerational trauma impacts families. PsychCentral. https://psychcentral.com/lib/how-intergenerational-trauma-impacts-families

Scuka, R. F., & Guerney, L. (2019). Filial therapy. *Play Therapy*, *14*(3). https://cdn.ymaws.com/www.a4pt.org/resource/resmgr/publications/pt_theories/Filial_Sept2019_FINAL.pdf

Sheely-Moore, A., & Bratton, S. (2010). A strengths-based parenting intervention with low-income African American families. *Professional School Counseling*, *13*(3), Article e2156759. https://doi.org/10.1177/2156759X1001300305

Stokes, M., Hope, E., Cryer-Coupet, Q., & Elliot, E. (2020). Black girl blues: The roles of racial socialization, gendered racial socialization, and racial identity on depressive symptoms among Black girls. *Journal of Youth and Adolescence*, *49*(11), 2175–2189. https://doi.org/10.1007/s10964-020-01317-8

Substance Abuse and Mental Health Services Administration (SAMHSA). (2018). National survey on drug use and health: African Americans. U.S. Department of Health and Human Services. https://www.samhsa.gov/data/sites/default/files/reports/rpt23247/2_AfricanAmerican_2020_01_14_508.pdf

US Census Bureau. (2022). Quick facts. https://www.census.gov/quickfacts/fact/table/US/PST120221

Whitaker, T. R., & Snell, C. L. (2016). Parenting while powerless: Consequences of "the talk." *Journal of Human Behavior in the Social Environment*, *26*(3–4), 303–309. https://doi.org/10.1080/10911359.2015.1127736

Index

For the benefit of digital users, indexed terms that span two pages (e.g., 52–53) may, on occasion, appear on only one of those pages
Boxes are indicated by *b* following the page number

A

Abrams, J. A., 204–5
accessibility, mental health
    services/treatment, 21–22,
    48–49, 454–55. *See also*
    under mental health
    services/treatment
achievement orientation, 136
"A Day at the Barbershop," 102
Adlerian group play therapy, 400–3
  Black Kids Count game, 402,
    408–18
  Let Me Be Great Chips, 402–3
Adlerian play therapy (AdPT), 105–
  6, 460–61
  Crucial Cs, 348, 401–2, 460–61
adultification bias, 4, 44–45
  Black boys, 258–61
    juvenile justice system, 265
  Black girls, 199, 201–4
    "fast" stereotype, 202–3
    fundamentals, 201–4
    loud, 202
    as racial stressor, 209
    strong, 203–4
  definition, 1
  incarcerated family member, 311–12

play therapy for
  Black girls, 199
  ecosystemic play therapy,
    104–5
adverse childhood events (ACEs),
    21–22, 393
  Black boys, 261–62
  bullying, witnessing, 124
  Child Trust Events Survey, 393
  Philadelphia Expanded ACEs,
    24–25
  Race-Based Traumatic Symptoms
    Scale, 24–25
  Race-Related Event Scale, 24–25
  racial trauma, 21–22
advocacy, teacher
  for Black students, 372
  implicit bias training, 372
African Grief Masks, 319, 323–29
age of mistake defense, 203–4
aggression. *See also* bullying
  Black boys, 253
  Black girls, punishment, 44
  childhood traumatic grief, 314
  grief as, playroom, 316–17
  learned behavior, 50
  in play therapy, Black boys, 267

as school mental health crisis
solution, 389–90
selection, 391–93
group therapy
phases, 393–96
final stage, 395
orientation and exploration
stage, 393–94
transition stage, 394–95
working stage, 395
for vicarious trauma, teacher,
374–75
Guerney, L., 108, 459
guilt theme
Black girls, 214
suicide risk, 344
Gurney, B., 108
Gurney, L., 108

H
Hailey, J., 130
hair, 126–27
Eurocentrism standards, 46, 205
maintenance, 126–27
policing, implicit bias, 205
truancy, Black children, 206–7
hair, Black girls
discrimination, 205–6
in schools, 206–7
truancy, 206–7
hair maintenance, 126–27
Hale, K., 126–27
Hall, J. G., 318–19
Halverson-Ramos, F., 110
hand games, for Black girl
empowerment, 213–14

Happy Teacher Revolution, 377
Headspace, 377
Heiko, R., 109
Heritage Youth Connection
Program, 403–5
outcomes, 404
overview, 403
program session outline, 403–4
Social Media Scavenger Hunt,
404–5, 419
Talk Me Up! card game, 405,
420–46
Hewitt, A. A., 254, 256–57
hip-hop artists, deaths of, 307,
308–9, 310–11
Hockenberry, S., 125
Hollingsworth, D., 337, 341–42
"home rules" *vs.* "school rules,"
128–29, 449–50
Homeyer, L. E., 111–12, 269, 271,
317, 398–400
homicide, Black youth, 16–17, 18,
307–8, 309–10
hotline calls, bias, 46
humanistic orientation, 135
humility, cultural. *See* cultural
humility
Hunter, A., 447–48
hyperactivity, misdiagnosis, 14–15
hypervigilance
Black boys, 260–61
community violence, 18, 262–63
on concentration, 18
from grief event, 309
PTSD, 7
race-based trauma, 24–25

definition, 448

racial socialization messages, 449–50

stress, 3–4, 8–9, 10, 448–53

therapeutic limit setting, 452–53

"the talk," 371–72, 448–49

internalized racism, 20

internet use, on suicide risk, 341

Irwin, V., 19, 123, 124–25, 126

I See You Cards, 385–86

J

Jacked Up Feelings, 352–53, 362–65

Jernberg, A. M., 107

Jezebel stereotype, 202–3

Jim Crow stereotypes, 260

Johnson, R. L., 45–46

joinin', 126–27

Jones, S., 137

Jungian analytical play therapy (JAPT), 109

Just Do You Bingo, 350, 359

juvenile justice system, 8–9, 16–17

Black boys, 265

Black girls, 210

diversion, 45

racial disparities, 11–12

K

Khubchandani, J., 338–39

King, W., 95

kinship-based social networks, 447–48

kinship bonds, 134–35

Kottman, T., 105–6, 348, 400–2, 460

L

Landreth, G. L., 38, 95, 99, 100–1, 107, 452–53

language

compassionate, 337

permissiveness, 100

profanity, 99–100

safety, 115–16

slang, 99

vernacular, 99

learning disability, misdiagnosis, 14–15, 314

Lee, J. M., 128

Leszcz, M., 393–94, 395

Let Me Be Great Chips, 402–3

LGBTQ+ students/youth, Black

attachment trauma, 130

bullying, 122–23, 124–25

among Black LGBTQ+ youth, 129–32

bullying, play therapy for, 123n.1, 139–41, 165

Mirror Affirmations, 140, 166

My Support Systems, 140–41, 167–68

Representin' Scavenger Hunt, 141, 169–73

Say My Name, 141, 174–98

mental health services

accessibility, 131–32

rejection, 6

suicide risk, 342

Lilly, J. P., 109

limit and boundaries theme, Black
boys, 267
limit setting, therapeutic, 452–53
Lindaman, S., 107
Lindsey, M., 200, 254–55, 337
loud, Black girls as, 202
Lowenstein, M., 111–12

M
Major Key Alert, 349
maladaptive coping skills. *See*
coping skills, maladaptive
Mammie stereotype, 201, 203–4
Mannarino, A. P., 313–14
Martin, Travon, 449
masculinity
toxic, Black boys, 255,
256–57
mass incarceration, 44–45, 135,
306, 311
McGill Johnson, A., 258–59, 265,
266
McNeil Smith, S., 8
Meany-Walen, K. K., 105–6, 380–
81, 400–1, 460
mechanical restraints, 14–15
media depictions, Black boys, 254
Memory Hearts, 320, 332–33
Memory Shoe Box, 319–20, 331
Memory T-Shirts, 319, 330
mental health, 35–37
Black Americans, 453–54
Black boys, 254–55
suicide, 254–55
Black caregivers, 453–54
Black girls, 199–200

caregiver, 454
COVID-19, 36–37
direct racial stressors on, 9–10
mis/over-diagnosis, 9, 21–22,
253, 267, 455
negative race-based interactions, 9
race-based stress on, 253
racial disparities, 35–36
racial trauma, 21–22
stigma, 200, 309, 455
mental health services/treatment,
49–51
accessibility, 21–22, 48–49,
454–55
Black girls, 200
Black LGBTQ+ youth, 131–32
family, church, and peer
alternatives, 335
filial therapy for, 459
play therapy for, 97–98
school social workers, 21–22
barriers, 454–55
bias, 45–47
Black youth, 35
group play therapy, 389–90
lack of, 9
plan development, 50–51
for race-based stress and trauma,
403
racial disparities, 35–36
teachers' role, 389–90
mentorship, 39, 135, 136, 340, 404
Mic Check, 394
microaggressions
definition, 31
race-related fatigue, 20–21

protection theme, 116–17
protective factors, Black community, 134–37
  humanistic orientation, 135
  kinship-based social networks, 447–48
  kinship bonds, 134–35
  religion, 136–37
  resilience, 135
  role flexibility, 135
  suffering, endurance of, 135
  village concept, 447–48
  work, education, and achievement orientation, 136
protective factors, for suicide risk, 342–43
psychoanalytic play therapy, 109
punishment. *See also* discipline, school
  Eurocentrism, 1–2
Punnett, A., 109
"Pushout: The Criminalization of Black Girls in Schools" (Morris), 209
Puzzanchera, C., 125
Puzzle Huddle, 102
puzzles, 102

R

race, defined, 31
race and culture conversation cards, 52
race-based stress, 4, 6–7, 8–9, 10–11, 462
  aggression, 114–15

  attachment-based play for, 136
  Black boys, 253, 254–55, 271–72
  Black girls, 199–200
  caregiver, 456, 457
  grief from, 321
  isolation from, 405–6
  mental health issues from, 253
  mental health services for, 403
  on parent–child relationship, 457
  play therapy for
    child-centered group play, 397
    cognitive play therapy, 349
    independent play, 115
    sand tray, in group play therapy, 399
    sand tray therapy, directive, 212–13
    Theraplay, 398
  on self-concept, 34
  on self-perceptions, negative, 34, 348
  self-regulation skills for, 254–55
  substance abuse, 318
  teacher psychoeducation on, 368
  vicarious trauma stressors, 10
Race-Based Traumatic Symptoms Scale (RBTSS), 24–25
Race-Related Event Scale, 24–25
race-related fatigue, 20–21
racial discrimination, 7. *See also* discrimination, racial
racial mistrust, 21
racial socialization, Black boys, paranoid/overreactive presentation, 260–61
racial socialization messages